THE IMPACT OF HUMAN RIGHTS LAW ON GENERAL INTERNATIONAL LAW

The Impact of Human Rights Law on General International Law

Edited by
MENNO T. KAMMINGA
and
MARTIN SCHEININ

OXFORD
UNIVERSITY PRESS

OXFORD
UNIVERSITY PRESS

Great Clarendon Street, Oxford OX2 6DP

Oxford University Press is a department of the University of Oxford.
It furthers the University's objective of excellence in research, scholarship,
and education by publishing worldwide in

Oxford New York

Auckland Cape Town Dar es Salaam Hong Kong Karachi
Kuala Lumpur Madrid Melbourne Mexico City Nairobi
New Delhi Shanghai Taipei Toronto

With offices in

Argentina Austria Brazil Chile Czech Republic France Greece
Guatemala Hungary Italy Japan Poland Portugal Singapore
South Korea Switzerland Thailand Turkey Ukraine Vietnam

Oxford is a registered trade mark of Oxford University Press
in the UK and in certain other countries

Published in the United States
by Oxford University Press Inc., New York

British Library Cataloguing in Publication Data

Data available

Library of Congress Cataloging in Publication Data

Data available

Typeset by Newgen Imaging Systems (P) Ltd., Chennai, India
Printed in Great Britain
on acid-free paper by
MPG Biddles Ltd., King's Lynn, Norfolk

ISBN 978–0–19–956522–1

1 3 5 7 9 10 8 6 4 2

Preface

This volume is the culmination of four years of work by the Committee on International Human Rights Law and Practice of the International Law Association (ILA), of which we had the honour to be Rapporteur and Chair, respectively. The Committee is composed of human rights experts from some 30 countries nominated by their national ILA branches. Together they represent a broad range of scholarship in human rights and international law. In our view the Committee therefore was an appropriate forum to carry out a review of the impact of international human rights law on general international law.

The impact of human rights law on general international law has been analysed in two earlier works: B. Simma, 'International Human Rights and General International Law: A Comparative Analysis' in *Collected Courses of the Academy of European Law*, vol. IV-2 (Kluwer, Dordrecht 1993) 153–256 and T. Meron, *The Humanization of International Law* (Martinus Nijhoff, Leiden/Boston 2006). With all due respect to the distinguished authors of these studies, we felt there was a need for a more systematic and comprehensive examination of the topic.

The present volume includes the Final Report of the Committee as adopted by the 2008 Conference of the ILA in Rio de Janeiro, and a number of articles representing elaborated versions of selected papers that were prepared by individual members of the Committee and that formed the basis for the Final Report. The individual contributions have benefited from the collective work of the Committee through joint workshops and other forms of interaction. This has resulted in certain common themes running through the volume as a whole.

We gratefully acknowledge the support provided by the Maastricht Centre for Human Rights and the University of Siena by hosting the 2006 and 2007 meetings of the Committee at which different drafts of the papers included in this book were discussed. We are also very grateful to Ms Annika Tahvanainen for her organizational help and to Ms Jane Flynn and Mr Wim Muller for their editorial assistance.

This book offers a stocktaking of a process that has only just started. General international law will continue to be challenged by international human rights law on a wide front. We hope many scholars and practitioners will continue to take up the challenge.

Menno T. Kamminga
Martin Scheinin

Contents

Table of contents

List of Abbreviations

ABA	American Bar Association
African J Intl Comp L	African Journal of International and Comparative Law
AC	Law Reports Appeal Cases
ACHPR	African Charter on Human and Peoples' Rights
AD	Annotated Digest
AJIL	American Journal of International Law
All ER	All England Law Reports
ASIL	American Society of International Law
Australian Ybk Intl L	Australian Year Book of International Law
BvR	File reference to a constitutional action before the German Constitutional Court (*Aktenzeichen einer Verfassungsbeschwerde zum Bundesverfassungsgericht*)
BYIL	British Year Book of International Law
CAT	Committee against Torture/Convention against Torture and Other Cruel, Inhuman or Degrading Treatment or Punishment
CEDAW	Committee on the Elimination of Discrimination against Women/Convention on the Elimination of All Forms of Discrimination against Women
CERD	Committee on the Elimination of Racial Discrimination/Convention on the Elimination of All Forms of Racial Discrimination
CESCR	International Covenant on Economic, Social and Cultural Rights
CFI	Court of First Instance (EU)
Chinese J Intl L	Chinese Journal of International Law
Connecticut J Intl L	Connecticut Journal of International Law
CRC	Convention on the Rights of the Child/Committee on the Rights of the Child
CSFR	Czech and Slovak Federal Republic
DC Cir	United States Court of Appeals for the District of Columbia Circuit
DRC	Democratic Republic of the Congo
ECHR	Convention for the Protection of Human Rights and Fundamental Freedoms (European Convention on Human Rights)
ECJ	European Court of Justice
ECmHR	European Commission of Human Rights
ECR	European Court Reports
ECtHR	European Court of Human Rights

ED Va	United States District Court for the Eastern District of Virginia
EHRR	European Human Rights Reports
EJIL	European Journal of International Law
ELR	European Law Reports
ETS	European Treaty Series
Finnish Ybk Intl L	Finnish Yearbook of International Law
FRY	Federal Republic of Yugoslavia
Ga J Intl Comp L	Georgia Journal of International and Comparative Law
GAOR	General Assembly Official Records
GYIL	German Yearbook of International Law
Harv Intl L J	Harvard International Law Journal
HLR	Harvard Law Review
HRC	Human Rights Council
HRCt	Human Rights Committee
HRLJ	Human Rights Law Journal
HRQ	Human Rights Quarterly
Human Rights L Rev	Human Rights Law Review
IACmHR	Inter-American Commission on Human Rights
IACtHR	Inter-American Court of Human Rights
ICCPR	International Covenant on Civil and Political Rights
ICJ	International Court of Justice
ICLQ	International and Comparative Law Quarterly
ICRC	International Committee of the Red Cross
ICTR	International Criminal Tribunal for Rwanda
ICTY	International Criminal Tribunal for the Former Yugoslavia
IHRR	International Human Rights Reports
ILA	International Law Association
ILC	International Law Commission
ILM	International Legal Materials
ILO	International Labour Organization
ILR	International Law Reports
ILSA J Intl Comp L	ILSA Journal of International and Comparative Law
Israel Ybk HR	Israel Yearbook on Human Rights
Italian Ybk Intl L	Italian Yearbook of International Law
JAAC	Jurisprudence des autorités administratives de la Confédération (Switzerland)
JICJ	Journal of International Criminal Justice
LJIL	Leiden Journal of International Law
LJN	Netherlands national jurisprudence number (*Landelijk Jurisprudentie Nummer*)
Melbourne J Int L	Melbourne Journal of International Law
Mich L Rev	Michigan Law Review
MRT	Moldavian Republic of Transdniestria
Nordic J Intl L	Nordic Journal of International Law

OJ	Official Journal of the European Communities
OR	Ontario Reports
PCIJ	Permanent Court of International Justice
RdC	Recueil des Cours
RGDIP	Revue Générale de Droit International Public
RIAA	Reports of International Arbitral Awards
Riv dir int	Rivisto di Diritto Internationale
RSC	Revised Statutes of Canada
RUDH	Revue Universelle des Droits de l'Homme
S Ct	Supreme Court Reporter
SC Res	Security Council Resolution
SCSL	Special Court for Sierra Leone
SDNY	United States District Court for the Southern District of New York
South African LJ	South African Law Journal
Tex. Crim. App.	Texas Court of Criminal Appeals
Texas L Rev	Texas Law Review
UN	United Nations
UN GAOR	United Nations General Assembly Official Records
UNGA	United Nations General Assembly
UNTS	United Nations Treaty Series
USC	United States Code
USSR	Union of Soviet Socialist Republics
UST	United States Treaties and Other International Agreements
VCLT	Vienna Convention on the Law of Treaties
WLR	Weekly Law Reports
Ybk ILC	Yearbook of the International Law Commission
YJIL	Yale Journal of International Law

Table of cases

PERMANENT COURT OF INTERNATIONAL JUSTICE

INTERNATIONAL COURT OF JUSTICE

INTERNATIONAL CRIMINAL TRIBUNALS

HUMAN RIGHTS COMMITTEE

COMMITTEE AGAINST TORTURE

EUROPEAN COMMISSION ON HUMAN RIGHTS

EUROPEAN COURT OF HUMAN RIGHTS

EUROPEAN COURT OF JUSTICE, INCLUDING THE COURT OF FIRST INSTANCE

INTER-AMERICAN COMMISSION ON HUMAN RIGHTS

INTER-AMERICAN COURT OF HUMAN RIGHTS

1

Final Report on the Impact of International Human Rights Law on General International Law

Menno T. Kamminga

1. Introduction

At the International Law Association's 2004 Conference in Berlin, the Executive Council entrusted the Committee on International Human Rights Law and Practice with the task of preparing a report on the relationship between general international law and international human rights law. This is the Committee's final report on the subject.[1] An interim report was presented at the Association's 2006 Toronto Conference.[2] That report was prepared at a Committee workshop held in Maastricht under the auspices of the Maastricht Centre for Human Rights. The present report was prepared at a workshop held at the Certosa di Pontignano near Siena, Italy at the kind invitation of Committee member Professor Riccardo Pisillo Mazzeschi.

Before starting its work the Committee considered two broad, alternative approaches to the study of the relationship between general international law and international human rights law. The first approach emphasizes the special, distinctive nature of international human rights law and assumes that the rules and principles of general international law, or at least some of them, are not applicable to it. This was associated with a more general trend of identifying so-called self-contained regimes within public international law and labelled the 'fragmentation' approach. The other approach is to take as the point of departure that international human rights law is part of general international law and that the two branches of law should be reconciled with each other as much as possible. This was labelled the 'reconciliation' approach. The Committee unanimously

---

[1] This chapter contains a slightly edited version of the Committee report that was adopted at the 2008 ILA Conference in Rio de Janeiro and that will in due course be published in *Report of the 73rd Conference of the International Law Association* (2008).

[2] *Report of the 72nd Conference of the International Law Association* (2006) 457.

considers that the reconciliation approach is preferable to the fragmentation approach, if only because it is overwhelmingly in conformity with international practice.

The relationship between general international law and international human rights law is obviously a two-way process. International human rights courts and UN human rights treaty bodies have often relied on norms of general international law, such as those contained, for example, in the Vienna Convention on the Law of Treaties. Increasingly, they also use other rules and principles of international law. However, this process is comparatively well known and well documented. The Committee considers that the reverse process, i.e. the impact of international human rights law on general international law, is a topic both less explored and more interesting.

International human rights law, in the sense of the present report, includes not merely human rights law *stricto sensu,* but any international norm capable of conferring rights and duties directly on individuals regardless of nationality, including under international humanitarian law and international criminal law.

General international law is a concept that is often used but rarely defined. It is the opposite of special international law (*lex specialis*), which governs particular topics (international trade law, law of the sea etc.). Examples of general international law are the law of treaties, as codified in the Vienna Convention on the Law of Treaties, and the law of state responsibility, as codified in the Articles on the Responsibility of States for Internationally Wrongful Acts.

At the beginning of the 21st century, one of the defining characteristics of the development of international law is the emergence on the global plane of the individual and other non-state actors (armed opposition groups, international organizations, international financial institutions, non-governmental organizations, multinational enterprises, etc.). Usually, discussion of this phenomenon is framed in terms of the increasing role played by non-state actors. Questions often arise as to the rights and obligations of these entities under international law and whether these rights and duties are enforceable at the international level. However, a more interesting question, in the view of the Committee, is whether the increasing role of non-state actors is also having an impact on the *substance* of international law. This process is sometimes referred to as the 'humanization' of international law.[3] Is international law changing from a state-centred system based on bilateral obligations, towards a normative system reflecting the interests and values of a wider range of actors, and of the international community? More specifically, are the changes beginning to affect general international law, or do they remain limited to the *lex specialis* of international human rights law, international humanitarian law, and international criminal law?

---

[3] The term was already employed more than 50 years ago in an article by Maurice Bourquin entitled 'L'humanisation du droit des gens', in *La technique et les principes du droit public: études en l'honneur de Georges Scelle* (Librairie générale de droit et de jurisprudence, Paris 1950) vol. I, 21.

There are few systematic examinations of the impact of international human rights law on general international law. Simma,[4] Cassese,[5] and Meron[6] are among the few scholars that have undertaken this task with varying degrees of intensity. The lack of broader scholarly interest is surprising in view of the importance of the topic. In order to become recognized and acquire legitimacy as the law of the world community, international law will have to become more reflective of the interests and values of a wider range of actors. Mere development of the *lex specialis* of human rights law, international humanitarian law, and international criminal law will not sufficiently serve this purpose because of the limitations imposed by general international law.

The Committee adopted the following method of work. First, it identified a set of legal issues developed by international human rights bodies (including international human rights treaty bodies, regional human rights courts and international criminal courts and tribunals) which are, at first sight, difficult to reconcile with traditional international law because they purport to reflect the interests of individuals rather than states. Next, the Committee considered whether these concepts have affected general international law or whether they have remained *lex specialis*. This was done primarily by examining the practice of two institutions that may be regarded as the guardians of general international law: the International Court of Justice and the International Law Commission. In quite a few cases, the ICJ and the ILC have either explicitly borrowed concepts and findings from human rights bodies or they have taken those approaches on board without identifying their source. The borrowing process is of course facilitated by the fact that an increasing number of ICJ judges and ILC members are themselves former members of international human rights bodies.

The present report was written by Menno Kamminga and is based on the following papers by members of the Committee discussing different aspects of the impact of human rights law on general international law: Martin Scheinin, *Human Rights Treaties and the Vienna Convention on the Law of Treaties*; Jan Wouters and Cedric Ryngaert, *The Impact of International Human Rights Law on the Process of the Formation of Customary International Law*; Sandesh Sivakumaran, *The Impact of International Human Rights Law on the Structure of International Obligations*; Thilo Rensmann, *The Impact of International Human Rights Law on the Immunity of States and their Officials*; Christina Cerna, *The Impact of International Human Rights Law on the Right to Consular Notification*; Jonas Christoffersen, *The Impact of International Human Rights Law on General Principles of Treaty Interpretation*; Ineke Boerefijn, *The Impact of International Human Rights Law on the International*

---

[4] B. Simma, 'International Human Rights and General International Law: A Comparative Analysis', in *Collected Courses of the Academy of European Law* vol. IV-2, 153–256 (Kluwer, Dordrecht 1993).

[5] A. Cassese, *International Law*, 2nd ed. (Oxford University Press, Oxford 2005) 396.

[6] T. Meron, *The Humanization of International Law* (Martinus Nijhoff Publishers, Leiden/ Boston 2006).

Regime of Treaty Reservations; Menno Kamminga, *The Impact of International Human Rights Law on the Law of State Succession in Respect of Treaties*; Riccardo Pisillo Mazzeschi, *The Impact of International Human Rights Law on the Law of Diplomatic Protection*. The report has benefited from comments and suggestions made by the following Committee members: Anne Bayefsky, Andrew Byrnes, John Dugard, Hurst Hannum, Matthias Herdegen, Mahulena Hofmann, Robert McCorquodale, Nicoletta Parisi, Sir Nigel Rodley, Charles Siegal, Geir Ulfstein and Ralph Wilde.

The Committee is well aware that the survey contained in the present report is incomplete and that the impact of international human rights law on general international law is a process that has only just started. Moreover, as will be seen below, in quite a few instances there have been challenges from international human rights law that have not resulted in noticeable impact on general international law. The Committee has nevertheless included those instances in its report because it regards them as instructive about the process.

The Committee considers that the impact of international human rights law on general international law is highly desirable in order to soften the international legal order's predominantly state-centred nature and to accommodate the special, non-reciprocal nature of international obligations in the field of human rights. However, the Committee has attempted not to engage in wishful thinking, 'human rightism'[7] or 'human rights triumphalism': the trap of attributing each and every innovation in international law to creative thinking by human rights lawyers. The Committee has tried to faithfully and succinctly record developments in a wide range of areas but it has been careful when drawing conclusions *de lege lata*. To prevent this report from being regarded as reflecting merely the narrow views of a group of human rights experts the Committee considers it important that it receives the imprimatur from the ILA Conference as a whole.

2. The Structure of International Obligations

Two concepts have strongly influenced the structure of international obligations: obligations *erga omnes* and peremptory norms (rules of *jus cogens*). Unlike some of the other notions discussed in this report, it cannot be maintained that international human rights bodies have had a significant impact on the development of these two concepts. Although international criminal tribunals and supervisory human rights bodies have occasionally made reference to them, they have mainly been shaped by the International Court of Justice and the International Law Commission respectively. Furthermore, although most *erga omnes* obligations and *jus cogens* rules are human rights norms, not all of them belong to this

---

[7] A. Pellet, ' "Human Rightism" and International Law' (2000) 10 Italian Ybk Intl L 3.

category. Finally, although the two concepts have had an important symbolic effect and have generated much interest among scholars and human rights activists they have not yet had much effect in practice. While the existence of the concepts is beyond doubt, the floodgates have not opened; states have remained reluctant to rely on them in their legal arguments.

2.1 Obligations *erga omnes*

Under traditional international law, a state can only protect its own rights and those of its own nationals. This fits uncomfortably with the notion of community interest. To help fill the gap, the International Court of Justice began using the concept of obligations *erga omnes*. The concept was introduced by the Court as an *obiter dictum* in the *Barcelona Traction* case, in an apparent response to widespread criticism of its refusal to recognize the *jus standi* of Ethiopia and Liberia in the *South West Africa* cases.[8] In its *obiter dictum* the Court suggested that the obligation not to commit or tolerate racial discrimination has an *erga omnes* character and therefore may be invoked by any state.[9] The finding represented a significant recognition by the Court of the existence of such a thing as the international community and the values and interests with which it is imbued. Since that time, the Court has appeared keen to make reference to obligations *erga omnes* in its findings, including the *East Timor*[10] and *Bosnian Genocide*[11] cases. In its advisory opinion on *The Wall* the Court went a step further and proceeded to draw legal consequences from the concept.[12] It observed that all states were under an obligation not to recognize the consequences of the breaches committed by Israel. As pointed out by Judge Kooijmans in his separate opinion, it would have been more appropriate to base this conclusion on the fact that the breaches committed amounted to violations of rules of *jus cogens*.[13]

The International Law Commission has also embraced the concept of obligations *erga omnes*. Article 48 of its Articles on Responsibility of States for Internationally Wrongful Acts provides that 'any State other than an injured State is entitled to invoke the responsibility of another State...if: (a) the obligation breached is owed to a group of States including that State, and is established for

---

[8] *South West Africa (Ethiopia v. South Africa; Liberia v. South Africa)*, Second Phase, Judgment of 18 July 1966, 1966 ICJ Reports 6.

[9] *Barcelona Traction, Light and Power Company, Limited* (New Application: 1962) *(Belgium v. Spain)*, Judgment of 5 February 1970, 1970 ICJ Reports 3, para. 33.

[10] *East Timor (Portugal v. Australia)*, Judgment of 30 June 1995, 1995 ICJ Reports 90, para. 29.

[11] *Application of the Convention on the Prevention and Punishment of the Crime of Genocide (Bosnia and Herzegovina v. Serbia and Montenegro)*, Preliminary Objections, Judgment of 11 July 1996, 1996 ICJ Reports 595, para. 31.

[12] *Legal Consequences of the Construction of a Wall in the Occupied Palestinian Territory*, Advisory Opinion of 9 July 2004, 2004 ICJ Reports 136, para. 159.

[13] Ibid., separate opinion of Judge Kooijmans, para. 40.

the protection of a collective interest of the group; or (b) the obligation breached is owed to the international community as a whole.'[14]

2.2 *Jus cogens*

Traditional international law is based on consent and there is no hierarchy of obligations: all obligations are of equal rank. In such a system there is no special place for community values that trump other norms such as in a domestic constitutional system. In order to fill this gap the International Law Commission introduced the concept of peremptory norms (*jus cogens*). Under Article 53 of the Vienna Convention on the Law of Treaties '[a] treaty is void if, at the time of its conclusion, it conflicts with a peremptory norm of general international law.' But the concept of *jus cogens* also has increasing relevance outside the field of the law of treaties; the ILC has included the concept in its Articles on Responsibility of States for Internationally Wrongful Acts. The Articles provide that states shall cooperate to bring to an end any serious breach arising under a peremptory norm of general international law.[15] The prohibitions against aggression, genocide, slavery, racial discrimination, crimes against humanity and torture and the right to self-determination are generally regarded as peremptory norms.[16]

The concept of *jus cogens* has, in recent years, been applied not only by international human rights courts (*Al-Adsani v. United Kingdom*[17]) and international criminal tribunals (*Prosecutor v. Furundžija*[18]), but also by other international courts such as the Court of First Instance of the European Communities (*Kadi v. Council*[19]) and by domestic courts (*Ex Parte Pinochet,*[20] and *Ferrini v. Germany*[21]).

The International Court of Justice, on the other hand, for reasons that are not difficult to guess has been reluctant to rely on the notion of *jus cogens* in its judgments.[22] In the *Arrest Warrant* case the Court declined to even discuss the argument raised

---

[14] Article 48, Articles on Responsibility of States for Internationally Wrongful Acts (adopted 12 December 2001) UNGA Res 56/83.

[15] Ibid., Articles 40 and 41.

[16] J. Crawford, *The International Law Commission's Articles on State Responsibility* (Cambridge University Press, Cambridge 2002) 188.

[17] *Al-Adsani v. United Kingdom* (App. No. 35763/97), ECtHR, Judgment of 21 November 2001, (2002) 34 EHRR 11, ECHR 2001-XI, para. 61.

[18] *Prosecutor v. Furundžija*, ICTY-95-17/1-T, Judgment of 10 December 1998, para. 153.

[19] Case T-315/01, *Kadi v. Council of the European Union and Commission of the European Communities* (CFI 21 September 2005), para. 226. At the time of writing the European Court of Justice had not yet adopted its judgment on appeal.

[20] *R v. Bow Street Metropolitan Stipendiary Magistrate, Ex parte Pinochet Ugarte (No. 3)*, UK House of Lords, [1999] 2 WLR 827.

[21] *Ferrini v. Federal Republic of Germany*, Italian Court of Cassation, Judgment of 11 March 2004, (2005) 99 AJIL 242.

[22] See in particular the separate opinion of Judge ad hoc Dugard in *Armed Activities on the Territory of the Congo (Democratic Republic of the Congo v. Rwanda)*, Judgment of 3 February 2006, 2006 ICJ Reports 6.

by Belgium, according to which immunity could not be invoked if a norm of *jus cogens* had been violated.[23] The Court referred to the concept of *jus cogens* in *Congo v. Rwanda,* but this occurred in a narrow context. The Court observed that the prohibition of genocide has the character of a peremptory norm but refused to accept that genocide could override the requirement of consent to jurisdiction.[24] In sum, the existence under general international law of the notion of *jus cogens* is beyond doubt, but its application in inter-state cases is still very rare.

3. The Formation of Customary International Law

The traditional approach to identifying a rule of customary international law is to rely on *opinio juris* to confirm state practice, or even to infer *opinio juris* from state practice. Accordingly, in the *North Sea Continental Shelf* cases, the Court observed that, in order for state practice to qualify as custom, the practice must 'be carried out in such a way, as to be evidence of a belief that this practice is rendered obligatory by the existence of a rule of law requiring it.'[25] Moreover, when weighing different types of state acts, the traditional approach is to attach more value to what states do (physical acts) than what they say (verbal acts). In his dissenting opinion in the *Fisheries* case Judge Reid wrote that '[t]he only convincing evidence of State practice is to be found in seizures, where the coastal state asserts its sovereignty over the waters in question by arresting a foreign ship'.[26]

In areas inspired by community values (*jus ad bellum,* armed conflict, human rights, the environment) this traditional approach is problematic. The significance to be attached to omissions is difficult to assess in these areas because it has be demonstrated that the abstention occurred out of a sense of legal obligation.[27] For example, in a debate on the lawfulness of cluster munitions, the traditional approach emphasizes that these weapons have been used by at least 23 states and that they are being produced by at least 34.[28] The new approach stresses the fact that these weapons are unlawful because they are indiscriminate.

Human rights treaty bodies and international criminal courts and tribunals have tended to follow an approach that is based on deduction from fundamental principles, rather than on induction from state practice. Moreover, when identifying

---

[23] *Arrest Warrant of 11 April 2000 (Democratic Republic of the Congo v. Belgium),* Judgment of 14 February 2002, 2002 ICJ Reports 3, para. 58.

[24] Ibid., para. 64.

[25] *North Sea Continental Shelf (Federal Republic of Germany v. Netherlands; Federal Republic of Germany v. Denmark),* Judgment of 20 February 1969, 1969 ICJ Reports 3, para. 77.

[26] *Fisheries (United Kingdom v. Norway),* Judgment of 18 December 1951, 1951 ICJ Reports 116, 191.

[27] J.-M. Henckaerts, 'Study on Customary International Law: A Contribution to the Understanding and Respect for the rule of Law in Armed Conflict' (2005) 87 *Review of the International Committee of the Red Cross* 175, 182.

[28] See U.S. Policy Regarding Cluster Munitions, (2007) 101 AJIL 501.

state practice, they emphasize what states say rather than what they do. There also is a tendency to regard the pronouncements of the supervisory bodies of human rights treaties and international tribunals as indications of state practice, especially if these pronouncements are acquiesced in by states (see Section 3.1 below).

The new approach was followed by the International Court of Justice in *Nicaragua*. In that case the Court observed that it 'must satisfy itself that the existence of the rule in the *opinio juris* of States is confirmed by practice' thus turning around the approach it had taken in the *North Sea Continental Shelf* cases.[29] Also in *Nicaragua,* the Court recognized that contrary practice does not undermine the formation of a rule of customary international law as long as the practice is condemned and the state in question does not claim to act as a matter of right.[30]

However, the new approach is by no means uncontroversial, as is illustrated by the reaction of the United States to the ICRC study *Customary International Humanitarian Law,* one of the most ambitious efforts ever undertaken to identify rules of customary international law. Two years after the publication of the study, a lengthy letter from the Legal Adviser of the US Department of State and his colleague of the US Department of Defense to the President of the ICRC complained that the study did not take sufficient account of battlefield practice. It argued 'that the Study places too much emphasis on written materials, such as military manuals and other guidelines published by States, as opposed to actual operational practice by States during armed conflict. Although manuals may provide important indications of State behaviour and *opinio juris*, they cannot be a replacement for a meaningful assessment of operational State practice in connection with actual military operations.'[31]

It follows that techniques for the identification of rules of customary international law differ depending on the subject matter. It should not be assumed that they are the same for commercial shipping as for warfare. As the international legal order becomes more and more concerned with areas governed by community values, the 'new' ways of identifying rules of customary international law will gain importance in due course.

4. Treaty Law

The International Law Commission's Study Group on Fragmentation of International Law has concluded that the Vienna Convention on the Law of Treaties is the appropriate instrument for dealing with problems of fragmentation

---

[29] *Military and Paramilitary Activities in and Against Nicaragua (Nicaragua v. United States of America)* (Merits), Judgment of 27 June 1986, 1986 ICJ Reports 14, para. 184.

[30] Ibid., para. 186.

[31] Letter from John Bellinger III, Legal Adviser, U.S. Department of State, and William J. Haynes, General Counsel, US Department of Defense, to Dr. Jakob Kellenberger, President, International Committee of the Red Cross, 3 November 2006, (2007) 46 ILM 514, 515. See also the response to this letter by J. M. Henckaerts, ICRC Legal Adviser, (2007) 46 ILM 959.

in international law. But even the Study Group recognizes that the VCLT's uniform rules for interpreting and applying different types of treaties are problematic.[32] Even at the time of its conclusion in 1969, the VCLT was criticized for its failure to distinguish between different types of treaties, in particular between 'bilateral' and 'non-bilateral' treaties. The Convention also did not take account of one of the special characteristics of multilateral treaties: that they may have their own monitoring bodies developing institutionalized practices of interpretation under the treaty in question. The provisions of the VCLT are therefore not always easily reconcilable with the special requirements of human rights treaties or other multilateral treaties establishing independent monitoring bodies. The special nature of the European Convention on Human Rights was famously characterized by the European Court of Human Rights in the following terms:

Unlike international treaties of the classic kind, the Convention comprises more than mere reciprocal engagements between Contracting States. It creates, over and above a network of mutual, bilateral undertakings, objective obligations which, in the words of the Preamble, benefit from a 'collective enforcement'.[33]

4.1 Treaty interpretation

It is sometimes suggested that the special nature of human rights treaties requires special rules of interpretation, which differ from the general rules of treaty interpretation. For example, the European Court of Human Rights has observed that, in interpreting the European Convention on Human Rights, 'regard must be had to its special character as a treaty for the collective enforcement of human rights and fundamental freedoms.'[34]

Such a claim for special treatment finds no support in the rules on treaty interpretation contained in the VCLT, however. When drafting general rules of interpretation the ILC specifically decided to omit from the VCLT a distinction between 'law-making' and other treaties.[35] This was in spite of the fact that the concept of treaties that pursue a common interest had already been recognized by the International Court of Justice. In its advisory opinion on *Reservations to the Genocide Convention* the Court famously observed:

In such a convention the contracting States do not have any interests of their own; they merely have, one and all, a common interest, namely, the accomplishment of those high purposes which are the *raison d'être* of the Convention. Consequently, in a convention of

[32] 'Fragmentation of International Law: Difficulties Arising from the Diversification and Expansion of International Law', Report of the Study Group of the International Law Commission, Finalized by M. Koskenniemi, 13 April 2006, UN Doc. A/CN.4/L.682, 250–251.

[33] *Mamatkulov and Askarov v. Turkey* (App. Nos. 46827/99 and 46951/99), ECtHR, Judgment of 4 February 2005, para. 100; *Loizidou v. Turkey* (Preliminary Objections) (App. No. 15318/89), ECtHR, Judgment of 23 March 1995, (1995) Series A No. 310, 20 EHRR 99, para. 70.

[34] *Soering v. United Kingdom* (App. No. 14038/88), ECtHR, Judgment of 7 July 1989, (1989) Series A No. 161, para. 87.

[35] Ybk ILC 1966 II, 219, para. 6.

this type one cannot speak of individual advantages or disadvantages to States, or of the maintenance of a perfect contractual balance between rights and duties.[36]

It would appear, however, that the principles for the interpretation of human rights treaties that have been relied upon by the European and Inter-American Courts of Human Rights do not differ substantially from the methods of treaty interpretation which are available under general international law, especially if it is assumed that the VCLT is not a complete codification of the customary international law on treaties, including its norms on treaty interpretation. It therefore cannot be said that there has been a significant impact from international human rights law on general international law in this field. For example, emphasis on the object and purpose of a treaty (the necessity 'to seek the interpretation that is most appropriate in order to realise the aim and achieve the object of the treaty, not that which would restrict to the greatest possible degree the obligations of the Parties')[37] is reflected in Article 31(1) of the VCLT. The principle of dynamic interpretation ('the Convention is a living instrument which...must be interpreted in the light of present-day conditions')[38] is reflected to a considerable extent in Article 31(3)(b) of the VCLT.

In one of its previous reports, the ILA Committee on International Human Rights Law and Practice suggested that human rights treaty body findings constitute 'subsequent practice in the application of the treaty which establishes the agreement of the parties regarding its interpretation' within the sense of Article 31(3)(b) of the VCLT, or, alternatively, that states' acquiescence in such findings constitutes such practice.[39] Although the International Court of Justice has not formally endorsed such an approach, it has implicitly adopted this course of action, for example in its advisory opinion on *The Wall*, in which it closely followed the findings of the UN human rights treaty bodies.

4.2 Treaty reservations

Under traditional international law, a state is bound by a treaty only to the extent that it has consented to be bound. From the point of view of international human rights law, this point of departure is problematic. Unlike most other treaties, human rights treaties create obligations of a non-reciprocal nature which establish rights for individuals. Reservations to human rights treaties

[36] *Reservations to the Convention on the Prevention and Punishment of the Crime of Genocide*, Advisory Opinion, of 28 May 1951, 1951 ICJ Reports 15, 23.

[37] *Wemhoff v. Germany* (App. No. 2122/64), ECtHR, Judgment of 27 June 1968, (1968) Series A No. 7, para. 8.

[38] *Tyrer v. United Kingdom* (App. No. 5856/72), ECtHR, Judgment of 25 April 1978, (1978) Series A No. 26, para. 31.

[39] Committee on International Human Rights Law and Practice, Final Report on the Impact of Findings of the United Nations Human Rights Treaty Bodies, *Report of the 71st Conference of the International Law Association* (2004) 621, 628–629.

therefore primarily affect the interests of individuals and not those of other states.

The approach to reservations taken by the UN human rights treaty bodies is reflected *inter alia* in guidelines adopted by the chairpersons of human rights treaty bodies[40] and a General Comment by the Human Rights Committee.[41] The line taken in these documents is similar to the attitude adopted earlier by the European Court of Human Rights.[42] The International Law Commission has worked on the issue of treaty reservations since 1994. Its work is not yet finished but it has already resulted in various draft guidelines. In his reports, ILC Special Rapporteur Alain Pellet has made frequent reference to the work on reservations carried out by the human rights treaty bodies. In 2007 there was even a meeting on the issue between the ILC and representatives of human rights treaty bodies.[43] Because of this frequent interaction, the impact of international human rights law on general international law in the area of treaty reservations is comparatively well documented. Three questions may be distinguished in this field: (1) What are the grounds for determining that a reservation is impermissible? (2) Who may determine whether a reservation is impermissible? and (3) What are the consequences of an impermissible reservation?

(1) In its advisory opinion on *Reservations to the Genocide Convention,* the International Court of Justice adopted the 'object and purpose' test to determine the validity of a reservation.[44] The test was subsequently included in Article 19(3) of the Vienna Convention on the Law of Treaties and is widely regarded as reflecting customary international law. ILC Special Rapporteur Alain Pellet has called it the 'pivot between the need to preserve the nature of the treaty and the desire to facilitate accession to multilateral treaties by the greatest number of States.'[45] From the point of view of international human rights law this test is not controversial, although in practice it may not always be easily applicable.

(2) Under Article 20 of the VCLT, a reservation is presumed permissible unless it is objected to by other states parties. This system was designed for treaties in which states have reciprocal interests, but it functions inadequately for human rights treaties. State parties to human rights treaties have little incentive to critically examine and object to reservations made by other states, since their own

---

[40] See, for example, Report of the meeting of the Working Group on Reservations, UN Doc. HRI/MC/2007/5.

[41] Human Rights Committee, General Comment No. 24, 4 November 1994.

[42] *Belilos v. Switzerland* (App. No. 10328/83), ECtHR, Judgment of 29 April 1988, (1988) Series A No. 132.

[43] Report of a meeting with human rights bodies, 15–16 May 2007, UN Doc. ILC(LIX)/RT/CRP.1.

[44] *Reservations to the Convention on the Prevention and Punishment of the Crime of Genocide,* Advisory Opinion of 28 May 1951, 1951 ICJ Reports 15.

[45] Tenth Report on Reservations to Treaties, by Alain Pellet, Special Rapporteur, UN Doc. A/CN.4/558/Add.1 (2005), para. 55.

direct interests are not affected. The Human Rights Committee, among others, has therefore taken the view that the task of determining the validity of reservations necessarily falls to the Committee.[46] ILC Special Rapporteur Alain Pellet has accepted that it makes sense for treaty bodies to perform this role. One of his draft guidelines provides as follows: 'Where a treaty establishes a body to monitor application of the treaty, that body shall be competent, for the purpose of discharging the functions entrusted to it, to assess the validity of reservations formulated by a State or an international organization.'[47] Although the ILC has not yet pronounced on this draft, the impact from international human rights law on general international law appears to have been straightforward in this case.

(3) Under Articles 20–21 of the VCLT a state objecting to a reservation has the option of either taking the view that the reservation precludes the entry into force of the convention between it and the reserving state, or to take the view that the convention will enter into force between it and the reserving state minus the provision burdened by the contested reservation. Neither of these options is attractive in respect of human rights treaties. The European Court of Human Rights has therefore decided that invalid reservations are severable.[48] The Human Rights Committee has adopted a similar position. It has observed that if it has determined that a reservation is incompatible with object and purpose of the ICCPR, the reservation is generally severable and the treaty is 'operative for the reserving party without the benefit of the reservation'.[49] The ILC has not yet formulated a draft guideline on this question and it remains to be seen whether it will follow the approach of the human rights treaty bodies. Clearly, however, of all the issues arising in respect of treaty reservations, this is the most controversial. The United States, the United Kingdom and France have already taken the unusual step of registering formal objections to the severability doctrine adopted by the Human Rights Committee.[50]

4.3 State succession in respect of treaties

In accordance with the 'clean slate' doctrine, under traditional international law a state is free to become or not to become a party to treaties that were binding on the predecessor state. Although the Vienna Convention on Succession of States in Respect of Treaties provides for the continuity of obligations in respect of all treaties, this position is not part of customary international law.[51] The only exception to the clean slate doctrine that is accepted under traditional international law

---

[46] Human Rights Committee, General Comment No. 24, 4 November 1994, para. 18.

[47] Tenth Report on Reservations to Treaties, by Alain Pellet, Special Rapporteur, UN Doc. A/CN.4/558/Add.1 (2005), paras. 166–171.

[48] *Belilos v. Switzerland* (App. No. 10328/83), ECtHR, Judgment of 29 April 1988, (1988) Series A No. 132, para. 60.

[49] Human Rights Committee, General Comment No. 24, para. 18.

[50] Report of the Human Rights Committee, UN Doc. A/50/40, vol. I (1996), Annex VI.

[51] Articles 31–35 of the Vienna Convention on Succession of States in Respect of Treaties (1978). See, for example, I. Brownlie, *Principles of Public International Law*, 5th ed. (Oxford University Press,

is the rule of the continuity of treaties relating to territorial regimes (including boundary regimes) as provided for in the Vienna Convention on Succession of States in Respect of Treaties.[52] That rule on territorial regimes has been qualified as a rule of customary international law by the International Court of Justice.[53]

In contrast, the UN human rights treaty bodies have taken the view that the special nature of human rights treaties entails that their protection devolves with territory and that protection is not affected by state succession.[54] Successor states therefore remain bound by human rights treaties from their date of independence and this is not dependent on any confirmation made by them. This therefore puts human rights treaties in the same league as treaties on territorial regimes.

However, although no state appears to have formally objected to the rule of automatic succession in respect of human rights treaties, so far the rule has not been formally enshrined under general international law. The rule is not reflected in the Vienna Convention on the Law of Treaties or the Vienna Convention on Succession of States in Respect of Treaties. Neither has it been endorsed by the International Court of Justice or the International Law Commission. In the *Bosnian Genocide* case, the Court decided not to respond to an argument in favour of automatic succession in respect of human rights treaties made by Bosnia-Herzegovina. Among the separate opinions to this judgment, only Judge Weeramantry expressed the view that there was indeed a rule of automatic succession with regard to the Genocide Convention. President Higgins has expressed sympathy for the idea in an academic article.[55]

5. International Law and Domestic Law

Under traditional international law, states are free to determine their relationship between international law and domestic law, so long as they ensure compliance with their international obligations. In accordance with this general principle, it has long been assumed that human rights treaties leave states parties the choice of means for the performance of their obligations.[56]

Oxford 1998) 663; A. Cassese, *International Law*, 2nd ed. (Oxford University Press, Oxford 2005) 78; M. N. Shaw, *International Law*, 5th ed. (Cambridge University Press, Cambridge 2003) 875.

[52] Articles 11–12 of the Vienna Convention on Succession of States in Respect of Treaties (1978).

[53] *Gabčíkovo-Nagymaros Project (Hungary v. Slovakia)*, Judgment of 25 September 1997, 1997 ICJ Reports 7, para. 123.

[54] Declaration by the 5th meeting of chairpersons of human rights treaty bodies, UN Doc. E/CN.4/1995/80, 4. Human Rights Committee, General Comment No. 26: Continuity of obligations, 8 September 1997.

[55] R. Higgins, 'The International Court of Justice and Human Rights' in K. Wellens (ed.), *International Law: Theory and Practice. Essays in Honour of Eric Suy* (Nijhoff, The Hague 1998) 691, 696–697.

[56] *Marckx v. Belgium* (App. No. 6833/74), ECtHR, Judgment of 13 June 1979, para. 58.

Subsequent practice of international human rights courts, however, demonstrates an apparent underlying assumption that their judgments may be applicable in the domestic legal sphere directly, without prior transformation into domestic law, despite a domestic legal rule to the contrary. For example, the European Court of Human Rights has ordered the return of property[57] and the immediate release of a detainee.[58] The Inter-American Court of Human Rights has ordered the opening of a school and a medical dispensary,[59] the release of a detainee,[60] and declared amnesty laws to be without legal effect.[61] Although these decisions may still require implementation by domestic authorities, their room for manoeuvre in such cases is very limited indeed.

States do not seem to have objected to these interventionist initiatives. In fact, an increasing number of constitutions, particularly in Eastern Europe, have made provisions of human rights treaties directly applicable in domestic law. However, it would be wrong to suggest that this type of judgment is now generally accepted. In *Avena* the International Court of Justice found that the United States was obliged to provide 'by means of its own choosing, review and reconsideration' of the convictions of the Mexican nationals sentenced to death without consular access.[62] Following this judgment, the US President ordered state courts to give effect to the decision 'in accordance with general principles of comity'.[63] However, the US Supreme Court subsequently decided that the ICJ decision was not enforceable in the absence of implementing legislation.[64]

6. Immunity

Immunity of the state and its (senior) officials from proceedings before a foreign court is based on the traditional maxim *par in parem non habet imperium*. It follows from the sovereign equality of states and is therefore one of the clearest examples of the 'statist' nature of international law.

In several recent cases this rule was challenged with human rights-based arguments but so far with little success, even before international human rights

---

[57] *Papamichalopoulos and Others v. Greece* (Just Satisfaction) (App. No. 14556/89), ECtHR, Judgment of 31 October 1995; *Brumarescu v. Romania* (Just Satisfaction) (App. No. 28342/95), ECtHR, Judgment of 23 January 2001.

[58] *Assanidze v. Georgia* (App. No. 71503/01), ECtHR, Judgment of 8 April 2004.

[59] *Aloeboetoe et al. v. Suriname* (Just Satisfaction), IACtHR, Judgment of 10 September 1993, (1994) Series C No. 15.

[60] *Loayza Tamayo* case, IACtHR, Judgment of 17 September 1997, (1997) Series C No. 33.

[61] *Barrios Altos* case (*Chumbipuma et al. v. Peru*), Judgment of 14 March 2001, (2001) Series C No. 75.

[62] *Avena and Other Mexican Nationals (Mexico v. United States of America)*, Judgment of 31 March 2004, 2004 ICJ Reports 12.

[63] Memorandum by the President for the US Attorney-General, 28 February 2005, (2005) 44 ILM 964.

[64] US Supreme Court, *Medellín v. Texas*, 552 US (2008), Judgment of 25 March 2008.

courts. In 2001, in *Al-Adsani*, the European Court of Human Rights decided that, even when acts of torture are alleged, a state enjoys immunity from civil suit in another state.[65] In 2006, in *Jones v. Saudi Arabia* the House of Lords endorsed this finding.[66] Decisions going the other way, such as *Ferrini*, carry less weight.[67]

In 2002, in the *Arrest Warrant* case, the International Court of Justice made a similar finding with regard to criminal proceedings. It held that incumbent heads of state, heads of government, and foreign ministers were immune from criminal proceedings before foreign courts even if they were charged with crimes under international law.[68] The Court did not attempt to balance the need for stable inter-state relations with the need to fight impunity for serious human rights violations. The International Law Commission has not pronounced on the issue yet.

No significant impact from international human rights law on general international law has therefore occurred so far in this area. Nevertheless, in view of the controversial nature of these decisions (*Al-Adsani* was decided by nine votes to eight and the *Arrest Warrant* decision was accompanied by 11 individual opinions) the law should be regarded as far from settled.

7. Diplomatic Protection

Under traditional international law, diplomatic protection is an instrument for the protection of persons and companies against injury by foreign states. However, because of its firmly established 'statist' nature, the cards are stacked heavily against the individual. As pointed out by the Permanent Court of International Justice in the *Mavrommatis* case, a state resorting to diplomatic action is asserting its own right to ensure, in the person of its subjects, respect for the rules of international law.[69] The underlying doctrine was repeatedly confirmed by the International Course of Justice, most recently in no uncertain terms in the *Barcelona Traction* case: 'The State must be viewed as the sole judge to decide whether its protection will be granted, to what extent it is granted, and when it will cease. It retains in this respect a discretionary power, the exercise of which may be determined by considerations of a political or other nature, unrelated to the particular case.'[70]

---

[65] *Al-Adsani v. United Kingdom* (App. No. 35763/97), ECtHR, Judgment of 21 November 2001, para. 61.

[66] *Jones v. Saudi-Arabia*, UK House of Lords, [2007] 1 AC 270.

[67] *Ferrini v. Federal Republic of Germany*, Italian Court of Cassation, Judgment of 11 March 2004, (2005) 99 AJIL 242.

[68] *Arrest Warrant of 11 April 2000 (Democratic Republic of Congo v. Belgium)*, Judgment of 14 February 2002, 2002 ICJ Reports 3.

[69] *Mavrommatis Palestine Concessions (Jurisdiction) (Greece v. United Kingdom)* 1924 PCIJ Series A, No. 2, 12.

[70] *Barcelona Traction, Light and Power Company, Limited* (New Application: 1962) *(Belgium v. Spain)* Second Phase, Judgment of 5 February 1970, 1970 ICJ Reports 44, para. 79.

It follows that, under the classic regime, a person injured by a foreign state who wishes to benefit from diplomatic protection faces several difficulties. First of all, states enjoy an entirely discretionary power as to whether to exercise diplomatic protection or not. Furthermore, only a person's state of nationality may exercise diplomatic protection on his behalf. Finally, if the state exercising diplomatic protection receives compensation, it is not obliged to transmit it to the injured person. These features of the system of diplomatic protection are particularly problematic if the individual has no alternative enforcement possibilities because domestic remedies are ineffective and remedies on the international plane are lacking.

Since diplomatic protection generally does not arise as an issue in the work of human rights treaty bodies and international criminal tribunals, there is not much pressure emanating from that side to change the system. Within the International Law Commission, the Special Rapporteur on Diplomatic Protection, John Dugard, has attempted to soften some of the system's harshest features, but with very limited success. Article 1 of the Draft Articles is drafted in such a way that it leaves open the question of whether a state exercising diplomatic protection does so in its own right, or that of its national, or both.[71] Proposals by the Special Rapporteur to include a provision in the Draft Articles providing for an obligation to exercise protection under certain circumstances, in particular when the injury results from a grave breach of a peremptory norm of international law, were not accepted by the ILC. The final version of the Draft Articles merely includes a provision *recommending* that states should give due consideration to the possibility of exercising diplomatic protection, especially when a significant injury has occurred; take into account, wherever feasible, the views of injured persons with regard to diplomatic protection and the reparation to be sought; and transfer to the injured person any compensation obtained for the injury from the responsible state subject to any reasonable deductions.[72] The accompanying Commentary duly explains that these are desirable practices which have not yet achieved the status of customary international law.

Attempts to convince the ILC to dispense with the rule that diplomatic protection may only be exercised by the state of nationality of the injured person were similarly unsuccessful. However, the Articles on Diplomatic Protection provide for some softening of the traditional rule. Article 8 introduces the possibility for a state to exercise diplomatic protection on behalf of stateless persons and recognized refugees who are lawfully and habitually resident on its territory.[73] The Commentary qualifies this provision as an exercise in the progressive development of the law.

---

[71] Art. 1, Draft Articles on Diplomatic Protection, Report of the 58th Session of the International Law Commission, UN Doc. A/61/10, para. 49.

[72] Art. 19, Draft Articles on Diplomatic Protection, Report of the 58th Session of the International Law Commission, UN Doc. A/61/10, para. 49.

[73] Ibid., Art. 8.

The International Court of Justice similarly has not shown much inclination to dispense with the nationality requirement. In *DRC v. Uganda*, Uganda alleged, by way of counter-claim, that Congolese troops had maltreated certain Ugandan nationals at Ndjili International Airport. The Court decided to treat this claim as an attempt to exercise diplomatic protection on behalf of these persons and declared it inadmissible because no evidence had been presented to identify them as Ugandan nationals.[74] As pointed out by Judge Simma in his separate opinion, the Court failed to observe that, instead of choosing the avenue of diplomatic protection, Uganda could also have invoked the responsibility of the DRC under Article 48(1)(a) of the Articles on Responsibility of States for Internationally Wrongful Acts. According to that provision, any state is entitled to invoke the responsibility of another state if 'the obligation breached is owed to a group of States including that State and is established for the protection of a collective interest of the group.' Such obligations were clearly at stake here since the abuses suffered by the injured individuals amounted to violations of obligations under international human rights law and international humanitarian law that have an *erga omnes* character. From the point of view of the clarification of the law it is regrettable that Uganda failed to take advantage of this possibility and that the Court failed to draw attention to it.

8. The Right to Consular Notification

Article 36(1)(b) of the Vienna Convention on Consular Relations provides for the right of a detained foreign national to be informed without delay that he may communicate with the consular officers of his own country. In its advisory opinion No.16, the Inter-American Court held that 'failure to observe this right is prejudicial to the due process of law and, in such circumstances, imposition of the death penalty is a violation of the right not to be deprived of life "arbitrarily"' as provided for in various human rights treaties.[75]

In the *La Grand* case, Germany, apparently inspired by this advisory opinion, argued that the right of the detainee to be informed had assumed the character of a human right. In response, the International Court of Justice observed that Article 36 creates individual rights for the detained individual and that consequently the reference to 'rights' in paragraph 2 must be read as applying not only to the rights of the sending state, 'but also to the rights of the detained individual.'[76] However, in *Avena* the Court took a more restrictive approach.

---

[74] *Armed Activities on the Territory of the Congo (Democratic Republic of the Congo v. Uganda)*, Judgment of 19 December 2005, 2005 ICJ Reports 168, para. 333.

[75] *The Right to Information on Consular Assistance in the Framework of the Guarantees of the Due Process of Law*, Advisory Opinion OC-16/99, 1 October 1999.

[76] *LaGrand (Germany v. United States of America)*, Judgment of 27 June 2001, 2001 ICJ Reports 466, para. 89.

Without referring to the Inter-American Court's advisory opinion—of which it clearly was aware—it declined to follow Mexico's suggestion to qualify the right to be informed of the right to consular access as a human right. It stated, rather sweepingly, that '[w]hether or not the Vienna Convention rights are human rights is not a matter that this Court need decide. The Court would, however, observe that neither the text nor the object and purpose of the Convention, nor any indication in the *travaux préparatoires*, support the conclusion that Mexico draws from its contention in that regard.'[77]

In this area, therefore, the impact from international human rights law on general international law has so far been very limited.

9. State Responsibility

Although the Articles on Responsibility of States for Internationally Wrongful Acts are mostly fairly traditional and state-centred, they are nevertheless generally more human rights-minded than the provisions of the Vienna Convention on the Law of Treaties—another result of the work of the International Law Commission. Presumably, this is partly due to the fact that they were adopted more than 30 years later, when international human rights law had developed stronger roots.

9.1 Attribution

An important question that has divided the International Court of Justice and the International Criminal Tribunal for the Former Yugoslavia for a number of years is what degree of control over an armed group is required for its conduct to become attributable to a state. In 1986, in the *Nicaragua* case, the World Court concluded that abuses committed by the *contras* in Nicaragua could not be attributed to the United States because the US had not exercised 'effective control' over this group.[78] In 1999, in the *Tadić* case, the Appeals Chamber of the ICTY criticized this test and took the view that the exercise of 'overall control' is sufficient to render analogous conduct attributable to the state.[79] In 2007, in the *Bosnian Genocide* case, the International Court of Justice responded. It explicitly rejected the ICTY's approach and reiterated its view that 'effective control' is the appropriate test on the grounds that the test adopted by the ICTY would stretch 'too far, almost to breaking point, the connection which must exist between the conduct of a State's organs and its international responsibility.'[80]

---

[77] Ibid., at para. 124.

[78] *Military and Paramilitary Activities in and Against Nicaragua (Nicaragua v. United States)* (Merits), Judgment of 27 June 1986, 1986 ICJ Reports 14, para. 115.

[79] *Prosecutor v. Tadić*, ICTY-94-1-A, Judgment of 15 July 1999, paras. 115–145.

[80] *Application of the Convention on the Prevention and Punishment of the Crime of Genocide (Bosnia and Herzegovina v. Serbia and Montenegro)*, Judgment of 26 February 2007, 2007 ICJ Reports, paras. 396–407 at 406.

On this question, therefore, there has been no impact from international human rights law on general international law. It appears obvious that the difference in approach is due to a difference in starting point. While the ICTY takes the individual victim as its point of departure, the World Court has the interests of states uppermost in its mind. The ILC has taken the side of the ICJ in this clash between international ,courts. Article 8 of the Articles on Responsibility of States for Internationally Wrongful Acts provides that '[t]he conduct of . . . a group of persons shall be considered an act of a State under international law if the . . . group of persons is in fact acting on the instructions of, or under the direction or control of, that State in carrying out the conduct.'

9.2 Positive obligations

International law's traditional approach is to emphasize a state's negative obligations, such as the prohibition of aggression reflected in Article 2(4) of the UN Charter and the prohibition of interference in internal affairs reflected in Article 2(7). The duty to exercise due diligence and state responsibility arising from an omission exist but they are underdeveloped.[81]

International humanitarian law and international human rights law, on the other hand, have long recognized the importance of positive obligations. For the protection of human rights and fundamental values, positive obligations are often more important than negative ones. Accordingly, under common Article 1 of the Geneva Conventions, parties undertake not only to respect but also 'to ensure respect' for the Conventions. Under Article 2 of the International Covenant on Civil and Political Rights, parties undertake not only to respect but also 'to ensure' the rights recognized in the Covenant. Under Article 2 of the International Covenant on Economic, Social and Cultural Rights, parties *inter alia* undertake to take steps through international cooperation to achieve the full realization of the rights contained in the Covenant. The precise content of the positive obligations hinted at in these provisions has been applied in numerous cases by international human rights courts including, most famously, the *Velásquez Rodríguez* case decided by the Inter-American Court of Human Rights.[82]

That the International Court of Justice has also often applied the positive obligations derived from primary rules contained in international human rights instruments is hardly surprising in view of the increasing number of cases in which it is being called upon to interpret those instruments. In its advisory opinion on *The Wall* the Court observed that it followed from common Article 1 of

---

[81] However, according to the commentary to the Articles on Responsibility of States for Internationally Wrongful Acts, cases in which the responsibility of states has been invoked on the basis of an omission have been 'at least as numerous' as those based on positive conduct. J. Crawford, *The International Law Commission's Articles on State Responsibility* (Cambridge University Press, Cambridge 2002) 82.

[82] *Velásquez Rodríguez* case, IACtHR, Judgment of 29 July 1988, (1989) 28 ILM 291.

the Geneva Conventions 'that every State party to that Convention, whether or not it is a party to a specific conflict, is under an obligation to ensure that the requirements of the instruments in question are complied with.'[83] In the *Bosnian Genocide* case the Court found Serbia guilty not of having committed genocide, but of having violated its obligation to prevent genocide and its obligation to cooperate with the International Criminal Tribunal for the Former Yugoslavia by transferring Ratko Mladić for trial.[84]

However, the concept of positive obligations has also made its way into secondary rules of general international law. The concept was incorporated, for example, into Article 41 of the Articles on Responsibility of States for Internationally Wrongful Acts: 'States shall cooperate to bring to an end through lawful means any serious breach within the meaning of Article 40.' This duty therefore arises in response to a serious breach of a peremptory norm of international law. The accompanying commentary expresses hesitation as to whether the positive duty of cooperation set out in Article 41 is already part of general international law, or whether it reflects progressive development.[85] At the same time, the 'responsibility to protect' was recognized by the UN General Assembly in the World Summit Outcome[86] and more recently the Security Council reaffirmed states' 'responsibility to protect populations from genocide, war crimes, ethnic cleansing, and crimes against humanity.'[87]

9.3 Crimes of state

Traditional international law does not distinguish between serious and less serious categories of internationally wrongful acts. Inspired by the codification of individual crimes under international law—in the draft Code of Crimes against the Peace and Security of Mankind[88] and subsequently in the Statute of the International Criminal Court—there has been some support for the codification of the concept of international crimes of state. The ILC introduced this concept in Article 19 of its Draft Articles on State Responsibility.[89] The provision divides internationally wrongful acts into international crimes and international delicts. However, the

---

[83] *Legal Consequences of the Construction of a Wall in the Occupied Palestinian Territory*, Advisory Opinion of 9 July 2004, 2004 ICJ Reports 136, para. 158. The Court's broad interpretation was criticized by Judge Kooijmans in his separate opinion.

[84] *Application of the Convention on the Prevention and Punishment of the Crime of Genocide (Bosnia and Herzegovina v. Serbia and Montenegro)*, Judgment of 26 February 2007, 2007 ICJ Reports.

[85] J. Crawford, *The International Law Commission's Articles on State Responsibility* (Cambridge University Press, Cambridge 2002) 249.

[86] General Assembly Resolution 60/1 (2005), World Summit Outcome, paras. 138–139.

[87] Security Council Resolution 1674 (2006), Protection of Civilians in Armed Conflict, para. 4.

[88] Ybk ILC 1976, vol. II, Part Two.

[89] Ybk ILC, 1976, vol. II, Part Two, 95–96. Adopted by consensus 'to the applause of the members of the Commission.' B.G. Ramcharan, *The Concept and Present Status of the Protection of Human Rights* (Martinus Nijhoff, Dordrecht 1989) 299.

proposal elicited considerable criticism from states. By way of compromise, the International Law Commission therefore proposed a more restricted version of the same underlying idea: 'serious breaches of obligations under peremptory norms of general international law.'[90] Peremptory norms, it may be recalled, include the prohibitions of aggression, genocide, slavery, racial discrimination, torture and the right to self-determination.[91] According to Article 41 of the Articles on Responsibility of States for Internationally Wrongful Acts, 'States shall bring to an end through lawful means any serious breach' within the meaning of this concept.

This result may therefore be regarded as an example of limited, but not insignificant, impact of international human rights law on general international law. While the term 'state crimes' has been consigned to the dustbin it is now generally accepted that certain breaches of international law are more serious than others and therefore entail more serious consequences.

10. Conclusions

This report is not an exhaustive list of instances in which international human rights law has had an impact on general international law or in which it has failed to do so. Moreover, the report has been a mere stocktaking; the process of international human rights law impacting the evolution of general international law is ongoing and likely to continue.

(1) The process is a response to a deeply and widely felt need to make the international legal order more responsive to the needs of a wider range of actors than just states, including the international community (understood as referring to humankind as a whole and not just the community of states).

(2) The impact of international human rights law upon general international law is not always generated by human rights law but sometimes merely by human rights 'thinking' by the International Court of Justice (obligations *erga omnes*) and the International Law Commission (*jus cogens*).

(3) The receptivity of the International Court of Justice and the International Law Commission to the process has been mixed. The Court has often been prepared to incorporate output from human rights treaty bodies and international criminal courts in its findings (most clearly in its advisory opinion on *The Wall* and in the *Bosnian Genocide* case). But in other cases the Court has been quite unwilling to balance traditional state interests against the interests of the individual, even when the latter are reflected in rules of *jus cogens* (such as in its advisory opinion on *Nuclear Weapons* and in the *Arrest Warrant* case).

---

[90] Article 40 of the Articles on Responsibility of States for Internationally Wrongful Acts.
[91] J. Crawford, *The International Law Commission's Articles on State Responsibility* (Cambridge University Press, Cambridge 2002) 188.

(4) It has been suggested that the Court's general approach is to acknowledge the existence of concepts derived from international human rights law, and thereby to 'educate' states, but to apply these concepts cautiously in order not to cause a backlash.[92] If this is indeed the Court's—or some of the judges'— underlying strategy it is understandable and deserving of support.

(5) For the International Law Commission, the question of the impact of international human rights law on general international law has particularly arisen in recent years in the context of its codification exercises on state responsibility, treaty reservations, and diplomatic protection. The ILC has not been fully averse to the process, but the actual steps it has taken have been rather modest, for example, by acknowledging that human rights treaty monitoring bodies have the authority to assess the validity of treaty reservations.

(6) An inquiry into the impact of international human rights law on general international law is to be distinguished from discussions about the so-called fragmentation of international law. The International Law Commission's Study Group on the Fragmentation of International Law regards the VCLT as the answer to any difficulties arising from the fragmentation of international law.[93] This position is debatable because the VCLT is not very human rights-oriented. In the end, human rights, rather than the VCLT, may be the ultimate unifying factor contributing to the coherence of international law.

(7) The permeation of international human rights law through general international law constitutes a quiet revolution which invariably targets international law's most 'statist' features.

---

[92] J. Dugard, *The Future of International Law: A Human Rights Perspective*, Valedictory Lecture, Leiden University, 20 April 2007, 9.

[93] *Fragmentation of International Law: Difficulties Arising from the Diversification and Expansion of International Law*, Report of the Study Group of the International Law Commission, Finalized by Martti Koskenniemi, 13 April 2006, UN Doc. A/CN.4/L.682, 15 and 262.

2

Impact on the Law of Treaties

*Martin Scheinin**

1. Introduction

This chapter discusses the relationship between the Vienna Convention on the Law of Treaties[1] and human rights treaties. The paper identifies alternative approaches in the issue and discusses their relative strengths and weaknesses. The paper is structured on the basis of five different approaches to the relationship in question. A brief concluding discussion follows their presentation and also addresses the question of the impact of human rights treaties upon the international law of treaties.

2. A Textual (Positivist) Approach to the Vienna Convention

An extreme positivist position in relation to the Vienna Convention would be to take it literally as a treaty that regulates treaty relationships between states in accordance with its own provisions—nothing less and nothing more. The application of such an approach would, somewhat surprisingly, result in a situation where the role of the VCLT is quite marginal and at the same time destructive in respect of the functioning of human rights treaties. This is, firstly, because the total number of states parties to the VCLT (108) is smaller than the number of states parties to any one of the six traditional UN human rights treaties, the latter ranging from 145 (CAT) to 193 (CRC).[2] The VCLT would be applicable only

---

* Professor of Public International Law, European University Institute (Florence).
[1] Adopted 23 May 1969, entered into force 27 January 1980, 1155 United Nations Treaty Series 331. Parties on 28 June 2008: 108 (Status of Multilateral Treaties Deposited with the Secretary-General, <http://untreaty.un.org/English/>).
[2] The six treaties referred to are the International Covenant on Economic, Social and Cultural Rights (CESCR; 16 December 1966, entered into force 3 January 1976, 993 UNTS 3), the International Covenant on Civil and Political Rights, (CCPR; 16 December 1966, entered into force 23 March 1976, 999 UNTS 171), the International Convention on the Elimination of All Forms of Racial Discrimination (CERD; adopted 21 December 1965, entered into force 4 January 1969, 660 UNTS 195), the Convention on the Elimination of All Forms of Discrimination against

in treaty relationships between states that also are parties to this Convention. Hence, under a textual reading, the VCLT would not at all apply in respect of a fairly large number of states that are parties to human rights treaties. And in respect of states that are parties to the VCLT, the VCLT would not govern their treaty relationships with states that are not parties to the VCLT.

Secondly, Article 4 of the VCLT contains a non-retroactivity clause according to which the Convention applies only to treaties which are concluded by states after the entry into force of the VCLT with regard to such states. Consequently, the VCLT would not apply in respect of many treaty relationships under human rights treaties between states that as such *are* parties to the VCLT but at least one of them ratified it later than the relevant human rights treaty.

To illustrate the consequences of these observations, let us, as an example, take a look at the 11 states that in the English alphabet start with the letter 'A'.[3] Due to the different ratification records of these states, there are, as of June 2008, 301 bilateral treaty relationships between these states under the six major human rights treaties. As four of the 11 states in question are not parties to the VCLT, and as many of the remaining seven states ratified the VCLT later than most of their human rights treaties, the VCLT is applicable in respect of less than 10 per cent of the total number of bilateral treaty relationships between the 11 states, to be exact in 22 relationships.[4] Even in respect of the CRC which internationally entered into force in 1990, i.e. almost ten years later than the VCLT, the Vienna Convention is applicable only in respect of six bilateral treaty relationships, although all of the 11 states in question are parties to the CRC and the total number of bilateral relationships is therefore 55.[5]

These consequences of the textual positivist approach demonstrate that it would be destructive not only for the coherence of human rights law but for public international law in general mechanically to apply the VCLT, in accordance with its own terms, in some but not all treaty relationships between states. This

---

Women (CEDAW; 18 December 1979, entered into force 3 September 1981, 1249 UNTS 13), the Convention against Torture and Other Cruel, Inhuman or Degrading Treatment or Punishment (CAT; 10 December 1984, entered into force 26 June 1987, 1465 UNTS 85), and the Convention on the Rights of the Child (CRC; 20 November 1989, entered into force 2 September 1990. 1577 UNTS 3). The recent additions to the family: the International Convention on the Protection of the Rights of All Migrant Workers and Members of Their Families (General Assembly resolution 45/158 of 18 December 1990), the Convention on the Rights of Persons with Disabilities (General Assembly resolution 61/106), or Optional Protocols to various treaties are not taken into account here. For the number of states parties, see Status of Multilateral Treaties Deposited with the Secretary-General, <http://untreaty.un.org/English/>, as visited 28 June 2008.

[3] Afghanistan, Albania, Algeria, Andorra, Angola, Antigua and Barbuda, Argentina, Armenia, Australia, Austria and Azerbaijan.

[4] The number of bilateral relationships in respect of which the VCLT is applicable under each of the six treaties is as follows: CESCR 1, CCPR 3, CERD 0, CEDAW 6, CAT 6 and CRC 6.

[5] Afghanistan, Angola, Antigua and Barbuda, and Azerbaijan are not parties to the VCLT. Albania, Andorra and Armenia ratified the VCLT later than the CRC. Consequently, the VCLT would be applicable in respect of the CRC in the relationships between Algeria, Argentina, Australia and Austria.

outcome demonstrates that a sensible relationship between human rights treaties and the VCLT can only be found by understanding the VCLT as something more—or something less—than a set of rules to be applied mechanically within the formal scope of application of the VCLT.

3. A Dogmatic Approach to the Vienna Convention

The non-retroactivity clause in Article 4 of the VCLT was central in the discussion above. However, that provision is more complex than was implied in its mechanical application above. The clause reads as follows:

Without prejudice to the application of any rules set forth in the present Convention to which treaties would be subject under international law independently of the Convention, the Convention applies only to treaties which are concluded by States after the entry into force of the present Convention with regard to such States.

The clause itself speaks against a mechanical positivist application of the VCLT, by referring to rules that would be applicable independently of the VCLT. The formulation reflects a more general understanding of the VCLT as a *codification, approximation,* or *illustration* of valid norms of customary international law in the field of the law of treaties. But if there is a close connection between the provisions of the VCLT and norms of customary law, what exactly is the nature of that connection? Are we speaking of a codification, approximation, *or* illustration?

One possible answer is to take the view that the International Law Commission managed to codify, in a comprehensive and exhaustive way, the customary norms on the law of treaties into the provisions of the VCLT, which therefore are for their substance applicable in respect of all treaties between states, irrespective of whether a particular state is a party to VCLT, or in which order it happened to ratify its international treaties.[6] For instance, Matthew Craven has described the VCLT as having come to assume 'almost canonical significance'.[7] Hence, the rules of the VCLT would be applicable in respect of any multilateral treaty, irrespective of the special characteristics of the treaty. The provisions of the VCLT, which were formulated on the basis of a rich variety

---

[6] For a pragmatic, rather than dogmatic approach leading to the same outcome, see, e.g. A. Aust, *Modern Treaty Law and Practice* (Cambridge University Press, Cambridge 2000) 10: 'To what extent does the Convention express rules of customary international law? A detailed consideration of this question is beyond the scope of this book, but it is, with certain exceptions, not of great concern to the foreign ministry lawyer in his day-to-day work. When questions of treaty law arise during negotiations, whether for a new treaty or about one concluded before the entry into force of the Convention, the rules set forth in the Convention are invariably relied upon even when the states are not parties to it.'

[7] M. Craven, 'Introduction', in M. Craven and M. Fitzmaurice (eds.), *Interrogating the Treaty: Essays in the Contemporary Law of Treaties* (Wolf Legal Publishers, Nijmegen 2005) 1.

of practices, would form a straitjacket in relation to treaty law. Such a dogmatic approach to the VCLT as a complete codification of customary law might lead to the denial of any need to adjust the applicable norms of the law of treaties to the nature of each treaty. For instance, as Articles 31–33 of the VCLT are silent on the relevance of any institutionalized practices of interpretation developed by an international monitoring body established through the treaty, such practices could be said to have no relevance for the interpretation of the treaty. And as Articles 19–21 are silent on the legal effect of impermissible reservations, there might be a temptation to apply the provisions of Article 21, which textually could be understood as referring only to permissible reservations,[8] in respect of any reservation.[9]

These expansive inferences rest upon the assumption that the VCLT would be a true codification of very firm rules of customary international law and that even textual lacunae could be filled by applying the provisions of the VCLT beyond their prescribed scope of application. Such an approach, which is here classified as dogmatic, represents a distorted view of international law and does not bear critical analysis. For instance, on the basis of the preparatory works of the VCLT it is quite clear that the adopted provisions on reservations and objections to reservations were never intended to govern the consequences of impermissible reservations,[10] and that the rules of customary law in respect of reservations to multilateral treaties were unclear at the time the VCLT was drafted. What came to be reflected in the VCLT is the majority view of the International Court of Justice in its Advisory Opinion in the *Reservations to the Genocide Convention* case.[11] That majority view, in turn, departed with reference to the 'special characteristics' of the Genocide Convention from what was referred to as the 'traditional concept', namely the requirement of consent by all parties for the permissibility of any reservation to a multilateral treaty.[12] If there was, at the time when the VCLT was drafted, customary law on the issue of the permissibility of reservations to

---

[8] Textually, Article 21 refers to reservations established 'in accordance with Articles 19, 20 and 23', i.e., to reservations that under Article 19 are permissible and are not, for instance, contrary to the object and purpose of the treaty.

[9] Greig has described the relationship between VCLT Articles 19 and 20 so that Article 19 was designed to place restrictions on the flexibility of entering reservations but its value was undermined by the open-ended nature of Article 20. D. Greig, 'Some Final Reflections', in M. Craven and M. Fitzmaurice (eds.), *Interrogating the Treaty* (2005) 261.

[10] Ybk ILC, 1966 II (UN Doc. A/CN.4/SER.A/1966/Add.1, 209). See also Greig (n. 9), 242.

[11] Reservations to the Convention on the Prevention and Punishment of the Crime of Genocide, Advisory Opinion of 28 May 1951, ICJ Reports 1951, 15. In this advisory opinion (p. 29), the ICJ stated by seven votes to five that a state that has entered a reservation which has been objected to by one or more of the parties to the convention can be regarded as a party to the Genocide Convention if the reservation is compatible with the object and purpose of the convention; 'otherwise, that State cannot be regarded as being a party to the Convention.'

[12] Ibid. For the 'traditional concept' based on the integrity of the treaty, see 22, and for the 'special characteristics' of the Genocide Convention calling for a more flexible approach, see 23.

multilateral treaties, the norm would have been that consent by all other parties is required for entering a reservation.

4. Human Rights Treaties as one of many Special Regimes

There are obvious reasons why human rights lawyers are uncomfortable with a dogmatic application of the VCLT, and why they wish to call for a modified application of the VCLT rules in respect of human rights treaties, such modified application taking due account of the special characteristics of human rights law. Although the VCLT is written as a general treaty applicable in any treaty relationships between states under international treaties, it contains many hidden assumptions that are not justified in respect of human rights treaties. Many of those hidden assumptions are unfounded also in respect of some other treaties, e.g. environmental treaties.[13] Among the most relevant of such hidden assumptions are the following:

(a) The VCLT is written as if only states and state interests mattered: it deals with reciprocal treaty relationships between states where every right by one state has as its correlate a duty of another state. There are no third parties involved—except perhaps third states[14]—and therefore states can legitimately for instance modify a multilateral treaty in their bilateral relationship through an agreement that represents a practice that is contrary to the wording of the treaty.[15]

(b) The VCLT is written as if states would have the sole responsibility to monitor each others' compliance with the treaty. There are no courts or other monitoring bodies involved in the interpretation, monitoring, or enforcement of a treaty. The VCLT regulates how states may react to each others' performance under a treaty but is silent on the role of any other actors. Human rights treaties, but also treaties on environmental law, trade law, or the law of the sea do not fit in the straitjacket woven by the dogmatic and expansive application of the VCLT.

These assumptions reflect the failure of the VCLT to afford attention to the classic distinction between contract treaties and law-making treaties.[16] Human rights

---

[13] See C. Redgwell, 'Reservations, Non-Compliance Procedures, and the "Policing" Role of Treaty Institutions' in M. Craven and M. Fitzmaurice (eds.), *Interrogating the Treaty* (2005) 197.

[14] See VCLT Article 36.

[15] See VCLT Article 41.

[16] The distinction is usually attributed to Triepel but is according to Craven actually traceable to Bergbolm. See M. Craven, 'What Happened to Unequal Treaties?' in M. Craven and M. Fitzmaurice (eds.), *Interrogating the Treaty* (2005) 75. In the same collection, D. Greig, 'Some Final Reflections' 258, suggests that the more parties an international treaty has, the more it comes to resemble a social contract based on its object and purpose.

treaties are only one but perhaps one of the clearest examples of law-making treaties that go beyond reciprocal binary relationships of rights and obligations between contracting states, as they have third-party beneficiaries, a high number of parties, autonomous monitoring mechanisms, and an aspiration to establish objectively binding normative international standards. The law of treaties, in contrast, has been described as 'the last bastion of contract-based international law'.[17]

Basing themselves on the fact that human rights treaties, although technically treaties between states, provide rights for third parties as beneficiaries, as well as on the existence of courts or expert bodies established under human rights treaties to monitor compliance with them, human rights lawyers call for a modified application of the VCLT rules in respect of human rights treaties. For instance, they may propose that monitoring bodies should have a say in assessing the permissibility and consequences of reservations. Or that the institutionalized practices of interpretation developed by a monitoring body established through a human rights treaty should affect the rules of interpretation under that treaty. Or that states should not be allowed to modify the treaty, with consequences for individuals as affected third parties, without following the amendment procedure prescribed by the treaty.

One conclusion drawn from this kind of uneasiness with the dogmatic application of the VCLT is to emphasize the *sui generis* nature of human rights treaties, describing them as a semi-autonomous or self-contained regime that operates according to rules that reflect its own characteristics and that as *lex specialis* deviate from (valid) rules of public international law as they are embodied in the VCLT. Similar conclusions may be drawn in relation to treaties on other branches of international law—such as environmental law or trade law. What results is an erosion of the unity of public international law, also called fragmentation of international law.[18]

However, it is submitted here that human rights law should not be reduced to one of many branches of international law, and that human rights lawyers should not join in the chorus singing the song of fragmentation. Where human rights lawyers are not satisfied with the dogmatic application of the Vienna Convention, they tend to call for stronger normativity for human rights treaties than that which a dogmatic reading of the VCLT seems to offer. They strive for some sort of 'objective' binding force of human rights treaties that would be above the zero-sum game states are playing under the VCLT, permitting states to modify the rules of the game whenever two or more states agree to do so. It would be contrary to this aspiration

---

[17] J. Brunnée, 'Reweaving the Fabric of International Law?' in M. Craven and M. Fitzmaurice (eds.), *Interrogating the Treaty* (2005) 120.

[18] Between 2002 and 2006 the International Law Commission conducted a study under the title 'Fragmentation of international law: difficulties arising from the diversification and expansion of international law', see International Law Commission, Report on the work of its fifty-sixth session (2004, A/59/10), Chapter X, International Law Commission, Report on the work of its fifty-seventh session (2005, A/60/10), Chapter XI, International Law Commission, Report of its Fifty-eighth session (2006, A/61/10), Chapter XII, and General Assembly resolution 61/34 (2006).

for stronger normativity to accept that human rights law is just one of many areas where the unity of public international law must give way to some specific characteristics of a branch of international law. Under the fragmentation approach, the quest for stronger normativity under human rights law than that which the law of treaties generally offers to treaties could, paradoxically, contribute to the weakening of international law in general. While the outcome of the International Law Commission's study on fragmentation of international law needs to be criticized for an over-emphasis of the role of the VCLT as an expression of generally applicable norms of the law of treaties,[19] its overall outcome of resorting back to the law of treaties appears to be the correct one. Hence, the challenge to human rights law is about its impact upon the general norms of the law of treaties.

5. Human Rights Norms as a Global Constitution

Many of the same arguments that human rights lawyers may offer as explanations for a trend of fragmentation may, however, also be presented to justify the opposite conclusion, namely a call for a more coherent and rigid structure of public international law. This approach would put forward the argument that human rights law is something more than just one branch of international law, namely a constitutional dimension of international law, representing objectively binding rules, that is, norms that are legally binding upon states irrespective of their continuing will to be bound. The European Court of Human Rights often refers to the constitutional nature of the ECHR,[20] and on the universal level one could speak of human rights treaties as an embryonic form of a global constitution. The VCLT may remain applicable according to its own terms in respect of those multilateral treaties that merely govern reciprocal relationships between states, with no third parties affected. But its provisions are insufficient and inadequate[21] for capturing

---

[19] For instance, the third conclusion of the study reads: 'When seeking to determine the relationship of two or more norms to each other, the norms should be interpreted in accordance with or analogously to the VCLT and especially the provisions in its Articles 31–33 having to do with the interpretation of treaties.' International Law Commission, Report of its Fifty-eighth session (2006, A/61/10), Chapter XII, Conclusion No. 3. In the view of the present author, it would have been much more proper here to refer to the law of treaties in general rather than the text of the VCLT.

[20] See, for instance, *Banković and Others against Belgium and Others* (Application No. 52207/99), ECtHR, Grand Chamber, inadmissibility decision of 12 December 2001: 'The Court's obligation, in this respect, is to have regard to the special character of the Convention as a constitutional instrument of European public order for the protection of individual human beings and its role, as set out in Article 19 of the Convention, is to ensure the observance of the engagements undertaken by the Contracting Parties' (para. 80).

[21] 'Inappropriate' and 'inadequate' were the words used by the Human Rights Committee in its General Comment No. 24 on reservations: 'As indicated above, it is the Vienna Convention on the Law of Treaties that provides the definition of reservations and also the application of the object and purpose test in the absence of other specific provisions. But the Committee believes that its provisions on the role of State objections in relation to reservations are inappropriate to address the problem of reservations to human rights treaties. Such treaties, and the Covenant specifically, are not a web of inter-State exchanges of mutual obligations. They concern the endowment of

the operation of human rights treaties that are more than just treaties between states, namely elements of an emerging global constitutional order.

This kind of approach to human rights law as a constitutional dimension of public international law may build its articulation partly with reference to the category of *jus cogens,* also recognized in the VCLT itself.[22] However, the formal supremacy of *jus cogens* human rights norms in respect of treaty provisions incompatible with such norms is a narrow and extreme case of the constitutional nature of human rights norms. In a more general sense, the constitutional nature of human rights norms rests on their close substantive link to fundamental moral values and to their structure with third parties as beneficiaries. Ultimately, the argument about human rights law as a global constitution rests on the special nature of human rights as such, and instead of calling for formal and absolute supremacy as in the special case of *jus cogens*, it may manifest itself in softer forms that afford a special status to human rights law in respect of 'merely' contractual treaties between states. For instance, the constitutional nature of human rights norms may in practice mean that they are applied as 'horizontal' norms that govern the interpretation of concepts and provisions found in treaties, including in the VCLT. Rather than speaking of a formal hierarchy of sources that would claim supremacy to human rights *treaties* in respect of other treaties, the constitutional dimension of human rights norms is based in their substantive content and, hence, represents a constitution in the substantive, rather than formal, sense.

By way of illustration, reference can be made to the notion of 'object and purpose' in the VCLT, Article 19. In respect of reservations to human rights treaties this notion can be interpreted broadly, and when combined with the principle of effective implementation of a human rights treaty this may lead to rather drastic consequences for states that choose to ratify human rights treaties but try to evade the resulting obligations by entering far-reaching reservations. Under a human rights treaty, a state may find itself in a situation where its reservation is declared impermissible[23] and treated as severable[24] from the state's acceptance to be

individuals with rights. The principle of inter-State reciprocity has no place, save perhaps in the limited context of reservations to declarations on the Committee's competence under Article 41. And because the operation of the classic rules on reservations is so inadequate for the Covenant, States have often not seen any legal interest in or need to object to reservations...' (para 17).

[22] VCLT Article 53.

[23] Human Rights Committee, General Comment No. 24: 'It necessarily falls to the Committee to determine whether a specific reservation is compatible with the object and purpose of the Covenant. This is in part because, as indicated above, it is an inappropriate task for States parties in relation to human rights treaties, and in part because it is a task that the Committee cannot avoid in the performance of its functions. In order to know the scope of its duty to examine a State's compliance under Article 40 or a communication under the first Optional Protocol, the Committee has necessarily to take a view on the compatibility of a reservation with the object and purpose of the Covenant and with general international law. Because of the special character of a human rights treaty, the compatibility of a reservation with the object and purpose of the Covenant must be established objectively, by reference to legal principles, and the Committee is particularly well placed to perform this task...' (para. 18).

[24] Human Rights Committee, General Comment No. 24, paragraph 18 *in fine*: 'The normal consequence of an unacceptable reservation is not that the Covenant will not be in effect at all

bound by the treaty, while the acceptance itself is understood to be irreversible.[25] Consent by an individual state would no longer be an absolute limit to state obligations under human rights treaties but would when needed be pushed aside by an objectively binding 'constitution'.[26] If the above explanation is correct, that it is the substantive *norms* of human rights that possess a constitutional quality, the modification of the rules governing the permissibility and consequences of reservations to human rights *treaties* would relate to human rights norms enshrined in human rights treaties, not just any provision of a human rights treaty.

6. Reconciling the Vienna Convention and Human Rights Treaties

The author of this chapter is attracted by the 'constitutional' approach just described, at least as a critical tool for addressing the shortcomings of a state-centred conception of evolving international law. As this approach will result in 'more law', rather than the erosion of international legal order which is the consequence of the fragmentation approach, the constitutional approach is much more appealing from a substantive human rights perspective than the preceding one.

Nevertheless, the author is at the same time mindful of the fact that the constitutional approach may be too radical for many scholars of public international law, not to mention international or domestic judges or governments. Therefore its proponents run a risk of being marginalized in a broader discourse about the place of human rights in world order. In order to avoid this risk, human rights lawyers need to strive for an approach that reconciles the rules of the VCLT with the special characteristics of human rights norms (or human rights treaties). Parallel to the elaboration of such a reconciliation approach, they may also resort to the critical nature of the constitutional approach as a justification for the need for a modified, instead of textual or dogmatic, application of the VCLT rules.

In short, the proposed reconciliation approach is based on the acceptance of the VCLT as a *reflection* of norms of customary law, through positive treaty provisions the wording of which was formulated with one ideal type of treaties

for a reserving party. Rather, such a reservation will generally be severable, in the sense that the Covenant will be operative for the reserving party without benefit of the reservation.'

[25] Human Rights Committee, General Comment No. 26: 'The Committee is therefore firmly of the view that international law does not permit a State which has ratified or acceded or succeeded to the Covenant to denounce it or withdraw from it.' (para. 5). Although the general comment includes references to the VCLT, it includes no mention of Article 54(b), providing for the right of a state to withdraw from a multilateral treaty with the consent of the other parties to the treaty.

[26] J. Merrills, 'The Mutability of Treaty Obligations' describes the severability approach taken by the European and Inter-American Courts of Human Rights and the Human Rights Committee as a paradigm shift where voluntarism is replaced by the demands of institutional effectiveness. In M. Craven and M. Fitzmaurice (eds.), *Interrogating the Treaty* (2005) 99. For further sources on the effect of reservations to human rights treaties, see, *inter alia*, C. Brölmann, 'Limits of the Treaty Paradigm', 32, in the same collection.

in mind. The drafters of the VCLT focused on inter-state relationships under a multilateral treaty that establishes no organ for its monitoring or enforcement and that merely regulates reciprocal relationships between states as rights-holders and obligation-bearers, with no affected third parties. Human rights lawyers can accept the full applicability of the provisions of the VCLT in respect of treaties that represent this ideal type of multilateral treaty.

However, when a treaty does not conform to all the described features of the ideal type, the rules of the VCLT do not represent a complete codification of rules of customary law but, rather, approximations of the applicable rules, subject to modified application whenever the specific characteristics of the treaty so require.

There are elements in the VCLT itself that appear to recognize that not all treaties conform to the ideal type of multilateral treaty that was the starting point in formulating the provisions. The clearest examples are constituent treaties of international organizations. Article 5 provides a rule, according to which the VCLT 'applies to any treaty which is the constituent instrument of an international organization and to any treaty adopted within an international organization without prejudice to any relevant rules of the organization'. And Article 20 on acceptance of and objections to reservations includes paragraph 3 according to which a reservation to a treaty that is a constituent instrument of an international organization 'requires the acceptance of the competent organ of that organization'.

Choosing an overly positivist mood, human rights lawyers could argue that at least some human rights treaties fall under VCLT Articles 5 and 20(3) as 'international organizations'. For instance, the International Covenant on Civil and Political Rights has its own membership[27] and establishes its own organs with defined competences.[28] Hence, any reservation would require the acceptance by the Human Rights Committee, which under the terms of the treaty appears to be the competent organ in respect of all functions that pertain to substantive interpretation of the human rights provisions in the treaty. Within environmental law, substantive multilateral treaties with a monitoring organ have actually been described as constituting treaties of an international organization, such as the Ozone Secretariat.[29]

Alternatively, and still within the positivist mood, human rights lawyers could argue that most human rights treaties are treaties 'adopted within an international organization' under the terms of VCLT Article 5. As a consequence, one would turn to 'relevant rules of the organization' as basis for a modified application of the provisions of the VCLT in issues such as reservations, interpretation and termination.

Instead of these fairly straightforward positivist answers, the reconciliation approach proposed in this Chapter would take VCLT Articles 5 and 20(3) as reflecting a more general principle: the recognition to adapt the application of the

[27] ICCPR Article 48.
[28] ICCPR Article 30 (3) (meeting of states parties), Article 28 (Human Rights Committee).
[29] See C. Brölmann, 'Limits of the Treaty Paradigm', in M. Craven and M. Fitzmaurice (eds.), *Interrogating the Treaty* (2005) 37.

VCLT to the specific features of a treaty. One would ask *why* the VCLT includes these two provisions in respect of constituent instruments of an international organization and whether the same justification applies in respect of some *other* category of treaties. According to literature, the justification for VCLT Article 20(3) lies in the essential need to preserve the integrity of an international organization.[30] Judging by the preparatory works of the VCLT, the justification for Article 20(3) was primarily addressed through the existence of a common monitoring organ established through the treaty, rather than the notion of 'international organization' as such.[31] The same arguments can very well be made in respect of human rights treaties that establish their own international monitoring organs and procedures, without a need to declare human rights treaties as falling, *stricto sensu*, under the notion of international organizations.

Another example of the reconciliation approach can be identified in respect of VCLT Articles 57 and 58 relating to the suspension of treaties. For instance in relation to the ICCPR these provisions should be read together with Article 4 of the ICCPR, defining derogation as the specific form of suspension that is allowed under the treaty and prescribing both substantive limits and procedural requirements for states that wish to resort to derogation. VCLT Articles 57(a) and 58(1)(a) explicitly refer to the provisions of the treaty as regulating suspension, and Article 58, which allows for suspension by agreement of certain but not all parties to a multilateral treaty, includes in Article 58(1)(b)(ii) a safeguard clause according to which such suspension must not be contrary to the object and purpose of the treaty.

Further, although VCLT Article 31, which contains the general rule of treaty interpretation, makes no mention of the relevance of institutionalized practices of interpretation developed through treaty monitoring organs in the exercise of their functions, it includes in Article 31(3)(b) a reference to 'any subsequent practice in the application of the treaty which establishes the agreement of the parties regarding its interpretation'. On the basis of the preparatory works, it appears clear that this clause does not merely refer to explicit acceptance by all states parties to a multilateral treaty but covers also the tacit approval of a practice engaging only some of the parties.[32] Hence, it would be legitimate to treat the outcomes of human rights treaty monitoring procedures, such as final views on individual complaints, concluding observations on state party reports, and general comments as codifications of earlier practice, as various forms of 'subsequent practice' in the meaning of VCLT Article 31(3)(b)—at least in the vast majority of instances where no formal objection is made by states parties.

---

[30] Aust, op. cit. (n. 6) 113.
[31] See Ybk ILC 1966 II (UN Doc. A/CN.4/SER.A/1966/Add.1), 207 where the argument is made that for the category of treaties in question the integrity of the instrument outweighs other considerations and it must be for the members of the organization, acting through its competent organ, to determine in how far any relaxation of the integrity of the instrument is acceptable.
[32] Ybk ILC 1966 II (UN Doc. A/CN.4/SER.A/1966/Add.1), 221–222.

7. Concluding Discussion

In the preceding sections of this Chapter, the *positivist* approach, the *dogmatic* approach and the *fragmentation* approach to the relationship between the VCLT and human rights treaties were rejected. Instead, the author expressed sympathy for the two remaining approaches, namely the *constitutional* and the *reconciliation* approaches. In the author's view the reconciliation approach has a strong basis in international law, including in a systematic reading and the drafting of the VCLT itself. The reconciliation approach is also more likely than the constitutional approach to meet acceptance beyond the circle of human rights scholars and human rights bodies, i.e. also within a broader discourse on public international law.

However, it is the view of the author that the constitutional approach has, in comparison to the reconciliation approach, two merits that justify its further consideration and elaboration, but rather within the reconciliation approach than as a real alternative to it. Firstly, the emphasis on the constitutional dimension of human rights represents a critical potential in respect of a state-centred doctrine of international law. Secondly, there may be areas where reconciliation does not suffice, i.e. where human rights treaties under their own terms and read in the light of their object and purpose call for the application of such norms in the field of the law of treaties that cannot be reconciled with the provisions of the VCLT but where one must accept that a *choice* between the rules derived from human rights treaties and the provisions of the VCLT must be made. One would not abandon the need to reconcile, but would be prepared to set aside the letter of the VCLT in order to reach a result that reconciles the international law of treaties with the constitutional dimension of human rights law.

One such area may be the potential severability of impermissible reservations.[33] The reconciliation approach may very well allow such an interpretation of the VCLT, including in the light of its Article 20(3), that recognizes the competence of monitoring organs established under human rights treaties to address and determine, at least for the purpose of their own functions, the permissibility of reservations by states. However, the next step, declaring an impermissible reservation severable, and holding the state bound by the treaty without the benefit of the reservation, might prove more difficult to reconcile with the VCLT regime, also taking into account the majority view in the ICJ Advisory Opinion in the *Reservations to the Genocide Convention* case.[34]

That said, it needs to be pointed out that the conclusion of severability has not been made merely by human rights scholars and human rights treaty bodies. Instead, it gains support also from the practice of at least certain states which, when objecting to reservations by other states, have concluded that the reserving

---

[33] On this issue see also Chapter 4 of this volume.
[34] See n. 11, above.

state is to be considered a party to the treaty in question, without the benefit of the reservation. Before the adoption of General Comment No. 24 by the Human Rights Committee in 1994, objections pronouncing the severability of the reservation had under the ICCPR been made by a number of states in respect of reservations by the Republic of Korea (1991)[35] and the United States (1992).[36] And much earlier, the United Kingdom applied what is here called severability in its objections to certain reservations entered under the 1949 Geneva Conventions on humanitarian law.[37]

In respect of the practical relevance of the various competing approaches described in this paper, it is interesting to note that two (France and the UK) of the three states (France, the UK and the USA)[38] that reacted to the Human Rights Committee's General Comment No. 24 by formally expressing their disagreement, had themselves on other occasions expressed the consequence of severability in their objections to reservations by other states. And many other states have, since the adoption of General Comment No. 24, supported the consequence of severability in their objections to reservations by some states. Such objections have been made in respect of reservations to the ICCPR or its Optional Protocols by at least Azerbaijan, Botswana, Guyana, Kuwait, Thailand, Trinidad and Tobago, and Turkey. Objections to these reservations, explicitly pronouncing severability as the consequence, were made by at least Denmark, Finland, Greece, the Netherlands, Norway, Poland, Portugal and Sweden.[39]

To the extent that severability as a consequence of an impermissible reservation represents the constitutional approach, and breaks the limits of any reconciliation between human rights treaties and the VCLT, there is also considerable

---

[35] Objection by the Czech and Slovak Federal Republic, 7 June 1991: '... does not recognize these reservations [to Articles 14 and 22] as valid. Nevertheless the present declaration will not be deemed to be an obstacle to the entry into force of the Covenant between the Czech and Slovak Federal Republic and the Republic of Korea.' See, also, the objection by the Netherlands. Status of Multilateral Treaties Deposited with the Secretary-General, <http://untreaty.un.org/English/access.asp>.

[36] The clearest examples of objections declaring severability are those by France and Italy. France, 4 October 1993: 'this United States reservation [to Article 6, paragraph 5] is not valid, inasmuch as it is incompatible with the object and purpose of the Convention. Such objection does not constitute an obstacle to the entry into force of the Covenant between France and the United States.' Italy, 5 October 1993: 'this reservation is null and void since it is incompatible with the object and the purpose of art. 6 of the Covenant... These objections do not constitute an obstacle to the entry into force of the Covenant between Italy and the United States.'

[37] See *Reservations to human rights treaties*; Final working paper submitted by Françoise Hampson, Sub-Commission on the Promotion and Protection of Human Rights (2004), UN Doc. E/CN.4/Sub.2/2004/42, paras 16–17.

[38] See Annual Report 1995 of the Human Rights Committee, UN Doc. A/50/40 vol. I 126–134 (the United States and the United Kingdom), Annual Report 1996 of the Human Rights Committee, A/51/40 vol. I, pp. 104–106 (France).

[39] For a brief account of state practice in the field of objections to reservations under the ICCPR, see M. Scheinin, 'Reservations to the International Covenant on Civil and Political Rights: Reflections on State Practice' in T. Koivurova (ed.), *Kansainvälistyvä oikeus: Juhlakirja, Professori Kari Hakapää*. [Law Going International: Essays in Honour of Professor Kari Hakapää.] (Rovaniemi, University of Lapland, Faculty of Law 2005), 479–488.

state practice supporting the constitutional approach. A new chapter in the book of state practice concerning reservations, and reflecting the growing impact of human rights law upon the law of treaties, was written subsequent to Bahrain's submission of a general reservation to the ICCPR in December 2006, *after* it had first in September 2006 acceded to the treaty. Both the substance of the reservation, subordinating the application of the ICCPR to Shariah, and the belated nature of the reservation triggered a record number (15) of objections by other states. While these objections generally declared Bahrain's reservation as impermissible, for being contrary to the rules and principles of the law of treaties, as well as the object and purpose of the ICCPR, most objecting states did not pronounce themselves on the legal consequences of the reservation they objected to as impermissible, beyond stating that the reservation did not preclude Bahrain from being considered a party to the ICCPR. Some states, however, were explicit in taking the position of severability, i.e. declaring that Bahrain is a party to the treaty without the benefit of its impermissible reservation. For instance, according to Mexico the reservation was 'invalid', and according to Sweden 'null and void'. In its objection the United Kingdom declared that the consequence of the late submission of the reservation by Bahrain had the consequence that the reservation 'shall have no effect'. Quite exceptionally, in view of the objections, the Secretary-General explicitly declared non-acceptance of the reservation made by Bahrain.[40]

As a more general conclusion it is submitted that the above discussion on different approaches to the relationship between the law of treaties and human rights treaties calls for caution whenever reference is made to the VCLT in the application of human rights treaties. Does a human rights court or expert body, or a scholar, or a state or intergovernmental organization, refer to the VCLT selectively, i.e. only when it suits the purposes of the actor? And what is the exact way these actors refer to the VCLT in the context of a human rights treaty: is the proposed way of applying the human rights treaty in question 'prescribed' by the VCLT, or is it merely the correct way to interpret the treaty itself, also 'reflected' in how relevant norms of the international law of treaties are formulated in the VCLT? In the view of the author, the correct answer is the latter one. Consequently, there is no need for human rights actors to be selective when making references to the law of treaties but, rather, to remain critical and consistent as to the way they refer to the VCLT and apply the law of treaties.

---

[40] 'In view of the below objections, the Secretary-General did not accept the reservation made by Bahrain in deposit.' This is the formulation used on the United Nations internet database on the status of multilateral treaties, see <http://untreaty.un.org/ENGLISH/bible/englishinternetbible/partI/chapterIV/treaty6.asp#N18>. For the text of the various objections, see also <http://www2.ohchr.org/english/bodies/ratification/4.htm>.

3

Impact on General Principles of Treaty Interpretation

*Jonas Christoffersen**

1. Introduction

Widespread is the view that the interpretation of human rights treaties is generally subject to special rules, deviating from generally accepted interpretative canons of international law. The view is most clearly expressed by the European Court of Human Rights, which claims that in interpreting the European Convention on Human Rights (ECHR) 'regard must be had to its special character as a treaty for the collective enforcement of human rights and fundamental freedoms'.[1]

In the following I argue, however, that the Court's method of interpretation is firmly rooted within the traditional canons of interpretation of general international law (Section 2) and that the method of subsidiary review does not deviate substantially from generally accepted methods of review in international law (Section 3). Accordingly, I suggest that general principles of treaty interpretation have had—and continue to have—tremendous impact on human rights law, whereas human rights law has not had much of an impact on general international law on the methodological plane, although the substance of human rights law—alongside all other branches of international law—will of course be part of the general body of international law.

I recognize that international lawyers over the last decades have faced growing concern over the special nature of international human rights law as part of a wider fear of fragmentaion of international law, and that contemporary international lawyers regularly consider international human rights law a special regime under international law.[2] While I have not been able to track down the source

---

* Associate professor in international human rights law at the University of Copenhagen.
[1] *Soering v.United Kingdom* (App. No. 14038/88), ECtHR, Judgment of 7 July 1989, (1989) Series A No. 161, para. 87.
[2] Conclusions of the Study Group on the Fragmentation of International Law adopted by the International Law Commission in its 58th Session and submitted to the General Assembly as part of the Commission's report covering the work of that session (UN Doc. A/61/10, para 251).

of the notion of a special doctrine of human rights interpretation, a good point of departure is Karel Vasak's 25-year-old suggestion that a developing, specific international law of protection was questioning certain traditional categories and solutions under general international law. International human rights law was, in Vasak's view, developing into a special branch of international law, although the special nature of human rights law stopped short of challenging the traditional state-centred structure of international law.[3] Vasak's point of departure was Wolfgang Friedmann's theory of the changing structure of international law. Friedmann recognized a development from the law of coexistence to the law of cooperation due, in part, to the increased focus in international law on the rights of individuals.[4] Friedmann recognized the significant progress achieved under the European Convention of Human Rights in 1964,[5] although he was sceptical about the possibility in practice of a global cooperation in the field of human rights.

The interaction between general canons of treaty interpretation and special means of human rights interpretation is of particular concern to international law, to the extent that human rights law breaks away from general international law by refuting its generally accepted norms. A (too) special nature of international human rights law is likely to erode the otherwise growing respect it is experiencing. This is particularly disturbing to the extent that other branches of international law would not place adequate weight on human rights in the interpretation of other sources. After all, human rights law forms part of general international law and is in dire need of support therefrom.

The European Court of Human Rights has sought to uphold the fine line between maintaining a link to general international law while at the same time separating itself therefrom. On the one hand, the Court has emphasized the international law background of the ECHR by stating that it 'should so far as possible be interpreted in harmony with other rules of international law of which it forms part'.[6] On the other hand, a 'special nature' discourse has been in action since the Court stated in 1989 that in 'interpreting the Convention regard must be had to its special character as a treaty for the collective enforcement of human rights and fundamental freedoms'.[7]

It is not an easy task to test the accuracy of the 'special nature' claim, because any comparison requires a common starting point. If an interpretation of a human

---

[3] K. Vasak, 'Towards a Specific International Human Rights Law' in K. Vasak and P. Alston (eds.), *The International Dimension of Human Rights* (Unesco, Paris 1982) 671–672.

[4] W. Friedmann, *The Changing Structure of International Law* (London, Stevens & Sons 1964), 40–44, 62 and 240–244; J. Crawford, 'The ILC's Articles on Responsibility of States for Internationally Wrongful Acts: A Retrospect' (2002) 96 AJIL 874, 887 points out that treaties may create individual rights that are not classified as human rights.

[5] Friedmann, *The Changing Structure of International Law* (1964), 63.

[6] *Fogarty v. United Kingdom* (App. No. 37112/97), ECtHR, Judgment of 21 November 2001, ECHR 2001-XI para. 35.

[7] *Soering v. United Kingdom* (App. No. 14038/88), ECtHR, Judgment of 7 July 1989, (1989) Series A No. 161, para. 87.

rights treaty favours the individual, is it then necessarily an individual-friendly interpretation in the sense that the interpretation goes further in the direction of the individual than the application of some other method of interpreation would go? Or is it just a straightforward interpretation based on general principles? I take the view that human rights law may be a special branch of international law to the extent that it provides different legal answers to similar problems compared to resolutions adopted under general international law.[8] It is, in my view, not sufficient to label human rights law as special when some other interpretation might be possible on the basis of general principles of interpretation. A verification or falsification of the 'special nature' claim thus requires in-depth analysis of the differences and similarities between the overarching general principles and the various branches of international law (trade law, sea law, communications law, human rights law, etc.); human rights law can only be considered special if it is demonstrated that different principles of interpretation are applicable in different fields of law.

In the following, I will address the issue from the perspective of the European Court of Human Rights. It is not possible within the scope of the present piece to include other human rights treaties, but I suggest that the answers provided would be similar. The scope of the following discussion is limited to the means of interpretation of the substance of human rights provisions thus leaving other issues (reservations, state succession etc.) to be discussed elsewhere.

2. General Doctrines of Treaty Interpretation

The 'special nature' claim must be tested against the content of general international law. General international law must be elucidated in order to arrive at a sufficiently well-founded appreciation of the ordinary or special character of human rights interpretative principles.

Extensive practice and literature exists on the construction of treaties and the delimitation of international legal reasoning. It is not required here to engage in a thorough and systematic analysis of the particular elements of the Vienna Convention on the Law of Treaties (VCLT) as the rules of the VCLT reflect a non-exhaustive approximation of general principles. One might conduct a technical analysis of the content of the particular rules, but substantive analysis is really called for to specify the precise impact of the various principles in different contexts. It may be taken for granted that the rules are applied differently in diverse areas of law, and that differences are not necessarily at variance with the VCLT. Put briefly, there is no one correct method of interpretation.

The International Law Commission (ILC) accordingly recognized the hermeneutic or subjective element inherent in the application of different methods of interpretation, observing that the process is 'not automatic but depends on the

---

[8] See ILC at n. 3, para. 12, point no. 2.

conviction of the interpreter' and that 'recourse to many of these principles is discretionary rather than obligatory and the interpretation of documents is to some extent an art, not an exact science'.[9] One might argue that the looseness of this proposition fits states' interests too well and leaves too much discretion to international arbiters, but it is more likely that the ILC sought to reconcile the disagreement among international lawyers as to the weight attached to: (i) the text as the expression of the intention of the parties, (ii) a subjective element distinct from the text, and (iii) the object and purpose of the treaty.[10]

The ILC emphasized 'the primacy of the text as the basis of interpretation, while at the same time giving a certain place to extrinsic evidence of the intentions of the parties and to the objects and purposes of the treaty as means of interpretation'.[11] Put differently, the various interpretative factors are not structured hierarchically and their application remains a matter of weighing the various interpretative principles. The limits to the scope of permissible interpretation cannot be entertained here, but the ILC observed that international courts should not 'revise treaties or . . . read into them what they do not, expressly or by implication, contain', which was taken to mean that 'an interpretation which ran counter to the clear meaning of the terms would not be to interpret but to revise the treaty'.[12]

The European Court of Human Rights adopted, in its earliest case law, ordinary rules on the interpretation of international treaties.[13] The Court expressly recognized in *Golder v. the United Kingdom* that the interpretation of the Convention should be 'guided by Articles 31 to 33 of the Vienna Convention of 23 May 1969 on the Law of Treaties' which articles were said to 'enunciate in essence generally accepted principles of international law'.[14] The ILC had emphasized that the distinction between primary and supplementary means of interpretation (Articles 31 and 32 respectively) did not entail 'a rigid line' as there is 'a general link' between the provisions, because of 'the unity of the process of interpretation'.[15]

---

[9] Ybk ILC 1966 II, 218, para. 4.

[10] Ibid., 218, para. 1.   [11] Ibid., 218, para. 2.

[12] Ibid., 221, cf. *Interpretation of Peace Treaties with Bulgaria, Hungary and Romania*, Advisory Opinion of 30 March 1950, 1950 ICJ Reports 65.

[13] *Lawless v. Ireland (No. 1) (Preliminary objection)* (App. No. 332/57), ECtHR, Judgment of 14 November 1960, (1960) Series A No. 1; *Lawless v. Ireland* (No. 3) (App. No. 332/57), ECtHR, Judgment of 1 July 1961, (1961) Series A No. 3, 53, para. 14; *Wemhoff v. Germany* (App. No. 2122/64), ECtHR, Judgment of 27 June 1968 (1968) Series A No. 7, para. 8; *Case 'relating to certain aspects of the laws on the use of languages in education in Belgium'* (*Belgian Linguistic* Case) (merits) (App. No. 1474/62; 1677/62; 1691/62; 1769/63; 1994/63; 2126/64), ECtHR, Judgment of 23 July 1968, (1968) Series A No. 6; *Ringeisen v. Austria* (App. No. 2614/65), ECtHR, Judgment of 16 July 1972, (1971) Series A No. 13.

[14] *Golder v. United Kingdom* (App. No. 4451/70), ECtHR, Judgment of 21 February 1975, (1975) Series A No. 18, para. 29; See also *Golder v. United Kingdom* (App. No. 4451/70) (1973) Series B No. 16, paras. 44–47; *National Union of Belgian Police v. Belgium* (App. No. 4464/70) (1974) Series B No. 17, para. 56; *Swedish Engine Drivers' Union v. Sweden* (App. No. 5614/72) (1974) Series B No. 18, para. 60.

[15] International Law Commission (1966), p. 220, para. 10. The Court described the process of interpretation as 'a single combined operation'; see *Golder v. United Kingdom* (App. No. 4451/70), ECtHR, Judgment of 21 February 1975, (1975) Series A No. 18, para. 30.

The general approach to the interpretation of the ECHR is illustrated by the express recognition in *Wemhoff v. Germany* that the ECHR should not be interpreted in a manner restricting 'to the greatest possible degree the obligations undertaken by the Parties'.[16] The Court also decided not to attach great weight to the preparatory works,[17] although it relied on them to confirm an interpretation in the *Belgian Linguistic* case.[18] The intention of the contracting parties has been emphasized on occasion,[19] but the Court has given primacy to the text of the Convention[20] read in the light of its object and purpose,[21] the principle of effectiveness,[22] and general principles of law.[23] The Court has expressly stated that the ECHR 'should so far as possible be interpreted in harmony with other rules of international law of which it forms part'.[24] This interpretative approach of the Strasbourg Court does not appear to deviate from that of general international law. Hence, although the International Court of Justice (ICJ) has resorted to the

[16] *Wemhoff v. Germany* (App. No. 2122/64), ECtHR, Judgment of 27 June 1968, (1968) Series A No. 7, 23, para. 8.

[17] *Lawless v. Ireland (No. 3)* (App. No. 332/57), ECtHR, Judgment of 1 July 1961, (1961) Series A No. 3, p. 53, para. 14; on the use of preparatory works in international law, see e.g. H. Lauterpacht, 'Restrictive Interpretation and the Principle of Effectiveness in the Interpretation of Treaties' (1949) 26 BYIL 63.

[18] *Case 'relating to certain aspects of the laws on the use of languages in education in Belgium'* (*Belgian Linguistic* Case) (merits) (App. No. 1474/62; 1677/62; 1691/62; 1769/63; 1994/63; 2126/64), ECtHR, Judgment of 23 July 1968, (1968) Series A No. 6, 30–31, para. 3.

[19] *Wemhoff v. Germany* (App. No. 2122/64), ECtHR, Judgment of 27 June 1968, (1968) Series A No. 7, 21, para. 4 and 23, para. 9; *Case 'relating to certain aspects of the laws on the use of languages in education in Belgium'* (*Belgian Linguistic* Case) (merits) (App. No. 1474/62; 1677/62; 1691/62;1769/63; 1994/63; 2126/64), ECtHR, Judgment of 23 July 1968, (1968) Series A No. 6, 35, para. 11; *De Wilde, Ooms and Versyp ('Vagrancy') v. Belgium (merits)* (App. No. 2832/66; 2835/66; 2899/66), ECtHR, Judgment of 18 June 1972, (1971) Series A No. 12, 8, para. 16.

[20] *Lawless v. Ireland (No. 3)* (App. No. 332/57), ECtHR, Judgment of 1 July 1961, (1961) Series A No. 3, para. 14; *Case 'relating to certain aspects of the laws on the use of languages in education in Belgium'* (*Belgian Linguistic* Case) (merits) (App. No. 1474/62; 1677/62; 1691/62; 1769/63; 1994/63; 2126/64), ECtHR, Judgment of 23 July 1968, (1968) Series A No. 6, 32, para. 6; *Wemhoff v. Germany* (App. No. 2122/64), ECtHR, Judgment of 27 June 1968, (1968) Series A No. 7, 23, para. 7; *Neumeister v. Austria* (App. No. 1936/63), ECtHR, Judgment of 27 June 1968, (1968) Series A No. 8; *Delcourt v. Belgium* (App. No. 2689/65), ECtHR, Judgment of 17 January 1970, (1970) Series A No. 11, 14, para. 25; *De Wilde, Ooms and Versyp ('Vagrancy') v. Belgium (merits)* (App. No. 2832/66; 2835/66; 2899/66), ECtHR, Judgment of 18 June 1972, (1971) Series A No. 12, 37, para. 68 and 39, para. 71; *Ringeisen v. Austria* (App. No. 2614/65), ECtHR, Judgment of 16 July 1971, (1971) Series A No. 13.

[21] *Wemhoff v. Germany* (App. No. 2122/64), ECtHR, Judgment of 27 June 1968, (1968) Series A No. 7, 23, para. 8; *Neumeister v. Austria* (App. No. 1936/63), ECtHR, Judgment of 27 June 1968, (1968) Series A No. 8, 39, para. 19, 40, para. 14; *Delcourt v. Belgium* (App. No. 2689/65), ECtHR, Judgment of 17 January 1970, (1970) Series A No. 11, 25, para. 15, *De Wilde, Ooms and Versyp ('Vagrancy') v. Belgium (merits)* (App. No. 2832/66; 2835/66; 2899/66), ECtHR, Judgment of 18 June 1972, (1971) Series A No. 12, 40–41, para. 76 and p. 41, para. 78.

[22] See *Golder v. United Kingdom* (App. No. 4451/70) (1975) Series A No. 18, paras. 34–35.

[23] Ibid., para. 35, for critical comments see Fitzmaurice dissenting opinion pp. 2 and 37; I. Sinclair, *The Vienna Convention on the Law of Treaties*, 2nd ed. (Manchester University Press, Manchester 1984) 133.

[24] *Fogarty v. United Kingdom* (App. No. 37112/97), ECtHR, Judgment of 21 November 2001, ECHR 2001-XI, para. 35.

notion of special regimes,[25] it has not applied a special doctrine in the interpretation of human rights treaties.[26]

3. Special Doctrines of Human Rights Interpretation

Despite relying on general canons of treaty interpretation, the Strasbourg Court has adopted the view that the ECHR must be interpreted in the light of its special character as a treaty for the collective enforcement of human rights and fundamental freedoms. It is this special doctrine that must be tested.

The speciality doctrine is based in essence on four different arguments or interpretative principles: (i) the principle of effectiveness; (ii) the notion of law-making treaties; (iii) the objective nature of states' obligations; and (iv) the doctrine of dynamic interpretation. It is my view that the 'special nature' claim cannot survive closer scrutiny as none of these four elements are particular to human rights treaties.

3.1 Practical and effective rights

The principle of effectiveness is at the heart of the Court's interpretative approach. The Court has always referred to the principle of effectiveness (*effet utile*)[27] and the principle of consequences (*effet conséquence*)[28] and it gave the doctrine a rhetorical

---

[25] *Legality of the Threat or Use of Nuclear Weapons (Merits)*, Advisory Opinion of 8 July 1996, 1996 ICJ Reports 226; *Legal Consequences of the Construction of a Wall in the Occupied Palestinian Territory*, Advisory Opinion of 9 July 2004, 2004 ICJ Reports 136.

[26] *LaGrand (Germany v. USA)*, 2001 ICJ Reports 466 and *Legal Consequences of the Construction of a Wall in the Occupied Palestinian Territory*, Advisory Opinion of 9 July 2004, 2004, ICJ Reports 226.

[27] *Case 'relating to certain aspects of the laws on the use of languages in education in Belgium'* (Belgian Linguistic Case) (merits) (App. No. 1474/62; 1677/62; 1691/62; 1769/63; 1994/63; 2126/64), ECtHR, Judgment of 23 July 1968, (1968) Series A No. 6, 31, para. 3; *De Wilde, Ooms and Versyp ('Vagrancy') v. Belgium (merits)* (App. No. 2832/66; 2835/66; 2899/66), ECtHR, Judgment of 18 June 1972, (1971) Series A No. 12, para. 16; *Golder v. United Kingdom* (App. No. 4451/70), ECtHR, Judgment of 21 February 1975, (1975) Series A No. 18, para. 26; *National Union of Belgian Police v. Belgium* (App. No. 4464/70), ECtHR, Judgment of 17 October 1975, (1975) Series A No. 19, para. 44; *Luedicke, Belkacem and Koc v. Germany* (App. No. 6210/73; 6877/75; 7132/75), ECtHR, Judgment of 28 November 1987, (1978) Series A No. 29, para. 42; for the earliest practice of the Commission, see *X. c. l'Autriche (dec.)*, ECmHR, (1959) 2 Yearbook 400, 405.

[28] See *Lawless v. Ireland (No. 3)* (App. No. 332/57), ECtHR, Judgment of 1 July 1961, (1961) Series A No. 3, 52, para. 14; *Neumeister v. Austria* (App. No. 1936/63), ECtHR, Judgment of 27 June 1968, (1968) Series A No. 8, para. 7; *Stögmüller v. Austria* (App. No. 1602/62), ECtHR, Judgment of 10 November 1969, (1969) Series A No. 9, 39, para. 3; *Delcourt v. Belgium* (App. No. 2689/65), ECtHR, Judgment of 17 January 1970, (1970) Series A No. 11; *Ringeisen v. Austria* (App. No. 2614/65), ECtHR, Judgment of 16 July 1971, (1971) Series A No. 13, para. 92; *Neumeister v. Austria (Article 50)* (App. No. 1936/63), ECtHR, Judgment of 7 May 1974, (1974) Series A No. 17, para. 30; *Golder v. United Kingdom* (App. No. 4451/70), ECtHR, Judgment of 21 February 1975,

twist observing in 1979 that the ECHR must protect rights that are practical and effective, not theoretical or illusory.[29]

The principle of effectiveness has been derived from the spirit of the ECHR[30] and is often linked to the doctrine of special interpretation.[31] The VCLT does not contain an express reference to the principle of effectiveness, but it is an ordinary canon of treaty interpretation applied in the interpretation and application of all kinds of treaties[32] and recognized by the ILC.[33] I accordingly fail to see that the 'special nature' claim can be based on the principle of effectiveness.

3.2 Law-making treaty

The Court first indicated the special nature of the ECHR in 1968, distinguishing it from ordinary treaties. In *Wemhoff v. Germany*, the Court faced the need to reconcile the French and English versions of the text of the ECHR and stated: 'Given that it is a law-making treaty, it is...necessary to seek the interpretation that is most appropriate in order to realise the aim and achieve the object of the treaty, not that which would restrict to the greatest possible degree the obligations undertaken by the Parties.'[34]

However, it was superfluous to consider the ECHR 'law-making' in order to reconcile the different textual versions of a treaty in the light of the aim and object of the treaty. VCLT Article 33(4) now proscribes the approach required in this instance and does not recognize the distinction between law-making and other treaties as the ILC did not 'consider it necessary' to draw the distinction.[35]

(1975) Series A No. 18, para. 36; *Engel and Others v. Netherlands* (App. No. 5100/71; 5101/71; 5102/71; 5354/72; 5370/72), ECtHR, Judgment of 8 June 1976 (1976) Series A No. 22, para. 81.

[29] *Airey v. Ireland* (App. No. 6289/73), ECtHR, Judgment of 9 October 1979, (1979) Series A No. 32, para. 24; compare *Delcourt v. Belgium* (App. No. 2689/65), ECtHR, Judgment of 17 January 1970, (1970) Series A No. 11, 18, para. 34.

[30] *Le Compte, van Leuven and de Meyere v. Belgium* (App. No. 6878/75; 7238/75), ECtHR, Judgment of 23 June 1981, (1981) Series A No. 43, para. 45; *Benthem v. Netherlands* (App. No. 8848/80), ECtHR, Judgment of 23 October 1985, (1985) Series A No. 97, para. 32; *Van Marle and Others v. Netherlands* (App. No. 8543/79; 8674/79; 8675/79; 8685/79), ECtHR, Judgment of 26 June 1986, (1986) Series A No. 101, para. 32; *Pudas v. Sweden* (App. No. 10426/83), ECtHR, Judgment of 27 October 1987, (1987) Series A No. 125-A, para. 31; *Bodén v. Sweden* (App. No. 10930/84), ECtHR, Judgment of 27 October 1987, (1987) Series A No. 125-B, para. 30; *Moreira de Azevedo v. Portugal*, (App. No. 11296/84) (1990) Series A No. 189, para. 66.

[31] *Soering v. United Kingdom* (App. No. 14038/88), ECtHR Judgment of 7 July 1989, (1989) Series A No. 161, para. 87. See also *Cruz Varas and Others v. Sweden* (App. No. 15576/89), ECtHR, Judgment of 20 March 1991, (1991) Series A No. 201, para. 94.

[32] Lauterpacht, 'Restrictive Interpretation and the Principle of Effectiveness in the Interpretation of Treaties' (1949) 26 BYIL 63 48–85.

[33] International Law Commission, Reports of the Commission to the General Assembly (1966), 219, para. 6.

[34] *Wemhoff v. Germany* (App. No. 2122/64), ECtHR, Judgment of 27 June 1968, (1968) Series A No. 7, 23, para. 8.

[35] Ybk ILC 1966 219, para. 5.

The Court has further distinguished its role from that of the ICJ in *Loizidou v. Turkey (Preliminary objections)* concerning the validity of Turkey's territorial restriction of its acceptance of the Court's jurisdiction. The Court found, *inter alia*, that the possibility of attaching restrictions to the acceptance of the optional jurisdiction of the International Court of Justice does not mean that restrictions are permissible under the ECHR. The Court rejected the analogous interpretation arguing that 'the context within which the ICJ operates is quite distinct from that of the Convention institutions', firstly, because the ICJ examines disputes between states, around the world, in any area of international law, and with reference to principles of international law and, secondly, because the role of the ICJ 'is not exclusively limited to direct supervisory functions in respect of a law-making treaty such as the Convention'.[36] The roles of the courts in The Hague and Strasbourg are dissimilar, but it would have been sufficient to argue that the ECHR does not contain a provision parallel to ICJ Statute Article 36 (3). It is accordingly difficult to see that the law-making-argument played any independent role in *Loizidou*.

Moreover, the law-making argument has been advanced in various other cases that do not appear to display any particular common denominator and the invocation of the argument seems to be a matter of form rather than substance.[37] I accordingly fail to see that the 'special nature' doctrine can be based on the claimed law-making nature of the ECHR.

3.3 Objective obligations

A third underpinning of the 'special nature' claim was forwarded by the Court in 1978 when it clarified 'the nature of the engagements placed under its supervision' as follows:

Unlike international treaties of the classic kind, the Convention comprises more than mere reciprocal engagements between contracting States. It creates, over and above a network of mutual, bilateral undertakings, objective obligations which, in the words of the Preamble, benefit from a 'collective enforcement'. By virtue of Article 24 [now Article 33], the Convention allows Contracting States to require the observance of those obligations without having to justify an interest deriving, for example, from the fact that a measure they complain of has prejudiced one of their own nationals.[38]

(Words in brackets added.)

---

[36] *Loizidou v. Turkey (Preliminary Objections)* (App. No. 15318/89), Judgment of 23 March 1995, (1995) Series A No. 310, 20 EHRR 99, para. 84.

[37] *Golder v. United Kingdom* (App. No. 4451/70), ECtHR, Judgment of 21 February 1975, (1975) Series A No. 18, para 36; *Sunday Times v. United Kingdom* (App. No. 6538/74), ECtHR, Judgment of 26 April 1979, (1979) Series A No. 30, para. 48; *Brogan and Others v. United Kingdom* (App. No. 11209/84; 11234/84; 11266/84; 11386/85), ECtHR, Judgment of 29 November 1988, (1988) Series A No. 145-B, para. 59; Judge de Meyer in *Pudas v. Sweden* (App. No. 10426/83), ECtHR, Judgment of 27 October 1987, (1987) Series A No. 125-A.

[38] *Ireland v. United Kingdom* (App. No. 5310/71), ECtHR, Judgment of 18 January 1978, (1978) Series A No. 25, para. 239; see similarly *Austria v. Italy (dec.)*, ECmHR, (1961) 4 Yearbook 116, 138.

The Court linked the objective nature of the obligations under the ECHR to the doctrine of special interpretation in *Soering v. the United Kingdom*.[39] The special nature of the ECHR is thus based in part on the collective enforcement system, i.e. the interstate complaint procedure.

The significance of the enforcement machinery to the interpretation of a given treaty is of general import to international human rights law and it has been argued that the objective nature of the obligations under human rights treaties has 'an impact' on the interpretation of the rights and freedoms protected, although it is not clarified what the impact may amount to.[40]

In my view, the notion might have grave consequences for the legitimacy of international human rights law and should be carefully considered. One should not take lightly the impact of a formal review mechanism on the substance of a human rights instrument. The reason is this: treaty provisions allowing for *actio populitaris* of states are uncommon in international law[41] and international law does not generally recognize any *actio popularis* of states.[42] In *Barcelona Traction*, the ICJ noted that 'on the universal level, the instruments which embody human rights do not confer on States the capacity to protect the victims of infringements of such rights irrespective of their nationality'.[43] Even where international law provides enforcement procedures, the international institutions are generally not competent to render binding interpretations.[44] In light of the general scarcity

---

[39] *Soering v. United Kingdom* (App. No. 14038/88), ECtHR Judgment of 7 July 1989, (1989) Series A No. 161, para. 87; see also e.g. *Mathieu-Mohin and Clerfayt v. Belgium* (App. No. 9267/81), ECtHR, 2 March 1987 (1987) Series A No. 113, para. 49; *Cruz Varas and Others v. Sweden* (App. No. 15576/89), ECtHR, Judgment of 20 March 1991, (1991) Series A No. 201, para. 94; *Loizidou v. Turkey (Preliminary Objections)* (App. No. 15318/89), Judgment of 23 March 1995, (1995) Series A No. 310, 20 EHRR 99, para. 70; *United Communist Party of Turkey and Others v. Turkey* (App. No. 133/1996/752/951), ECtHR, Judgment of 30 January 1998, ECHR 1998-I, para. 28; *Mamatkulov and Abdurasulovic v. Turkey* (App. Nos. 46827/99 and 46951/99), Judgment of 6 February 2003, para. 92; *Yasa v. Turkey* (App. No. 63/1997/847/1054), ECtHR, Judgment of 2 September 1998, ECHR 1998-VI, para. 64.

[40] A. Orakhelashvili, 'Restrictive Interpretation of Human Rights Treaties in the Recent Jurisprudence of the European Court of Human Rights' (2003) 14 EJIL 529, 533; M. K. Addo and N. Grief, 'Is There a Policy Behind the Decisions and Judgments Relating to Article 3 of the European Convention on Human Rights?' (1995) 20 ELR 178, 183 presents the argument that, in the context of Article 3, the 'doctrine' of collective guarantee 'means that all states must observe and respect the prohibitions there laid down', but that is to equalize the collective guarantee with the binding force of the Convention.

[41] G. L. Weil, *The European Convention on Human Rights: Background, Development and Prospects* (A. W. Sijthoff, Leiden 1963) 198. An example is Article 227 para. 1 EC (Article 170 EC Treaty).

[42] See e.g. P. van Dijk, *Judicial Review of Governmental Action and the Requirement of an Interest to Sue: A Comparative Study of the Requirement of an Interest to Sue in National and International Law* (Sijthoff & Noordhoff, The Hague 1980); M. Ragazzi, *The Concept of International Obligations Erga Omnes* (Clarendon Press, Oxford 1997) 210–214; N. Jørgensen, *The Responsibility of States for International Crimes* (Clarendon Press, Oxford 2000) 220.

[43] *Barcelona Traction, Light and Power Company, Limited (Belgium v. Spain)* 1970 ICJ Reports 3, para. 91.

[44] On the global level, inter-state complaint procedures are found in e.g. CERD (Article 11), ICCPR (Article 41), CAT (Article 21), but not in e.g. CEDAW, CESCR and CRC. Individual

of enforcement procedures under international law, it is not surprising that international law does not link the content of a legal obligation to the means of enforcement.[45] If the interpretation by international courts and/or monitoring bodies is considered special, the legitimacy of internationally adopted interpretations might decrease. Interpretations should be able to stand in their own right and international monitoring bodies should not be seen to lift themselves up by the bootstraps.

A general link between the interpretation of the substantive provisions of human rights treaties and the access to collective or individual means of enforcement is further contradicted by impracticality. If inferences were drawn from enforcement as to substance, it would have to be assumed that the nature of the applicable interpretative principles of e.g. the ECHR changed on 7 August 1950 when the Committee of Ministers agreed on the optional enforcement machinery,[46] on 5 July 1955 when the jurisdiction of the Commission was accepted, on 3 September 1958 when the Court's jurisdiction was established, or at whatever later stage each of the contracting parties recognized the Commission's and/or the Court's jurisdiction. The intertemporal problem is no longer pertinent under the ECHR, but it may still arise in respect of treaties that entail optional enforcement procedures. Drawing inferences from the enforcement procedures might in theory lead to different interpretations in situations where not all contracting parties have accepted the optional jurisdiction of an institution.

Admittedly, the access to an international enforcement machinery may in practice lead to a dynamic development of international human rights law, perhaps because independent international lawyers are less likely than national lawyers to interpret treaties restrictively. Yet, the perfectly legitimate development of international law by means of generally recognized doctrines of interpretation (see Section 3.4 below) cannot be considered dependent on the existence of any kind of enforcement machinery. I accordingly fail to see that the 'special nature' claim can be based on the objective nature of human rights obligations and/or the attached enforcement system.

---

complaint procedures are attached to e.g. CERD (Article 14), ICCPR (Optional Protocol No. 1), CAT (Article 22), CEDAW (Optional Protocol), but not e.g. CESCR and CRC. On a regional level, inter-state complaints may be lodged under the African Charter (Article 47) and the Inter-American Convention (Article 45). Individual petitions are accepted under the African Charter (Article 55: Commission, Protocol, Court) and the Inter-American Convention (Article 33). Only the regional Courts have jurisdiction to render binding judgments (ECHR Article 46, ACHR Article 63, and IACHR Protocol Article 3). See e.g. C. Tomuschat, *Human Rights: Between Idealism and Realism* (Oxford University Press, Oxford 2003) 159–170.

[45] No link is drawn by e.g. van Dijk, *Judicial Review of Governmental Action and the Requirement of an Interest to Su: A Comparative Study of the Requirement of an Interest to Sue in National and International Law* (Sijthoff & Noordhoff, The Hague 1980) 335–336; M. Kamminga, *Inter-State Accountability for Violations of Human Rights* (University of Pennsylvania Press, Philadelphia 1992) 156–163.

[46] Council of Europe, *Collected Edition of the Travaux Préparatoires*, vol. 3 (1961) 770.

3.4 Dynamic interpretation

The final and perhaps most important foundation of the 'special nature' claim is the dynamic interpretation of international human rights treaties. It was contemplated at the drafting stage of the ECHR that it should be interpreted in the light of general principles, not at the time of conclusion, but 'at any given moment'.[47] Professor Max Sørensen observed in 1975 that the ECHR is a 'living legal instrument'[48] and in 1978 the Court adopted the now well-known phrase that 'the Convention is a living instrument which ... must be interpreted in the light of present-day conditions'.[49] The principle of evolutive interpretation was later linked to the doctrine of special interpretation.

The Court had indicated the relevance of comparative and evolutive interpretation in 1968[50] and 1975[51] and relied increasingly on the doctrine in the late 1970s.[52] The link between comparative interpretation and the margin of appreciation was made expressly in *Handyside v. the United Kingdom*.[53] The notion of evolutive and comparative interpretation is (unfortunately) often linked to the doctrine of the margin of appreciation,[54] although comparative interpretation

---

[47] P.-H. Teitgen in Council of Europe, *Collected Edition of the Travaux Préparatoires*, vol. 1 (1961) 131.

[48] M. Sørensen, 'Do the Rights set Forth in the European Convention on Human Rights in 1950 Have the Same Significance in 1975?' *Proceedings of the 4th International Colloquy about the European Convention on Human Rights—organised by the Ministry of Foreign Affairs of Italy and the Secretariat General of the Council of Europe (Rome 5–8 November 1975)* (Council of Europe, Strasbourg 1975) 106.

[49] *Tyrer v. United Kingdom* (App. no. 5856/72), ECtHR, Judgment of 25 April 1987, (1978) Series A No. 26, para. 31.

[50] *Case 'relating to certain aspects of the laws on the use of languages in education in Belgium'* (*Belgian Linguistic* Case) (merits) (App. No. 1474/62; 1677/62; 1691/62; 1769/63; 1994/63; 2126/64), ECtHR, Judgment of 23 July 1968, (1968) Series A No. 6, 34, para. 10.

[51] *National Union of Belgian Police v. Belgium* (App. No. 4464/70), ECtHR, Judgment of 17 October 1975, (1975) Series A No. 19, para. 39; see Eissen, 'Oral Intervention', *Proceedings of the 4th International Colloquy about the European Convention on Human Rights—organised by the Ministry of Foreign Affairs of Italy and the Secretariat General of the Council of Europe (Rome 5–8 November 1975)* (Council of Europe, Strasbourg 1975); *Swedish Engine Drivers' Union v. Sweden* (App. No. 5614/72), ECtHR, Judgment of 6 February 1974, (1974) Series A No. 20; *Schmidt and Dahlström v. Sweden* (App. No. 5589/72), ECtHR, Judgment of 6 February 1976, (1976) Series A No. 21. The Commission had adopted a somewhat more daring approach by referring to a number of international instruments, see *National Union of Belgian Police v. Belgium* (App. No. 4464/70) (1974) Series B No. 17, paras. 63–69 and *Swedish Engine Drivers' Union v. Sweden* (App. No. 5614/72) (1974) Series B No. 18, paras. 65–71.

[52] *Engel and Others v. Netherlands* (App. No. 5100/71; 5101/71; 5102/71; 5354/72; 5370/72), ECtHR, Judgment of 8 June 1976, (1976) Series A No. 22, paras. 59 and 81.

[53] *Handyside v. United Kingdom* (App. No. 5493/72), ECtHR, Judgment of 7 December 1976, (1976) Series A No. 24, para. 48.

[54] *Engel and Others v. Netherlands* (App. No. 5100/71; 5101/71; 5102/71; 5354/72; 5370/72), ECtHR, Judgment of 8 June 1976 (1976) Series A No. 22, para. 24 and para. 72 with reference to *Case 'relating to certain aspects of the laws on the use of languages in education in Belgium'* (*Belgian Linguistic* Case) (merits) (App. No. 1474/62; 1677/62; 1691/62; 1769/63; 1994/63; 2126/64), ECtHR, Judgment of 23 July 1968, (1968) Series A No. 6, 34, para. 10.

is a generally applicable means of interpretation applicable beyond the scope of the margin of appreciation. The doctrine of comparative interpretation refers to national and international standards[55] and has occasionally prompted the Court to restrict the retrograde effect of its judgment.[56]

The Court remains of the view that the special nature of the ECHR justifies its dynamic interpretation. In *Zarb Adami v. Malta* concerning discrimination on the basis of sex, the Court said:

> Since the Convention is first and foremost a system for the protection of human rights, the Court must however have regard to the changing conditions in Contracting States and respond, for example, to any emerging consensus as to the standards to be achieved.[57]

It is, in other words, the (special) system of human rights protection that justifies dynamic interpretation and *vice versa*.

However, the use of comparative material was not new to the European judiciary in the 1970s[58] and other sources of international law are likewise interpreted dynamically. In the advisory opinion in the *Namibia* case, the ICJ noted that some concepts are 'by definition evolutionary' and 'not static', and the ICJ must therefore 'take into consideration the changes which have occurred in the supervening half-century, and its interpretation cannot remain unaffected by the subsequent development of law, through the Charter of the United Nations and by way of customary law. Moreover, an international instrument has to be interpreted and applied within the framework of the entire legal system prevailing at the time of the interpretation'.[59]

The ICJ thus implicitly adopted the view of the ILC, which had amended the text of the draft Article 31(3)(c) of the VCLT from 'international law in force at the time of its conclusion' to read 'any relevant rules of international law applicable in

---

[55] *Marckx v. Belgium* (App. No. 6833/74), ECtHR, Judgment of 13 June 1979, (1979) Series A No. 31, para. 41.

[56] Ibid. The Court was inspired by the Court of Justice of the European Communities and expressly referred to Case 43/75 *Gabrielle Defrenne v. Société anonyme belge de navigation aérienne Sabena* [1976] ECR 455; see P. H. Teitgen, 'The Temporal Effect of the Judgments of the European Court of Human Rights and the Court of Justice of the European Communities' (1980) 1 HRLJ 36; see further *Christine Goodwin v. United Kingdom* (App. No. 28957/95), ECtHR, Judgment of 11 July 2002, ECHR 2002-VI, § 120; *Grant v. United Kingdom* (App. No. 32570/03), ECtHR, Judgment of 23 May 2006, paras. 41–43.

[57] *Zarb Adami v. Malta* (App. No. 17209/02), ECtHR, Judgment of 20 June 2006, para. 74; *Ünal Tekeli v. Turkey* (App. No. 29865/96), ECtHR, Judgment of 16 June 2004, para. 54; *Christine Goodwin v. United Kingdom* (App. No. 28957/95), ECtHR, Judgment of 11 July 2002, ECHR 2002-VI, para. 74; *Stafford v. United Kingdom* (App. No. 46295/99), ECtHR, Judgment of 28 May 2002, ECHR 2002-IV, para. 68.

[58] Joined cases 7/56, 3/57 to 7/59 *Dineke Algera, Giacomo Cicconardi, Simone Couturaud, Ignazio Genuardi, Félicie Steichen v. Common Assembly of the European Coal and Steel Community* [1957] REC 81.

[59] *Legal consequences for States of the Continued Presence of South Africa in Namibia (South West-Africa) notwithstanding Security Council Resolution 276,* Advisory Opinion of 21 June 1971, 1971 ICJ Reports 16, 31.

the relations between the parties'.[60] The adopted wording reflected an acceptance by the ILC of the 'evolution of the law on the interpretation of legal terms',[61] an approach which may be required by good faith.[62] In the *Oil Platforms* case concerning the United States' use of force in order to protect its interests under an economic relations and consular rights treaty with Iran, the ICJ confirmed the interpretation of the treaty in the light of general international law on the use of force, which 'forms an integral part of the task of interpretation'.[63]

The doctrine of dynamic interpretation has recently attracted renewed interest. McLachlan has concluded, on the basis of an extensive survey of international practice, that the integral process of interpretation of, in particular, open-textured language calling for programmatic interpretation may take account of relevant international law either in the (negative) sense of avoiding conflicts between different sources of international law or in the (positive) sense of informing one source of international law of the meaning of another source. The scope of evolutionary interpretation will necessarily depend on the specific treaty's terms and nature, object and purpose as well as the parties' intention.[64]

It is, for this reason alone, fairly difficult—if not impossible—to compare the permissible scope of evolutionary interpretation under various human rights and other treaties. The doctrine may be controversial, but a degree of development must be permissible, partly because the practical need for comparative interpretation can hardly be ignored, partly because of the long-standing and overwhelming state practice accepting the dynamic interpretation of the ECHR. It should not be overlooked in this context that the interpretation of treaties may take account of 'any subsequent practice in the application of the treaty which establishes the agreement of the parties regarding its interpretation', see VCLT Article 31(3)(b). The VCLT is not confined, based on the preparatory works,[65] to the explicit acceptance by the parties of a particular interpretation. In the context of the ECHR, there is no question of the long-standing and wide-ranging acceptance by the Committee of Ministers of the principle of evolutionary interpretation, which is confirmed moreover as recently as in the explanatory report to Protocol No. 14:[66] the legitimacy of a degree of evolutionary interpretation cannot be contested.

---

[60] ILC (1966) Annual Report, 222.

[61] Ibid., 222.

[62] H. Waldock, 'The Effectiveness of the System set up by the European Convention on Human Rights' (1980) 1 HRLJ 1, 4–5; ILC (1966) *Annual Report*, 222.

[63] *Oil Platforms (Islamic Republic of Iran v. United States of America)*, Judgment of 6 November 2003, 2003 ICJ Reports 161, para. 41. The application of the doctrine of evolutionary interpretation of general international law is not uncontroversial, see C. McLachlan, 'The Principle of Systematic Integration and Article 31(3)(c) of the Vienna Convention' (2005) 54 ICLQ 279, 306–309.

[64] McLachlan (2005) 54 ICLQ 279, 309–319.

[65] ILC (1966) *Annual Report*, 222, para. 15.

[66] Council of Europe, Explanatory Report to Protocol No. 14 to the Convention for the Protection of Human Rights and Fundamental Freedoms, amending the control system of the Convention (2004), para. 13.

The ECHR is interpreted extensively in the light of comparative national and international law as well as a variety of soft-law standards. It is clear that the comparative and evolutionary interpretation of the ECHR goes far beyond avoiding conflicts with other areas of international law. The scope of the evolutionary interpretation of the ECHR is not uncontested and a large study could be made out of the legitimate scope of dynamic interpretation.[67] That task cannot be undertaken and it may suffice here to note that the ILC has recently left open a potentially wide margin of interpretation suggesting that the scope of evolutionary interpretation depends on the nature of the treaty, the concrete facts of each case, and the appropriate weight given to international law in the circumstances.[68] In light of the general acceptability in international law of evolutionary interpretation,[69] a special doctrine of interpretation neither was, nor is needed to adopt this method.[70] I accordingly fail to see that the 'special nature' claim can be based on the doctrine of dynamic interpretation.

3.5 A wider European perspective

Vasak noted in 1982 that international human rights law is an unstable law in a process of constant change and facing constant challenges.[71] The comparative interpretation of international (human rights) law entails a recognition of the indeterminacy and development of law. International (human rights) law is sensitive to external influences, tolerates amendment along the way, and does not amount to frozen politics.[72]

The room for judicial development is wider in international law compared to national law due to the lack of international law-making procedure and the slow development of international standards.[73] The need to develop international law and the claim of judicial neutrality makes comparative interpretation necessary. The claim of neutrality is commonly expressed in terms of the condemnation of

---

[67] See e.g. R. Toma, *La réalité judiciaire de la Cour européenne des droits de l'Homme: Activisme et retenue judiciaires* (Nomos, Baden-Baden 2003) observing that the dilemma of activism and restraint is apparent rather that substantial as the role of restraint is to limit the dynamic and evolutionary interpretation, which is necessarily attached to the ECHR.

[68] ILC Report on the Work of its Fifty-Seventh Session, GAOR Sixtieth Session Supp. No. 10 (2005) (UN Doc. A/60/10), ch. XI, 220, para. 478; International Law Commission, Report of the Study Group, Fragmentation of International Law: Difficulties Arising from the Diversification and Expansion of International Law (Finalized by Martti Koskenniemi) (2006) UN Doc. A/CN.4/L.682, 206–244.

[69] See e.g. E. McWhinney, *Judicial Settlement of International Disputes: Jurisdiction, Justiciability and Judicial Law-Making on the Contemporary International Court* (Martinus Nijhoff Publishers, Dordrecht 1991).

[70] See e.g. Ibid.

[71] Vasak, *Towards a Specific International Human Rights Law* (1982) 672.

[72] L.D. Eriksson, 'The Indeterminacy of Law or Law as a Deliberate Practice' in A. Hirvonen (ed.), *Polycentricity: The Multiple Scenes of Law* (Pluto Press, London/Sterling/Virginia 1998) 46.

[73] H. Lauterpacht, *The Function of Law in the International Community* (Clarendon Press, Oxford 1933) 256.

judges' enforcement of their own views, opinions, and preferences. The neutrality claim makes inevitable the inclusion of societal standards in the decision-making process and in legal reasoning.[74]

The special nature of human rights treaty law depends on whether a wide variety of different legal issues are in practice resolved in a special manner compared to the traditional, general doctrines of international law. The doctrine of special interpretation reflects a general tendency to view international human rights law as a branch of international law that calls for a special approach to interpretation. It is in my view doubtful whether the view is sustainable as regards the interpretation of substantive rights and freedoms under the ECHR.

It might be fruitful at this junction to draw a parallel to the European Court of Justice's (ECJ's) vision of Community law as a special legal system.[75] The ECJ's attempt to bring life to the text of the treaties was exposed to resistance and criticism. The first major works on the political integration of the ECJ appeared in the late 1960s[76] and the ECJ was subjected to criticism of judicial activism in the 1980s.[77] Members of the ECJ have defended the practice by attempting to show that the case law fell within generally recognized principles of interpretation.[78] A number of books and articles have attempted to analyse the ECJ's activities on the basis of a comparison with generally accepted canons of interpretation of international law.[79] The ECJ has not officially explained its departure from the discourse of general international law. It has been argued that the ECJ misunderstood the potential of international legal reasoning,[80] but the introduction of a new legal discourse may reflect an attempt to obtain greater freedom of adjudication.[81]

---

[74] W. Sadurski, *Moral Pluralism and Legal Neutrality* (Kluwer Academic Publishers, Dordrecht/Boston/London 1990) 44–47.

[75] Case 26/62, *NV Algemene Transport en Expeditie Onderneming van Gend en Loos v. Nederlandse Administratie der Belastingen* [1963] ECR 13; Case 6/64 *Flaminio Costa v. E.N.E.L.* [1964] ECR 585.

[76] A.W. Green, *Political Integration by Jurisprudence: The Work of the Court of Justice of the European Communities in European Political Integration* (A.W. Sijthoff, Leiden 1969).

[77] H. Rasmussen, *On Law and Policy in the European Court of Justice: A Comparative Study in Judicial Policymaking* (Martinus Nijhoff Publishers, Dordrecht/Boston/Lancaster 1986).

[78] H. Kutscher, *Methods of Interpretation as seen by a Judge at the Court of Justice* (Court of Justice of the European Communities, Luxembourg 1976) 6.

[79] A. Bredimas, *Methods on Interpretation and Community Law* (North-Holland Publishing Company, Amsterdam/New York/Oxford 1978); C. Gulmann., 'Methods of Interpretation of the European Court of Justice' (1980) 24 *Scandinavian Studies of Law* 187, 190; L.N. Brown and T. Kennedy, *The Court of Justice of the European Communities, 4th ed.* (Sweet and Maxwell, London 1994) 294–322.

[80] O. Spiermann, 'The Other Side of the Story: An Unpopular Essay on the Making of the European Community Legal Order' (1999) 10 EJIL 763; see also D. Wyatt, 'New Legal Order, or Old?' (1982) 7 ELR 147.

[81] J. Weiler, 'Rewriting *Van Gend & Loos*: Towards a Normative Theory of ECJ Hermeneutics' in O. Wiklund (ed.), *Judicial Discretion in European Perspective* (Nordstedts Juridik/Kluwer Law International, Stockholm 2003).

The same thing can be said about the European Court of Human Rights; the Court may have preferred the development of a new line of reasoning to supplement the 'traditional' arguments based on the VCLT, because a 'special' approach to interpretation may be helpful to avoid criticisms of the Court's judicial activity. A new discourse might not be met by the same prejudicial conceptions about the scope of legitimate treaty interpretation. The argument that the Court transgressed the boundaries of ordinary canons of interpretation could be deflected by the argument that the ECHR is a special treaty, which is not subject to the ordinary canons of interpretation, and which accordingly leaves a wider scope of interpretation to the Court. These observations are admittedly speculative, but a strict analysis of the adopted methods of interpretation does not support the 'special nature' claim.

4. The Subsidiary Review under the ECHR

The 'special nature' claim could likewise be based on the European Court of Human Rights' general recourse to the principle of subsidiarity (margin of appreciation) in its review of the contracting states' observance of their obligations under the ECHR.[82] The subsidiarity principle was established in 1968 in the *Belgian Linguistic case* when the Court observed that:

it cannot assume the role of the competent national authorities, for it would thereby lose sight of the subsidiary nature of the international machinery of collective enforcement established by the Convention. The national authorities remain free to choose the measures which they consider appropriate in those matters which are governed by the Convention. Review by the Court concerns only the conformity of these measures with the requirements of the Convention.[83]

The Court later added in the *Handyside case* that 'it is in no way the Court's task to take the place of the competent national courts but rather to review under Article 10 the decisions they delivered in the exercise of their power of appreciation' and that 'the machinery of protection established by the Convention is subsidiary to the national systems safeguarding human rights'.[84]

The international review of states' observance of international obligations is not easily addressed, as the underlying distinction between a general interpretation and the specific application of the interpretation to a particular case is slippery

---

[82] For the Inter-American Court, see D.R. Pinzón, The 'Victim' Requirement, the Fourth Instance Formual and the Notion of 'Person' in the Individual Complaint Procedure of the Inter-American Human Rights System (2001) 7 ILSA J Intl Comp L 1.

[83] *Case 'relating to certain aspects of the laws on the use of languages in education in Belgium'* (*Belgian Linguistic* Case) (merits) (App. No. 1474/62; 1677/62; 1691/62; 1769/63; 1994/63; 2126/64), ECtHR, Judgment of 23 July 1968, (1968) Series A No. 6, 35, para. 10 *in fine*.

[84] *Handyside v. United Kingdom* (App. No. 5493/72), ECtHR, Judgment of 7 December 1976, (1976) Series A No. 24, para. 50.

and perhaps illusive. It is not possible here to address the nature and impact of the subsidiarity principle, but it is clear that subsidiary review by international tribunals may leave an increased scope of discretion to domestic authorities e.g. by refraining from declaring a violation, provided the absence of arbitrariness or other error of appreciation is not manifest.

I will argue, nonetheless, that the Court's method of review does not deviate from what might be a generally accepted method of review under general international law. Rather, the gap between the general interpretation and the specific application of international law was sought to be narrowed by the European Court of Human Rights when it refined its method of international review in the 1970s. In other words, despite the general opinion among international (human rights) lawyers of the particular nature of the Court's subsidiary review and attached margin of appreciation, I do not consider the doctrine special.

4.1 Interpretation and review in general international law

When the European Court laid the foundation of its subsidiary review in the 1970s, it faced the argument that its review should be limited to ascertaining whether the domestic courts acted 'reasonably, in good faith and within the limits of the margin of appreciation left to the Contracting States.'[85]

If the Court had thus restricted its review of the states' transgression of limits on their power of appreciation and confined its supervisory role to a standard of good faith and reasonableness, it would admittedly not have been foreign to international law. An international review restricted to observing whether national authorities acted in good faith, with due care, and in a reasonable manner, corresponded to a classical description in international law of the binding force of international obligations. Hence, when Fitzmaurice was the ILC's special rapporteur during the drafting of the VCLT, the draft provision on the binding force of treaties (*pacta sunt servanda*) had the following wording: 'A treaty must be carried out in good faith, and so as to give it a reasonable and equitable effect according to the correct interpretation of its terms.'[86]

The qualification concerning reasonable and equitable effect reflected the view, first, that a treaty must not be given its maximum effect and, secondly, that once the 'correct' interpretation had been established it becomes 'the duty of the parties to carry it out reasonably, equitably and in good faith'.[87] When Waldock presented his third report in 1964, the qualification had been left out of the text of what is now VCLT Article 26, but Waldock relied on the distinction between interpretation and application and found it 'desirable to underline a little that the obligation to observe treaties is one of good faith and not *stricti juris*.'[88] The

---

[85] Ibid., para 48, Argument of the Government and the majority of Commission.
[86] ILC Fourth Report by G. G. Fitzmaurice: Law of Treaties Ybk ILC 1959-II 37, 42.
[87] Ibid., 54, para. 18.
[88] ILC Third Report by Sir Humphrey Waldock on the Law of Treaties, Ybk ILC 1964-II 5, 7.

review by international institutions of the observation of international obligations would, according to Waldock's view, be limited to determining whether the
treaty has been observed in good faith, since that is all that is required by international law.

The exact determination of the requirement of good faith in general international law is hard to specify, but Waldock referred to Chapter 3 of Bin Cheng's
General Principles of International Law.[89] Bin Cheng expressed the view that a
state's sovereign right to legislate must not deprive individual rights of their practical effect.[90] Bin Cheng accordingly took the view that the 'reasonable and bona
fide' exercise of the right to legislate in matters governed by international law entails
the search for 'a reasonable balance between the conflicting interests involved.'[91]

The principle of good faith might thus be seen to respect the international
obligations undertaken by states while at the same time restricting those obligations by placing limits on the scope of review of international tribunals. If this
approach had been adopted by the Strasbourg Court, its role would be restricted
to determining whether the national authorities have acted reasonably and equitably rather than in strict accordance with the ECHR.

4.2 Interpretation and review under the ECHR

The Court rejected in *Sunday Times v. United* Kingdom the argument that its
review should be limited to issues of good faith and reasonableness. The majority
of 11 judges reiterated that 'it is in no way the Court's task to take the place of the
competent national courts'[92] and added:

This does not mean that the Court's supervision is limited to ascertaining whether a
respondent State exercised its discretion reasonably, carefully and in good faith. Even a
Contracting State so acting remains subject to the Court's control as regards the compati-
bility of its conduct with the engagements it has undertaken under the Convention. The
Court still does not subscribe to the contrary view which, in essence, was advanced by the
Government and the majority of the Commission in the Handyside case.[93]

In the same issue, the minority of nine judges expressed the following opinion:

The margin of appreciation involves a certain discretion and attaches primarily to the
evaluation of the danger that a particular exercise of the freedom safeguarded by Article
10(1) could entail for the interests listed in Article 10(2) and to the choice of measures

---

[89] Ibid., 8, footnote 12.
[90] B. Cheng, *General Principles of Law as applied by International Courts and Tribunals*
(Stevens & Sons Limited, London 1953) 117.
[91] Ibid., 131–132.
[92] *Sunday Times v. United Kingdom* (App. No. 6538/74), ECtHR, Judgment of 26 April 1979,
(1979) Series A No. 30, para 59 with reference to *Handyside v. United Kingdom* (App. No. 5493/72),
ECtHR, Judgment of 7 December 1976, (1976) Series A No. 24, para. 50.
[93] *Sunday Times v. United Kingdom* (App. No. 6538/74), ECtHR, Judgment of 26 April 1979,
(1979) Series A No. 30, para. 59; see n. 92 above.

intended to avoid that danger.... For the purposes of such an evaluation—to be made with due care and in a reasonable manner, and which of necessity will be based on facts and circumstances prevailing in the country concerned and on the future development of those facts and circumstances—the national authorities are in principle better qualified than an international court (reference omitted).[94]

Having pointed out that the exercise of discretion must be made with due care and in a reasonable manner, the minority added:

[The Court's] supervision is concerned, in the first place, with determining whether the national authorities have acted in good faith, with due care and in a reasonable manner when evaluating those facts and circumstances, as well as the danger that might thereby be occasioned for the interests listed in Article 10(2); further and above all, it seeks to ensure that, in a society that means to remain democratic, the measures restricting freedom of expression are proportionate to the legitimate aim pursued... (reference omitted).[95]

The minority accordingly ascribed to a standard of review that seems to follow Waldock's opinion, whereas the majority chose a different path. In the light of the absence of clear support behind Waldock's view, the majority's opinion cannot be considered to entail a departure from general international law.

4.3 The nature of subsidiary review

What is more, the subsidiary review of the Strasbourg Court is widely misunderstood as the ECHR in many instances leaves to the contracting parties a measure of implementation freedom, discretion, or margin of appreciation not as a consequence of the Court's subsidiary review, but in the absence of international standards. The implementation freedom/discretion/margin of appreciation generally reflects the nature of the obligations undertaken by the states, namely obligations of result leaving the choice of means to states.

The subsidiary review is a different thing that concerns the Court's review and depends in essence on five general qualifications:

The normative qualification

The factual qualification

The procedural qualification

The legitimacy qualification

The absent qualification

The qualifications are well known to legal doctrine as factors affecting the margin of appreciation (principle of subsidiarity). Legal doctrine thus recognized as

---

[94] Joint dissenting opinion, para. 7.

[95] Joint dissenting opinion, paras. 7–8. Judge Fitzmaurice had expressed a similar standpoint in his dissenting opinion in *Golder v. United Kingdom* (App. No. 4451/70), ECtHR, Judgment of 21 February 1975, (1975) Series A No. 18, para. 10 concerning Article 8(2).

relevant factors the quality of the assessment of evidence and facts,[96] the quality of the decision-making procedures,[97] the legitimacy of the domestic decision-maker,[98] as well as the substance of the ECHR.

The normative qualification is not generally a qualification of subsidiary review. The argument runs that the states' measure of discretion (margin of appreciation) is enlarged where 'it is not possible to find in the domestic law of the various Contracting States a uniform European conception of morals.'[99] The absence or presence of a uniform or similar European standard concerns the general interpretation of the ECHR rather than the application of the ECHR to the circumstances of specific cases. The mere fact that protection might be offered in some contracting states does not mean that the ECHR should offer protection, although this is often suggested.[100] The seemingly endless reiteration in legal doctrine of the significance of common European standards pertains to the substantive content of the ECHR and does not, in principle, have anything to do with the subsidiarity review on the international plane.

The factual qualification follows from the view expressed in the *Belgian Linguistic* case, namely that a proper interpretation and application of the ECHR must take account of the specific elements pertaining in a given society or in a particular case. In the *Handyside* case, the Court observed that the requirement of the ECHR 'varies from time to time and from place to place'.[101] The underlying view is that the interpretation and application of the ECHR may vary depending on the position of different institutions that have disparate appreciation of facts and varied acquaintance with societal issues emerging in different situations. The qualification is of course of particular relevance in cases concerning complex appreciations of evidence and facts.

The procedural qualification is based on the fact that 'the Convention leaves to each Contracting State, in the first place, the task of securing the rights and liberties it enshrines. The institutions created by it make their own contribution to this task but they become involved only through contentious proceedings and once all domestic remedies have been exhausted (Article 26)'.[102] Recently, the procedural

---

[96] Y. Shany, 'Toward a General Margin of Appreciation Doctrine in International Law?' (2006) 16 EJIL 907, 913.

[97] D. Feldman, 'Establishing the Legitimacy of Judicial Procedures for Protecting Human Rights' (2001) 13 *European Review of Public Law* 139.

[98] P. Mahoney, 'Judicial Activism and Judicial Self-Restraint in the European Court of Human Rights: Two sides of the Same Coin' (1990) 11 HRLJ 57, 81.

[99] *Handyside v. United Kingdom* (App. No. 5493/72), ECtHR, Judgment of 7 December 1976, (1976) Series A No. 24, para. 48.

[100] J.A. Sweeney, 'Margins of Appreciation: Cultural Relativity and the European Court of Human Rights in the Post-Cold War Era' (2005) 54 ICLQ 459, 466.

[101] *Handyside v. United Kingdom* (App. No. 5493/72), ECtHR, Judgment of 7 December 1976, (1976) Series A No. 24, para. 48.

[102] Ibid., para. 48; compare with J.B. Thayer, 'The Origin and Scope of the American Doctrine of Constitutional Law' (1893) 7 HLR 129, 152 (the courts are the 'ultimate arbiter..., so far as litigated cases bring the questions before them').

qualification has gained increasing significance pursuant to the view that the Court may relax its review, provided domestic authorities have followed adequate procedures aimed at securing respect for the standards of the ECHR.[103]

The legitimacy qualification is the most complex one. The point of departure can be the Court's view expressed in the *Handyside* case in 1976: 'By reason of their direct and continuous contact with the vital forces of their countries, State authorities are in principle in a better position than the international judge to give an opinion on the exact content of these requirements as well as on the "necessity" of a "restriction" or "penalty" intended to meet them'.[104]

The Court's assessment of the proper standard of protection of the ECHR is accordingly made subsidiary to the assessment of domestic authorities, because they are better placed due to their 'direct and continuous contact with the vital forces of their countries.' The Court in *Handyside* developed the argument of the *Belgian Linguistic* case, namely that it 'cannot disregard those legal and factual features which characterise the life of the society in the State.' The *Handyside* Court focused more directly on the legitimacy of the substantive interpretation by pointing to the domestic authorities' 'direct and continuous contact with the vital forces of their countries'.

It is clear that the absence of common standards, the better factual insight of national authorities, as well as the adequate nature of procedures followed at the domestic level argue against the Court's finding of a violation. Yet, the legitimacy argument has independent value going beyond the normative, factual, and procedural qualification. The very fact that the contested measure has a certain institutional legitimacy on the domestic level may be taken into account.

The Court expressly addressed the democratic legitimacy attached to domestic decision-making for the first time in *Hatton and Others v. United Kingdom* concerning noise pollution emanating from night flights to and from Heathrow airport. The Grand Chamber reiterated what it called 'the fundamentally subsidiary role of the Convention' in the following way: 'The national authorities have direct democratic legitimation and are, as the Court has held on many occasions, in principle better placed than an international court to evaluate the local needs and conditions.... In matters of general policy, on which opinions within a democratic society may reasonably differ, the role of the domestic policy maker should be given special weight...' (references omitted).[105]

The Court thus confirmed its exercise of self-restraint vis-à-vis domestic authorities, not only by reason of the absence of sufficiently high international

---

[103] L. Wildhaber, 'A Constitutional Future for the European Court of Human Rights' (2002) 23 HRLJ 161.

[104] *Handyside v. United Kingdom* (App. No. 5493/72), ECtHR, Judgment of 7 December 1976, (1976) Series A No. 24, para. 48.

[105] *Hatton and Others v. United Kingdom* (App. No. 36022/97), ECtHR, Judgment of 7 August 2003, ECHR 2003-VIII, para. 97; see also *Fretté v. France* (App. No. 36515/97), ECtHR, Judgment of 26 February 2002, ECHR 2002-I, para. 41.

standards etc., but also by reason of the different institutional legitimacy of the Court and domestic authorities.

In the controversial judgment *Hirst v. United Kingdom (No. 2)* concerning convicted criminals' right to vote, legitimacy has been found by the Court to vary according to the quality of the domestic, democratic procedures. A Chamber of the Court noted that the lack of clear consensus on the protection of prisoners' voting rights 'underlines the importance of the margin of appreciation afforded to national legislatures in laying down conditions governing the right of franchise.' The normative qualification of domestic discretion was thus based on a comparative interpretation of the ECHR. However, the Chamber further addressed the interaction between democratic legitimacy and procedure as follows:

That said however, the Court does not consider that a Contracting State may rely on the margin of appreciation to justify restrictions on the right to vote which have not been the subject of considered debate in the legislature and which derive, essentially, from unquestioning and passive adherence to a historic tradition. The Court has had occasion in many cases to underline the importance, in the interpretation and application of Convention rights, of 'democratic values'..., including the crucial role played by elected representatives in defending the interests of the electorate.... The right to vote for those elected representatives must also be acknowledged as being the indispensable foundation of a democratic system. Any devaluation or weakening of that right threatens to undermine that system and it should not be lightly or casually removed. (References omitted.)[106]

The majority of the Grand Chamber used slightly different language to address the weight placed in the Court's review on a considered domestic decision-making process:

As to the weight to be attached to the position adopted by the legislature and judiciary in the United Kingdom, there is no evidence that Parliament has ever sought to weigh the competing interests or to assess the proportionality of a blanket ban on the right of a convicted prisoner to vote. It is true that the question was considered by the multi-party Speaker's Conference on Electoral Law in 1968 which unanimously recommended that a convicted prisoner should not be entitled to vote. It is also true that the Working Party, which recommended the amendment to the law to allow unconvicted prisoners to vote, recorded that successive Governments had taken the view that convicted prisoners had lost the moral authority to vote and did not therefore argue for a change in the legislation. It may perhaps be said that, by voting the way they did to exempt unconvicted prisoners from the restriction on voting, Parliament implicitly affirmed the need for continued restrictions on the voting rights of convicted prisoners. Nonetheless it cannot be said that there was any substantive debate by members of the legislature on the continued justification in light of modern day penal policy and of current human rights standards for maintaining such a general restriction on the right of prisoners to vote.[107]

---

[106] *Hirst v. United Kingdom (No. 2)* (App. No. 74025/01), ECtHR, Judgment of 30 March 2004, para. 40.
[107] Ibid., para. 79.

The reasoning of the Chamber as well as the Grand Chamber is of general applicability and in line with the mindset expressed in *Handyside* and *Hatton* and the Court's view could be generalized as follows: 'A Contracting State may rely on the margin of appreciation to justify restrictions on a right which has not been the subject of considered debate in the legislature and which derives, essentially, from unquestioning and passive adherence to a historic tradition.'

The significance of domestic legitimacy and procedures cannot be pursued here.[108] The point is mainly that the subsidiarity principle may be qualified by the democratic legitimation of domestic policy- and decision-maker. The legitimacy is accordingly an independent factor in the weighing and balancing of conflicting considerations.

Finally, the subsidiary review might be adopted for no apparent reason; the qualification may simply be absent. Since the unqualified application of the subsidiarity principle is not based on any particular considerations there is no reason to address it in detail, although it should be kept in mind. The absence of any particular qualification is perhaps best demonstrated by the Court's restraint in respect of domestic authorities' interpretation of international law. In *Prince Hans Adam II*, the Court stated that the principle of subsidiarity applies to the interpretation of 'general international law and international agreements'.[109] In *Slivenko v. Latvia*, the Court declared more generally:

The Court reiterates that it is primarily for the national authorities, notably the courts, to interpret and apply domestic law.... This also applies where international treaties are concerned; it is for the implementing party to interpret the treaty, and in this respect it is not the Court's task to substitute its own judgment for that of the domestic authorities, even less to settle a dispute between the parties to the treaty as to its correct interpretation. Nor is it the task of the Court to re-examine the facts as found by the domestic authorities as the basis for their legal assessment. The Court's function is to review, from the point of view of the Convention, the reasoning in the decisions of the domestic courts rather than to re-examine their findings as to the particular circumstances of the case or the legal classification of those circumstances under domestic law. (reference omitted.)[110]

The Court thus extended the scope of the principle of subsidiarity to the interpretation of international law, despite the fact that domestic authorities might

---

[108] See further *B. and L. v. United Kingdom* (App. No. 36536/02), ECtHR, Judgment of 13 September 2005, para. 39; *Draon v. France* (App. No. 1513/03), ECtHR, Judgment of 6 October 2005, para. 108; *Maurice v. France* (App. No. 11810/03), ECtHR, Judgment of 6 October 2005, para. 117; *Ždanoka v. Latvia* (App. No. 58278/00), ECtHR, Judgment of 16 March 2006, para. 134.

[109] *Prince Hans-Adam II of Liechtenstein v. Germany* (App. No. 42527/98), ECtHR, Judgment of 12 July 2001, ECHR 2001-VIII, para. 50.

[110] *Slivenko v. Latvia* (App. No. 48321/99), ECtHR, Judgment of 9 October 2003, para. 105; see also *Waite and Kennedy v. Germany* (App. No. 26083/94), ECtHR, Judgment of 18 February 1999, ECHR 1999-I, para. 54; *Beer and Regan v. Germany* (App. No. 28934/95), ECtHR, Judgment of 18 February 1999, para. 44; *Drieman and Others v. Norway* (App. No. 33678/96), ECtHR, Decision of 4 May 2000, 9; *Federation of Offshore Workers' Trade Unions and Others v. Norway* (App. No. 38190/97), ECtHR, Decision of 27 June 2002, ECHR 2002-VI, 16.

not necessarily have any special expertise in comparison to an international court nor be better placed in the interpretation of international law.[111]

The interpretation of international law is in various ways an unavoidable aspect of the Court's exercise of its jurisdiction as the ECHR refers to international law in various provisions.[112] Pursuant to VCLT Article 31(3)(c), the interpretation of the ECHR must take account of 'any relevant rules of international law applicable in the relations between the parties' and international law further plays a part in the comparative interpretation of the ECHR. The Court has recognized that the ECHR 'should as far as possible be interpreted in harmony with other rules of international law'.[113] The Court's view is quite understandable, although it is likely to meet its limits in case of conflicts between the contracting parties' obligations under the ECHR and according to other sources of international law.

The factors affecting the Court's subsidiary review have been considered in great detail in the Court's practice and in legal literature. The measure of discretion of states flowing from the Court's subsidiary review is addressed by means of a special terminology—margin of appreciation—that is yet to be embraced by other branches of international law.[114] However, there is little, if any, reason to think that the Court's method of review deviates substantially from that of other comparable international tribunals.

5. Conclusions

The overall conclusion drawn here is that the principles governing the interpretation and application of human rights treaties are not special. This conclusion runs counter to the view adopted by many international (human rights) lawyers who might tend to focus on the impact of the special legal regime on the overall evolution of public international law. Yet, the speciality of human rights law

---

[111] In *Melchior v. Germany* (App. No. 66783/01), ECtHR, Decision of 2 February 2006, 10–11 concerning, *inter alia*, the interpretation of an agreement between Denmark and Germany relating to the restitution of property rights, the Court argued that the interpretation of the agreement 'was primarily up to the domestic courts', because the agreement had been incorporated into German law.

[112] Article 7(1) on retrospective criminal law; Article 15(1) on derogation; Article 35(1) on exhaustion of domestic remedies; Protocol no. 1 Article 1(1).

[113] *Al-Adsani v. United Kingdom* (App. No. 35763/97), ECtHR, Judgment of 21 November 2001, (2002) 34 EHRR 11, ECHR 2001-XI, para. 55; see also *Fogarty v. United Kingdom* (App. No. 37112/97), ECtHR, Judgment of 21 November 2001, ECHR 2001-XI, para. 35; *McElhinney v. Ireland* (App. No. 31253/96), ECtHR, Judgment of 21 November 2001, ECHR 2001-XI, para. 36; *Manoilescu and Dobrescu v. Romania and Russia* (App. No. 60861/00), ECtHR, Judgment of 3 March 2005, para. 70 (the words 'as far as possible' not repeated); *Bosphorus Hava Yolları Turizm ve Ticaret Anonim Şirketi (Bosphorus Airways) v. Ireland* (App. No. 45036/98), ECtHR, Judgment of 30 June 2005, ECHR 2005-VI, para. 150.

[114] Shany, (2006) 16 EJIL 907.

should not be assumed, but be firmly demonstrated before any impact is sought to be determined.

While the interpretative principles applicable to international human rights treaties do not deviate substantially from the general canons of interpretation under international law, the degree of dynamic interpretation may not be identical in different areas of international law. Yet, one cannot say the ECHR has been developed more aggressively than e.g. the individual rights under the European Union treaty complex. Moreover, the subsidiary method of review adopted by the European Court of Human Rights demonstrates the desire to narrow the gap between abstract interpretation of international treaties and the specific application thereof in international adjudication.

At the end of the day, the interpretation of the ECHR is informed by principles generally accepted by the international legal system. It is crucial that the gradual adjustment of the international legal system takes place in good faith and a spirit of cooperation.[115] The Strasbourg Court has accordingly paid respect to the view of other actors on the international plane, just as the ICJ has laid emphasis on the views expressed by the monitoring bodies under the various UN instruments.[116]

The very foundation of a coherent development of international law is common interpretative principles and there is, in my view, no need to nourish the doctrine of special human rights interpretation. The special interpretation discourse is not likely to disappear, but we should recognize it as form rather then substance, unless important substantive arguments of principle warrant a departure from general principles of international law.

[115] R. Higgins, 'The ICJ, the ECJ, and the Integrity of International Law' (2003) 52 ICLQ 1, 10–12 and 19.
[116] *Legal Consequences of the Construction of a Wall in the Occupied Palestinian Territory*, Advisory Opinion of 9 July 2004, 2004 ICJ Reports 136.

4

Impact on the Law on Treaty Reservations

*Ineke Boerefijn**

1. Introduction

The major United Nations human rights treaties have been widely ratified, but have also attracted large numbers of reservations and declarations.[1] It is a fundamental rule of public international law that states can only be bound by a treaty to the extent that they consent to be bound. Consequently, states have, in principle, the freedom to formulate reservations to treaties, provided that these are not prohibited by the treaty concerned, or otherwise not permitted as being contrary to the object and purpose of the treaty. In their work, human rights treaty monitoring bodies have been confronted with reservations affecting the scope of applicability of human rights guarantees, sometimes limiting applicability to a large extent. In the fulfilment of their monitoring role they have addressed various questions on the validity of reservations.

This contribution examines a number of pertinent aspects concerning reservations to treaties, including the question of validity of reservations and the competence of the treaty monitoring bodies to assess the validity and the consequences of their findings. These issues have been discussed extensively by the monitoring organs, in academic literature, and in the work of the International Law Commission (ILC). The main focus of this Chapter is on the United Nations human rights treaty bodies and the way in which they deal with reservations under the reporting procedure. Since this procedure is mandatory for all states parties, it provides the monitoring bodies with an opportunity to address all reservations systematically. Their concluding comments are therefore worth examining in this context. Furthermore, the United Nations monitoring bodies have

* Senior lecturer, Netherlands Institute of Human Rights, School of Law, Utrecht University.

[1] For an overview of the substance of reservations and declarations to the main United Nations human rights treaties see the 'Treaty bible' at <http://untreaty.un.org/ENGLISH/bible/englishinternetbible/partI/chapterIV/chapterIV.asp>. This contribution will not deal with the definition of reservations. According to Article 2(1)(d) of the Vienna Convention on the Law of Treaties the term reservation means 'a unilateral statement, however phrased or named, made by a State, when signing, ratifying, accepting, approving or acceding to a treaty, whereby it purports to exclude or to modify the legal effect of certain provisions of the treaty in their application to that State.'

adopted relevant general comments in which they have dealt with the issue of reservations in general terms. The Meeting of Chairpersons of Human Rights Treaty Bodies established a Working Group on Reservations that formulated recommendations for the treaty bodies on the way to address reservations. In addition, practice developed under the individual complaints procedures of the United Nations treaties and the European Convention on Human Rights is taken into account.

The ILC has been discussing the question of reservations since 1994[2] and is in the process of formulating guidelines. For two reasons the ILC pays particular attention to human rights treaties. First, their non-reciprocal character distinguishes them from other treaties, they 'do not lend themselves to reservations and objections and, in particular, the objecting State cannot be released from its treaty obligations *vis-à-vis* citizens of the reserving State.'[3] Second, human rights treaties have established monitoring bodies, and questions have been raised as to their competence with regard to assessing the validity of reservations. It must be noted that the work of the ILC is not yet completed. The Commission has provisionally adopted draft guidelines and commentaries thereto on the issues dealt with are in Sections 4–7 of this Chapter. The ILC has not yet adopted draft guidelines on the role of the monitoring organs, dealt with in Section 8; the Special Rapporteur of the ILC has submitted proposals on this issue. Nevertheless, the latter also provide an interesting overview of the impact of international human rights law on the law on treaty reservations.

This Chapter begins with a section on general aspects of the reservations regime and the validity of reservations to human rights treaties (Sections 2 and 3). Section 4 deals with the 'object and purpose' rule, paying specific attention to general human rights treaties. Section 5 deals with various types of reservations that (potentially) affect the implementation of the entire treaty. Subsequently, Section 6 addresses reservations to norms that have a special status, such as peremptory norms and non-derogable norms. Section 7 addresses reservations affecting the role of monitoring bodies. Section 8 then deals with the competence of the monitoring bodies to examine reservations and determine their validity, as well as the consequences of their findings. Each of these sections will first examine the position of the human rights treaty monitoring bodies, followed by a discussion of the views of the ILC, its Special Rapporteur and, if available, the International Court of Justice. Each Section concludes with a brief assessment of the impact of international human rights law on the position of the ILC and the Special Rapporteur. Section 9 provides an overall assessment of the impact of international human rights law on the law on reservations to treaties.

---

[2] The General Assembly endorsed the ILC's decision to deal with the issue of reservations in Resolution 48/31, Report of the International Law Commission on the work of its forty-fifth session (1993), para. 7. ILC member Mr. Alain Pellet was appointed Special Rapporteur on this issue.

[3] International Law Commission, First report on the law and practice relating to reservations to treaties by Mr. Alain Pellet, Special Rapporteur UN Doc. A/CN.4/470 (1995), para. 138.

2. Ratification and the Obligation to Implement Treaty Obligations

The act of ratification or accession imposes an obligation on the state to give effect to the standards included in the treaty and to fulfil its obligations with respect to the monitoring procedures established by it.[4] The ratification by the state is an expression of its consent to be bound, and of its intention to act in conformity with the terms of the treaty. The duty to give effect requires a variety of implementation measures, which can include amending existing legislation and adopting new legislation, providing access to a remedy in case of a violation, and awareness raising of the general public and relevant professional groups. State organs should interpret domestic standards in conformity with the treaty, which requires, *inter alia,* that individuals should be able to invoke the rights included in the treaty before domestic courts.[5]

The large number of reservations, and the far-reaching impact of some reservations, raises questions as to whether states genuinely consent to be bound. Persuasion by the international community may play a role in states' decisions to ratify human rights treaties. Documents resulting from World Conferences and resolutions adopted by the General Assembly and the Commission on Human Rights (now replaced by the Human Rights Council) consistently call upon states to ratify the main human rights instruments.[6] For example, Article 26 of the Vienna Declaration and Programme of Action (1993) urges the universal ratification of human rights treaties, and encourages all states 'to avoid, as far as possible, the resort to reservations.'[7] In the process of ratification, as well as in the formulation of permissible reservations, states can seek assistance from the Office of the High Commissioner for Human Rights. This may have resulted in states ratifying a treaty for no other reason than to enhance their international image.[8]

It can be argued that reservations to human rights treaties are undesirable since these treaties contain minimum standards. However, prohibiting reservations to human rights treaties altogether could result in vague formulations of treaty obligations due to continued disagreement on strong and unambiguous language, and could result in a lower number of ratifications. Permitting reservations allows

---

[4] This obligation is included in Article 26 of the Vienna Convention on the Law of Treaties (adopted 23 May 1969, entered into force 27 January 1980) 1155 UNTS 331, which requires states parties to perform a treaty in good faith.

[5] On the obligation to 'give effect' see Human Rights Committee, General Comment No. 31, 'The Nature of the General Legal Obligation Imposed on States Parties to the Covenant', in Compilation of General Comments and General Recommendations adopted by Human Rights Treaty Bodies (2006), UN Doc. HRI/GEN/1/Rev.8, 233–238.

[6] The Human Rights Council has not yet adopted a resolution on this issue.

[7] Vienna Declaration and Programme of Action, A/CONF.157/23 (1993), para. 26.

[8] W. Schabas, 'Reservations to Human Rights Treaties: Time for Innovation and Reform' (1994) 32 *Annuaire canadien de droit international* 39, 41.

states that are unwilling or unable to accept the full extent of all obligations to become a party to a treaty.[9]

3. Validity of Reservations under Human Rights Treaties[10]

The major United Nations human rights treaties either permit reservations, provided that they meet certain criteria,[11] or are silent on the issue.[12] Treaty provisions that refer to reservations explicitly provide that reservations which are incompatible with the object and purpose of the treaty shall not be permitted. Article 20 of the Convention on the Elimination of Racial Discrimination (CERD) contains the most detailed provision in this respect, to the effect that a reservation which inhibits the work of any of the bodies established by the Convention is not allowed. Further, it states that 'a reservation shall be considered incompatible or inhibitive if at least two thirds of the States parties to this Convention object to it.'

Among the substantive United Nations human rights instruments, only the Second Optional Protocol to the Covenant on Civil and Political Rights, on the abolition of the death penalty, prohibits reservations, with the exception of reservations providing for the application of the death penalty in war time, pursuant to a conviction for a most serious crime of a military nature committed during wartime (Article 2(1)). Out of 64 states parties, only two maintain a reservation: Azerbaijan and Greece. Upon accession, Azerbaijan reserved the right to allow the application of the death penalty 'for the grave crimes, committed during war or in condition of the threat of war', which was objected to by five other states parties, holding that this reservation exceeded the scope of Article 2. Subsequently, Azerbaijan amended its reservation, now using terms that have not been objected to.

---

[9] J. Klabbers, 'On human rights treaties, contractual conceptions and reservations' in: I. Ziemele (ed.), *Reservations to Human Rights Treaties and the Vienna Convention Regime: Conflict, Harmony or Reconciliation* (Martinus Nijhoff, Leiden/Boston 2004) 181.

[10] The International Law Commission has had quite some debate on the appropriate terminology. Using 'permissible' and 'impermissible' raises issues on international responsibility. It decided to use the more neutral terms 'valid' and 'invalid'. International Law Commission, Tenth report on reservations to treaties by Mr. Alain Pellet, Special Rapporteur, UN Doc. A/CN.4/558 (2005), paras. 6–8. These terms are used throughout this contribution.

[11] Article 20 Convention on the Elimination of Racial Discrimination; Article 28 Convention on the Elimination of Discrimination Against Women; Article 51 Convention on the Rights of the Child; Article 91 Convention on the Protection of the Rights of all Migrant Workers and Members of their Families; Article 46 Convention on the Rights of Persons with Disabilities and Article 14 of the Optional Protocol to this Convention.

[12] Covenant on Civil and Political Rights; Covenant on Economic, Social and Cultural Rights; Convention Against Torture; and Convention for the Protection of All Persons from Enforced Disappearance. Articles 28(1) and 30(2) CAT permit specific declarations relating to the inquiry procedure and the settlement of disputes, respectively.

States can only formulate[13] reservations when signing, ratifying, accepting, approving or acceding to a treaty (VCLT Article 19(1)), not at any other stage.[14] States that have second thoughts cannot formulate a reservation after they are already a party to a treaty; they would have to then denounce and re-ratify with a reservation. It must be borne in mind, however, that denunciation of human rights treaties is not always possible.[15] A reservation may be withdrawn at any time; practice shows that indeed some states have withdrawn their reservations over time, however, they constitute a minority.[16] A number of recent human rights instruments that establish additional monitoring procedures to human rights treaties set a new trend. These instruments prohibit reservations, but allow states not to accept all monitoring procedures by 'opting out'.[17] It is striking that the large majority of states that become parties to these instruments do not use the opting-out clause and thus accept all monitoring procedures. This structure may therefore turn out to be an important step ahead in limiting the number of reservations.

In the context of the reporting procedure, treaty bodies encourage states parties to review their reservations with a view to withdrawing even permissible reservations on the policy basis that reservations 'diminish the scope of protection afforded by treaties and should thus be construed narrowly and removed if at all possible.'[18] Similar encouragement towards withdrawal of reservations can be found in the resolutions of political organs.[19] Practice of both states and treaty monitoring bodies thus shows a trend towards limiting the number and scope of reservations.

---

[13] The term 'formulate' in the Vienna Convention on the Law of Treaties was chosen deliberately. A reservation is 'made' only after it has been accepted by the other states. Tenth report on reservations to treaties UN Doc. A/CN.4/558 (2005), para. 14.

[14] For practical reasons, the UN Secretary-General permits states to formulate their reservations afterwards, rather than encouraging states to write their reservations on the original copy of a treaty. These are then accepted as 'late reservations'. See P. Kohona, 'Some Notable Developments in the Practice of the UN Secretary-General as Depositary of Multilateral Treaties: Reservations and Declarations' (2005) 99 AJIL 433, 435.

[15] Human Rights Committee, General Comment No. 26, 'General comment on issues relating to the continuity of obligations to the International Covenant on Civil and Political Rights', in Compilation of General Comments and General Recommendations adopted by Human Rights Treaty Bodies (2006) UN Doc. HRI/GEN/1/Rev.8, 212–213.

[16] UN Treaty Bible, <http://untreaty.un.org>.

[17] See Article 28 CAT, Article 10 of the Optional Protocol to the Convention on the Elimination of Discrimination Against Women, and Article 30 of the Optional Protocol to CAT.

[18] Seventeenth Meeting of Chairpersons of the Human Rights Treaty Bodies, Fourth Inter-Committee Meeting of the Human Rights Treaty Bodies, The Practice of Human Rights Treaty Bodies with Respect to Reservations to International Human Rights Treaties, UN Doc. HRI/MC/2005/5 (2005), para. 7.

[19] See, *inter alia*, General Assembly Resolution 60/149, *International Covenants on Human Rights* (2005), para. 7; *Convention on the Elimination of All Forms of Discrimination against Women* (2005), para. 6; Human Rights Council Resolution 4/1, 'Question of the realisation in all countries of economic, social and cultural rights, in Human Rights Council', in *Report to the General Assembly on the fourth session of the Human Rights Council,* UN Doc. A/HRC/4/123, para. 3(a).

4. The 'Object and Purpose' of Human Rights Treaties

The 'object and purpose' test is crucial in determining whether or not a specific reservation is valid. The term finds its origin in the ICJ's Advisory Opinion in the *Reservations to the Genocide Convention* case,[20] and was subsequently included in the VCLT. It is now considered to be the 'pivot between the need to preserve the nature of the treaty and the desire to facilitate accession to multilateral treaties by the greatest possible number of States.'[21] It is not always easy to establish what exactly constitutes the object and purpose of a human rights treaty. As was observed by Lijnzaad, 'the claim that a particular reservation is contrary to object and purpose is easier made than substantiated.'[22] Perceptions on the 'object and purpose' of a treaty can evolve over time.[23] For treaties dealing with a single issue, such as the Convention Against Torture, it may be relatively easy to define its *raison d'être,* however, for a general treaty, such as the ICCPR, this is not the case. According to the Human Rights Committee:

In an instrument which articulates very many civil and political rights, each of the many articles, and indeed their interplay, secures the objectives of the Covenant. The object and purpose of the Covenant is to create legally binding standards for human rights by defining certain civil and political rights and placing them in a framework of obligations which are legally binding for those States which ratify; and to provide an efficacious supervisory machinery for the obligations undertaken.[24]

This does not provide much guidance for determining which rights may or may not be subjected to reservations. In this context, the Human Rights Committee pays specific attention to norms that have acquired a special status in international human rights law, including peremptory norms and norms that belong to customary international law, against which no reservations may be made. This issue will be further addressed in section 60. The HRCt considers that reservations to the obligation to respect and ensure the rights, and to do so on a non-discriminatory basis (Article 2 (1)) would not be acceptable, as such reservations

---

[20] *Reservations to the Convention on the Prevention and Punishment of the Crime of Genocide,* Advisory Opinion of 28 May 1951, 1951 ICJ Reports 15.

[21] International Law Commission, Tenth Report of the Special Rapporteur, Addendum, UN Doc. A/CN.4/558/Add.1 (2005), para. 55.

[22] L. Lijnzaad, *Reservations to UN-Human Rights Treaties: Ratify and Ruin?* (Martinus Nijhoff, Dordrecht 1995) 82–83.

[23] W. Schabas, 'Reservations to the Convention on the Rights of the Child' (1996) 18 HRQ 472, 479.

[24] Human Rights Committee, General Comment No. 24, General comment on issues relating to reservations made upon ratification or accession to the Covenant or the Optional Protocols thereto, or in relation to declarations under Article 41 of the Covenant, in Compilation of General Comments and General Recommendations adopted by Human Rights Treaty Bodies (2006), UN Doc. HRI/GEN/1/Rev.8, 200–207 at 206, para. 7. Further on this issue, see R. Moloney, 'Incompatible Reservations to Human Rights Treaties: Severability and the Problem of State Consent' (2004) 5 Melbourne J Int L 155.

would not pass the object and purpose test.[25] In the consideration of Kuwait's initial report, the HRC examined the 'interpretative declaration' regarding Articles 2(1) and 3 ICCPR, on non-discrimination and equal treatment generally and discrimination specifically against women respectively, which reads:

Although the Government of Kuwait endorses the worthy principles embodied in these two articles as consistent with the provisions of the Kuwait Constitution in general and of its article 29 in particular, the rights to which the articles refer must be exercised within the limits set by Kuwaiti law.[26]

In its concluding observations, the Human Rights Committee appears to apply two criteria, referring to both the special status of Articles 2 and 3, and the broad wording of the 'declaration'. It stated that Articles 2 and 3 constitute core rights and overarching principles of international law that cannot be subject to limits set by Kuwaiti law. It further noted that such broad and general limitations would undermine the object and purpose of the entire Covenant. It concluded that the declaration contravened Kuwait's essential obligations under the Covenant and was therefore without legal effect and did not affect the powers of the Committee.[27]

Further, the Human Rights Committee has observed that reservations to a supportive guarantee, such as the right to an effective remedy, are not valid, as this is an integral part of the structure of the ICCPR and underpins its efficacy. It considers reservations that affect the Committee's monitoring role also incompatible with the object and purpose of the ICCPR.[28]

Reservations to norms not categorized as peremptory or part of customary international law can nevertheless affect the object and purpose of a treaty. Human rights treaties are not a listing of separate unrelated rights and obligations, but a means to achieve the goal of respect, promotion, and protection of human rights. A reservation to a single treaty provision can therefore be incompatible with the object and purpose of the treaty.[29] An example of a reservation to one provision that affects the enjoyment of other rights constitutes Kuwait's reservation to Article 7(a) of the Women's Convention, which excludes women from the right to be eligible for election and to vote. The Committee on the Elimination of Discrimination Against Women considered this reservation incompatible with the object and purpose of the Convention.[30] CEDAW did not justify this finding, but it is clear that

---

[25] Human Rights Committee, General Comment No. 24, para. 9.

[26] UN Treaty Bible, <http://untreaty.un.org>.

[27] Human Rights Committee, Concluding Comments on Kuwait, in Report of the Human Rights Committee, GAOR A/55/40 (2000), Vol. I, paras. 456–457.

[28] Human Rights Committee, General Comment No. 24, para.11.

[29] Françoise Hampson, Reservations to Human Rights Treaties: Final Working Paper, UN Doc. E/CN.4/Sub.2/2004/42, para. 50.

[30] CEDAW, Concluding Observations on Kuwait, in Report of the Committee on the Elimination of Discrimination against Women, GAOR A/59/38 (2004), para. 61. The reservation was withdrawn on 9 December 2005.

Article 7 contains an important right for women. Excluding women from participating in political life has serious consequences for their role in other fields of public life, in influencing policy making, and hence also in their role in private life.[31] The Committee on the Elimination of Racial Discrimination considers Article 4 (prohibition of the dissemination of racist ideas) as a key provision of a mandatory nature.[32] It refers to this status when it urges states parties to withdraw their reservations to this provision; it does not, however, use terminology such as invalid, unacceptable, impermissible, or incompatible. It must be noted that there are few examples of this nature, since the treaty bodies do not lightly draw the conclusion that a reservation is incompatible with the object and purpose of the treaty. Nevertheless, it is clear that they take the view that a precisely worded reservation, affecting the application of a narrowly defined part of a treaty, can be incompatible with the object and purpose of the treaty.

The ILC considers that establishing the object and purpose of a treaty is very difficult; attempts made in scholarly writing to define a general method are 'disappointing.'[33] According to the ILC, the main rule is that a reservation is incompatible with the object and purpose of the treaty if it affects an essential element of the treaty that is necessary to its general thrust, in such a way that the reservation impairs the *raison d'être* of the treaty.[34] This concerns the 'fundamental core' that is to be preserved in order to avoid the 'effectiveness' of the treaty as a whole being undermined.[35] The ILC has considered it useful to draft a guideline specifically on the object and purpose of general human rights treaties such as the ICCPR, CESCR and ECHR. Provisionally adopted draft guideline 3.1.12 reads:

> To assess the compatibility of a reservation with the object and purpose of a general treaty for the protection of human rights, account shall be taken of the indivisibility, interdependence and interrelatedness of the rights set out in the treaty as well as the importance that the right or provision which is the subject of the reservation has within the general thrust of the treaty, and the gravity of the impact the reservation has upon it.[36]

The reference to the indivisibility, interdependence and interrelatedness of rights resembles the Human Rights Committee's reference to the 'interplay' of rights, and is language commonly used in the international human rights discourse since its inclusion in the 1993 Vienna Declaration.[37] In the commentary, the ILC

---

[31] On the importance of Article 7 for the exercise of other rights see CEDAW, General Recommendation No. 23, Political and Public Life, in Compilation of General Comments and General Recommendations adopted by Human Rights Treaty Bodies (2006), UN Doc. HRI/GEN/1/Rev.8 (1997), 318–329.

[32] Committee on the Elimination of Racial Discrimination, General Recommendation No. XV on Article 4 of the Convention, in Compilation of General Comments and General Recommendations adopted by Human Rights Treaty Bodies (2006), UN Doc. HRI/GEN/1/Rev.8, 248–249, at 248, para. 2.

[33] Report of the International Law Commission, GAOR A/62/10 (2007), 73.

[34] Ibid., 66.   [35] Ibid., 74 (footnotes omitted).   [36] Ibid., 65.

[37] Vienna Declaration and Programme of Action (1993) Part I, Article 5: 'All human rights are universal, indivisible and interdependent and interrelated.'

specifies that the wording is taken from this Declaration and that it 'emphasises the global nature of the protection afforded by general human rights treaties and is intended to prevent their dismantling.'[38]

The reference to the importance of the central rights in the general thrust of the treaty recognizes, according to the ILC, 'that certain rights protected by these instruments are no less important than other rights—and, in particular, non-derogable ones.'[39] Although in this section of the commentary no explicit reference is made to the HRCt's general comment on reservations, this element can be regarded as an affirmation of the HRCt's position that rights which are not qualified as non-derogable can be of such importance that they may not be subjected to reservations.[40]

With respect to the third element, concerning the gravity of the impact of reservations, the ILC observes that 'even in the case of essential rights, reservations are possible if they do not preclude protection of the rights in question and do not have the effect of excessively modifying their legal regime.'[41] The HRCt's general comment does not distinguish between reservations that have a grave impact on a right and those that have a minor impact. It appears, however, that the HRCt would not wish to distinguish between minor and grave reservations to essential rights, but seeks to persuade states parties to limit any reservation to such rights. This issue is further discussed in the sections dealing with norms that have acquired a special status in international human rights law.

The commentary to this draft guideline further pays attention to the validity of reservations, with reference to states parties' tacit acceptance of many reservations, and treaty bodies' absence of concern about certain reservations. The ILC concludes that general reservations to one of the protected rights are not invalid as such.[42] The draft guideline may serve as a sort of safety net to evaluate reservations that do not fall within the scope of the other guidelines. Unlike the treaty bodies, the ILC does not display any inclination to keep reservations to a minimum and to aim for the ultimate withdrawal of all reservations; rather, the commentary stresses the acceptability of reservations.

5. Reservations Affecting Implementation of the Treaty in its Entirety

Article 27 of the Vienna Convention on the Law of Treaties (VCLT) provides that a state may not invoke the provisions of its internal law as justification for its failure to

---

[38] Report of the International Law Commission GAOR A/62/10 (2007), 116.
[39] Ibid.
[40] Human Rights Committee, General Comment No. 24, para. 10.
[41] Report of the International Law Commission GAOR A/62/10 (2007), 116.
[42] Ibid., 114.

perform its obligations under a treaty. While the possibility of formulating reservations may be considered as an exception to this rule,[43] since reservations are made because of the non-conformity of domestic law with international law, the 'right' to formulate reservations can never go so far as to give priority to domestic law in general, since this would not constitute implementation of the treaty in good faith. Various types of reservations can affect the implementation of a treaty in its entirety. It is difficult to further categorize reservations of this nature, but for the sake of clarity, a distinction is made between reservations to the provisions containing the general duty to give effect, reservations that accord domestic law a superior status, and generally worded reservations that (potentially) affect the implementation of the treaty as a whole. Clearly, there is overlap between the categories.

5.1 Reservations to the provision 'to give effect'

First, there are reservations that explicitly state that the core provision containing the obligation to take all necessary implementation measures shall not be complied with. For example, upon ratification of the Women's Convention, Brunei made 'reservations with respect to . . . Article 2, in order to ensure its implementation within the bounds of the provisions of the Islamic Shariah.' This particular reservation has not been examined by CEDAW, since Brunei has not submitted a report. In its statement on reservations, CEDAW has stated that Article 2 is central to the object and purpose of the Women's Convention, and that reservations to this provision are not permissible.[44] Some reservations explicitly affect Article 2; others are drawn so widely that they encompass Article 2. In its practice under the reporting procedure, CEDAW categorically states that reservations that affect Article 2 are incompatible with the object and purpose of the Convention.

The Human Rights Committee has taken the same view. In its general comment on reservations it has stated that reservations to ICCPR Article 2(2), which obliges states to take the necessary steps at the domestic level to give effect to the rights of the Covenant, are not acceptable.[45]

The ILC has not addressed this issue in a separate guideline, but it is covered by the guideline addressing the status of internal law in relation to international law, which is dealt with in the next section.

---

[43] Lijnzaad, *Reservations to UN-Human Rights Treaties* (1995) 87; Schabas (1996) 18 HRQ 472, 479.

[44] Committee on the Elimination of Discrimination Against Women, Statements on Reservations to the Convention on the Elimination of All Forms of Discrimination against Women, in Report of the Committee on the Elimination of Discrimination against Women, GAOR, A/53/38/Rev.1 (1998), Part Two, Chapter I. A, paras. 6, 8 and 16. On CEDAW's practice see H. Schöpp-Schilling, 'Reservations to the Convention on the Elimination of all forms of Discrimination Against Women: An Unresolved Issue or (No) New Developments?' in I. Ziemele (ed.), *Reservations to Human Rights Treaties and the Vienna Convention Regime: Conflict, Harmony or Reconciliation.* (Martinus Nijhoff, Leiden / Boston 2004), 3–40.

[45] Human Rights Committee, General Comment No. 24, para. 9.

5.2 Reservations according superior status to domestic law

Second, there are reservations that provide in general terms that domestic law will be interpreted in such a way that it is not affected by the ratification of the treaty. This is largely similar to the first type distinguished, although formulated differently, and not containing an explicit reference to provisions such as ICCPR Article 2 and Article 2 of the Women's Convention. In its general comment on reservations, the Human Rights Committee has stated on this aspect that 'reservations should not seek to remove an autonomous meaning to Covenant obligations, by pronouncing them to be identical, or to be accepted only in so far as they are identical, with existing provisions of domestic law.'[46] In its practice under the reporting procedure, it has criticized the United States of America. Upon conclusion of the examination of the initial report, it stated that 'the State party's reservations, declarations and understandings to the Covenant…taken together,…intended to ensure that the United States has accepted only what is already the law of the United States.'[47] It did not, however, conclude that this rendered the reservations invalid.

The Committee on the Rights of the Child (CRC) chooses mild language in assessing the validity of reservations in its concluding observations. Where Iran went so far as to say that it reserved the right 'not to apply any provisions or articles of the Convention that are incompatible with Islamic Laws and the international legislation in effect', the Committee merely stated that this reservation negated many provisions of the Convention and it expressed its concern about the compatibility with object and purpose.[48] Although the CRC has regularly referred to the Vienna Declaration and Programme of Action and to Article 27 of the VCLT in its encouragement to states to withdraw the reservations, it does not provide a further motivation for its findings. It is noteworthy that the Committee seems to prefer to comment on the 'necessity' of reservations, rather than their permissibility or validity. States parties are more critical in their objections against these reservations than the CRC. With respect to the reservation of Iran (and similar reservations of a number of other states), The Netherlands submitted the following objection:

The Government of the Kingdom of the Netherlands considers that such reservations, which seek to limit the responsibilities of the reserving State under the Convention by invoking general principles of national law, may raise doubts as to the commitment of these States to the object and purpose of the Convention and moreover, contribute to

---

[46] Ibid., para. 19.

[47] Human Rights Committee, Concluding Comments on the United States of America, in Report of the Human Rights Committee, GAOR A/50/40, Vol. I (1995), para. 279. The Committee declared some of the specific reservations by the United States incompatible with the object and purpose of the ICCPR.

[48] Committee on the Rights of the Child, Concluding Observations on the Islamic Republic of Iran, CRC/C/15/Add.254 (2005), para. 6.

undermining the basis of international treaty law. It is in the common interest of States that treaties to which they have chosen to become parties should be respected, as to object and purpose, by all parties. The Government of the Kingdom of the Netherlands therefore objects to these reservations.[49]

Upon ratification of the Women's Convention, Saudi Arabia submitted a reservation that provides that 'In the case of contradiction between any term of the Convention and the norms of Islamic law, the Kingdom is not under obligation to observe the contradictory terms of the Convention.' The Committee on the Elimination of Discrimination Against Women considered this reservation to be 'drawn so widely that it is contrary to the object and purpose of the Convention.'[50] It did not indicate precisely why it reached the conclusion, whether the main concern was the impact on Article 2 of the Convention, on the treaty as a whole, the vague terminology, or all of these taken together. States have sometimes been very clear on this criterion in their objections. Finland, for example, has objected against various Islamic reservations, on the ground of the 'general principle of treaty interpretation according to which a party may not invoke the provisions of its internal law as justification for failure to perform a treaty.'[51]

Treaty body practice on this type of reservation shows that the claimed superior status of domestic law is not a criterion often applied in the examination of the validity of a reservation. CEDAW has included it in its statement on reservations, providing that neither traditional, religious nor cultural practice, nor incompatible domestic laws and policies could justify violations of the Convention. However, in its practice under the reporting procedure, no reference is made to this criterion; the Committee either simply states that such reservations are incompatible with the object and purpose of the Convention without further motivation, or it applies the criterion of precision, by making reference to the incompatibility of 'general reservations'.

The ILC's provisionally adopted draft guideline 3.1.11 deals with reservations relating to internal law:

A reservation by which a State or an international organisation purports to exclude or to modify the legal effect of certain provisions of a treaty or of the treaty as a whole in order to preserve the integrity of specific norms of the internal law of that State or rules of that organisation may be formulated only insofar as it is compatible with the object and purpose of the treaty.[52]

This type of reservation is distinguished from the one referred to in draft guideline 3.1.7 on generally worded reservations (see below, Section 5.3), regarding which the ILC reiterates that they are problematic because of the impossibility of

---

[49] UN Treaty Bible, <http://untreaty.un.org>.

[50] Committee on the Elimination of Discrimination Against Women, Concluding Observations on Saudi Arabia, CEDAW/C/SAU/CO/2 (2008), para. 9.

[51] UN Treaty Bible, <http://untreaty.un.org>.

[52] Report of the International Law Commission, GAOR A/62/10 (2007), 65.

assessing compatibility. The question underlying draft guideline 3.1.11 is whether a precisely worded reservation could be justified by considerations arising from domestic law. The ILC recalls that reservations are often made because treaty obligations are incompatible with domestic law, and finds objections by states on the ground that provisions of internal law may not be invoked as a justification of a failure to perform a treaty unconvincing. Its position is that reservations may not be 'a cover for not actually accepting any new international obligation.'[53] The reference to 'certain provisions of a treaty' is deliberate, and expresses that the preservation of particular norms of internal law is acceptable, provided that these are not incompatible with the object and purpose of the treaty concerned. This section of the commentary does not contain references to the Islamic reservations, even though these give priority to domestic law over international law in general terms. In the absence of consistent treaty body practice no conclusion can be drawn on the impact of their work. The formulation of this draft guideline (reservations are permitted, unless ...) illustrates the ILC's different general attitude towards reservations, as it does not support the treaty bodies' position that the ultimate goal is universal ratification without any reservations.

5.3 Vague and generally worded reservations

The third criterion concerns generally worded reservations that (potentially) affect the implementation of the treaty as a whole. In its general comment, the Human Rights Committee has stated:

Reservations must be specific and transparent, so that the Committee, those under the jurisdiction of the reserving State and other States parties may be clear as to what obligations of human rights compliance have or have not been undertaken. Reservations may thus not be general, but must refer to a particular provision of the Covenant and indicate in precise terms its scope in relation thereto.[54]

The HRCt has applied the criterion 'specific and transparent' in the individual complaints procedure, *inter alia* when it examined a communication on Article 10(2), to which Australia made a reservation, reading 'In relation to paragraph 2(a) the principle of segregation [of accused persons and convicted persons] is accepted as an objective to be achieved progressively'.[55] The Committee noted that the reservation is specific and transparent, and that its scope is clear. It stated that while it would be desirable for all states parties to withdraw reservations expeditiously,

[53] Ibid., 110–112.

[54] Human Rights Committee, General Comment No. 24, para. 19. This is comparable to the European Court of Human Rights' interpretation of Article 57 (former Article 64) of the European Convention on Human Rights. In the *Belilos* judgment it considered that 'reservation of a general character' means 'in particular a reservation couched in terms that are too vague or broad for it to be possible to determine their exact meaning and scope.' *Belilos v. Switzerland*, (App. No. 10328/83), ECtHR, Judgment of 29 April 1988, (1988) Series A No. 132, para. 55.

[55] UN Treaty Bible, <http://untreaty.un.org>.

the ICCPR does not contain a timeframe for the withdrawal of reservations.[56] It thus declared the communication inadmissible. Specific and transparent reservations can thus legitimately exist and preclude the Committee from examining a communication. Unfortunately, the Committee did not apply all criteria adopted in its general comment, in particular not those that point out that reservations should not be maintained indefinitely. Australia ratified the ICCPR in 1975 and, especially in light of the fact that the reservation contains the term 'progressively', there was ample room for the Committee to consider that 25 years should have been sufficient to realize the objective of ICCPR Article 10(2)(a).

Lack of precision appears to constitute the main concern of approximately ten Western states that regularly object against generally worded reservations to the Women's Convention and the Convention on the Rights of the Child.[57] For example, the Government of Norway objected to the general reservation by Saudi Arabia to the Women's Convention by stating that 'due to its unlimited scope and undefined character, this part of the reservation is contrary to object and purpose of the Convention.'[58]

The concluding observations on Qatar's state report illustrate the Committee Against Torture's apparent reluctance to declare reservations incompatible with the object and purpose of the Convention. Qatar formulated a broad reservation, to 'any interpretation of the provisions of the Convention that is incompatible with the precepts of Islamic law and the Islamic religion', against which twelve objections have been submitted. The Committee Against Torture expressed its concern, because of the 'broad and imprecise nature' of the reservation. It observes that it 'consists of a general reference to national law without specifying its contents and does not clearly define the extent to which the reserving State has accepted the Convention, thus raising questions as to the State party's overall implementation of its treaty obligations.' It recommended re-examination of the reservation with a view to withdrawing it.[59]

From the perspective of protection of individual rights and the need for monitoring bodies to fulfil their tasks, reservations must be formulated as narrowly and precisely as possible. CEDAW and the Human Rights Committee appear to be a step ahead of other treaty bodies in drawing conclusions on the compatibility of generally worded reservations with the object and purpose of a treaty. States parties that have formulated objections have drawn similar conclusions to the two treaty bodies. It would be helpful if the treaty bodies would be more precise in their explanations, and specify whether their findings are based on the refusal

---

[56] *Cabal and Pasini v. Australia,* (1020/2002), HRCt, 7 August 2003, Report of the Human Rights Committee, GAOR A/58/40, Vol. II (2003), Annex V, section DD, para. 7.4.

[57] Cooperation between member states of the Council of Europe takes place on the basis of Committee of Ministers Recommendation No. R (99) 13 on responses to inadmissible reservations to international treaties. In addition to Council of Europe member states, Mexico has also submitted a considerable number of objections to generally worded reservations under CEDAW.

[58] UN Treaty Bible, <http://untreaty.un.org>.

[59] CAT, Concluding observations on Qatar, CAT/C/QAT/CO/1 (2006), para. 9.

to implement or to state that domestic law shall not be affected, or because of the general terms that have been used.

With respect to vague or general reservations, ILC draft guideline 3.1.7 reads: 'A reservation shall be worded in such a way as to allow its scope to be determined, in order to assess in particular its compatibility with the object and purpose of the treaty.'[60]

The commentary points out that such reservations affect the entitlement of other states to take a position on such reservations, in most cases because they refer to undefined domestic provisions. It is therefore the impossibility of assessing the compatibility with the object and purpose of the treaty concerned, rather than the certainty that they are incompatible, which makes them fall within the scope of Article 19(c) of the VCLT. In the commentary to this rule, references are made to state practice under human rights treaties, as well as to the Human Rights Committee's general comment on reservations, and the case law of the European Commission and Court of Human Rights.[61]

The practice of human rights treaty bodies has had a distinct impact on the work of the ILC. Like the ILC, human rights treaty bodies regard the impossibility of determining the precise scope and effect of a generally worded reservation as problematic. However, unlike the ILC, they have pointed out that the vagueness is not the only concern, but that such reservations demonstrate the state party's refusal to accept the core obligation 'to give effect' to the treaty provisions. Further, the treaty bodies and the ILC draw different conclusions as regards validity. Whereas treaty bodies regard such reservations as incompatible with the object and purpose of the treaty concerned, the ILC notes that it would seem difficult to maintain that they are invalid *ipso jure*, because of the impossibility of assessing whether or not the conditions for substantive validity have been fulfilled.[62] The ILC's primary concern thus relates to the interests of other states parties in establishing the extent to which the reserving state considers itself to be bound, rather than to the impact of the reservation for individuals on the enjoyment of human rights. On many occasions, the intention of the state is very clear indeed: it does not intend to make any significant changes in its domestic law, for example, because it seeks to uphold the special position of religious laws. Rightfully, the treaty bodies have been critical towards such reservations also for other reasons than the lack of precision. In this respect we therefore see little impact of international human rights law on the work of the ILC. In light of the ILC's acceptance that reciprocity does not really play a role in human rights treaties, it would have been appropriate to take a less state-centred approach and to address the question of vague and generally worded reservations to human rights treaties separately, in order to take into account the special nature of these treaties.

---

[60] Report of the International Law Commission, GAOR A/62/10 (2007), 64.
[61] Ibid., 82 *et seq.*   [62] Ibid., 82–88.

6. Reservations to Norms that have Acquired Special Status

6.1 Reservations affecting *jus cogens* norms

The Vienna Declaration reaffirmed that all human rights are 'universal, indivisible and interdependent and interrelated',[63] which makes it difficult to argue that some rights are more important than other rights, or that there is a hierarchy among human rights. Nevertheless, it must be assumed that the object and purpose test necessitates a certain distinction between the various treaty provisions.[64]

According to the Human Rights Committee, reservations to norms of a peremptory character would not be compatible with the object and purpose of the Covenant.[65] Under Article 53 of the VCLT, a peremptory norm is 'a norm accepted and recognised by the international community of states as a whole as a norm from which no derogation is permitted and which can be modified only by a subsequent norm of general international law having the same character.' Concluding that reservations to peremptory norms are not permitted is uncontroversial, but then the next question is, which rights fall in this category?[66] It would fall outside the scope of the present Chapter to examine which rights form part of *jus cogens*,[67] or to examine the practice of the various treaty bodies in an in-depth manner.[68]

The Human Rights Committee's concluding observations on reservations to ICCPR Articles 6(5) and 7 (prohibition of imposition of the death penalty on persons who were minors at the time the offence was committed, and prohibition of torture, cruel, inhuman or degrading treatment, respectively) are an example of precisely formulated reservations that were considered incompatible with the object and purpose of the treaty concerned.[69] No explanation was provided, but it is quite likely that the conclusion was based on the fact that both provisions are non-derogable under ICCPR Article 4(2) and form part of *jus cogens*.

The ILC considers that a reservation to a customary norm is not invalid *per se*, provided that the reservation does not affect the binding nature of this norm. The fact that a provision reflects a customary norm is 'a pertinent factor in establishing

---

[63] Article 5 Vienna Declaration (1993).

[64] Lijnzaad, *Reservations to UN-Human Rights Treaties* (1995) 83.

[65] Human Rights Committee, General Comment No. 24, para. 8; see also E. Klein, 'A Comment on the Issue of Reservations to the Provisions of the Covenant Representing (peremptory) Rules of General International Law', in I. Ziemele (ed.), *Reservations to Human Rights Treaties and the Vienna Convention Regime: Conflict, Harmony or Reconciliation.* (Martinus Nijhoff, Leiden/Boston 2004) 59–65.

[66] See also Schabas, (1994) 32 *Annuaire canadien de droit international* 49.

[67] See Chapter 7 of this volume on the Structure of International Obligations.

[68] This has been done for HRCt (CCPR), CEDAW, CAT and CERD in I. Ziemele (ed.), *Reservations to Human Rights Treaties and the Vienna Convention Regime* (2004).

[69] HRCt, Concluding Comments on the United States of America, GAOR A/50/40, Vol. I (1995), para. 14.

the validity' of the reservation concerned.[70] On reservations to a rule of *jus cogens* the ILC states that 'a reservation cannot exclude or modify the legal effect of a treaty in a manner contrary to a peremptory norm of general international law.'[71] The ILC position on reservations to *jus cogens* norms differs somewhat from the position taken by the Human Rights Committee. Whereas the HRCt states that such reservations are, as such, incompatible with the object and purpose of the ICCPR,[72] the ILC holds the view that this cannot be maintained in such general terms.[73] The ILC achieves the same result, namely invalidity, but does not use the 'object and purpose' rule. Instead, the ILC relies on the general rules of public international law that do not allow states in any way to undermine the status of this category of rules, and concludes that any reservation to a provision which formulates a rule of *jus cogens* is null and void *ipso jure*.[74] It is difficult to establish what impact practice in international human rights organs has had on the formulation of this particular draft guideline, since hardly any reservations to *jus cogens* norms seem to exist.[75]

6.2 Reservations to non-derogable norms

In its general comment on reservations, the Human Rights Committee recalled the great importance of non-derogable rights, but stressed that not all rights of profound importance have in fact been made non-derogable. It observed that while 'there is no automatic correlation between reservations to non-derogable provisions, and reservations which offend against the object and purpose of the Covenant, a State has a heavy onus to justify such a reservation.'[76] In its work under the reporting procedure, it has urged Germany to withdraw its reservation to Article 15(1) (prohibition of retroactive punishment) with reference to the non-derogable status of this provision.[77]

With respect to reservations to provisions relating to non-derogable rights, the ILC takes as a starting point that these are undesirable, but not necessarily invalid:

A State or international organisation may not formulate a reservation to a treaty provision relating to non-derogable rights unless the reservation in question is compatible with the

---

[70] Report of the International Law Commission, GAOR A/62/10 (2007), 65, Draft Guideline 3.1.8.

[71] Ibid., 65, Draft Guideline 3.1.9.

[72] HRCt, Concluding Comments on the United States of America, GAOR A/50/40, Vol. I (1995), para. 8.

[73] Report of the International Law Commission, GAOR A/62/10 (2007), p. 101.

[74] Ibid., 101–102.

[75] Unlike the right to freedom from racial discrimination, the right to freedom from sex discrimination has not achieved the status of *jus cogens*. See H. Charlesworth, 'Whose Rule? Women and the International Rule of Law' in S. Zifcak (ed.), *Globalisation and the Rule of Law* (Routledge, London/New York 2006) 83, 86.

[76] HRCt, General Comment No. 24, para. 10.

[77] HRCt, Concluding Observations on Germany, CCPR/CO/80/DEU (2004), para. 10.

essential rights and obligations arising out of that treaty. In assessing that compatibility, account shall be taken to the importance which the parties have conferred upon the rights at issue by making them non-derogable.[78]

The commentary to the guidelines shows that the ILC considers reservations to non-derogable rights as 'suspect', but not as invalid *per se*. It takes the view that it is necessary to be very cautious, which is why it drafted the first sentence of the guideline in the negative (reservations are not compatible, unless …). When non-derogable provisions concern norms of *jus cogens*, the rule described in the previous Section applies. Although the ILC is critical on the terminology used by the Human Rights Committee, the core of both rules is the same. Determining the validity of reservations to non-derogable rights that do not form part of *jus cogens* is subjected to a test stricter than the 'essential element' test developed for determining whether reservations are contrary to the 'object and purpose' of the treaty.

7. Reservations Affecting the Monitoring Role of International Organs

With respect to the supervisory procedures, the Human Rights Committee has pointed out explicitly that its monitoring role constitutes an essential element of the Covenant, which is also directed to securing the enjoyment of the rights. Reservations 'that purport to evade that essential element in the design of the Covenant' are incompatible with the object and purpose of the Covenant.[79] According to the HRCt, states may not reserve the right not to present a report or seek to reject the HRCt's competence to interpret the requirements of provisions of the Covenant.[80] With respect to the validity of reservations under the Optional Protocol, the HRCt takes the position that the object and purpose of this treaty is to recognize the competence of the Committee to receive and consider communications from individuals who claim to be victims of a violation by a state party of any of the rights in the Covenant. It observed that

a reservation to an obligation of a State to respect and ensure a right contained in the Covenant, made under the first Optional Protocol when it has not previously been made in respect of the same rights under the Covenant, does not affect the State's duty to comply with its substantive obligation. A reservation cannot be made to the Covenant through the vehicle of the Optional Protocol but such a reservation would operate to ensure that the State's compliance with that obligation may not be tested by the Committee under the first Optional Protocol. And because the object and purpose of the first Optional Protocol is to allow the rights obligatory for a state under the Covenant to be tested before the Committee, a reservation that seeks to preclude this would be contrary to the object and

---

[78] Report of the International Law Commission, GAOR A/62/10 (2007), 65, Draft Guideline 3.1.10.
[79] HRCt, General Comment No. 24, para. 11.   [80] Ibid.

purpose of the first Optional Protocol, even if not of the Covenant. A reservation to a substantive obligation made for the first time under the first Optional Protocol would seem to reflect an intention by the State concerned to prevent the Committee from expressing its views relating to a particular article of the Covenant in an individual case.[81]

Various member states of the Council of Europe have made a reservation to Article 5(2)(a) of the Optional Protocol, to the effect that the Human Rights Committee is not only precluded from examining communications if 'the same matter' is being examined by the European Court of Human Rights, but also cases where the examination by the Court has been concluded. According to the HRCt, 'Insofar as the most basic obligation has been to secure independent third party review of the human rights of individuals, the Committee has, where the legal right and the subject matter are identical under the Covenant and under another international instrument, viewed such a reservation as not violating the object and purpose of the first Optional Protocol.'[82]

In the *Loizidou* judgment, the European Court of Human Rights examined Turkey's reservation to (then) Articles 25 and 46 of the European Convention, aimed at restricting *ratione loci* the right of individual complaint. It considered that 'States could not qualify their acceptance of the optional clauses thereby effectively excluding areas of their law and practice within their "jurisdiction" from supervision by the Convention institutions.'[83]

A reservation by Trinidad and Tobago to the Optional Protocol to the ICCPR and the Human Rights Committee's response thereto has drawn much attention. Trinidad and Tobago had been confronted with various findings of a violation of Articles 6 (right to life), 10 (right to humane treatment in detention), and 14 (right to a fair trial) in communications submitted by prisoners facing the death penalty. The state party denounced the Optional Protocol, and re-acceded with a reservation to Article 1 of the Optional Protocol, providing that 'the Human Rights Committee shall not be competent to receive and consider communications relating to any prisoner who is under sentence of death in respect of any matter relating to his prosecution, his detention, his trial, his conviction, his sentence or the carrying out of the death sentence on him and any matter connected therewith.'[84] The reservation was examined in the case of *Rawle Kennedy v. Trinidad and Tobago*. The Human Rights Committee considered that the reservation singled out a group of individuals for lesser procedural protection, and that this constituted discrimination, in contravention of the basic principles of

---

[81] Ibid., para. 13.

[82] Ibid., para. 14. On the Committee's practice, see M. Scheinin, 'Reservations by States under the International Covenant on Civil and Political Rights and its Optional Protocols, and the Practice of the Human Rights Committee', in: I. Ziemele (ed.), *Reservations to Human Rights Treaties and the Vienna Convention Regime* (Martinus Nijhoff Publishers, Leiden 2004) 41, 55–57.

[83] *Loizidou* v. *Turkey* (Preliminary Objections) (App. No. 15318/89), ECtHR, Judgment of 23 March 1995, (1995) Series A No. 310, para. 77.

[84] UN Treaty Bible, <http://untreaty.un.org>.

the ICCPR and its Optional Protocols. It concluded that the reservation was incompatible with the object and purpose of the Optional Protocol, and that the communication was admissible.[85] Subsequently, Trinidad and Tobago denounced the Optional Protocol altogether, which is a result that was probably foreseen by the Committee. This is indeed an undesirable effect of the Committee's decision, but accepting this type of reservation, against which a number of states parties[86] had objected, would have undermined the Committee's own position.

On this issue, the judgment of the International Court of Justice (ICJ) in the case of the *Democratic Republic of the Congo v. Rwanda* is relevant. The ICJ examined, among others, the compatibility of Rwanda's reservations to Article IX of the Genocide Convention and Article 22 of the Convention on the Elimination of Racial Discrimination (CERD) with the object and purpose of the respective treaties. The ICJ attached much value to the fact that the reservations do not affect substantive obligations relating to acts of genocide and racial discrimination, but only the jurisdiction of the Court. It considered that the reservations could not be deemed to be incompatible with the object and purpose of the Genocide Convention and the CERD.[87] The Court included a more general finding by stating that 'there exists no peremptory norm requiring States to consent to such jurisdiction in order to settle disputes relating to the Convention on Racial Discrimination.'[88] It reiterated that 'the mere fact that rights and obligations *erga omnes* or peremptory norms of general international law *(jus cogens)* are at issue in a dispute cannot in itself constitute an exception to the principle that its jurisdiction always depends on the consent of the parties.'[89] As a consequence, the absence of a treaty monitoring body under the Genocide Convention results in a gap in the monitoring of the implementation of some of the most fundamental human rights. In a separate opinion five judges argued that it is not self-evident that a reservation to Article IX of the Genocide Convention is permissible. They submit that the Court has an important role under the Convention and that, clearly, states parties have a role in monitoring compliance with the treaty obligations. Article IX offers a state that believes another state is committing genocide the chance to come to the Court. The five judges stress that Article IX 'speaks not only of disputes over the interpretation and application of the Convention, but over the "fulfilment of the Convention".'[90]

---

[85] Human Rights Committee, *Kennedy* v. *Trinidad and Tobago*, Admissibility Decision of 2 November 1999, Comm. No. 845/1999, GAOR A/55/40, Vol. II (2000), Annex XI, sect. A, para. 6.7. For a discussion of the Committee's reasoning and the dissenters' position, which argued that the case should have been declared inadmissible, see Scheinin, 'Reservations by States under the International Covenant on Civil and Political Rights' (2004), 49–51.

[86] See objections by France, Germany, Ireland, Italy, The Netherlands, Spain and Sweden.

[87] International Court of Justice, *Armed Activities on the Territory of the Congo (Democratic Republic of the Congo v. Rwanda)*, Judgment of 3 February 2006, 2006 ICJ Reports 6, paras. 67, 77, 78.

[88] Ibid., paras. 69 and 78.   [89] Ibid., para. 125.

[90] Ibid., Joint separate opinion of Judge Higgins, Judge Kooijmans, Judge Elaraby, Judge Owada, and Judge Simma, paras. 28–29.

The provisionally adopted ILC guideline on the issue of reservations to dispute settlement and monitoring procedures provides that:

A reservation to a treaty provision concerning dispute settlement or the monitoring of the implementation of the treaty is not, in itself, incompatible with the object and purpose of the treaty, unless:

(i) The reservation purports to exclude or modify the legal effect of a provision of the treaty essential to its *raison d'être;* or

(ii) The reservation has the effect of excluding the reserving State or international organisation from a dispute settlement or treaty implementation monitoring mechanism with respect to a treaty provision that it has previously accepted, if the very purpose of the treaty is to put such a mechanism into effect.[91]

The commentary to the provisions cites the ICJ judgment, the HRCt's general comment on reservations and views in the *Rawle Kennedy* case and the *Loizidou* judgment of the European Court of Human Rights, and states in so many words that the body of case law led the Commission to the formulation of this rule.[92]

The first sentence of the ILC draft guideline reflects the ICJ's finding in the judgment on the *Armed Activities on the Territory of the Congo.* There are major differences between the Human Rights Committee's general comment and this draft guideline. Unlike the HRCt, the ILC takes as a starting point that a reservation concerning the monitoring of the implementation of the treaty is not incompatible with the object and purpose of the treaty. It formulates two exceptions: first, the reservation should not affect substantive provisions of the treaty concerned. The phrase 'the very purpose' in the second exception is confusing. While a number of monitoring procedures are laid down in an additional protocol (such as the Optional Protocol to the Women's Convention), most procedures form part of the treaty that also contains the substantive provisions, as is the case for the reporting procedure under all human rights treaties, and for complaints procedures under the CERD and CAT. In such cases, the monitoring procedure is not 'the very purpose' of the treaty, but one of the essential elements. The ILC draft guideline is ambiguous, and does not fully reflect the position taken by the HRCt.

The ICJ judgment apparently has had a greater impact on the ILC draft guideline than the HRCt's general comment. The Court's judgment was based on the fact that the reservation affected only its own competence, not the norms on genocide and racial discrimination. The absence of practice from the Committee on the Elimination of Racial Discrimination on this issue may have prevented a more progressive interpretation of public international law by the Court. It would therefore be useful if treaty bodies encouraged states parties to withdraw reservations

---

[91] Report of the International Law Commission, GAOR A/62/10 (2007), 66, Draft Guideline 3.1.13.

[92] Ibid., 120.

on dispute settlement by the International Court of Justice, where applicable. Where there is no treaty body, as in the case of the Genocide Convention, there is a gap in the monitoring of the implementation of treaty obligations if states maintain their reservation to Article IX. Neither the ICJ nor the ILC show any inclination to contribute to closing the gap.

8. Determination of the Validity of Reservations

There are various questions relating to the roles and competencies of the treaty monitoring bodies. For the purpose of this analysis, two aspects will be distinguished: first, the competence to discuss reservations and the provisions to which these apply; and the ability to make findings and formulate recommendations is addressed. Second, the competence to attach consequences to the conclusion that a reservation is invalid is dealt with. It is recalled that on this aspect the ILC has not yet adopted draft guidelines with accompanying commentary. The following Sections thus mainly refer to the Special Rapporteur's work.

8.1 The competence to examine reservations and formulate recommendations

Article 20 of the VCLT provides that, under treaties that permit reservations, no subsequent acceptance by other contracting states is required. Otherwise, a reservation is presumed to be acceptable, subject to the right of states to challenge validity. This system was designed for treaties that contain obligations based on reciprocity, and in which states have specific interests as contracting parties. Human rights treaties are of an entirely different nature, in which the interests of states are different. As a result, the majority of states parties cannot or do not rigorously examine the validity of reservations and submit objections only when a reservation is incompatible with the object and purpose of the treaty. Practical obstacles also affect the effectiveness of this system. States that wish to object have only a little time to do so, since they must submit their objections within one year after ratification. States that become parties after the treaty has entered into force cannot enter objections against reservations by states that were parties before them. States which consider that a reservation may have been acceptable twenty years' ago, but has become impermissible over time, cannot submit an objection. Changes of opinion on valid reservations cannot be expressed by states parties in this setting.

States may have various motives when deciding whether or not to object to reservations. An explanation for the low number of objections by contracting states is that states are not really interested in how other states treat individuals within their territory, but that they are interested in the right to make reservations themselves. As a consequence, states care more about the right to make reservations, than about the right to object.[93] The VCLT system favours states that formulate reservations, even invalid reservations. If states object to reservations without attaching consequences to their objections, the reserving state—even if it is breaching international law—gets what it wants.[94]

Even though the large majority of states parties do not lodge objections against reservations, it may not be assumed that all reservations that are not the subject of objections are thus valid. It is clear that the aim of the VCLT is to ensure that reservations that are incompatible with the object and purpose of the treaty are prohibited. However, the system codified in the VCLT is inappropriate on this point. The Human Rights Committee's general comment on reservations, adopted in 1994, constitutes a landmark document on this issue. The Committee concluded that it has the competence:

> to determine whether a specific reservation is compatible with the object and purpose of the Covenant. This is in part because, as indicated above, it is an inappropriate task for States parties in relation to human rights treaties, and in part because it is a task that the Committee cannot avoid in the performance of its functions. In order to know the scope of its duty to examine a State's compliance under article 40 or a communication under the first Optional Protocol, the Committee has necessarily to take a view on the compatibility of a reservation with the object and purpose of the Covenant and with general international law. Because of the special character of a human rights treaty, the compatibility of a reservation with the object and purpose of the Covenant must be established objectively, by reference to legal principles, and the Committee is particularly well placed to perform this task.[95]

The division of roles between states parties and treaty monitoring bodies differs significantly from the drafters' intentions. While 'every State Party has a legal interest in the performance by every other State Party of its obligations',[96] treaty-based monitoring of compliance with human rights obligations is in practice not performed by states parties but is left to the treaty monitoring bodies. States apparently prefer to discuss human rights records in the framework of political organs. The Human Rights Committee has called on states parties to act more as contracting parties, as compliance with Covenant obligations should be considered as 'a reflection of legitimate community interest.'[97] State practice concerning reservations is useful because, in assessing the validity of reservations, treaty bodies use objections that have been submitted by states parties to seek guidance.[98] It is therefore important that states parties continue to play their role in assessing the validity of reservations and submit their objections when necessary.

---

[93] E. Swaine, 'Reserving' (2006) 31 YJIL 307, 327.

[94] J. Klabbers, 'Accepting the Unacceptable? A New Nordic Approach to Reservations to Multilateral Treaties', (2000) 69 Nordic J Intl L 179.

[95] HRCt, General Comment No. 24, para. 18.

[96] HRCt, General Comment No. 31, para. 2.   [97] Ibid.

[98] HRCt, General Comment No. 24. para .17.

In the debate on the competence of treaty bodies to 'determine' validity of reservations, it is often overlooked that treaty monitoring bodies are not precluded from asking questions about legislation and practice concerning the provision to which a reservation has been made, and why states are unable to amend domestic legislation and bring it in line with the treaty. This competence is derived from the provisions on the reporting procedure. States are under an obligation to report on the progress made in the implementation of the treaty and on factors and difficulties in the implementation (see for example ICCPR Article 40). The existence of a reservation indicates that there is 'a factor or difficulty' in implementing the treaty, and that the state party concerned must explain its motivation for entering and maintaining the reservation. A procedure for dealing with reservations in the context of the reporting procedure was agreed on by the Meeting of Chairpersons of the Human Rights Treaty Bodies. Treaty bodies will request information in their lists of issues on the nature and scope of reservations, the motivation for formulating and maintaining reservations, the precise effect and plans to limit and withdraw reservations. In the dialogue, treaty bodies will clarify their concern. In their concluding observations they will welcome withdrawal of reservations and acknowledge ongoing reviews, express concern about the maintenance of reservations, and encourage the complete withdrawal of reservations.[99] It would be beyond the scope of this paper to examine the practice in an in-depth manner.[100] In the consideration of reports treaty bodies can easily avoid the 'determination' of the validity of a reservation.

The competence of the treaty bodies to examine reservations was accepted by the ILC Special Rapporteur at an early stage of his work. In his second report, Pellet argued that the fact that human rights treaties establish monitoring bodies is one main aspect that distinguishes them from other treaties. These organs could not perform the functions vested in them if they could not determine the exact extent of their competence *vis-à-vis* states. They must have the possibility to assess their own competence, and therefore the exact extent of the commitments entered into by the state concerned.[101] While there has been discussion in the ILC as to whether treaty bodies without decision-making power could at all monitor the validity of reservations,[102] the Commission agreed in its preliminary conclusions on reservations, that 'where these treaties [i.e. human rights treaties] are silent on

[99] Nineteenth Meeting of Chairpersons of the Human Rights Treaty Bodies, Sixth Inter-Committee Meeting of the Human Rights Treaty Bodies, Report of the Meeting of the Working Group on Reservations, UN Doc. HRI/MC/2007/5, para. 9.

[100] An overview of recent practice is available in Nineteenth Meeting of Chairpersons of the Human Rights Treaty Bodies, Sixth Inter-Committee Meeting of the Human Rights Treaty Bodies, Report on Reservations, UN Doc. HRI/MC/2007/5/Add.1, Annex 2, The practice of the human rights treaty bodies with respect to reservations—concluding observations/comments (January–April 2007).

[101] ILC, Second Report on Reservations to Treaties by Alain Pellet, Special Rapporteur, UN Doc. A/CN.4/477/Add.1 (1996), paras. 202–210.

[102] ILC, Preliminary Conclusions of the International Law Commission on Reservations to Normative Multilateral Treaties Including Human Rights Treaties, in Report of the International Law Commission, GAOR A/52/10 (1997), para. 133 *et seq.*

the subject, the monitoring bodies established thereby are competent to comment upon and express recommendations with regard, *inter alia,* to the admissibility of reservations by States, in order to carry out the functions assigned to them.'[103] The ILC calls upon states to cooperate with the monitoring bodies and give due consideration to their recommendations.[104] In his tenth report, the Special Rapporteur stated that the time had come to 'revisit' some of the Preliminary Conclusions, without taking any decisive action that would lead to a change in their meaning. He proposes to formulate a guideline that begins with a general provision recalling that the various modalities of verification are mutually reinforcing, in particular where treaty monitoring bodies exist. The proposed draft guideline refers to treaty monitoring bodies as competent to rule on the validity of reservations. In a sub-guideline the Special Rapporteur added: 'Where a treaty establishes a body to monitor application of the treaty, that body shall be competent, for the purpose of discharging the functions entrusted to it, to assess the validity of reservations formulated by a State or an international organisation.'[105]

This text affirms the practice that the treaty bodies have developed over the years; it reflects that there is a plurality of bodies competent to assess the validity of reservations. The main difference as compared to the Special Rapporteur's previous position is that the powers are cumulative and not exclusive of each other.[106] The impact of the practice of human rights treaty bodies is thus clearly visible.

With respect to the plurality, it is noteworthy that the ILC proposes a larger role for the Secretary-General of the United Nations as depository for reservations to treaties, which is an administrative task that consists of receiving and circulating texts.[107] The International Law Commission has suggested that the depository should draw the attention of the reserving state to what constitutes, in his opinion, a manifest invalidity. If the state maintains the reservation, the depository shall communicate it to other states parties, indicating the nature of legal problems raised by the reservation.[108]

8.2 The competence to determine validity and the consequences thereof

The second part of this section deals with the most controversial aspect, which is the effect of the finding by a treaty body that a reservation is invalid. The matter is not resolved in the VCLT. States objecting to reservations generally add that

---

[103] Ibid., para. 157(5). Some ILC members continued to disagree with this position, see para. 150.

[104] Ibid., para. 157(9).

[105] ILC, Tenth Report of the Special Rapporteur, Addendum, UN Doc. A/CN.4/558/Add.2 (2005), paras. 166–171.

[106] Ibid., para. 172.

[107] In accordance with Article 77 of the Vienna Convention on the Law of Treaties.

[108] Tenth Report of the Special Rapporteur (2005), para. 159 *et seq.* with further references. This is reflected in Draft Guideline 2.1.8, provisionally adopted by the ILC, see Report of the International Law Commission, GAOR A/57/10 (2005), para. 437.

their objections do not constitute an obstacle to the entry into force of the treaty between the reserving and the objecting state. Sometimes states—especially Scandinavian states—go further by indicating that the treaty enters into force in its entirety and that the reserving state cannot benefit from the reservation.[109] The Human Rights Committee's general comment on reservations states:

> The normal consequence of an unacceptable reservation is not that the Covenant will not be in effect at all for a reserving party. Rather, such a reservation will generally be severable, in the sense that the Covenant will be operative for the reserving party without benefit of the reservation.[110]

At the time of the adoption of this general comment this position was not established practice among all treaty monitoring bodies. Opinions differed especially on the final sentence of the above quotation. For the first time, a general comment attracted objections from states parties. According to the United States of America, the Committee's position was 'completely at odds with established legal practice and principles' and a state that withholds its consent to be bound by a provision 'cannot be presumed, on the basis of some legal fiction, to be bound by it.'[111] In its statement on reservations, adopted in 1998, CEDAW assigned itself a more limited role than the HRCt. It stated that it had an important role to play, but did not go beyond this and considered that it would continue to encourage states parties to review their reservations and express its concern about impermissible reservations.[112]

Since then, the views on this aspect have changed, at least among the treaty monitoring bodies. The Working Group on Reservations established by the Meeting of Chairpersons of Human Rights Treaty Bodies stated that, for the purpose of discharging their functions, treaty bodies are competent to 'assess the validity of reservations and, in the event, the implications of a finding of invalidity of a reservation, particularly in the examination of individual communications or in exercising other fact-finding functions in the case of treaty bodies that have such competence.'[113] This is in line with the position taken by the European Court of Human Rights, which held in the *Belilos* judgment that 'the silence of

---

[109]　See for example the objections by Norway against the reservation by Qatar to the Convention Against Torture, UN Treaty Bible, <http://untreaty.un.org>, which reads in the final sentence: 'The Convention thus becomes operative between Norway and Qatar without Qatar benefiting from the said reservation.' On objections by states generally, see Kohona, (2005) 99 AJIL 433, 443–444; and on the Nordic practice Klabbers, (2000) 69 Nordic J Intl L 179.

[110]　HRCt, General Comment No. 24, para. 18.

[111]　Observations on General Comment No. 24 (52), on issues relating to reservations made upon ratification or accession to the Covenant or the Optional Protocols thereto, or in relation to Article 41 of the Covenant, United States of America. Reprinted in Report of the Human Rights Committee, GAOR A/50/40, Vol. I (1996) 126, 129–130. The United Kingdom and France also submitted observations.

[112]　Committee on the Elimination of Discrimination Against Women, Statements on Reservations to the Convention on the Elimination of All Forms of Discrimination against Women, in Report of the Committee on the Elimination of Discrimination against Women, GAOR, A/53/38/Rev.1 (1998), paras. 22–24.

[113]　Report of the Working Group on Reservations, UN Doc. HRI/MC/2007/5, para. 16–5.

the depositary and the Contracting States does not deprive the Convention institutions of the power to make their own assessment.'[114] The Court determined that the 'interpretative declaration' submitted by Switzerland was invalid, and that consequently Switzerland was bound by the Convention.[115]

The different status of the United Nations treaty monitoring bodies as compared to the regional human rights courts has resulted in debates on their competence. The reactions to the HRCt's conclusion on the consequences of finding Trinidad and Tobago's reservation incompatible with object and purpose, and subsequent conclusion that the Committee was not precluded from examining the communication, show that this is one of the most controversial issues in the debate on reservations to human rights treaties.[116] The HRCt's conclusion overstepped the line that many have drawn.

In support of the Human Rights Committee's position it can be argued that the act of ratification confirms the state's intention to be bound and to give effect to the rights and freedoms guaranteed in the treaty concerned. It would be inappropriate for a treaty body or other states parties to conclude that the reserving state would not be bound at all and invalidate the ratification.[117] Rather than render the consent to be bound ineffective, 'the severance approach nullifies the reservations but leaves the consent to be bound unaffected.'[118] Also, nullifying a ratification as a consequence of declaring a reservation invalid would constitute an undesirable effect from the perspective of protecting minimum human rights standards. Allowing states to join a human rights treaty with incompatible reservations would 'repudiate or downgrade its normative, or standard-setting, base.'[119] There are reasons to take into account that human rights treaties are a special category of treaties. Where the protection of the individual and not that of sovereign states is at issue, there are 'compelling policy reasons why "the thing may rather have effect than be destroyed".'[120]

The practice of other states parties is relevant information for the monitoring body in determining the validity of a reservation. This holds true for state

---

[114] *Belilos v. Switzerland* (App. No. 10328/83), ECtHR, Judgment of 29 April 1988, (1988) Series A No. 132, para. 47.

[115] Ibid., para. 60.

[116] See the dissenting opinions to the admissibility decision in *Kennedy v. Trinidad and Tobago*, GAOR A/55/40, Vol. II (2000), Annex XI, sect. A, and critically former Committee member, and one of the dissenters, E. Klein, 'A Comment on the Issue of Reservations to the Provisions of the Covenant Representing (peremptory) Rules of General International Law' in Ziemele, *Reservations to Human Rights Treaties and the Vienna Convention Regime* (2004), and a response from M. Scheinin, 'Reservations by States under the International Covenant on Civil and Political Rights', in the same volume, 48–51.

[117] See also Scheinin, 'Reservations by States under the International Covenant on Civil and Political Rights' (2004) 51.

[118] C. Redgwell, 'Reservations to Treaties and Human Rights Committee General Comment No. 24 (52)' (1997) 46 ICLQ 390, 407.

[119] R. Goodman, 'Human Rights Treaties, Invalid Reservations, and State Consent' (2002) 96 AJIL 531, 534.

[120] Schabas, (1994) 32 *Annuaire canadien de droit international* 39, 74.

practice in objecting to reservations, as well as their practice in accepting provisions unconditionally. In *Loizidou*, the European Court of Human Rights pointed out that Turkey 'must have been aware, in view of the consistent practice of Contracting Parties under Articles 25 and 46 . . . to accept unconditionally the competence of the Commission and Court, that the impugned restrictive clauses were of questionable validity under the Convention system and might be deemed impermissible by the Convention organs.' The Court also pointed to the objections that had been submitted to the Turkish declarations, which supported the observation concerning Turkey's awareness of the legal position. The Court saw a willingness on the part of Turkey 'to run the risk that the limitation clauses at issue would be declared invalid by the Convention institutions without affecting the validity of the declarations themselves.'[121]

The Working Group on Reservations of the Meeting of Chairpersons of Human Rights Treaty Bodies agrees that an invalid reservation is to be considered null and void. It has added that as a consequence, 'a State will not be able to rely on such a reservation and, unless its contrary intention is incontrovertibly established, will remain a party to the treaty without the benefit of the reservation.'[122] The position taken by the Human Rights Committee has thus now been endorsed by the Working Group, and subsequently by the Inter-Committee meeting,[123] which is an important development in international human rights law.

CEDAW has examined reports from a number of states parties with reservations that were considered incompatible with object and purpose. It has urged states parties to withdraw these reservations and to bring domestic legislation in line with the Convention. For example, after welcoming the withdrawal by the Syrian Arab Republic of a significant number of its reservations, it expressed its concern about the remaining reservations, that affected, *inter alia,* Articles 9 and 16 of the Convention and which are deemed by CEDAW to be incompatible with the object and purpose of the Convention.[124] In its concluding observations it addressed issues relating to these provisions and recommended that Syria 'modify or repeal, without delay and within a clear time frame, discriminatory legislation, including discriminatory provisions in its Personal Status Act, Penal Code and Nationality Act.'[125] CEDAW's practice shows that this Committee also takes the view that states parties cannot benefit from invalid reservations. In its work under the Optional Protocol to the Convention CEDAW has not yet been confronted with invalid reservations. This is likely to happen, since states parties

---

[121] *Loizidou v. Turkey (Preliminary Objections)* (App. No. 15318/89), Judgment of 23 March 1995, (1995) Series A No. 310, 20 EHRR 99, para. 95.

[122] Report of the Working Group on Reservations, UN Doc. HRI/MC/2007/5, para. 16(7).

[123] Report of the Chairpersons of the Human Rights Treaty Bodies on Their Nineteenth Meeting, UN Doc. A/62/224 (2007), Annex, Report of the Sixth Inter-Committee Meeting of Human Rights Treaty Bodies, para. 48 (v).

[124] CEDAW, Concluding Observations on the Syrian Arab Republic, UN Doc. CEDAW/C/SYR/CO/1 (2007), para. 12.

[125] Ibid., para. 18.

such as Libya and Bangladesh have ratified the Optional Protocol. CEDAW will then have to decide if it will adhere to the same position as the Human Rights Committee.[126]

According to one of the early reports of the Special Rapporteur of the ILC, only the reserving state can determine whether the invalid reservation constitutes an essential element of its consent to be bound. It then has two options: either to withdraw or amend the reservation, or to terminate its participation in the treaty. He argued that 'no organ can take the place of the reserving State in determining the latter's intentions regarding the scope of the treaty obligations it is prepared to assume.'[127] He maintained that the general rules apply also to human rights treaties. The question is not how states can be kept on board, but whether or not they have consented to be bound.[128] The object and purpose of human rights treaties do not transfer them into 'international "legislation" which would bind States against their will.'[129] The ILC Preliminary Conclusions (adopted in 1996) state that 'the legal force of the findings made by monitoring bodies in the exercise of their power to deal with reservations cannot exceed that resulting from the powers given to them for the performance of their general monitoring role.'[130]

The Special Rapporteur proposed to add to the guideline concerning the competence of treaty monitoring bodies that '[t]he findings made by such a body in the exercise of this competence shall have the same legal force as that deriving from the performance of its general monitoring role.'[131] This formulation seems to reflect the concern about the human rights treaty bodies' interpretation of their mandate.

This particular aspect has not yet been settled in the ILC. In his tenth report (2005) the Special Rapporteur stated, as a guideline, that a reservation formulated in spite of the prohibition arising from the provisions of the treaty or from its incompatibility with the object and purpose of the treaty is not valid. He further suggested that a reservation that does not fulfil the conditions of validity is 'null and void'.[132] However, due to the controversy on the issue among its members, the Commission has not been able to take a position on whether the nullity of the reservation invalidates the consent to be bound itself.[133] Some members consider severability to be 'an appropriate sanction for a manifestly impermissible reservation', while others considered it to be unacceptable as affecting the free will of states.[134]

---

[126] See further Schöpp-Schilling, 'Reservations to the Convention on the Elimination of all forms of Discrimination Against Women' (2004).

[127] Second report of the Special Rapporteur, UN Doc. A/CN.4/477/Add.1 (1996), para. 252, and discussion in paras. 234–251.

[128] Ibid., para. 226.   [129] Ibid., para. 229.

[130] ILC, Preliminary Conclusions of the International Law Commission on Reservations to Normative Multilateral Treaties Including Human Rights Treaties, in Report of the International Law Commission, GAOR A/52/10 (1997), para. 157(8).

[131] Tenth Report of the Special Rapporteur, UN Doc. A/CN.4/558/Add.1 (2005), para. 171.

[132] Ibid., para. 187, Draft Guideline 3.3 and 3.3.2.

[133] Ibid., para. 200.

[134] Report of the International Law Commission, GAOR A/52/10 (1997), para. 142.

In a meeting of the International Law Commission and human rights bodies, this particular aspect was addressed. The report of this meeting shows that differences of opinion continued to exist. One of the ILC members urged the treaty bodies to be cautious, since a restrictive attitude towards the reserving state could lead to 'political difficulties', such as withdrawal from the Optional Protocol to the ICCPR.[135]

The Special Rapporteur is a proponent of state action to further codify the mandate of the monitoring bodies, as is evidenced in another rule, where he states that states should insert clauses, or adopt protocols, specifying the nature and, where appropriate, the limits of the competence of such bodies to assess the validity of reservations.[136] The latter draft guideline is confusing and superfluous. If it is accepted that the treaty monitoring bodies have the authority to examine reservations, take a position thereon and formulate recommendations, it is not necessary to start the cumbersome process of negotiating new treaty provisions. Clearly, this draft guideline does not at all reflect the position of the treaty bodies, as they consider that these functions are within their mandate, without the need for a specific provision.

Developments in international human rights law have clearly influenced the discussion on this matter in the International Law Commission. The concern among various members is based on the Human Rights Committee's approach to impermissible reservations, which has now also been supported by the Inter-Committee Meeting. In the light of the current drafts formulated by the Special Rapporteur and the discussions in the ILC, it is unlikely that the ILC will endorse the position taken by the HRC and the Working Group on Reservations. To the ILC, the principle of state consent to be bound constitutes an obstacle to a progressive development to combat invalid reservations.

9. Assessing Impact

The reservations issue constitutes a concern for all treaty bodies and has been a subject of discussion in the Meeting of Chairpersons of the Human Rights Treaty Bodies, which resulted in the adoption of guidelines for future practice in the examination of reservations. The work of the Special Rapporteur and the International Law Commission on the issue of reservations is still a work in progress, especially on the question of the consequences of invalid reservations. The present Section will attempt to assess to what extent practice in international

---

[135] Alain Pellet, Meeting with Human Rights Bodies (15 and 16 May 2007), UN Doc. ILC(LIX)/RRT/CRP.1, para. 24.

[136] Tenth report of the Special Rapporteur, UN Doc. A/CN.4/558/Add.1 (2005) 31, Draft Guideline 3.2.2. This text is based on the Preliminary Conclusions of the ILC, GAOR A/52/10 (1997), para. 157(7).

human rights law-making and treaty interpretation has had an impact on general public international law.

International human rights law has evidently played a role in the drafting of the guidelines on reservations by the International Law Commission. The Special Rapporteur has made ample use of general comments and general recommendations, concluding observations and state practice in objecting (or not) to reservations.

9.1 General approach towards reservations

From the perspective of the promotion and protection of human rights, the aim of universal ratification is worth pursuing. This is meaningful only if the number of reservations is minimized and their impact limited. As stated by the Working Group on Reservations established by the Meeting of Chairpersons of the Human Rights Treaty Bodies, 'reservations that are not permitted, including those that are incompatible with the object and purpose of the treaty, do not contribute to attainment of the objective of universal ratification.'[137] The Working Group agreed on encouraging 'the complete withdrawal of reservations, the review of the need for them or the progressive narrowing of scope through partial withdrawals of reservations.'[138] Treaty bodies' practice is based on the point of departure that it is desirable to keep states on board, which they consider preferable over declaring them not to be bound, or seeking a declaration from them to that effect. Even if withdrawal is not achieved overnight, the effect of a dialogue can be that discussions at the national level are started, both within the government and civil society. At the international level, the strategy developed by the Working Group on Reservations and endorsed by the Meeting of Chairpersons of the Human Rights Treaty Bodies should be welcomed.[139] To enhance the credibility of their work, it is necessary that treaty bodies become more precise in their conclusions on reservations and rely on international law in the formulations of their motivations for concluding that reservations are not valid.

Political organs have reaffirmed this aim repeatedly since the World Conference on Human Rights. State practice shows a mixed picture. Since 1993 many ratifications have been accompanied by—to say the least—dubious reservations and the number of states that formulate objections to reservations remains limited. Yet, it is also clear that a substantial number of reservations have been withdrawn. Some instruments establishing new supervisory mechanisms prohibit reservations altogether, or discourage them by means of an opting-out clause.

The draft ILC guidelines do not reflect the overall aim of achieving universal ratification without reservations. Looking at the draft guidelines as a set, it is clear that the ILC is much more concerned about the interests of the state than

---

[137] Report of the Working Group on Reservations, UN Doc. HRI/MC/2007/5, para. 16–4.
[138] Ibid., para. 16–9, under c(iv).   [139] Ibid., para. 16–9.

the individual. It attaches superior value to the principle that states can be bound only to the extent that they consent to be bound, that may not be watered down by declaring their reservations invalid all too easily. Formulations of the draft guidelines show that the overall approach is to accept reservations, unless they are incompatible. This shows that there is no general discouragement of reservations, which is very different from the approach taken by the treaty bodies.

The idea that human rights treaty bodies aim to keep states 'on board' is not acceptable to the Special Rapporteur and the ILC. This is evident in particular in the discussions on the mandate of the treaty bodies, in which the ILC has not endorsed the position of the treaty bodies, and it is not likely that it will do so. In this area the trend in international human rights law thus has not influenced the position of the Special Rapporteur and the ILC.

9.2 Interpretation of the object and purpose rule

International human rights organs have addressed reservations that potentially undermine the enjoyment of human rights at the domestic level in various ways. Some organs, notably the Human Rights Committee and the Committee on the Elimination of Discrimination Against Women, have been critical of reservations that potentially undermine the general obligation to give effect to a treaty. Among the treaty bodies there are differences, which may be diminished in the future when the recommendations of the Working Group on Reservations are implemented. A harmonized approach could contribute to further withdrawals by states of invalid reservations.

Treaty bodies have used different formulations, some were more cautious than others, and on various occasions, explanations were even absent. Nevertheless, there are examples of general comments and concluding observations that state clearly that reservations which affect the general obligation to implement are not valid, no matter in which terms they have been formulated, be it because they explicitly reserve the implementation of CEDAW Article 2 , accord superior status to domestic law, or because they are vague and general. The latter criterion has been referred to the most frequently in the work of the treaty bodies. The reluctance, and often outright refusal, by states to ensure that international norms prevail over domestic norms does not get the attention it deserves, either from the treaty bodies, or from the Special Rapporteur and the ILC. So far, reservations stating that a treaty in its entirety is interpreted as not being contradictory to national law, have been categorized as being too general and too vague, instead of a cover not to accept any new obligation. However, even if such reservations were elaborated in detail, specifying which provisions of family law or criminal law would not be affected by the ratification, such reservations would be unacceptable.

The issue of vague and general reservations is particularly acute for human rights treaties. The deliberations of the ILC and the studies of the Special

Rapporteur clearly show that the general comments and concluding observations have played a role, as many examples are cited. Whereas the human rights treaty bodies consider that vague and general reservations are as such incompatible with the object and purpose of the treaty concerned, this has not been accepted by the ILC. It has stated that it is not possible to draw this conclusion, because of the lack of insight into the effect of the reservation. It is noteworthy here that the ILC's primary concern about vague and general reservations is that these cause problems for other contracting states in assessing the extent to which the reserving state is bound. The ILC does not address the consequences for the individuals who should enjoy the human rights guaranteed by the treaty, which is another illustration of the ILC's state-centred attitude.

The analysis in Section 6 showed that it is not easy to indicate precisely on which issues developments concerning norms that have acquired a special status in international human rights law have had an impact on general public international law, because there is not much practice concerning reservations to such norms. With respect to *jus cogens* norms, the Human Rights Committee and the ILC have taken a different approach, but reach the same conclusion. Also with respect to non-derogable norms, the terminology differs, but the end result is similar.

9.3 The competence of the monitoring bodies

The practice of the treaty bodies of discussing reservations, be it in terms of necessity or in terms of validity, is accepted by states parties. The treaty bodies' recommendations to states parties to withdraw their reservations is a useful strategy befitting the reporting procedure. States parties' ratification is an expression of their consent to be bound, which is confirmed by participating in the reporting procedure. This least far-reaching step has been accepted by the Special Rapporteur of the International Law Commission, and found a place in the draft guidelines that have been submitted to the ILC. On this issue, the analysis showed an impact of the work of the human rights treaty bodies; the draft guideline formulated by the Special Rapporteur reflects their practice, and he has even explicitly stated that he has revisited his position. It is clear that the reference to treaty monitoring bodies is mainly a reference to human rights organs. However, the suggestion to adopt additional provisions or protocols defining the competence of the treaty bodies with respect to reservations undermines the well-established practice of the treaty bodies, as that could be used to argue in the future that, under treaties which do not have such clauses, the treaty monitoring bodies would not have the mandate to consider reservations, which would constitute a major step back.

Differences of opinion are most evident when it comes to the consequences of finding a reservation invalid. Clearly, the work of the treaty bodies has influenced the debates, as that has focused on the position taken by the Human

Rights Committee, which has now largely been supported by the Meeting of Chairpersons. The human rights treaty bodies have taken the position that states that have formulated invalid reservations should not benefit from the reservations, but that this does not affect their consent to be bound, unless contrary intention is incontrovertibly established. The Special Rapporteur has not yet formulated a draft guideline, as he considered that the time was not yet right to do so. It thus has had 'an impact', but it is unlikely that the ILC will endorse the position of the human rights treaty bodies. This aspect also demonstrates the state-oriented approach of the ILC and the Special Rapporteur.

10. Final Remarks

The ILC has singled out the question of reservations to treaties, and has focused on developments in that area exclusively. However, it is useful to look at the issue of reservations not in isolation, but to take into account the entire range of developments in the work of the human rights treaty bodies. The monitoring functions of the treaty bodies have advanced significantly over the years and today they play a role in international human rights law that was unimaginable at the time of the conclusion of the drafting of the instruments. The mandate of the treaty bodies has developed gradually, and the monitoring procedures have evolved into a regime that plays a crucial role in the promotion and protection of human rights. Interpretations by treaty bodies of rights and obligations were not foreseen, often simply because the problems they were confronted with were not the subject of discussion at the time of drafting the treaties. These developments have not been taken into account by the ILC. It would be useful for the Commission to do so, as they have affected the status of the treaty monitoring in international human rights law. Of course, they are not judicial bodies, but their comments and recommendations—especially where the seven treaty bodies take joint positions— cannot easily be set aside.

The determination of the validity of a reservation and implementing the consequences of such a finding falls equally within the sphere of the competence of the treaty bodies, as developed over the years. In developing their roles, the monitoring bodies have filled the gap that emerged as a result of the inadequate functioning of the VCLT regime. Consultation and coordination among treaty bodies, through the meeting of chairpersons of human rights treaty bodies, has ensured that there is conformity to a large extent in the working methods of the treaty bodies, thus strengthening the steps that have been taken. The treaties leave ample room for the development of the tasks of the treaty bodies. Determining the validity of reservations and attaching consequences to this finding is perfectly in line with other developments in the monitoring machinery.

The reservations issue is a question that all treaty bodies have in common. Their cooperation and the harmonization of their practice is in itself a step forward, and crucial in the further development of practice relating to reservations to human rights treaties. While states continue to play a role in monitoring the validity of reservations, the role of the human rights treaty monitoring bodies has expanded significantly. The acknowledgement of their mandate is based on their expertise and their unique role under the treaties. Concluding observations are not always sufficiently precise in pointing out the problem concerning a reservation. In their work, the treaty bodies can be more specific, and in their recommendations they can provide guidance on the ways in which domestic laws need to be changed. It would be useful if they would continue to discuss their practice, and adopt common positions on similar reservations. In due time, a joint general comment on reservations to human rights treaties would be valuable. In such a document, the treaty bodies could elaborate on the specificities of human rights treaties and the consequences thereof for the human rights regime. Such a general comment should take the individual's position as a starting point, instead of the interests of the state.

5

Impact on State Succession in
Respect of Treaties

*Menno T. Kamminga**

1. Introduction

In accordance with the consent-based nature of traditional international law a new state is free to become or not to become a party to treaties that were binding on the predecessor state. It is true that the 1978 Vienna Convention on Succession of States in Respect of Treaties provides for the continuity of obligations in respect of all treaties that were binding on the predecessor state.[1] However, the Convention's approach in this respect has attracted little support from states and does not appear to reflect customary international law. The Convention entered into force only in 1996 and so far only 21 states have become parties to it (although, interestingly, this group includes many of the recent successor states).[2] Contrary to the approach taken in the Vienna Convention, most states favour a 'clean slate' approach in respect of treaty succession.[3]

* Professor of International Law, Maastricht University. Director, Maastricht Centre for Human Rights. This is an updated and modified version of a paper that appeared in *The Status of International Treaties on Human Rights*, Venice Commission, Collection Science and Technique of Democracy, No. 42, Strasbourg: Council of Europe Publishing, 2006, 31–41.

[1] Arts. 31–35, Vienna Convention on Succession of States in Respect of Treaties, adopted 22 August 1978, entered into force 6 November 1996, 1946 UNTS 3, reproduced at 17 ILM (1978) 1488.

[2] Current parties (as of June 2008) to the Vienna Convention on Succession of States in Respect of Treaties are: Bosnia and Herzegovina, Croatia, Cyprus, Czech Republic, Dominica, Ecuador, Egypt, Estonia, Ethiopia, Iraq, Liberia, Montenegro, Morocco, Saint Vincent and the Grenadines, Serbia, Seychelles, Slovakia, Slovenia, the Former Yugoslav Republic of Macedonia, Tunisia and Ukraine.

[3] For example, on Austria, see H. Tichy, 'Two Recent Cases of State Succession—An Austrian Perspective' (1992) 4 *Austrian Journal of Public and International Law* (1992) 117, 123–124; on the Netherlands, see A. Bos, 'Statenopvolging in het bijzonder met betrekking tot verdragen' (1995) 111 *Mededelingen van de Nederlandse Vereniging voor Internationaal Recht* 55; on the United States, see *Restatement (Third) of the Foreign Relations Law of the United States* (1987), para. 210(3), Reporters' Note 4. In the same vein, I.Brownlie, *Principles of Public International Law*, 5th ed. (Oxford University Press, Oxford 1998) 663; A. Cassese, *International Law*, 2nd ed. (Oxford

There is one generally accepted exception to the clean slate doctrine. This applies in respect of treaties establishing boundaries and other territorial regimes. According to Articles 11 and 12 of the Vienna Convention on Succession of States in Respect of Treaties, such treaties are not affected by a succession of states. Unlike the principle on the continuity of obligations under treaties generally, the principle of the continuity of treaties on territorial regimes has attracted widespread support. In the *Gabčíkovo-Nagimaros* case the International Court of Justice identified it as a rule of customary international law.[4]

The question that arises is whether human rights treaties represent a second exception to the clean slate doctrine. International practice during the past two decades provides considerable evidence to test this hypothesis. During the 1990s the Union of Soviet Socialist Republics (USSR), the Socialist Federal Republic of Yugoslavia (FRY) and the Czech and Slovak Federal Republic (CSFR) disintegrated into in a large number of separate states. Among the many legal questions raised by this disintegration process was its effect on adherence to human rights treaties. The USSR, FRY and CSFR had all been parties to the main UN human rights treaties. Were the successor states emerging from these three states automatically bound by these treaties? Or were they free to adhere or not to adhere to them?

Based on a review of the practice of states, international organizations, and human rights treaty bodies during the first half of the 1990s it will be shown in this paper that the inhabitants of a territory cannot be deprived of the rights previously granted to them under a human rights treaty as a result of the fact that another state has assumed responsibility for the territory. This continuity of obligations under human rights treaties occurs automatically, *ipso jure*, and therefore does not require formal notification by the successor state. However, in practice confirmations by the successor state that it considers itself bound by the human rights treaties to which its predecessor was a party tend to be welcomed by the depositories and the supervisory bodies of human rights treaties because they help to clarify any ambiguities that may exist.

Since 1993, the question of the continuity or otherwise of obligations arising out of human rights treaties has been addressed by a wide range of international authorities, including the UN Commission on Human Rights, the UN human rights treaty bodies and the International Court of Justice.

(1) In 1993, 1994 and 1995, the UN Commission on Human Rights adopted three successive resolutions, introduced by the Russian Federation and adopted without a vote, entitled 'Succession of States in respect of international human rights treaties'.[5] In those resolutions the Commission referred to the 'special

---

University Press, Oxford 2005) 78; M.N. Shaw, *International Law,* 5th ed. (Cambridge University Press, Cambridge 2003) 875.

[4] *Gabčíkovo-Nagymaros Project* (*Hungary v. Slovakia*), Judgment of 25 September 1997, 1997 ICJ Reports 7, para. 123.

[5] Resolutions 1993/23, 1994/16 and 1955/18.

nature' of human rights treaties and their 'continuing applicability' to successor states. The resolutions called on successor states that had not yet done so 'to confirm to appropriate depositories that they continue to be bound by obligations under international human rights treaties'.

(2) The supervisory bodies of UN human rights treaties have adopted a series of general statements in support of automatic state succession in respect of the treaties within their purview. Most importantly, in 1994 the 5th meeting of chairpersons of human rights treaty bodies declared that:

successor States were automatically bound by obligations under international human rights instruments from the respective date of independence and that observance of the obligations should not depend on a declaration of confirmation made by the Government of the successor State.[6]

In the same vein, the Human Rights Committee, the supervisory body of the International Covenant on Civil and Political Rights observed in its General Comment on continuity of obligations:

once the people are accorded the protection of the rights under the Covenant, such protection devolves with territory and continues to belong them, notwithstanding change in government of the State party, including dismemberment in more than one State or State succession . . . The Committee is therefore firmly of the view that international law does not permit a State which has ratified or acceded to the Covenant to denounce it or withdraw from it.[7]

(3) In the literature, the doctrine of automatic succession in respect of human rights treaties has generally been cautiously supported.[8] However, while it is generally agreed that the doctrine is desirable, questions have been raised whether there is sufficient evidence of state practice and *opinio juris* to make it into a rule of customary international law.

The strongest and most articulate scepticism has been voiced in an article by Akbar Rasulov.[9] He argued that '[t]he *opinio juris* currently held by the successor states strongly disfavours any automaticity of succession'. He also pointed

---

[6] UN Doc. E/CN.4/1995/80 at 4.

[7] HRCt, General Comment No. 26: Continuity of obligations, 8 September 1997.

[8] M.N. Shaw, 'State Succession Revisited' (1994) 5 Finnish Ybk Intl L 34, 84 (one is on the verge of widespread international acceptance of the principle that human rights treaties continue to apply within the territory of a predecessor State irrespective of a succession). P. Pazartzis, 'State Succession to Multilateral Treaties: Recent Developments' (1998) 3 *Austrian Review of International & European Law* 397, 414 (principle of obligatory succession to human rights treaties seems to be developing). B. Stern, 'Les questions de succession d'Etats dans l'affaire à l'Application de la Convention pour la prevention et la repression du crime de genocide devant la Cour internationale de Justice', in N. Ando et al. (eds.), *Liber Amicorum Shigeru Oda* (2002) 285, 297 ('Il s'agit d'une règle en devenir, qui est encore controversée'). F. Ruiz Ruiz, 'The Succession of States in Universal Treaties on the Protection of Human Rights and Humanitarian Law' (2003) 7 *International Journal of Human Rights* 42, 69 (presumption in favour of continuity of human rights treaties).

[9] A. Rasulov, 'Revisiting Succession to Humanitarian Treaties: Is There a Case for Automaticity?' (2003) 14 EJIL 141–170.

out that existing international practice is limited to East European and Central European states and that no general conclusions should therefore be drawn from it about the existence of a rule of customary international law. Finally, according to Rasulov the human rights treaty bodies have not been consistent in their attitude towards state succession. More specifically, he maintained that the doctrine of automatic succession in respect of human rights treaties is ultimately unpersuasive because:

(a) Human rights treaty bodies insist on confirmations by successor states thereby creating the impression that without such confirmations treaty obligations would not continue;
(b) Human rights treaty bodies accept that successor states often accede rather than succeed to human rights treaties thereby creating the impression that their guiding principle is not continuity of obligations but freedom of choice.

More recently, the Final Report of the International Law Association's Committee on the Law of State Succession also concluded that automatic state succession in respect of human rights treaties is not a rule of customary international law.[10]

Without attempting an exhaustive survey I will concentrate in this contribution on practice under the European Convention on Human Rights and the International Covenant on Civil and Political Rights because the most thorough consideration of the underlying issues has occurred within the context of these two treaties.

2. Practice under the European Convention on Human Rights

Even sceptics agree that practice under the European Convention on Human Rights with regard to the former Czechoslovakia provides ample support for the doctrine of automatic state succession in respect of human rights treaties.[11]

On 1 January 1993, the Czech and Slovak Federal Republic dissolved into two independent states: the Czech Republic and the Slovak Republic. The CSFR had been a party to the European Convention on Human Rights since 18 March 1992. According to Article 66 of the Convention, only members of the Council of Europe could become parties to the Convention. On 30 June 1993, the Council of Europe's Committee of Ministers therefore admitted the two new states as members. At the same time the Committee decided that, in accordance with their express wishes, the two states were to be regarded as succeeding to

---

[10] Final Report of the Committee on the Law of State Succession, forthcoming in *Report of the 73rd Conference of the International Law Association* (Rio de Janeiro 2008).

[11] Rasulov, supra n. 9, at 165–167.

the Convention retroactively, with effect from 1 January 1993, i.e. from their date of independence.[12] The unorthodox procedure followed in this case apparently reflected the strong desire on the part of both the existing members of the Council of Europe and its two new members to ensure seamless continuity of obligations under the Convention.[13]

Subsequent official records confirm this interpretation. The chart of signatures and ratifications of the Council of Europe's Treaty Office lists the Czech Republic and Slovakia as having been parties to the Convention since 1 January 1993. A footnote mentions that the dates of signature and ratification listed are by the former Czech and Slovak Federal Republic. There is no reference to any notifications by the Czech Republic or Slovakia. In other words, the continuity of obligations in this case has indeed occurred *ipso jure*, without action on the part of the two successor states.

Consistent with the attitude adopted by the Committee of Ministers, the European Court of Human Rights has on numerous occasions considered individual petitions against the Czech Republic and against Slovakia for violations that occurred since 18 March 1992, i.e. the date on which ratification of the Convention and recognition of the right of individual petition by the former Czech and Slovak Federal Republic took effect.[14] The standard formula employed in judgments of the Court describing the facts of such cases is: 'The period to be taken into consideration began on 18 March 1992, when the recognition by the former Czech and Slovak Federal Republic, to which Slovakia [the Czech Republic] is one of the successor States, of the right of individual petition took effect.' This 'purist' approach to state succession allowing for accountability of conduct by the predecessor state apparently has not prompted any objections by the Czech Republic or Slovakia.

It is true that practice with regard to state succession under the European Convention on Human Rights has been limited to the case of the former Czech and Slovak Federal Republic. But in view of the firm precedents that have now been set by the Committee of Ministers and the European Court of Human Rights it seems highly unlikely that on future occasions a different course of action would be followed by these two institutions.

---

[12] Council of Europe Doc. H/INF(94) 1.

[13] See, J.F. Flauss, 'Convention européenne des droits de l'homme et succession d'Etats aux traités: une curiosité, la décision du Comité des Ministres du Conseil de l'Europe en date du 30 juin 1993 concernant la République tchèque et la Slovaquie' 6 RUDH (1994) 1–5.

[14] See, for example, *Matter v. Slovakia* (App. No. 31534/96), ECtHR, Judgment of 5 July 1992, para. 52; *Nemec and others v. Slovakia* (App. No. 48672/99), ECtHR, Judgment of 15 November 2001, para. 30; *Gajdúšek v. Slovakia* (App. No. 40058/98), ECtHR, Judgment of 18 December 2001, para. 51; *Chovančík v. Slovakia* (App. No. 54996/00), ECtHR, Judgment of 17 June 2001, para. 18; *Beňačková v. Slovakia* (App. No. 53376/99), ECtHR, Judgment of 17 June 2003, para. 20; *Konečný v. Czech Republic* (App. Nos. 47269/99, 64656/01 and 65002/01), ECtHR, Judgment of 26 October 2004, para. 4; and *Škodáková v. Czech Republic* (App. No. 71551/01), ECtHR, Judgment of 21 December 2004, para. 30.

3. Practice under the International Covenant
on Civil and Political Rights

Of the various human rights treaty bodies the Human Rights Committee, the supervisory body of the International Covenant on Civil and Political Rights, has devoted most attention to the questions of principle raised by a succession of states. By the beginning of 1993, most states belonging to the former Soviet Union and Yugoslavia had either succeeded or acceded to the Covenant. At its session in March/April 1993 the Committee addressed the states that had not yet taken such action by declaring that:

all the people within the territory of a former State party to the Covenant remained entitled to the guarantees of the Covenant, and that, in particular, Armenia, Georgia, Kazakhstan, Kyrgyzstan, Tajikistan, the former Yugoslav Republic of Macedonia, Turkmenistan and Uzbekistan were bound by the obligations of the Covenant as from the dates of their independence.[15]

The Committee added that reports under Article 40 of the Covenant accordingly became due one year after these dates and it requested that such reports be submitted to it.[16] The Committee had earlier adopted a similar decision with regard to Bosnia-Herzegovina, Croatia, and the Federal Republic of Yugoslavia.[17] The Committee therefore regarded the states in question as having succeeded automatically and treated them as such by insisting that they submit implementation reports.

The Committee's approach has been remarkably successful. By the end of the 1990s all the above-mentioned states had either formally succeeded or acceded to the Covenant with the exception of Kazakhstan (see below).

While the Committee has reluctantly accepted that a successor state may opt to *accede* rather than *succeed* to the Covenant, it insists that accession takes effect retroactively to the date when the state became independent.[18] This means that it regards Armenia (acceded in 1993), Azerbaijan (acceded in 1992), Georgia (acceded in 1994), Kyrgyzstan (acceded in 1994), Tajikistan (acceded in 1999), Turkmenistan (acceded in 1997) and Uzbekistan (acceded in 1995) not as parties from the customary three months after the receipt of the instrument of accession but as having been parties since 1991 when each of them became independent.

Although these states therefore acceded to the Covenant up to eight years after their independence the Committee's attitude that these notifications take effect retroactively to their date of independence has not been challenged.[19] However, the Committee has accepted that reports submitted by these successor states

---

[15] UN Doc. A/49/40, para. 49.   [16] Ibid.
[17] Ibid., para. 48.   [18] Ibid., note b.
[19] R. Hanski and M. Scheinin, 'The Work of the Human Rights Committee under the International Covenant on Civil and Political Rights and its Optional Protocol' in R. Hanski and

be labelled 'initial' reports. In other words, it has not insisted for example that reports by successor states of the Soviet Union be labelled 'fourth' reports because the USSR had submitted its 'third' report before breaking up in 1991. On the other hand, the Committee has insisted that reports by the successor states cover events since their independence and it has made a point of mentioning this in its concluding observations.[20] In the case of Azerbaijan, the Committee specifically recorded its appreciation that that country's delegation when addressing questions by members of the Committee 'did not deny accountability for events that occurred in the country after the date of independence but before the date of accession'.[21] The records reveal no objections to this attitude and the states in question therefore appear to have acquiesced in it. Some states have submitted reports that specifically covered the period since independence rather than merely the period since their accession.[22]

The last former republic of the USSR to clarify its position was Kazakhstan. Kazakhstan became independent on 16 December 1991 but it only proceeded to sign the Covenant on 2 December 2003 and to ratify it on 24 January 2006. This would appear to suggest that Kazakhstan did not consider itself in any way bound by the Covenant. However, this did not daunt the Committee. Until its date of ratification the Committee continued to treat Kazakhstan as having remained a party to the Covenant by way of succession and it listed the country as such in its annual reports. It also continued to invite Kazakhstan to present its (initial) report. In a footnote in its annual reports the Committee pointed out:

Although a declaration of succession has not been received, the people within the territory of the State—which constituted part of a former State party to the Covenant—continue to be entitled to the guarantees enunciated in the Covenant in accordance with the Committee's established jurisprudence.[23]

In contrast, in the UN document entitled 'Multilateral Treaties Deposited with the Secretary-General', prepared by the Treaty Section of the UN Office of Legal Affairs, Kazakhstan was not listed as a party to the Covenant. The documents therefore reflect a fundamental difference of approach between the UN Office of Legal Affairs, which carries out depositary functions on behalf of the Secretary-General, and the Human Rights Committee, the body elected by the parties to supervise the implementation of the Covenant. While the Office of Legal Affairs has followed a passive approach consisting of recording the intentions of states,

---

M. Scheinin, *Leading Cases of the Human Rights Committee* (Institute for Human Rights, Turku/Åbo 2003) 8.

[20] See, for example, Concluding observations on the initial report of Armenia, UN Doc. CCPR/C/79/Add.100, Concluding observations on the initial report of Kyrgyzstan, UN Doc. CCPR/CO/69/KGZ, and Concluding observations on the initial report of Uzbekistan, UN Doc. CCPR/CO/71/UZB.

[21] Concluding observations on the initial report of Azerbaijan, UN Doc. CCPR/C/79/Add.38.

[22] Initial report by Uzbekistan, UN Doc. CCPR/C/UZB/99/1.

[23] E.g. UN Doc. A/59/40 (vol. I) Annex I, note d.

the Human Rights Committee has relied on a principled philosophy that is independent from the conduct of states.

Significantly, when Kazakhstan finally ratified it did so without any reservations. In fact, none of the successor states that have acceded to the Covenant has entered any reservations. Arguably, this reflects the *opinio juris* that in view of the continuity of obligations which pertains, a successor state is not entitled to enter reservations that had not been made by the predecessor state.

In spite of its innovative actions, the Human Rights Committee's attitude has been less radical than that of the European Court of Human Rights. Unlike the European Court, the Committee has not always insisted on holding successor states explicitly accountable for unlawful conduct by the predecessor state. However, this may be partly due to the fact that the nature of the reporting procedure generally does not force treaty bodies to make specific determinations on a state party's obligations *ratione temporis*.

4. The Attitude of the International Court of Justice

The International Court of Justice has so far avoided taking a position one way or the other although it was offered the opportunity to do so in the *Bosnian Genocide* case. In response to an argument of automatic succession in respect of human rights treaties made by Bosnia-Herzegovina[24] the Court observed:

Without prejudice as to whether or not the principle of 'automatic succession' applies in the case of certain types of international treaties or conventions, the Court does not consider it necessary, in order to decide on its jurisdiction in this case, to make a determination on the legal issue concerning State succession.[25]

In their separate opinions to this judgment only one individual judge expressed clear views on the issue of automatic succession in respect of human rights treaties. Judge Weeramantry argued that there was indeed a principle of automatic succession in regard to the Genocide Convention. Judge Higgins has expressed sympathy for the idea in an academic article.[26]

Based on the references in the judgment to the humanitarian nature of the Genocide Convention at least one author has suggested that the Court 'appeared to endorse, tacitly, at least, the conclusion drawn by Bosnia-Herzegovina as to automatic succession'.[27] In my opinion, it would be inappropriate to draw such

[24] *Application of the Convention on the Prevention and Punishment of the Crime of Genocide* (Preliminary Objections) *(Bosnia-Herzegovina v. Yugoslavia)*, Judgment of 11 July 1996, 1996 ICJ Reports 595, para. 21.
[25] Ibid., para. 23.
[26] R. Higgins, 'The International Court of Justice and Human Rights', in K. Wellens (ed.), *International Law: Theory and Practice. Essays in Honour of Eric Suy* (Nijhoff, The Hague 1998), 691, 696–697.
[27] M.C.R. Craven, 'The Genocide Case, the Law of Treaties and State Succession' (1997) 68 BYIL 127, 152.

an inference. It should however be pointed out that in its more recent advisory opinion on *The Wall* the Court demonstrated a tendency to closely follow the practice of the treaty bodies when interpreting human rights treaties.[28] One might therefore speculate that, if obliged to make up its mind, the Court would follow the treaty bodies' line in favour of automatic succession but this is no more than speculation.

5. Concluding Observations

Human rights treaty bodies have taken the view that the protection accorded by human rights treaties devolves with territory and is not affected by state succession. Successor states therefore remain bound by human rights treaties from their date of independence and this is not dependent on any confirmation made by them.

This regime represents a significant exception to the general rule of non-continuity of treaty obligations. In effect, it puts human rights treaties in the same league as treaties establishing boundaries and other territorial regimes.

Although only two human rights treaties have been surveyed in any detail in this paper the approach taken by the supervisory bodies is broadly consistent as evidenced by the 1994 joint statement by the chairpersons of UN treaty bodies.[29] While the actual practice of the supervisory bodies has not been entirely uniform, inconsistencies relate to matters of detail and not to matters of principle.

Practice under the European Convention on Human Rights has been the most principled and far reaching. Within six months of the collapse of the Czech and Slovak Federal Republic the Council of Europe's Committee of Ministers reacted by deciding that the Czech Republic and the Slovak Republic were to be regarded as having succeeded to the Convention retroactively from their date of independence. The European Court of Human Rights followed suit by holding the two new states accountable for any breaches committed by the predecessor state.

The UN human rights treaty bodies have generally been more restrained in their attitude to state succession. They have accepted that successor states accede rather than succeed to their treaties and that there may be significant delays in this process; they have accepted that successor states submit implementation reports that are labelled 'initial' even if the predecessor state had already submitted one or more reports in the past; and they have not held successor states accountable for breaches by the predecessor state. In other words, while they have firmly insisted on continuity of substantive obligations they have adopted a pragmatic approach towards achieving this result and they have not insisted on full continuity of accountability.

---

[28] *Legal Consequences of the Construction of a Wall in the Occupied Palestinian Territory*, Advisory Opinion of 9 July 2004, 2004 ICJ Reports 136, paras. 109–112 and 136.

[29] Supra n. 6.

It may be argued that notifications by the successor state have a constitutive rather than confirmative character and therefore are incompatible with the *automatic* nature of treaty succession in respect of human rights treaties. The repeated calls upon successor states to 'confirm' their obligations under human rights treaties by political bodies such as the UN Commission on Human Rights and expert bodies such as the UN treaty bodies would support such an interpretation.

But in my view calls on states to 'confirm' their obligations do not serve such a constitutive function. For example, in 1977 the UN General Assembly called on member states to reinforce their support for the Declaration against Torture by making unilateral declarations by which they would agree to comply with the Declaration.[30] Thirty-three states made such declarations. It has never been suggested that by calling on states to make such declarations the General Assembly was in fact undermining the prohibition of torture under customary international law. On the contrary, human rights lawyers widely regarded the declarations that were made as reinforcing the prohibition.[31]

Significantly, the three resolutions on state succession in respect of human rights treaties adopted by the UN Commission on Human Rights in which states were called upon to 'confirm' that they continue to be bound, also refer to the 'special nature' of human rights treaties and their 'continuing applicability' to successor states. Any constitutive nature of such confirmations would be difficult to reconcile with such language.

While the Human Rights Committee has reluctantly accepted that a successor state may opt to *accede* rather than *succeed* to the International Covenant on Civil and Political Rights, it insists that accession takes effect retroactively to the date when the successor state became independent.

The exceptional case of Kazakhstan, rather than serving to undermine the doctrine of automatic succession, has enabled the Human Rights Committee to demonstrate the ultimate consequence of the doctrine by treating Kazakhstan as a state party retroactively to its date of independence.

It is true that international practice relating to succession of states in respect of human rights treaties has been limited to the 20-odd Central and East European states that gained their independence as a result of the collapse of the USSR, the FRY and the CSFR in the 1990s. Practice relating to Hong Kong and Macau, while fully consistent with the doctrine of automatic succession to human rights treaties, does not have the same evidentiary value because continuity of obligations in respect of these territories is based on bilateral agreements between China and the United Kingdom and China and Portugal, respectively. In view of the widespread support from states and the lack of opposition from successor states it would however be unduly restrictive to assume European regional custom only.

---

[30] UN General Assembly Res. 32/64, 8 December 1977.
[31] See N.S. Rodley, *The Treatment of Prisoners under International Law*, 2nd ed. (Clarendon Press, Oxford) 42–43, 61–62.

It is also true that the doctrine of the continuity of obligations under human rights treaties is driven primarily by the human rights treaty bodies, in particular the Human Rights Committee. Similarly, the continuity of treaties in the field of international humanitarian law is driven by the International Committee of the Red Cross and the continuity of treaties in the field of international labour law is driven primarily by the International Labour Office. It is uncertain whether successor states would have embraced the doctrine if they had been left to make up their own minds. But it is legally significant that the practice of the treaty bodies has not been objected to by states. This contrasts, for example, with the treaty bodies' practice relating to reservations, which has been strongly objected to by some states.[32]

The doctrine is evidence of the special status of human rights treaties in international law. It demonstrates that obligations under human rights treaties not only enjoy a superior ranking in comparison to other international standards but that they are also permanent and inalienable. In other words, while states may come and go obligations under human rights treaties remain as they are. Charles de Gaulle's celebrated words '*Les traités, voyez vous, sont comme les jeunes filles et comme les roses, ça dure ce que ça dure*' apparently are not applicable to human rights treaties.

However, the doctrine of automatic succession in respect of human rights treaties has not been endorsed—or rejected for that matter—by the International Court of Justice or the International Law Commission. In the *Bosnian Genocide* case, the Court passed up an opportunity to take a position on the doctrine. The Vienna Convention on Succession of States in Respect of Treaties still provides for automaticity for treaties on territorial regimes but not for human rights treaties. There are no current initiatives to amend the Convention in order to change this situation. It must therefore be concluded that the doctrine of automatic succession in respect of human rights treaties has so far remained *lex specialis*. There is no strong evidence that it has become part of general international law.

---

[32] Compare the objections to Human Rights Committee General Comment No. 24 by the United States, and the United Kingdom (1995 Annual Report of the Human Rights Committee, UN Doc. A/50/40 vol. I, 126–134) and France (1996 Annual Report of the Human Rights Committee, UN Doc. A/51/40 vol. I, 104–106).

6

Impact on the Process of the Formation of Customary International Law

Jan Wouters* and Cedric Ryngaert**

1. Introduction

It is often argued, especially by human rights-oriented lawyers, that the method of customary law formation in the field of human rights and international humanitarian law is structurally different from the traditional method of customary law formation in public international law.[1] Whereas the latter requires both consistent state practice and *opinio juris* (i.e. the sense of legal obligation), the former would allow *opinio juris* to play a more important role than state practice, which is often defective as far as human rights and humanitarian law are concerned. If state practice is played down, human rights and humanitarian rules may obviously more easily be identified as customary norms. This then widens the protective net cast by relevant treaty law, a process that was not expected in the early years of international human rights protection.[2]

* Professor of International Law and International Organisations, Director, Leuven Centre for Global Governance Studies and Institute for International Law, Leuven University; *Of Counsel,* Linklaters, Brussels.

** Lecturer in Public International Law, Utrecht University and Leuven University; member of the Dutch Research School for Human Rights and of the Leuven Centre for Global Governance Studies and Institute for International Law, Leuven University.

[1] E.g. J.F. Flauss, 'La protection des droits de l'homme et les sources du droit international', in Société française pour le droit international, *La protection des droits de l'homme et l'évolution du droit international*, actes colloque SFDI de Strasbourg (Pedone, Paris 1998) 65; T. Meron, *The Humanization of International Law* (Martinus Nijhoff, Leiden/Boston 2006) 370; special issues 1 and 2 of the *Georgia Journal of International and Comparative Law* (1995–1996) 1–426; for negations and critiques of this structural difference, however, see J.L. Goldsmith and E.A. Posner, *The Limits of International Law* (Oxford University Press, Oxford 2005) 132–133 (arguing, from an international relations perspective, that '[m]odern [human rights] customary international law does not constrain States any more or less than traditional customary international law did'); M. Byers, *Custom, Power and the Power of Rules* (Cambridge University Press, Cambridge 1999) 165 (below n. 74).

[2] R.B. Lillich, 'The Growing Importance of Customary International Human Rights Law' (1995–1996) 25 Ga J Intl Comp L 1.

This contribution looks at the 'human rights method' of ascertaining customary international law, with its emphasis on *opinio juris* over state practice, with a
favourable eye. It will point out that, while it is primarily a doctrinal construct, it
actually draws support from the International Court of Justice's 1986 *Nicaragua*
judgment. Before wading into conceptual waters, in a second Section, drawing
in particular on a study by the International Committee of the Red Cross, it will
show how this method works in practice in the field of international humanitarian law. In the third and most important Section, an attempt will be made at con-
ceptualising the specific character of human rights and humanitarian customary
law formation as opposed to classical positivist customary law formation. This
Section will present 'modern positivism'—an approach that combines customary
law with broadly drawn general principles of law—as an attractive method that
furthers humanitarian and ethical interests while remaining within the confines
of positivist international law. In a fourth and final Section, our focus will turn
to the applicability of modern positivism beyond the strict human rights and
humanitarian law fields. It will be argued that the more important the common
interests of states or humanity are, the greater the weight that may be attached to
opinio juris as opposed to state practice. If the stakes are high, inconsistent state
practice may be glossed over, and a high premium may be put on states' statements and declarations, *inter alia* in multilateral fora, in identifying customary
law combined with general principles of law.

2. The *Nicaragua* Method of Ascertaining Customary International Law

It is widely believed that the 'human rights' method of ascertaining customary
international law finds its roots in progressive US doctrine dissatisfied with the
US Government dragging its feet as to ratifying universal human rights treaties.[3]

---

[3] Notably Sections 701 and 702 of the *Restatement (Third) of U.S. Foreign Relations Law* (1987)
on the 'Customary Law of Human Rights'. Note 2 to Section 701 observes that 'the practice of
states that is accepted as building customary international law of human rights includes some forms
of conduct different from those that build customary law generally'. Customary international law
may enable municipal courts to give effect to the substantive protections of human rights treaties
to which the state is not a party, especially in states, such as the US, where customary international
law is the 'law of the land'; *The Paquete Habana*, 175 US 677, 20 S Ct 290. In the US municipal
system, customary human rights law takes on a specific significance in the context of private litigation based on the Alien Tort Claims Act (28 USC Section 1350) by virtue of which '[t]he district
courts shall have original jurisdiction of any civil action by an alien for a tort only, committed in
violation of *the law of nations* or a treaty of the United States' (emphasis added). The *law of nations* is
generally considered to be synonymous with general international law, i.e. customary international
law and general principles of law (Flauss, 'La protection des droits de l'homme et les sources du
droit international' (1998) 50). It has also been advanced, not surprisingly from a French perspective, that the human rights method is actually an instrument of US foreign policy, as the customary
international law values to be promoted are actually synonymous with US constitutional values.
Flauss, 'La protection des droits de l'homme et les sources du droit international' (1998) 51.

However, emphasis on *opinio juris* to the detriment of actual state practice may be found in the practice of international courts as well. The International Court of Justice (ICJ)'s *Nicaragua* judgment is most commonly cited in this context. In *Nicaragua*, the ICJ held, in relation to the customary norms on the use of force, that '[t]he Court must satisfy itself that the existence of the rule in the *opinio juris* of States is confirmed by practice.'[4] In so doing, it signalled that ascertaining *opinio juris* logically precedes the analysis of state practice. In addition, the Court appeared to gloss over inconsistencies in state practice,[5] thereby creating the impression that, as long as *opinio juris* is not in doubt, the consistency of state practice, a cherished and arguably primordial element of a customary rule, is not to be the first consideration. Under *Nicaragua*, inconsistent conduct is to be viewed as the violation of an established rule—a rule having crystallized primarily on the basis of strong *opinio juris*—rather than as evidence of a newly emerging rule. This is at odds with the conventional view of customary international law, which emphasizes state practice over *opinio juris*,[6] and does, accordingly, not brook contrary practice.[7]

---

[4] *Military and Paramilitary Activities in and Against Nicaragua (Nicaragua v. United States) (Merits)*, Judgment of 27 June 1986, 1986 ICJ Reports 14, 98, para. 184.

[5] Ibid. 98, para. 186 ('It is not to be expected that in the practice of States the application of the rules in question should have been perfect, in the sense that States should have refrained, with complete consistency, from the use of force or from intervention in each other's internal affairs. The Court does not consider that, for a rule to be established as customary, the corresponding practice must be in absolutely rigorous conformity with the rule. In order to deduce the existence of customary rules, the Court deems it sufficient that the conduct of States should, in general, be consistent with such rules, and that instances of State conduct inconsistent with a given rule should generally have been treated as breaches of that rule, not as indications of the recognition of a new rule. If a State acts in a way prima facie incompatible with a recognised rule, but defends its conduct by appealing to exceptions or justifications contained within the rule itself, then whether or not the State's conduct is in fact justifiable on that basis, the significance of that attitude is to confirm rather than to weaken the rule.'). The fact that uncertainties or contradictions do not necessarily threaten the existence of a rule of customary international law was recognised as early as 1951 by the ICJ, see *Fisheries (United Kingdom v. Norway)*, Judgment of 18 December 1951, 1951 ICJ Reports 116, 138 ('The Court considers that too much importance need not be attached to the few uncertainties or contradictions, real or apparent, which the United Kingdom Government claims to have discovered in Norwegian practice. They may be easily understood in the light of the variety of the facts and conditions prevailing in the long period which has elapsed since 1812, and are not such as to modify the conclusions reached by the Court [relating to the existence of a rule of customary international law].').

[6] In the classical view, the 'subjective' requirement of *opinio juris* may sometimes even be dispensed with, e.g. ILA, Committee on Formation of Customary (General) International Law, Final Report, Statement of Principles Applicable to the Formation of General Customary International Law, *Report of the 69th Conference* (London 2000) 714, 742 (stating that 'it is not always and probably not even usually, *necessary* to prove the existence of any sort of subjective element in addition to the objective element [. . .]').

[7] O. Schachter, 'New Custom: Power, *Opinio Juris* and Contrary Practice' in J. Makarczyk (ed.), *Theory of International Law at the Threshold of the 21st Century: Essays in Honour of Krzysztof Skubiszewski* (Kluwer Law International, The Hague/London/Boston 1996) 531, 538 ('The notion that contrary practice should yield to *opinio juris* challenges the basic premise of customary law.'); Schachter supports the *Nicaragua* approach, however: O. Schachter, *International Law in Theory and Practice* (Martinus Nijhoff, Dordrecht/Boston/London 1991) 340.

The question now arises whether there is good reason to extrapolate the *Nicaragua* dictum to other fields of international law. After all, in *Nicaragua*, the ICJ was called upon to ascertain the customary rules on the use of force. These rules are amongst the international rules that are most routinely violated by states (and surely so during the Cold War, which provided the backdrop for the *Nicaragua* case, when the United States and the Soviet Union were fighting global proxy wars), in spite of states invariably paying lip service to the sanctity of international peace. Doubtless, in international law on the use of force, there is a yawning gap between what states practise and what they preach. As far as treaty law is concerned, in particular Article 2(4) of the UN Charter, this may not subtract from the continuing validity of the prohibition on the use of force, as for desuetude, the required counter-consensus will prove to be elusive. Yet as far as customary international law is concerned, the gap is more problematic, as contrary state practice may prevent a rule on the prohibition on the use of force from crystallizing as a norm of customary law, or undermine the continuing validity of the prohibition of the use of force if such a prohibition had previously crystallized. If, however, a subject matter is regulated by treaty law of universal application, one would be hard-pressed to find a customary norm on the same subject matter to be at variance with the treaty norm, especially if the need for regulation is advocated by all members of the international community. If the *opinio juris* in favour of the norm, either in its conventional or its customary form, is undisputed, the customary norm will apply in parallel with the conventional norm. In the *Nicaragua* case, given the parties' and all states' UN Charter commitments and their support for General Assembly resolutions, and particularly the Friendly Relations Declaration, the ICJ duly established *opinio juris* as to the binding character of the abstention from the threat or use of force against the territorial integrity or political independence of any state.[8]

As a matter of principle, the *Nicaragua* method, emphasizing *opinio juris* over state practice in ascertaining customary international law, may be applicable to other fields of international law. Yet obviously, some fields lend themselves more easily to the application of the *Nicaragua* method. In particular, human rights and international humanitarian norms are, like the prohibition of the use of force, evidenced by strong *opinio juris*, enshrined in international conventions, and characterized by inconsistent state practice. These features make such norms prime candidates for application of the *Nicaragua* method. In Section 4, it will be examined whether the *Nicaragua* method—which will be characterized as the 'modern positivist method'—could also apply to other fields of international law.

---

[8] *Nicaragua (Merits)*, 1986 ICJ Reports 14, 89–90, para. 188; Kirgis has argued that the ICJ's 'primary reliance on normative words rather than on a combination of words and consistent deeds' in *Nicaragua* may be explained by 'the need for stability', F.L. Kirgis, 'Custom on a Sliding Scale' (1987) 81 AJIL 146, 147.

Quite clearly, under *Nicaragua*, the existence of the customary rule in the *opinio juris* of states should still be confirmed by practice. Faced with the challenge of inconsistent physical practice—e.g. states engaging in torture, states targeting civilians in times of war—emphasis may be placed rather on *verbal* state practice. In statements, states will ordinarily deny that they engage in torture or target civilians, or will apologize for any transgressions, as the political and moral fall-out of defending gross violations of human rights and humanitarian norms is considerable.

It may be noted here that *opinio juris* and verbal state practice are difficult to separate.[9] Often, the same statement may count as evidence of state practice and *opinio juris*. If, in addition, emphasis is methodologically placed on verbal state practice, and physical state practice is played down, it may appear that invoking state practice as a separate element to prove the existence of a customary norm is mostly superfluous. Nonetheless, ascertainment of *opinio juris*, the first step of the test under *Nicaragua*, might of itself imply ascertainment of state practice, as determining *opinio juris* is mainly based on the statements of states. An analysis of such statements may kill two birds with one stone: it may satisfy the requirement of *opinio juris* and the requirement of state practice at the same time.[10]

3. Ascertaining Customary International Humanitarian Law

In this second Section, it will be shown why, how, and by whom emphasis is put on verbal state practice, which often at the same time reflects *opinio juris*, rather than physical or battlefield practice in ascertaining customary international humanitarian law. Attention will also be devoted to the criticism this has provoked.

It was in the 1995 *Tadić* (Appeals) case before the International Criminal Tribunal for the Former Yugoslavia (ICTY) that an international tribunal most eloquently set out the practical reasons for downplaying battlefield practice in the process of ascertaining customary law:

When attempting to ascertain State practice with a view to establishing the existence of a customary rule or a general principle, it is difficult, if not impossible, to pinpoint the actual behaviour of the troops in the field for the purpose of establishing whether they

---

[9] Also *Report of the 69th Conference of the International Law Association* (2000), 718.

[10] Roberts, for her part, has opposed this method, discounting statements from the state practice analysis, on the ground that they 'often fuse *lex lata* and *lex ferenda*'. Instead, she only takes statements into account when ascertaining *opinio juris*, A.E. Roberts, 'Traditional and Modern Approaches to Customary International Law: A Reconciliation' (2001) 95 AJIL 757, 789. Roberts's state practice analysis, however, takes into consideration 'reasons for a lack of protest over breaches'. Ibid. It is hard to see then why protests themselves, as a modality of 'statements', ought to be discounted. Protests could, in the authors' view, certainly be deprived of any normative aspirations (*opinio juris*), and thus qualify as state practice.

in fact comply with, or disregard, certain standards of behaviour. This examination is rendered extremely difficult by the fact that not only is access to the theatre of military operations normally refused to independent observers (often even to the ICRC) but information on the actual conduct of hostilities is withheld by the parties to the conflict; what is worse, often recourse is had to misinformation with a view to misleading the enemy as well as public opinion and foreign Governments. In appraising the formation of customary rules or general principles one should therefore be aware that, on account of the inherent nature of this subject-matter, reliance must primarily be placed on such elements as official pronouncements of States, military manuals and judicial decisions.[11]

The result of the *Tadić* method is that 'humanizing' customary norms of international humanitarian law will be more easily ascertained. Indeed, battlefield practice—which is often far less humane than may appear from the lofty wording of official statements and military manuals—is not considered to substantially contribute to the formation of customary international law if contrary verbal or written practice is available. The *Tadić* method takes the *Nicaragua* method one step further: not only does it play down inconsistent state practice, notably on the battlefield, in the face of more humane verbal state practice and *opinio juris*; it even seems to deem battlefield practice methodologically irrelevant because of its untrustworthiness.

The *Nicaragua* and *Tadić* methods are echoed by the influential study of the International Committee of the Red Cross (ICRC) on customary international humanitarian law (2005). In this study, the ICRC has indicated that the *Nicaragua* finding 'is particularly relevant for a number of rules of international humanitarian law where there is overwhelming evidence of verbal state practice supporting a certain rule found alongside repeated evidence of violations of that rule.'[12] While the ICRC does not exclude physical acts in its selection of state practice, the 161 rules of customary international humanitarian law which it identifies are based overwhelmingly on verbal acts and *opinio juris*.[13]

The ICRC's heavy reliance on verbal acts has, not surprisingly, elicited a response from a state that *has* troops on the ground, and that could cite abundant battlefield practice: the United States. The US Government could no longer lie

---

[11] *Prosecutor v. Tadić*, ICTY-94–1-AR72, Decision on the defence motion for interlocutory appeal on jurisdiction, 2 October 1995, para. 99.

[12] J.M. Henckaerts and L. Doswald-Beck, ICRC, *Customary International Humanitarian Law. Volume I: Rules* (Cambridge University Press, Cambridge 2005) xxxviii. Compare also ibid. xl ('*Opinio juris* plays an important role…in certain situations where the practice is ambiguous, in order to decide whether or not that practice counts towards the formation of custom.').

[13] Verbal acts taken into account by the ICRC study include military manuals, national legislation, national case law, instructions to armed and security forces, military communiqués during war, diplomatic protests, opinions of official legal advisors, comments by governments on draft treaties, executive decisions and regulations, pleadings before international tribunals, statements in international organisations and at international conferences and government positions taken with respect to resolutions of international organisations. Physical acts taken into account by the ICRC study include, for example, battlefield behaviour, the use of certain weapons and the treatment provided to different categories of persons; Ibid. xxxii.

low; it had to react to the ICRC study in order to safeguard US national interests, because the ICRC, having limited international legal personality, gives authoritative interpretations to the laws of war, and even believes that its own practice—the ICRC's official statements—may *also* count as state practice evidencing norms of customary international humanitarian law.[14] The US was, in particular, concerned about the applicability of the 1977 Additional Protocols to the Geneva Conventions—to which the US is not a party—as customary international law, and about the applicability of the Geneva Conventions and the Additional Protocols as customary international law in internal armed conflicts.

On November 3, 2006, John B. Bellinger, the Legal Adviser of the US Department of State, and William J. Haynes, General Counsel of the US Department of Defense, sent a letter to Jakob Kellenberger, the President of the ICRC, venting their concern over the methodology used to ascertain rules and over whether the authors have proffered sufficient facts and evidence to support those rules.[15] In this letter, which contains a preliminary assessment of the ICRC study, the US took issue with both the ICRC's assessment of state practice and its assessment of *opinio juris*. The substance of the criticism does not surprise: the state practice cited by the ICRC is arguably 'insufficiently dense to meet the "extensive and virtually uniform" standard generally required to demonstrate the existence of a customary rule', the study 'places too much emphasis on written materials, such as military manuals and other guidelines published by States, as opposed to actual operational practice by States during armed conflict', it 'gives undue weight to statements by non-governmental organisations and the ICRC itself', and it should not establish *opinio juris* 'when the evidence of a State's sense of legal obligation consists predominantly of military manuals.'[16]

US protest makes clear that the method of ascertaining customary international humanitarian law espoused by the ICRC, a method that places emphasis

[14] Ibid. xxxv; a role for NGOs in the formation of customary international law is also advocated by I.R. Gunning, Modernising Customary International Law: The Challenge of Human Rights, (1990–1991) 31 Va J Int'l L 211 (notably as far as international refugee law is concerned).

[15] The letter was made public in March 2007, reproduced at (2007) ILM 514; for a response see J.M. Henckaerts, 'Customary International Humanitarian Law: a Response to US Comments', (2007) 89 *International Review of the Red Cross* 473. For an early critical technical assessment by a US Department of Defense official writing in his own name see W. Hays Parks, 'The ICRC Customary Law Study: a Preliminary Assessment' (2005) ASIL Proc. 208–212.

[16] Letter Bellinger/Haynes, (ibid), 2–4 (the letter clarifies: 'Rather than indicating a position expressed out of a sense of a customary legal obligation, in the sense pertinent to customary international law, a State's military manual often (properly) will recite requirements applicable to that State under treaties to which it is a party. Reliance on provisions of military manuals designed to implement treaty rules provides only weak evidence that those treaty rules apply as a matter of customary international law in non-treaty contexts. Moreover, States often include guidance in their military manuals for policy, rather than legal, reasons. For example, the United States has long stated that it will apply the rules in its manuals whether the conflict is characterised as international or non-international, but this clearly is not intended to indicate that it is bound to do so as a matter of law in non-international conflicts. Finally, the Study often fails to distinguish between military publications prepared informally solely for training or similar purposes and those prepared and approved as official government statements.').

on verbal state practice and is quick to find sufficient state practice and *opinio juris* when morality demands regulatory intervention, does not go unchallenged. US concerns signal that the traditional formal method of ascertaining customary international law has not yet given way to a purportedly more subjective method informed by humanitarian sensitivities. The influence of humanitarianism and morality on the 'modern' method of ascertaining customary international law will be the subject of the next Section.

4. The 'Modern Positivist' Approach

4.1 Methodology and value preferences

A choice of methodology is often not value- or politically neutral. This also holds true in law and international law. Scholar/lawyer A may have a preference for method 1 because it best serves his or her moral or political proclivities, while scholar/lawyer B may opt for method 2 because that method best transmits his or her value preferences. Quite conceivably, both A and B will term their own method 'objective', and another method 'subjective'. For our purposes, scholar/lawyer A may prefer the traditional method of ascertaining customary international law that emphasizes dense state practice and *opinio juris*, and that puts a high premium on physical state practice, because that method best serves the sovereign interests of the state he or she defends or identifies with. Scholar/lawyer B, for his or her part, may prefer the modern method of ascertaining customary international law that emphasizes *opinio juris* over state practice, and verbal state practice over physical state practice, because that method best serves the protection of human rights and the globalization of values.[17]

Persons without a vested interest, such as scholars, judges and ICRC legal advisors tend to be lawyers of the 'B' mould, whereas state officials tend to be lawyers of the 'A' mould. This explains why the ICJ, the ICTY, the ICRC, and arguably the majority of writers, as discussed above, appear to have swooned for the modern method,[18] and why the US has been so critical towards the ICRC study on

---

[17] The influence of the observational standpoint on the method of ascertaining customary international law the observer uses was also highlighted in the 2000 ILA Report on the Formation of Customary Law: ILA, Final Report of the Committee on Formation of Customary Law (2000) 716, no. 7 ('In studying the customary process, it is necessary to be aware of the issue of the observational standpoint. By this reference is not mainly made to the (obvious) need to identify for oneself and for others one's own assumptions and goals. Rather, the suggestion is that different *functions* may lead the persons performing them to adopt a somewhat different attitude to the sources [...]') (footnote omitted; original emphasis).

[18] The ICRC, relying on the ICTY and the ICJ, did not hide the influence of human and community values on its method of ascertaining customary law, see ICRC Study on *Customary International Humanitarian Law* (2005) xlii ('It appears that international courts and tribunals on occasion conclude that a rule of customary international law exists when that rule is a desirable one

customary international humanitarian law.[19] Because the modern approach is less formalistic than the traditional approach, and allows moral considerations to seep in, it could easily be submitted that it is less rigorous and less 'objective', but is that really so?

4.2 Positivism, naturalism, and their discontents

Positivism is the school of legal thought underlying our contemporary system of law and international law. Because it excludes non-legal factors from the process of ascertaining what the law is, and analyses whether states have actually consented to the law, 'positive international law' is supposedly objective. Under a positivist approach to customary international law, state practice and *opinio juris* are meticulously analysed, and a customary norm is only established when state consent, albeit tacit, can be identified.

The classical positivist approach may, however, pose serious difficulties for the legal protection and promotion of human rights. As already noted, state practice in the field of human rights is often inconsistent, especially at a universal level.[20] This has prompted the courts and the doctrine to emphasize *opinio juris* over state practice, and verbal over physical state practice. In so doing, they may believe that they still apply the classical positivist paradigm. Yet in reality, they may give *opinio juris* undue weight—or even conjure up firm *opinio juris* when there is only weak evidence—and unjustifiably turn a blind eye to physical state practice. In reality, evidence of *opinio juris* and state practice may be utterly insufficient for a norm of customary human rights law to be articulated. A return to a controversial natural law approach, which allows law to be established on the basis of moral or religious apriori, may then seem the only solution; because human rights protection is a moral imperative, the law should be adjusted accordingly.[21] Naturally, this approach may confound the *lex lata* and the *lex ferenda*,[22] threaten

for international peace and security or for the protection of the human person, provided that there is no important contrary *opinio juris*.').

[19] The content of the Bellinger/Haynes letter, discussed above, is hardly neutral, as its authors, as US officials, are supposed to defend the national interest of the United States in drafting legal opinions.

[20] At a regional level, state practice may be more consistent, and the classical positivist approach may not pose such difficulties. Flauss, 'La protection des droits de l'homme et les sources du droit international' (1998) 66–67 (noting that *regional* customary law could be formed pursuant to the classical method, e.g. among the member states of the Council of Europe).

[21] Also M. Koskenniemi, 'The Pull of the Mainstream' (1990) 88 Mich L Rev 1946, 1953 (noting that the customary law formation in the field of human rights is determined by an 'anterior—though in some respects largely shared—criterion of what is right and good for human life'). For criticism, amongst others, A. Pellet, 'Droits-de-l'hommisme' et droit international, Conférence commémorative Gilberto Amado, 18 July 2000, 4 (charging that the adherents of the new school 'feraient mieux de laisser aux « activistes des droits de l'homme »... le soin de changer le droit plutôt qu'à s'y essayer eux-mêmes...', and lambasting 'la recherche abusive du particularisme').

[22] E.g. Roberts, (2001) 95 AJIL 757, 761–763 (not regretting this tendency though, noting that law always has a normative dimension, relating to what the law *ought to be*).

state sovereignty,[23] and lower the level of legal certainty positivism has conferred on the law.

4.3 General principles of law and 'modern' positivism

Clearly, it is mainly the inconsistency of states' human rights practice that complicates the formation of customary human rights norms. If only international law sources or concepts could be found that de-emphasize state practice. Fortunately for activist lawyers, these exist. For one, rules of *jus cogens* or peremptory norms are in no need of consistent state practice. They only need to be 'accepted and recognised by the international community of states *as a whole*' as norms 'from which no derogation is permitted'.[24] This implies that states *ut singuli* need not have accepted and recognized these rules to be bound by them. Inconsistent state practice is, accordingly, no bar to the general binding character of a norm of *jus cogens*. *Jus cogens* is a useful legal device to sidestep the difficulties posed by the requirements for customary law formation in the human rights field: quite some number of human rights norms are arguably *jus cogens* norms, e.g. the prohibition of torture, the prohibition of genocide, etc.[25] Nonetheless, it requires a stretch to subsume *all* human rights under the *jus cogens* heading. Yet here another international legal concept may come to the rescue: general principles of law.

'General principles of law recognized by civilized nations' are a source of law that the ICJ is authorized to apply under the Court's Statute.[26] As a source of international law, general principles could be conceived of as principles of law common to municipal systems. Alternatively, they could be conceived of as genuine principles of international law, irrespective of analogies at the municipal law level. Under both conceptions of general principles, actual state practice is arguably not the main consideration, unlike the situation with respect to the crystallization of customary rules.[27] Being principles, they need not be uniformly practised.

Human rights norms could be characterized as general principles under both conceptions: either they could be viewed as municipal constitutional law analogies, or they could be viewed as general principles in their own right. Professor

---

[23] On this in particular Pellet, 'Droits-de-l'hommisme' et droit international (2000) 6–7 (denouncing the violation of states' rights not to be bound by a norm, and arguing that human rights activists rather than lawyers should push the boundaries of the law).

[24] Article 53 of the Vienna Convention on the Law of Treaties (emphasis added).

[25] See for a list of *jus cogens* norms: Ybk ILC 1966, II, 248. The prohibition of torture as a *jus cogens* norm was recognised by, amongst others, the ICTY Trial Chamber in *Prosecutor v. Furundžija*, ICTY-95-17/1-T, Judgment of 10 December 1998, paras. 153–156.

[26] Article 38(1)(c) of the ICJ Statute.

[27] Under the first conception, only municipal, as opposed to *international* state practice, is relevant. Under the second conception, general principles of international law are, as Brownlie has noted, 'primarily abstractions from a mass of rules and have been so long and so generally accepted as to be no longer *directly* connected with State practice.' I. Brownlie, *Principles of Public International Law*, 4th ed. (Clarendon Press, Oxford 1990) 19.

Henkin is the main proponent of the first approach. Henkin has put forward the idea of a 'non-conventional' law of human rights. This law is neither treaty law nor customary international law. In Henkin's own words, 'it is not based on "custom" or on state practice at all', it 'is not based on consent', and 'it binds particular states regardless of their objections.'[28] Instead, international human rights law is 'constitutional' in the sense that it derives from national constitutional rights.[29] These rights are articulated in contemporary 'liberal national constitutions'. Through the concept of general principles of law (which Henkin himself does not explicitly use), they could be considered as a source of public international law.

Henkin's 'non-conventional' international human rights law has, not surprisingly, been assailed as contrary to established doctrine, particularly by Professor D'Amato. D'Amato has criticized Henkin for 'inventing' a new source of international law, as national constitutions are, in themselves, not recognized as a source of international law.[30] He has, in addition, pointed out that hardly any of the liberal constitutions mention the human rights on Henkin's list.[31] In all fairness, D'Amato's criticism is exaggerated. Under a less formal conception of constitutional law, municipal constitutional law could also encompass certain international human rights-related criminal offences in the penal code, such as the prohibition of genocide, slavery and torture. Moreover, while national constitutions are indeed, *as such*, not a source of international law, they could surely become so if they 'piggyback' on the concept of general principles of law. As to the argument that Henkin only takes (Western) liberal constitutions into account, it could be replied that non-Western constitutions nowadays boast as many, if not more, articles on fundamental freedoms as Western constitutions. The 2006 Constitution of the Democratic Republic of the Congo, for instance, contains no less than 51 articles on 'human rights and fundamental liberties',[32] whereas Belgium, hardly an illiberal state, has a mere 25 articles on 'the Belgians and their rights'.[33] While human rights practice may be uneven, democratic, rule of law-based states, which now constitute the majority of states,[34] recognize human rights principles in their constitutions and laws.[35] States' widespread recognition

---

[28] L. Henkin 'Human Rights and State Sovereignty', (1995–96) 25 Ga J Intl Comp L 31, 38.

[29] Ibid., 40.

[30] A. D'Amato, 'Human Rights as Part of Customary International Law: A Plea for Change of Paradigms' (1995–96) 25 Ga J Intl Comp L 47, 56.

[31] Ibid., 54.

[32] Articles 11–61 of the Constitution of the Democratic Republic of the Congo, proclaimed 18 February 2006.

[33] Articles 8–32 of the Coordinated Constitution of Belgium, 17 February 1994.

[34] The NGO Freedom House considered 123 countries to be electoral democracies in its 2007 Freedom in the World survey. See <http://www.freedomhouse.org/template. cfm?page=368&year=2007>.

[35] Communist constitutions also recognize human rights, albeit to a lesser extent. The Constitution of Vietnam, for instance, stipulates in its Article 50 that '[i]n the Socialist Republic of Vietnam human rights in the political, civic, economic, cultural and social fields are respected',

of these principles, even in the absence of strict respect for them in practice, combined with the increasing relevance of human rights in inter-state relations, may suffice to elevate them to general principles of law.[36]

Under the second conception of general principles, general principles of international law are established not on the basis of municipal law analogies but top-down, from international practice. Human rights may also be qualified as general principles under this conception, which emphasizes the practice of states in and *vis-à-vis* international fora, organizations, and institutions. Alston and Simma are the main advocates of reliance on such general principles to ground the legally binding character of international human rights law in the absence of treaty law.[37] They interestingly believe that recourse to general principles allows us to remain within the confines of positivism, with its emphasis on state *consent* in the creation of (international) norms:

In contrast to . . . natural law views, the recourse to general principles . . . remains grounded in a consensualist conception of international law. Consequently, what is required for the establishment of human rights obligations *qua* general principles is essentially the same kind of convincing evidence of general acceptance and recognition . . . in order to arrive at customary law. However, this material is not equated with State practice but is rather seen as a variety of ways in which moral and humanitarian considerations find a more direct and spontaneous 'expression in legal form'.[38]

yet it puts heavy emphasis on the citizens' duties in the remainder of the Constitution. The Cuban Constitution also recognizes human rights (Articles 45–66), with an emphasis on socio-economic rights. The Chinese Constitution has a chapter on fundamental rights and duties of citizens (Articles 33–56), although Article 51 may deprive citizens' rights of much of their substance: 'The exercise by citizens of the People's Republic of China of their freedoms and rights may not infringe upon the interests of the state, of society and of the collective, or upon the lawful freedoms and rights of other citizens.'

[36] For criticism of the normative objectivity of general principles of law in view of the possible lack of state practice see Schachter, *International Law in Theory and Practice* (1991) 338 ('Constitutions with human rights provisions that are little more than window-dressing can hardly be cited as significant evidence of practice of "general principles" of law.'); T. Meron, *The Humanization of International Law* (2006) 374 ('Absent conforming practice, the identification of the general principles may be subjective, even arbitrary.').

[37] B. Simma and P. Alston, 'The Sources of Human Rights Law: Custom, *Jus Cogens* and General Principles' (1992) Australian Ybk Intl L 82, 102 ('Principles brought to the fore in this "direct way", so to speak, would (and should) then percolate down into domestic fora, instead of being elevated from the domestic level to that of international law by way of analogy.'). Also B. Simma and A.L. Paulus, 'The Responsibility of Individuals for Human Rights Abuses in Internal Conflicts: A Positivist View' (1999) 93 AJIL 302, 307 ('Increasingly, general principles of international law establish themselves from the top down, as it were; that is, not by deduction from domestic law but by proclamation in international fora.'); O. Schachter, *International Law in Theory and Practice* (1991) 340 (submitting that 'one must look for "practice" and *opinio juris* mainly in the international forums where human rights issues are actually discussed, debated and sometimes resolved by general consensus.'); J.I. Charney, 'Universal International Law' (1993) 87 AJIL 529, 538 ('Rather than state practice and *opinio juris*, multilateral forums often play a central role in the creation and shaping of contemporary international law.').

[38] Simma and Alston, (1992) Australian Ybk Intl L 82, 105 (footnotes omitted).

4.4 ICJ support for 'modern positivism'

Alston and Simma have a number of pronouncements of the ICJ on the role of humanitarian considerations in international law, often in passing, on their side. Most notably, in its very first judgment on the merits (1949), the ICJ pointed out, in the *Corfu Channel* case, that 'elementary considerations of humanity' are 'general and well-recognised principles' of international law.[39] The *Corfu Channel* dictum was cited approvingly by the Court in the 1986 *Nicaragua* (merits) judgment.[40] In the 1980 *Tehran Hostages* case, the Court cited 'the fundamental principles enunciated in the Universal Declaration of Human Rights'—which is of itself not binding—to support the illegality of wrongful deprivation of a person's freedom.[41]

It was, obviously, precisely in the *Nicaragua* case that the ICJ came up with the controversial dictum cited above, that '[t]he Court must satisfy itself that the existence of the rule in the *opinio juris* of States is confirmed by practice',[42] and thereby hinted that *opinio juris* may be more important than state practice in the formation of customary international law. Yet the subject matter of both dicta was different. The customary law dictum related to the rules governing the use of force, whereas the dictum on general principles related to rules of international humanitarian law. It is not entirely clear why the ICJ relied on customary law in order to identify the rules on the use of force and on general principles in order to identify rules of humanitarian law. Possibly, it faced difficulties in ascertaining state practice, battlefield practice in particular, like the ICTY did in the *Tadić* case (Section 2 above). By relying on general principles, the Court could

---

[39] *Corfu Channel (United Kingdom v. Albania)*, Judgment of 9 April 1949, 1949 ICJ Reports 4, 22 ('The obligations incumbent upon the Albanian authorities consisted in notifying, for the benefit of shipping in general, the existence of a minefield in Albanian territorial waters and in warning the approaching British warships of the imminent danger to which the minefield exposed them. Such obligations are based, not on the Hague Convention of 1907, No. VIII, which is applicable in time of war, but on *certain general and well-recognised principles*, namely: *elementary considerations of humanity*, even more exacting in peace than in war; the principle of the freedom of maritime communication; and every State's obligation not to allow knowingly its territory to be used for acts contrary to the rights of other States.') (emphasis added).

[40] *Nicaragua Case (Merits)* 1986 ICJ Reports 14, 112, para. 215; 113–114 para. 218. 'Elementary considerations of humanity' were also relied upon by the ICTY in the *Tadić* case *Prosecutor v. Tadić*, ICTY-94–1-AR72, Decision on the defence motion for interlocutory appeal on jurisdiction, 2 October 1995, para. 119) ('Indeed, *elementary considerations of humanity* and common sense make it preposterous that the use by States of weapons prohibited in armed conflicts between themselves be allowed when States try to put down rebellion by their own nationals on their own territory.').

[41] *United States Diplomatic and Consular Staff in Iran (United States v. Iran)*, Judgment of 24 May 1980, 1980 ICJ Reports 3, 42, para. 91 ('Wrongfully to deprive human beings of their freedom and to subject them to physical constraint in conditions of hardship is in itself manifestly incompatible with the principles of the Charter of the United Nations, as well as with the fundamental principles enunciated in the Universal Declaration of Human Rights'); Schachter has argued that the Court only 'rhetorically relied on the Declaration as a touchstone of legality', O. Schachter, *International Law in Theory and Practice* (1991) 339.

[42] *Nicaragua Case (Merits)* 1986 ICJ Reports 14, 98, para. 184.

sidestep the problems inherent in ascertaining customary law. Alternatively, the field of international humanitarian law lends itself specifically to the application of humanitarian principles, on which the 1949 Geneva Conventions are after all based.[43] Humanitarian concerns and principles have informed the development of the conventional law of war, so that it is only logical to reach back to them in case there is no applicable treaty law, rather than to ascertain the existence of customary norms that are themselves based on these very concerns and principles.

It may be noted that the most cogent defence of human rights as general principles of law in the ICJ's records was formulated in the dissenting opinion of Judge Tanaka in the 1966 *South West Africa* cases.[44] Unlike Alston and Simma, Tanaka did not shy away from taking an openly natural law approach to general principles of law: he did not require 'the consent of States as a condition of the recognition of the general principles'.[45] Alston and Simma, in contrast, anchor their general principles approach in *positive* law; they are not willing to give up the consensualist underpinnings of contemporary international law.[46] The question arises whether Tanaka's and Alston and Simma's approaches are in the end very different from each other; for what is that 'legal form' in which moral and humanitarian considerations ought to be clothed (a form required by a positivist-minded ICJ in the *South West Africa* cases)?[47]

4.5 Putting modern positivism to the test

In a later article by Simma and his co-author Paulus, the 'modern positivist' 'general principles' approach is put to the test by means of a discussion of the

[43] Ibid., 113–114, paras 218 ('the Geneva Conventions are in some respects a development, and in other respects no more than the expression, of [fundamental general principles of humanitarian law]'), and 220 ('an obligation [to respect and to ensure respect for the Geneva Conventions in all circumstances] does not derive only from the Conventions themselves, but from the general principles of humanitarian law to which the Conventions merely give specific expression').

[44] *South West Africa (Ethiopia v. South Africa; Liberia v. South Africa)*, Judgment of 18 July 1966, 1966 ICJ Reports 6, 298 (Tanaka diss.) ('As an interpretation of Article 38, paragraph 1(c), we consider that the concept of human rights and of their protection is included in the general principles mentioned in that Article.').

[45] Ibid., (adding that 'States which do not recognise this principle or even deny its validity are nevertheless subject to its rule. From this kind of source international law could have the foundation of its validity extended beyond the will of States, that is to say, into the sphere of natural law and assume an aspect of its supra-national and supra-positive character.').

[46] However, like Tanaka, and Henkin for that matter, Simma and Alston consider general principles of law to be the source of international law that confers a binding character on *jus cogens* norms. Simma and Alston, (1992) Australian Ybk Intl L 82, 105; *South West Africa Cases*, 298 (Tanaka diss.); Henkin, (1995–96) 25 Ga J Intl Comp L 31, 38 (submitting that 'international non-conventional human rights law is *jus cogens*, or is like *jus cogens*'). The use of general principles of international human rights law should not be reserved for *jus cogens* norms—as Henkin seems to imply—though, lest principles that do not rise to the level of *jus cogens* may not be relied upon. Cf below Section 4 for the difference between *jus cogens* and 'higher norms'.

[47] *South West Africa*, 1966 ICJ Reports 6, 34, para. 51.

responsibility of individuals for human rights abuses in internal conflicts.[48] Under the classical positivist approach towards customary international law, such responsibility may not easily be established, since, as Simma and Paulus themselves admit, 'the state practice involved is anything but firm'.[49] Few states have indeed held persons criminally liable for their transgressions of the laws of war in internal, as opposed to international, conflicts. Relevant state practice could, accordingly, hardly be termed 'extensive and virtually uniform'.[50]

However, if verbal state practice in and *vis-à-vis* international fora is taken into account, another picture emerges. Modern positivism allows for the consideration of statements by states in international fora, of the (tacit) acceptance of international tribunals' statutes and judgments, and of the widespread adoption of treaties dealing with the subject matter. Individual criminal responsibility for war crimes committed in non-international armed conflicts may then be established as a matter of international law on the basis of its inclusion in conventions such as the Statute of the International Criminal Court, on the basis of statutes of and trials in international criminal tribunals (the International Criminal Tribunal for Rwanda, ICTY, and the Special Court for Sierra Leone), of the adoption of legislation criminalizing war crimes committed in internal armed conflicts, of statements of states supporting individual criminal responsibility, and of UN practice (Security Council, General Assembly, Human Rights Commission/Council).

This is exactly how the ICRC has established the customary law status of individual criminal responsibility for war crimes committed in internal armed conflicts in Rule 151 of its 2005 Study.[51] Simma and Paulus, while also concluding that such responsibility is acquired under international law, do not, however, follow the customary law track, at least not exclusively. As already noted, because the stringent state practice requirement of traditional customary law may undermine the binding character of human rights and humanitarian concerns, a method that de-emphasizes state practice *as it was known* had to be found. This method is the 'general principles' method advocated by Alston and Simma. However, in Simma and Paulus's conception, general principles do not seem to suffice *in themselves* to ground the binding character of human rights and humanitarian concerns. Their use of the traditional customary law categories of state practice and *opinio juris* makes clear that 'general principles' in fact constitute a legal device employed to *buttress* the customary law method. This method would, on its own, not yield the desirable outcome, if the classical understanding of state practice were to be used.[52]

---

[48] Simma and Paulus, (1999) 93 AJIL 302.

[49] Ibid., 312.

[50] *North Sea Continental Shelf (Federal Republic of Germany v. Netherlands; Federal Republic of Germany v. Denmark)*, Judgment of 20 February 1969, 1969 ICJ Reports 3, 43, para. 74.

[51] ICRC Study on *Customary International Humanitarian Law* (2005) 551–555.

[52] Simma and Paulus, (1999) 93 AJIL 302, 313 ('On the basis of a modern positivism—hence also taking into account the practice of international institutions and accepting as *opinio juris* the legal views expressed by states in international organisations—one can defend the ICTY

In order to understand the practical operation of this modern positivist method *vis-à-vis* the traditional positivist method, it might be useful to develop another example: universal jurisdiction over war crimes. The ICRC confirms in Rule 157 of its 2005 Study that 'States have the right to vest universal jurisdiction in their national courts over war crimes.'[53] Universal jurisdiction is commonly defined as jurisdiction based solely on the nature of a crime 'without regard to where the crime was committed, the nationality of the alleged or convicted perpetrator, the nationality of the victim, or any other connection to the State exercising such jurisdiction'.[54] The ICRC finds evidence for the legality of the exercise of universal jurisdiction in the national legislation and (scarce) case law, but also in military manuals and treaties such as the Genocide Convention and the Statute of the International Criminal Court, which conventions do not even provide for the exercise of universal jurisdiction. Arguably, the international community's desire not to let core crimes go unpunished, a desire which has been translated in the international criminalization of heinous acts and in widespread state support for international criminal tribunals, may, as Kress (who draws on Simma and Paulus) submits, 'be seen as a strong indication in favour of a customary State competence to exercise universal jurisdiction'.[55]

That the modern positivist approach is controversial, especially in the eyes of powerful states, is stating the obvious. Reference has already been made to the virulent US criticism of the ICRC study on customary international humanitarian law. While the US has taken issue with the study's method *in general*, it has also criticized specific rules 'found' by the ICRC study. Rule 157, the rule on universal jurisdiction over war crimes, is one of them. Relying on a traditional positivist approach, the US has pointed out that there is in fact 'very little evidence of actual prosecutions of war crimes not connected to the forum state', as only six states have claimed jurisdiction based on customary rights.[56] In a 2004 report on universal jurisdiction, the American Bar Association has been similarly wary of universal jurisdiction.[57] In this report, emphasis was put rather on the recognized

---

jurisprudence and the Rwanda Statute *on the basis of a combination of developing customary law and existing general principles.*') (emphasis added).

[53] ICRC Study on *Customary International Humanitarian Law* (2005) 604–607.

[54] Principle 1 (1) of the Princeton Principles on Universal Jurisdiction (2001), reprinted in S. Macedo (ed.), *Universal Jurisdiction* (Philadelphia: University of Pennsylvania Press, 2004) 21.

[55] C. Kress, 'Universal Jurisdiction over International Crimes and the *Institut de Droit international*' (2006) JICJ 561, 573.

[56] Letter Bellinger/Haynes (2007) 17–22.

[57] American Bar Association, Section of Individual Rights and Responsibilities, Report on universal criminal jurisdiction, adopted by the House of Delegates, 9 February 2004, available at <http://www.abanet.org/leadership/2004/dj/103a.pdf>. The Mission of the American Bar Association is to be the national representative of the U.S. legal profession. It is the largest voluntary professional association in the world. With more than 400,000 members, the ABA provides law school accreditation, continuing legal education, information about the law, programmes to assist lawyers and judges in their work, and initiatives to improve the legal system for the public. <http://www.abanet.org/about>.

role that 'specially affected States' are, under ICJ case law,[58] allowed to play in the formation of customary international law.[59] Because US military forces are deployed worldwide, the US may, as a specially affected state, arguably play a more important role in the formation of the customary laws of war, including the law on universal jurisdiction over war crimes.[60] As the US does *not* exercise universal criminal jurisdiction over war crimes, a norm of permissive customary law on the subject should, in the US view, not easily be established. The latter view is, not surprisingly, categorically rejected in the ICRC study.[61] This rejection supports the modern positivist approach espoused by the ICRC, as it reduces the strength of contrary state practice, as well as the fall-out of US views on a finding of *opinio juris* in favour of a morally desirable customary rule. At any rate, US opposition demonstrates that the modern positivist approach towards customary law is not yet acquired; the traditional state-centred approach will probably remain the preferred approach of powerful states wishing to avoid international regulation without their explicit and unambiguous consent.

5. Impact on General International Law

Clearly, doctrinal rigour is not of the utmost importance for modern positivists; treaty practice, custom and general principles are liberally combined so as to achieve the desired result: increased promotion and protection of human rights.[62] Does such a method truly deserve the epithet 'positivism' (whether modern or not)?

It should be recalled that, while general principles of law are a *positive* source of law, they are undoubtedly the source of law most open to moral influences. As Simma and Paulus admit, 'the ethical standpoint of the observer—and the lawyer—will almost necessarily inform the answers provided . . . in the application of general principles of law.'[63] If the existence of general principles is in essence in

---

[58] *North Sea Continental Shelf Cases,* 1969 ICJ Reports 3, 43, para. 74.

[59] See ABA Report (2004) 6 ('Just as coastal states are the primary relevant states for purposes of customary law on maritime territorial boundaries, states with forces experienced in armed conflict are the primary relevant states for purposes of the customary international law of war.').

[60] Letter Bellinger/Haynes (2007) 2–3.

[61] ICRC Study on *Customary International Humanitarian Law* (2005) xxxviii (arguing that 'all States have a legal interest in requiring respect for international humanitarian law by other States, even if they are not a party to the conflict').

[62] E.g. the terminology of Flauss, 'La protection des droits de l'homme et les sources du droit international' (1998) 69–71 (both referring to 'une forme suprême de droit coutumier', and pointing out that, in view of the widespread violations of human rights, general principles of law are 'l'instrument le plus indiqué pour donner une expression juridique directe aux considérations éthiques et humanitaires', and then settling for 'un « dépassement » des deux sources de droit international général visées par l'article 38 (1b et c) du CIJ [*i.e.* customary international law and general principles]'.).

[63] Simma and Paulus, (1999) 93 AJIL 302, 316.

the ethical eye of the beholder, subjectivity, anathema to 'objective' positive law, seems to prevail. The moral imperative of putting an end to impunity serves, for instance, as the basic source for a finding of criminal responsibility for individuals who have committed war crimes in internal armed conflicts, or for the legality of exercising universal jurisdiction over such crimes. International practice is subsequently selectively resorted to so as to bring a foregone moral conclusion to an acceptable legal level, to clothe moral considerations in a supposedly 'legal form'. Deduction trumps induction, the preferred method of legal positivism.[64]

In the field of international human rights and humanitarian law, classical positivism appears to have given way to a more ethics-based 'modern positivism'. As Schachter has indeed pointed out, '[i]t would not be inappropriate to consider [human rights] norms as a species of "higher law" evidenced by the positions taken by the generality of governments and by the juridical bodies.'[65] Norms may be elevated to 'higher law' if they constitute 'prohibitions of State conduct that are strongly supported and important to international order and human values.'[66] Because of their importance, the formation of these norms should not strictly follow the ordinary consensualist rules of international law formation. Human rights are the prime candidates for this 'higher law' approach, as '[a]t the very heart of the human rights movement is the postulate that the fundamental rights which are recognised by the international community are superior to the claims of governments.'[67]

The question now arises whether what may be warranted for the *lex specialis* of human rights or humanitarian law could also be extrapolated to other fields of international law. Phrased differently, what is the impact of the formation of the sources of human rights and humanitarian law on the formation of the sources of general international law?

It is submitted here that the abstract definition of 'higher law', as proposed by Schachter, might surely encompass more norms than just human rights norms, humanitarian norms, or norms governing the use of force. 'Higher law' may, amongst others, encompass certain norms of international environmental law.[68] For instance, strong support is emerging for tighter regulation of greenhouse gas emissions lest the world heads for an environmental and human catastrophe.[69] Strong *opinio juris*, even in the face of weak state practice, may in due course possibly translate into a legally binding prohibition for all states to emit

---

[64] Also Roberts, (2001) 95 AJIL 757, 763.

[65] O. Schachter, 'New Custom: Power, *Opinio Juris* and Contrary Practice' (1996) 540.

[66] Ibid., 538.

[67] Also Schachter, *International Law in Theory and Practice* (1991) 342.

[68] However Roberts, (2001) 95 AJIL 757, 783 (arguing that the 'moral considerations involved in environmental pollution are strong but not as compelling as the moral imperative against torture', and that, hence, 'a customary environmental norm will require greater conformity with state practice, and is more likely to be undermined by conflicting practice than a customary prohibition on torture').

[69] For very recent evidence thereof see G8 Chair's summary, G8 Summit, Heiligendamm, 8 June 2007, available at <http://www.g-8.de/nsc_true/Content/EN/Artikel/__g8-summit/anlagen/chairs-summary,templateId=raw,property=publicationFile.pdf/chairs-summary>.

disproportionate amounts of greenhouse gases (even if developing countries have, as for now, no specific commitments to that effect under the Kyoto Protocol).

It may be noted that 'higher law' is not synonymous with *jus cogens*. Arguably, the threshold for a rule to establish itself as *jus cogens* is higher than the threshold for a rule to establish itself as 'higher law' through a flexible application of customary international law and general principles. For the latter category, evidence of state practice and *opinio juris* is, in line with the classical customary law method, still required, although state practice will, as noted above, more readily be ascertained than in the classical view. 'Higher law' and *jus cogens* do, however, share the common aim of doing justice to global values which the traditional bilateralism of international law and international relations fail to sufficiently protect. The prevalence of violations of human rights, humanitarian norms, and environmental rules to some extent, is precisely so high because they tend to occur in a municipal setting. They typically do not affect bystander states, which thus have no incentive to bring pressure to bear on the violating state to end its deviant behaviour.[70] Moreover, in the absence of protest, relevant state practice may not materialize and international law may not come into being. Regulation might, however, be highly desirable to safeguard the immediate and long-term interests of humanity and mankind.

In an international community that increasingly values multilateralism over bilateralism, and that values obligations towards the international community as a whole (obligations *erga omnes*) over reciprocal obligations; classical methods of law formation based on state consent and extensive and uniform state practice may be relaxed somewhat if 'the stakes are high'.[71] Ethical considerations are allowed a comeback—or perhaps their role is only made more explicit—and they are integrated in the system of positive law. Modern positivism becomes a porous construct; while, in name, it is committed to the identification of law as objectively posited by states, it opens itself up to ethical influences, plugging the undesirable gaps left by defective state practice. As values globalize, it is to be expected that this modern positivism, developed in the context of human rights and humanitarian law, will increasingly infiltrate other areas of international law. After all, the list of customary human rights and humanitarian law norms has also expanded over the years.[72]

Conversely, areas where 'the stakes are not so high', where the absence of a rule may not give rise to a disruption of world public order, may not be 'in need of' modern positivism. One may think here of more technical rules of public international law, e.g. in some areas of the law of the sea or the law of jurisdiction. There, customary rules will still be established on the basis of classical positivism,

---

[70] Also O. Schachter, *International Law in Theory and Practice* (1991) 336 ('States do not usually make claims on other States or protest violations that do not affect their nationals. In that sense, one can find scant State practice accompanied by *opinio juris*.').

[71] Borrowing from Kirgis, (1987) 81 AJIL 146, 148.

[72] O. Schachter, *International Law in Theory and Practice* (1991) 340.

with its strong emphasis on consistent state practice and lesser emphasis on *opinio juris*.[73] Yet where common interests and values ought to be safeguarded, as Byers has noted, '[t]he weighing of supporting, ambivalent and opposing State practice may be seen as a facilitative, and not as a compulsory, exercise'.[74] Put differently, state practice is selectively used to justify a customary norm that is not morally neutral.[75] As a result, when it is undeniable that a rule of international law may further the common interests of humanity or the community of states, the weight of the requirement of consistent state practice may, if need be, justifiably be played down, and the weight of the requirement of *opinio juris* may be played up,[76] with the caveat that only 'clear-cut and unequivocal' *opinio juris* may be taken into account,[77] and substantial consistent state practice is identified.[78] These caveats ensure respectively that *opinio juris* is widespread and beyond discussion among states, and that customary law norms do not become wholly utopian.

If international law may be formed in a different fashion when the world's common interests are at stake, the question as to the role of the persistent objector rule may have to be addressed. Under the modern approach, in the face of basic moral values cementing the international community, not every single state's express consent to be bound by a norm of international law, a cornerstone of classical international law, is required for the state practice requirement to be met.[79] It may then only be a small step to submit that the persistent objector rule (which has it that a state that persistently and openly dissents from a customary rule while it is crystallizing will not be bound by that rule) does not apply in the context of 'higher law'. Nonetheless, while persistent objection to *jus cogens* may indeed be off-limits,[80] as we write, there probably does not exist an exception

[73] Compare ibid., ('Where the stakes are not as high, international decision makers have not been as quick to find restrictive customary rules', citing the *North Sea Continental Shelf* Cases on maritime delimitation and the *Lotus* Case, *S.S. 'Lotus' (France v. Turkey)*, 1927 PCIJ, Series A, No. 10, on criminal jurisdiction).

[74] Byers, *Custom, Power and the Power of Rules* (1999) 163. The term 'common interests' is used by Byers, who refers to 'fundamental principles of international law' which are 'conspicuously in the common interests of most if not all States'. For Byers, these interests are not the interests of 'humanity', but essentially of states. This leads him to conclude that the fundamental principles conveying these interests 'are entailed, or necessarily implied, by an international legal system in which the principal actors are sovereign States,' and hence, that the special method of customary law formation in the field of human rights fits the classical state-centred conception of public international law. Ibid., 165.

[75] Roberts, (2001) 95 AJIL 757, 765.

[76] International Law Association, Committee on Formation of Customary (General) International Law, Final Report (2000) 751–752 (noting that 'a substantial manifestation of acceptance by States that a customary rule exists may compensate for a relative lack of practice').

[77] Ibid., 753.

[78] Compare Roberts, (2001) 95 AJIL 757, 775–778 (explaining that in interpreting custom, the threshold criterion of fit, which guarantees descriptive accuracy and is based on state practice, ought always to be fulfilled, yet also asserting that state practice may be rather broadly construed in this exercise).

[79] Ibid., 766.

[80] E.g. Meron, *The Humanization of International Law* (2006) 376.

to the persistent objector rule for other 'fundamental principles of international law'.[81] Accordingly, while, in the real world, there is not much evidence of states opting out of fundamental principles, the availability of persistent objection in the context of customary international human rights and international humanitarian law may theoretically undermine the latter's universal aspirations. It is also this persistent influence of the persistent objector rule that sets customary international law, and general principles formation for that matter, apart from *jus cogens* formation.

Clearly, under the modern approach to customary law, state consent remains important. It is submitted here that, somewhat counter-intuitively perhaps, it is in fact more important than under the traditional approach. Modern customary law is often based on declarations and treaties with nearly universal participation, whereas traditional custom is often based on the practice of a limited number of (powerful) states.[82] Somewhat surprisingly, the democratic content of the *opinio juris* requirement may offset the perceived deficiencies of inconsistent state practice in the formation of modern custom. Ironically, in the final analysis, modern positivism may be considered as more positive and more consent-based than traditional positivism.

In conclusion, the method of ascertaining customary law in the field of human rights and humanitarian law may in due course have an impact on general international law, in particular in fields where the stakes are high. In these fields, such as international environmental law, where truly global or planetary interests—as opposed to the aggregated interests of individual states—are at stake, extrapolation is undoubtedly desirable to safeguard humanity's common values and destiny. In these fields, the traditional requirement of consistency of state practice may be played down a bit, provided that a strong *opinio juris*, democratically informed by global state consent, has crystallized in international fora.

---

[81] The United Kingdom has advanced such an exception in its written pleadings in the *Fisheries Case*, ICJ Pleadings, II, 426–7, but it was not addressed by the Court. The ILA's Committee on Formation of Customary (General) International Law has submitted that '[t]o the extent that the "fundamental principle" in question forms part of the *jus dispositivum* and not the *jus cogens*, there seem to be no other precedents to support the British position' (above n. 6, 740, footnote omitted).

[82] Roberts, (2001) 95 AJIL 757, 767–768. Also International Law Association, Committee on Formation of Customary (General) International Law, Final Report (2000) 734, Rule 14 (ii) ('Subject to the rules about persistent objection...for a specific State to be bound by a rule of general customary international law it is not necessary to prove that it participated actively in the practice or deliberately acquiesced in it.').

7

Impact on the Structure of International Obligations

*Sandesh Sivakumaran**

1. Introduction

International obligations traditionally have been viewed as reciprocal and non-hierarchical. They were generally considered bilateral with the injured state alone being able to institute proceedings in the event of their violation. Norms were norms and any relativity between them was rejected. Over time, particularly in the second half of the 20th century, there has been movement away from the strict bilateral and non-hierarchical nature of the international obligation. Concepts such as obligations *erga omnes* and *jus cogens* norms have garnered acceptance and have restructured international obligations. There has been movement towards different types of obligations—obligations owed to a single state or to the international community as a whole—and varying levels of norms—ordinary and peremptory. Norms for the protection of the human person have been central to these shifts.

This chapter will assess the extent to which international human rights law has impacted upon the structure of international obligations, focusing on obligations *erga omnes* and *jus cogens* norms.

PART I: STANDING

2. The Classical Model

Traditionally, a state could protect only its own rights and those of its nationals, the latter being considered part of the former. The International Court of Justice, and the Permanent Court of International Justice before it, not infrequently referred to the general rule that '[b]y taking up the case of one of its subjects and by

* Lecturer at the School of Law and Fellow of the Human Rights Law Centre, University of Nottingham.

resorting to diplomatic action or international judicial proceedings on his behalf, a State is in reality asserting its own rights—its right to ensure, in the person of its subjects, respect for the rules of international law.'[1] Indeed, the famous dictum continued: 'Once a State has taken up a case on behalf of one of its subjects before an international tribunal, in the eyes of the latter the State is sole claimant'.[2] The dispute between an individual and a third state was thus translated into a dispute between the state of nationality of the individual and the third state, the injury to the individual being eclipsed by the injury to the national state.

The movement from the individual to the state presupposed a certain nexus between the individual and the state. Traditionally, the concept of nationality fulfilled that link. As the Permanent Court explained, 'it is the bond of nationality between the State and the individual which alone confers upon the State the right of diplomatic protection'.[3] Accordingly, and importantly for the classical model, a state could not exercise diplomatic protection on behalf of foreign nationals,[4] for it did not suffer any injury upon the injury to the foreign national.

The very idea of diplomatic protection thus rested on two bases. First, the third state should have violated its obligation 'towards the national State in respect of its nationals' and secondly, only the state to whom the obligation was owed could bring a claim alleging its breach.[5] These two bases made it near impossible for an altruistic state that sought to protect the nationals of a third state, or a state that had bonds of, say, ethnicity with nationals of a third state, to espouse a judicial claim on their behalf. Absent the bond of nationality, little could be done by way of the institution of judicial proceedings.

This classical approach reached its high point in the infamous second phase of the *South West Africa* cases. As is well known, Ethiopia and Liberia instituted proceedings against South Africa in relation to the latter's conduct in South West Africa. The applicants alleged that South Africa, through its conduct and particularly its policy of apartheid, violated its obligations under the mandate. The case was thus brought 'on behalf of' the inhabitants of South West Africa and not on behalf of Ethiopian or Liberian nationals. In its judgment on preliminary objections, the Court found that Ethiopia and Liberia had standing to bring the case.[6] In the second phase, however, a differently constituted Court distinguished between the applicants' standing and their legal interest in the subject matter of the claim and

---

[1] *Mavrommatis Palestine Concessions (Jurisdiction) (Greece v. United Kingdom)* 1924 PCIJ Series A, No. 2, 12. See also e.g. *Case Concerning the Payment of Various Serbian Loans Issued in France (France v. Kingdom of the Serbs, Croats and Slovenes)* 1929, PCIJ Series A, No. 20; *Case Concerning the Payment in Gold of the Brazilian Federal Loans Issued in France (France v. Brazil)* 1929 PCIJ, Series A No. 20–21, 17; *Nottebohm (Liechtenstein v. Guatemala)* 1955 ICJ Reports 4, 24.

[2] Mavrommatis, ibid.

[3] *Panevezys-Saldutiskis Railway Case (Estonia v. Lithuania)* 1939 PCIJ Series A/B, No. 76, 16.

[4] Ibid.

[5] *Reparation for Injuries Suffered in the Service of the United Nations*, Advisory Opinion of 11 April 1949, 1949 ICJ Reports 174, 181–182.

[6] *South West Africa (Ethiopia v. South Africa; Liberia v. South Africa)*, Preliminary Objections, Judgment of 21 December 1962, 1962 ICJ Reports 319.

found the necessary interest to be lacking.[7] The Court drew a distinction between the 'special interests' provisions of the mandate, namely the rights of missionaries who were nationals of League of Nations member states to practise their calling in the mandated territory and the 'conduct' provisions of the mandate, which related to the treatment by the mandatary of the inhabitants of the mandated territory. The Court found that Ethiopia and Liberia had a legal interest in the 'special interests' provisions of the mandate but not in the 'conduct' provisions of the mandate.[8]

The Court was not wholly averse to the idea of intangible rights or non-material interests but it required such rights or interests to be 'clearly vested' in those who claimed them and that was found not to be the case of individual members of the League of Nations.[9] The Court thought it 'remarkable' if 'so important a right, having such potentially far-reaching consequences... had been created indirectly, and in so casual and almost incidental a fashion, by an ordinary jurisdictional clause'.[10] The jurisdictional clause under the mandate was considered singularly unexceptional and could not support a claim for a legal interest with respect to the 'conduct' provisions. Accordingly, Ethiopia and Liberia, not having suffered injury themselves, could not show the required interest in the subject matter of the claim in order to bring judicial proceedings.

3. The Impact of Obligations *Erga Omnes*[11]

A mere four years after the judgment of the Court in the second phase of *South West Africa*, a judgment that had received trenchant criticism, the Court essentially revisited its finding. In the *Barcelona Traction* case, the Court reasoned:

When a State admits into its territory foreign investments or foreign nationals, whether natural or juristic persons, it is bound to extend to them the protection of the law and assumes obligations concerning the treatment to be afforded them. These obligations, however, are

---

[7] The distinction between standing and legal interest in the two phases has been criticized. See e.g. J. Dugard, '*South West Africa Cases*, Second Phase 1966' (1966) 83 South African LJ 429; R. Higgins, 'The International Court and South West Africa: the Implications of the Judgment' (1966) 42 *International Affairs* 573.

[8] *South West Africa Cases (Ethiopia v. South Africa; Liberia v. South Africa)*, Second Phase, Judgment of 18 July 1966, 1966 ICJ Reports 6. On the dispute generally, see J. Dugard, *The South West Africa/Namibia Dispute* (University of California Press, Berkeley 1973).

[9] *South West Africa*, Second Phase, ibid, para. 44.

[10] Ibid., para. 63.

[11] The concept of obligations *erga omnes* means many things to many people, sometimes even different things to the same institution. The ICJ has used it in a number of different respects, for example *Nuclear Tests (Australia v. France)*, Judgment of 20 December 1974, 1974 ICJ Reports 253, paras 50 and 52; *Application of the Convention on the Prevention and Punishment of the Crime of Genocide (Bosnia and Herzegovina v. Yugoslavia)*, Preliminary Objections, Judgment of 11 July 1996, 1996 ICJ Reports 595, para. 31; *Legal Consequences of the Construction of a Wall in the Occupied Palestinian Territory*, Advisory Opinion of 9 July 2004, 2004 ICJ Reports 136, paras 154–159. In this paper, it refers solely to its orthodox usage, namely the 'very specific issue of jurisdictional *locus standi*': *Palestinian Wall*, Separate Opinion of Judge Higgins, para. 37.

neither absolute nor unqualified. In particular, an essential distinction should be drawn between the obligations of a State towards the international community as a whole, and those arising vis-à-vis another State in the field of diplomatic protection. By their very nature the former are the concern of all States. In view of the importance of the rights involved, all States can be held to have a legal interest in their protection; they are obligations *erga omnes*.

Such obligations derive, for example, in contemporary international law, from the outlawing of acts of aggression, and of genocide, as also from the principles and rules concerning the basic rights of the human person, including protection from slavery and racial discrimination. Some of the corresponding rights of protection have entered into the body of general international law (*Reservations to the Convention on the Prevention and Punishment of the Crime of Genocide, Advisory Opinion*[12]); others are conferred by international instruments of a universal or quasi-universal character.[13]

Given that the subject matter of the case did not require any such comment, this passage, with its reference to legal interests, may be seen as reflecting a certain reaction on the part of the Court to its earlier judgment in *South West Africa*.[14] According to the Court, there are certain obligations that are owed to the international community as a whole. All states have a legal interest in their protection without the need for a special interest or a particular injury. On this basis, Ethiopia and Liberia would have been able to challenge South Africa's conduct in South West Africa. In two short paragraphs, the Court fundamentally changed the way in which a claim may be espoused.

Such was the potential for change that Judge de Castro famously remarked that the passage 'should be taken *cum grano salis*', writing: 'I am unable to believe that by virtue of this dictum the Court would regard as admissible, for example, a claim by state A against state B that B was not applying "principles and rules concerning the basic rights of the human person" . . . with regard to the subjects of state B or even state C.'[15]

3.1 Human rights and obligations *erga omnes*

The *Barcelona Traction* dictum is of considerable import, not only for what it means for the rules of jurisdictional *locus standi* but also in its move away from the bilateral and towards the community.[16] The Court expressly recognized the

---

[12] 1951 ICJ Reports 23.

[13] *Barcelona Traction, Light and Power Company, Limited (Belgium v. Spain)* (New Application: 1962), Judgment of 5 February 1970, 1970 ICJ Reports 3, 32.

[14] A number of commentators have taken this view, for example J. Crawford, *The Creation of States in International Law* (Oxford University Press, Oxford 2006) 103; J. Dugard, '1966 And All That: The South West Africa Judgment Revisited in the East Timor Case' (1996) 8 African J Intl Comp L 549, 553–554; O. Schachter, *International Law in Theory and Practice* (Martinus Nijhoff, The Hague 1991) 344.

[15] *Nuclear Tests*, 1974 ICJ Reports 253, Dissenting Opinion of Judge de Castro 387. For a similar view, see F.A. Mann, 'The Doctrine of *Jus Cogens* in International Law' in F.A. Mann (ed.), *Further Studies in International Law* (Clarendon Press, Oxford 1990) 91.

[16] See B. Simma, 'From Bilateralism to Community Interest in International Law' (1994) VI 250 RdC 217.

existence of an international community and went on to imbue that community with interests and values. These community interests relate primarily to the protection of the human person. Indeed, of the obligations mentioned, all but one relates directly to human rights and even that one is not altogether removed. Today, the obligation to respect the right to self-determination,[17] certain (unspecified) obligations of international humanitarian law,[18] protection from torture,[19] and other peremptory norms,[20] may be added to the list of community values and obligations *erga omnes*. That most obligations *erga omnes* relate to the protection of the human person is not surprising given that '[i]n these fields, the law does not create reciprocal obligations between States in the bilateralist manner.'[21] The list is not a model of clarity. Debate has surrounded the phrase 'basic rights' of the human person and the extent to which the Court was intending to distinguish between basic rights and other rights.[22] A later paragraph of the *Barcelona Traction* judgment is also seemingly inconsistent with the passage cited above.[23] Still, the impact of these two paragraphs is potentially great. It has been described as sounding 'the death knell of narrow bilateralism and sanctified egoism for the sake of the universal protection of certain fundamental norms relating, in particular, to human rights.'[24]

The idea that a state has a legal interest in the treatment of foreign nationals does have a certain history. Diplomatic representations, for example, have long been brought on behalf of foreign nationals.[25] There exists less by way of the institution of judicial proceedings on behalf of foreign nationals but even in this respect there has not been silence. As the Court noted in its *Reparation* opinion, 'even in inter-State relations, there are important exceptions to the rule [on diplomatic protection], for there are cases in which protection may be exercised by a State on behalf of persons not having its nationality.'[26] These cases relate primarily, though not exclusively,[27] to the protection of the human person.

---

[17] *East Timor (Portugal v. Australia)*, Judgment of 30 June 1995, 1995 ICJ Reports 90, para. 29; *Legal Consequences of the Construction of a Wall in the Occupied Palestinian Territory*, Advisory Opinion of 9 July 2004, 2004 ICJ Reports 136, paras 88, 156.

[18] *Palestinian Wall*, ibid, para. 155.

[19] *Prosecutor v. Furundžija*, ICTY-95-17/1-T, Judgment of 10 December 1998, para. 151.

[20] See Part 2.

[21] Report of the Study Group of the International Law Commission, Fragmentation of International Law: Difficulties Arising from the Diversification and Expansion of International Law, UN Doc. A/CN.4/L.682, para. 391.

[22] On which, see T. Meron, 'On a Hierarchy of International Human Rights' (1986) 80 AJIL 1; M. Ragazzi, *The Concept of International Obligations* Erga Omnes (Clarendon Press, Oxford 1997) 139–145.

[23] Para. 91. For reconciliation, see Simma (1994) 250 RdC 217, 296.

[24] P. Weil, 'Relative Normativity in International Law' (1983) 77 AJIL 413, 432.

[25] See M.T. Kamminga, *Inter-State Accountability for Violations of Human Rights* (University of Pennsylvania Press, Philadelphia 1992) Chapter 1.

[26] *Reparation for Injuries*, 1949 ICJ Reports 174, 181.

[27] *Case of the S.S. 'Wimbledon' (United Kingdom and others v. Germany)* 1923, PCIJ Series A, No. 1; *Interpretation of the Statute of the Memel Territory (United Kingdom and others v. Lithuania)*, 1932, PCIJ Series A/B, No. 47 and No. 49. See generally *South West Africa, Preliminary Objections*,

The Constitution of the International Labour Organization provides that 'Any of the Members shall have the right to file a complaint with the International Labour Office if it is not satisfied that any other Member is securing the effective observance of any Convention which both have ratified in accordance with the foregoing articles.'[28] Even prior to the judgment of the Court in *South West Africa*, two Commissions of Inquiry had been established pursuant to a complaint filed under the aforementioned provision of the Constitution.[29] The first was established to adjudicate upon a complaint by Ghana that Portugal was not 'securing the effective observance in her African territories of Mozambique, Angola and Guinea of Convention No. 105 [on Forced Labour], which both Portugal and the Republic of Ghana have ratified.'[30] A second examined the complaint of Portugal against Liberia alleging non-compliance with ILO Convention No. 29 on Forced Labour. No special interest was required of either Ghana or Portugal. The Governing Body, in deciding to appoint the second Commission, noted that the filing of such a complaint 'represents the exercise of a constitutional right provided for in the Constitution of the International Labour Organisation.'[31] Judge Jessup observed in relation to the first complaint: '[t]he fact which this case establishes is that a State may have a legal interest in the observance, in the territories of another State, of general welfare treaty provisions and that it may assert such interest without alleging any impact upon its own nationals or its direct so-called tangible or material interests.'[32]

Treaties 'having a broad humanitarian interest'[33] are another example. Article IX of the Genocide Convention provides that '[d]isputes between the Contracting Parties relating to the interpretation, application or fulfilment of the present Convention, including those relating to the responsibility of a state for genocide or for any of the other acts enumerated in article III, shall be submitted to the International Court of Justice at the request of any of the parties to the dispute.' The European Convention on Human Rights similarly provides that '[a]ny High Contracting Party may refer to the Court any alleged breach of the provisions of the Convention and the protocols thereto by another High Contracting Party.'[34] Early

---

1962 ICJ Reports 319, Separate Opinion of Judge Jessup, 425; *South West Africa, Second Phase*, 1966 ICJ Reports 6, Dissenting Opinion of Judge Jessup, 511; C. Tams, *Enforcing Obligations* Erga Omnes *in International Law* (Cambridge University Press, Cambridge 2005) 75–79; E. Schwelb, The *Actio Popularis* and International Law (1972) 2 Israel Ybk HR 46, 54–55.

[28] Constitution of the International Labour Organization, Article 26(1).

[29] See Kamminga, *Inter-State Accountability for Violations of Human Rights* (1992) 148; S. Leckie, 'The Inter-State Complaint Procedure in International Human Rights Law: Hopeful Prospects or Wishful Thinking?' (1988) 10 HRQ 249, 277–289.

[30] Complaint by the Government of Ghana concerning the Observance by the Government of Portugal of the Abolition of Forced Labour Convention, 1957 35 ILR 285, 286.

[31] Complaint by the Government of Portugal concerning the Observance by the Government of Liberia of the Forced Labour Convention, 1930 36 ILR 351, 358.

[32] *South West Africa, Preliminary Objections,* 1962 ICJ Reports 319, Separate Opinion of Judge Jessup 428.

[33] Ibid., 426.

[34] Convention for the Protection of Human Rights and Fundamental Freedoms, Article 33 (ex-Article 24).

use of this provision included the *Pfunders* case in which the European Commission of Human Rights noted that 'the High Contracting Parties have empowered any one of their number to bring before the Commission any alleged breach of the Convention, regardless of whether the victims of the alleged breach are nationals of the applicant State or whether the alleged breach otherwise particularly affects the interests of the applicant State'.[35] Foreshadowing the idea of an international community with particular interests and values, the European Commission observed that when a state party refers an alleged breach under ex-Article 24 of the Convention, it 'is not to be regarded as exercising a right of action for the purposes of enforcing its own rights, but rather as bringing before the Commission an alleged violation of the public order of Europe.'[36] The referring state in such a situation is 'fulfilling its role as one of the collective guarantors of Convention rights.'[37]

The inter-war minorities treaties, of which the 1919 Treaty between Poland and the Principal Allied and Associated Powers formed the model, constitutes a third example. The Polish minorities treaty afforded certain minority rights to inhabitants of Poland. Article 12 of that treaty provided that: 'Poland agrees that any member of the Council of the League of Nations shall have the right to bring to the attention of the Council any infraction, or any danger of infraction, of any of these obligations'. The Article went on to provide that Poland agrees that any 'difference of opinion as to questions of law or fact arising out of these articles' may be referred to the PCIJ by 'any one of the Principal Allied and Associated Powers or any other Power, a member of the Council of the League of Nations'.[38] The latter part of this Article thus gave standing to those members of the Council of the League that were not Principal Allied or Associated Powers and therefore not a party to the treaty in question. Standing was thus derived, not from the treaty but from membership in the Council of the League of Nations.

3.2 Obligations *erga omnes* in practice

Given that all states have a legal interest in the protection of certain rights, it may have been thought that the floodgates would open, or at the very least that the traditional system of diplomatic protection would have been overtaken. After all, 'Foreign Offices of the world' had been 'advised to review their acceptances of the optional clause' consenting to the jurisdiction of the Court.[39] However, as Schachter presciently forecast, states would 'hesitate to open a Pandora's box

---

[35] *Austria v. Italy (dec.)*, ECmHR, (1961) 4 Yearbook 116, 140. See also *Denmark, France, The Netherlands, Norway and Sweden v. Turkey (dec.)*, ECmHR, (1983) 26 Yearbook 30.

[36] *Austria v. Italy*, ibid., 140. See also *Denmark, France, The Netherlands, Norway and Sweden v. Turkey*, ibid., 30.

[37] D.J. Harris, M. O'Boyle and C. Warbrick, *Law of the European Convention on Human Rights* (Butterworths, London 1995) 585.

[38] Treaty of Peace Between the United States of America, the British Empire, France, Italy, and Japan and Poland (1919) 13 AJIL Supp. 423, 429.

[39] Mann, *The Doctrine of Jus Cogens in International Law* (1990) 91.

which would allow every member of the now numerous community of States to become a "prosecutor" in judicial proceedings on behalf of the human rights of all persons.'[40] Indeed, the issue has been raised in only a handful of cases and for various reasons the Court has not had occasion to explore the concept.

In the *Nuclear Tests* case, Australia and New Zealand argued that there was an obligation against atmospheric nuclear testing and that such an obligation was an obligation *erga omnes*.[41] The dispute was eventually considered moot and the precise contention of the applicants was not considered, but a number of individual judges commented upon the argument. Judge Sir Garfield Barwick observed that '[i]f this submission were accepted, the Applicant would, in my opinion, have the requisite legal interest, the *locus standi* to maintain this basis of its claim.'[42] In *Armed Activities on the Territory of the Congo,* Judge Simma noted that a state has standing to bring a claim on behalf of an individual whose human rights have been violated and who may or may not possess the nationality of that state.[43] The issue was not considered by the full Court. In the *Bosnia Genocide* case, Bosnia and Herzegovina requested the Court rule on 'acts of genocide and other unlawful acts allegedly committed against "non-Serbs" outside its own territory' by Serbia and Montenegro. The Court recognized that '[i]nsofar as that request might relate to non-Bosnian victims, it could raise questions about the legal interest or standing of the Applicant in respect of such matters and the significance of the *jus cogens* character of the relevant norms, and the *erga omnes* character of the relevant obligations.'[44] However, given the Court's other findings, it did not pronounce on the issue.

Obligations *erga omnes* also have their limits. The fact that a state has a legal interest in the subject matter of a claim does not mean that the Court automatically has jurisdiction to hear the case. In *East Timor*, the Court noted that 'the *erga omnes* character of a norm and the rule of consent to jurisdiction are two different things.'[45] The indispensible third party rule, for example, will apply equally to a case concerning obligations *erga omnes* as to a case involving a strictly bilateral obligation.[46] This has been described as avoiding any 'radical restructuring

---

[40] Schachter, *International Law in Theory and Practice* (1991) 345.

[41] *Nuclear Tests (Australia v. France)* ICJ Pleadings: Vol. I, 334–5; *Nuclear Tests (New Zealand v. France)* ICJ Pleadings: Vol. II, 204.

[42] *Nuclear Tests (Australia v. France)*, 1974 ICJ Reports 253, Dissenting Opinion of Judge Sir Garfield Barwick 437. See also Joint Dissenting Opinion of Judges Onyeama, Dillard, Jiménez de Aréchaga and Sir Humphrey Waldock 369–370, which Tams (*Enforcing Obligations Erga Omnes* (2005) 181) views as 'cautious endorsement' of the applicants' position.

[43] *Armed Activities on the Territory of the Congo (Democratic Republic of the Congo v. Uganda)*, Judgment of 19 December 2005, 2005 ICJ Reports 168, Separate Opinion of Judge Simma, para. 35.

[44] *Application of the Convention on the Prevention and Punishment of the Crime of Genocide (Bosnia and Herzegovina v. Serbia and Montenegro)*, Judgment of 26 February 2007, 2007 ICJ Reports, para. 185.

[45] *East Timor*, 1995 ICJ Reports 90, para. 29.

[46] Ibid., cf Dissenting Opinion of Judge Weeramantry 213–216; Separate Opinion of Judge Ranjeva 131.

of the hierarchy of international norms, by favouring procedural requirements over substantive change.'[47] However, the distinction has been reaffirmed in later cases with the added statement that 'the mere fact that rights and obligations *erga omnes* may be at issue in a dispute would not give the Court jurisdiction to entertain that dispute.'[48]

Despite the reticence of the Court, the idea of obligations *erga omnes* has spread to other international bodies and may be considered an established part of the international legal architecture. The International Law Commission (ILC)'s Articles on State Responsibility provide the most important example, Article 48 of which provides:

Any State other than an injured State is entitled to invoke the responsibility of another State...if:

(a) the obligation breached is owed to a group of States including that State, and is established for the protection of a collective interest of the group; or
(b) the obligation breached is owed to the international community as a whole.[49]

The Commentary to this provision reveals that the Article is intended to give effect to the relevant passage in *Barcelona Traction* and is 'a deliberate departure' from the second phase of *South West Africa*.[50] In a similar vein, the Commentary to the ILC's Draft Articles on Diplomatic Protection provides that 'customary international law allows States to protect the rights of non-nationals by protest, negotiation and, if a jurisdictional instrument so permits, legal proceedings.'[51]

For its part, the *Institut de droit international* has observed that: '[i]n the event of there being a jurisdictional link between a State alleged to have committed a breach of an obligation *erga omnes* and a State to which the obligation is owed, the latter State has standing to bring a claim to the International Court of Justice or other international judicial institution in relation to a dispute concerning compliance with that obligation.'[52]

---

[47] C. Chinkin, '*The East Timor Case (Portugal v. Australia)*' (1996) 45 ICLQ 712, 721–722. See also C. Chinkin, *Third Parties in International Law* (Clarendon Press, Oxford 1993) 211–212. Cf C. Tomuschat, 'Article 36', in A. Zimmerman, C. Tomuschat and K. Oellers-Frahm (eds.), *The Statute of the International Court of Justice: A Commentary* (Oxford University Press, Oxford 2006) 606.

[48] *Armed Activities on the Territory of the Congo (New Application: 2002) (Democratic Republic of the Congo v. Rwanda)*, Judgment of 3 February 2006, 2006 ICJ Reports 6, paras 64 and 125.

[49] ILC, Articles on Responsibility of States for Internationally Wrongful Acts, GA Res 56/83, Annex, Article 48. See also R. Ago, Fifth Report on State Responsibility, Ybk ILC 1976-II (Part I) 28–29; J. Crawford, Third Report on State Responsibility, UN Doc. A/CN.4/507 (15 March 2000) 29–55.

[50] ILC, Commentary to the Draft Articles on Responsibility of States for Internationally Wrongful Acts, Commentary to Article 48(8) and fn 725. See also International Law Commission, Commentary to the Draft Articles on Diplomatic Protection, UN Doc. A/61/10, Commentary to Article 16(2).

[51] Commentary to Draft Articles on Diplomatic Protection, ibid., Article 16(2).

[52] Institut de droit international, Resolution on 'Obligations *erga omnes* in International Law' (Krakow 2005) Article 3.

Treaty-based non-special interest provisions also continue apace.[53] Various international and regional human rights instruments authorize inter-state applications, however, some of these require separate acceptance on the part of states parties and even then are used infrequently.[54] For this reason, states have been urged to utilize this procedure more effectively. The UN Human Rights Committee has reminded states parties 'of the desirability of making the dec-laration contemplated in article 41' of the International Covenant on Civil and Political Rights and has reminded those that have made the declaration 'of the potential value of availing themselves of the procedure under that article.'[55] At the Inter-American level, Judge Cançado Trindade has stated that 'there could hardly be better examples of mechanism for application of the obligations *erga omnes* of protection (at least in the relations of the States Parties *inter se*) than the methods of supervision foreseen *in the human rights treaties themselves*, for the exercise of the collective guarantee of the protected rights.'[56] The Parliamentary Assembly of the Council of Europe has also appealed to states to use Article 33 of the European Convention on Human Rights 'as a matter of urgency and to refer to the European Court of Human Rights alleged breaches by the Russian Federation of the provisions of the Convention and its Protocols.'[57]

PART 2: HIERARCHY OF NORMS

Domestic legal systems have some form of hierarchy of norms, whether expressed through a constitutional provision, or ideas of public policy or public order. These 'higher' norms take precedence over other norms in the event and to the extent of any inconsistency between them. Thus, legislation may be rendered invalid or contracts void for violation of a higher norm.

There has been much discussion and considerable disagreement as to whether this was also true of the international legal system. Some took the view that there was no distinction within norms, only between norms and non-norms.[58] Emphasis was placed on the voluntarist nature of international law and the com-plete freedom of states to interact with one another. Others opined that certain norms as higher or peremptory have a long history at the international level,

---

[53] For a recent example, see Agreement between the Government of the Federal Democratic Republic of Ethiopia and the Government of the State of Eritrea, Article 5(9), (2001) 40 ILM 260.

[54] International Covenant on Civil and Political Rights, Article 41; American Convention on Human Rights, Article 45; Convention against Torture and Other Cruel, Inhuman or Degrading Treatment or Punishment, Article 21.

[55] UN Human Rights Committee, General Comment No. 31, Nature of the General Legal Obligation Imposed on States Parties to the Covenant, UN Doc. CCPR/C/21/Rev.1/Add.13, para. 2.

[56] *Las Palmeras v. Colombia* (Preliminary Objections), IACtHR, Judgment of 4 February 2000, Series C No. 67, Separate Opinion of Judge Cançado Trindade, para. 14.

[57] Recommendation 1456 (2000), para. 18.

[58] See e.g. Weil, (1983) 77 AJIL 413, 421.

the idea even being described as 'older than modern international law itself'.[59] Critics of the concept queried its utility, uncertainties surrounding its formation and content, and its impact on 'ordinary' norms.[60] Those in favour felt that the concept of higher norms was an inevitable part of an international system that was not purely consensual and which reflected basic values of the international community. While states may disregard many rules in their relations with one another, they remained subject to these basic values.

4. Identification of Peremptory Norms

Today, the debates revolve around the content of the category of peremptory norms and their impact. It is commonplace to read that, although the category of peremptory norms is accepted, their identification remains shrouded in mystery. Contrary to this popular belief, there is relative agreement on the core norms that have peremptory status; the only disagreement relates to those norms at the threshold of such status. There is agreement both on the types of norms that have peremptory status as well as on the concrete norms themselves.[61]

Hersch Lauterpacht, as Special Rapporteur of the ILC on the law of treaties, first proposed that '[a] treaty, or any of its provisions, is void if its performance involves an act which is illegal under international law and if it is declared so to be by the International Court of Justice'. Lauterpacht took the view that the test for illegality was 'inconsistency with such overriding principles of international law which may be regarded as constituting principles of international public policy'.[62] Along similar lines, the next Special Rapporteur, Fitzmaurice, opined that *jus cogens* norms 'involved not only legal rules but considerations of morals and of international good order.'[63] The ILC itself observed that it is the 'particular nature of the subject matter' that determines whether a norm has the character of *jus cogens*,[64] and more recently and most clearly that peremptory norms are 'substantive rules of conduct that prohibit what has come to be seen as intolerable because of the threat it presents to the survival of States and their peoples and the most basic human values.'[65]

So much for the types of norms that are capable of being peremptory. What of the norms themselves? The prohibition on the unlawful use of force is considered

---

[59] Study Group of the ILC, *Fragmentation of International Law*, UN Doc. A/CN.4/L.682, 182.

[60] See e.g. Weil, (1983) 77 AJIL 413; G. Schwarzenberger, 'International *Jus Cogens*' (1964–65) 43 Texas L Rev 455; A. D'Amato, 'It's A Bird, It's A Plane, It's *Jus Cogens*' (1990–91) 6 Connecticut J Intl L 1.

[61] The meanings attributed to *jus cogens* norms are fewer than those of obligations *erga omnes*. To the extent that there are different meanings, discussion in this part will be limited to 'substantive *jus cogens*' and not on what some have termed 'systemic' or 'structural *jus cogens*'.

[62] H. Lauterpacht, First Report on the Law of Treaties, Ybk ILC 1953-II, 155.

[63] G. Fitzmaurice, Third Report of the Law of Treaties, Ybk ILC 1958-II, 41.

[64] ILC, Commentary to Draft Articles on the Law of Treaties, Ybk ILC 1966-II, 248.

[65] Commentary to Articles on State Responsibility, Article 40(3).

by some to represent the classic example of a *jus cogens* norm. Peremptory status is supported by the International Law Commission and the views of individual judges of the Court in such cases as *Nicaragua, Oil Platforms* and the *Wall*.[66] The full Court itself, in *Nicaragua*, stated that: 'The International Law Commission, in the course of its work on the codification of the law of treaties, expressed the view that "the law of the Charter concerning the prohibition of the use of force in itself constitutes a conspicuous example of a rule in international law having the character of *jus cogens*".'[67] This passage is considered by some to show that the Court itself has affirmed the existence of *jus cogens* norms; to others the Court was doing no more than repeating the view of the ILC. At best the position is ambiguous and the Court may well have been deliberate in its ambiguity.

As for other norms considered by international tribunals to have peremptory status, 'the position of the individual is involved, and... the rules contravened are rules instituted for the protection of the individual.'[68] In 2006, for the first time explicitly, the Court, rather than individual members of the Court, identified a norm as having peremptory status. In *Congo v. Rwanda*, the Court stated that the prohibition of genocide is a norm which 'assuredly' has the character of a peremptory norm.[69] This has been the consistent view of the *ad hoc* international criminal tribunals as well as the International Law Commission.[70] It should not go unnoticed that the first time in which the Court explicitly referred to a norm of *jus cogens* was in the context of genocide, the very worst offence that may be committed against the human person, the prohibition of which Judge ad hoc Lauterpacht had described as 'one of the few undoubted examples of *jus cogens*.'[71]

More contentious is the idea that fundamental human rights have the status of peremptory norms. Some have gone further and claimed that all human rights

---

[66] H. Waldock, Second Report on the Law of Treaties, Ybk ILC 1963-II, 52–53; Commentary to Draft Articles on the Law of Treaties, Ybk ILC 1966-II, 247–248; ILC, Commentary to Draft Articles on the Law of Treaties between States and International Organizations or between International Organizations, Ybk ILC 1982-II, 56; Commentary to Articles on State Responsibility, Article 40(4) and Article 26(5); *Military and Paramilitary Activities In and Against Nicaragua*, 1986 ICJ Reports 14, Separate Opinion of Judge Nagendra Singh 153 and Separate Opinion of Judge Sette-Camara 199–200; *Oil Platforms (Islamic Republic of Iran v. United States of America)*, Judgment of 6 November 2003, 2003 ICJ Reports 161, Separate Opinion of Judge Simma, para. 9 and Dissenting Opinion of Judge Elaraby, para. 1.1; *Legal Consequences of the Construction of a Wall in the Occupied Palestinian Territory*, 2004 ICJ Reports 136, Separate Opinion of Judge Elaraby, para. 3.1.

[67] *Nicaragua*, 1986 ICJ Reports 14, 100.

[68] Fitzmaurice, Third Report, Ybk ILC 1958-II, 40.

[69] *Congo v. Rwanda*, 2006 ICJ Reports 6, para. 64.

[70] See e.g. *Prosecutor v. Kupreškić et al*, ICTY-95–16-T, Judgment of 14 January 2000, para. 520; *Prosecutor v. Kayishema and Ruzindana*, ICTR-95–1-T , Judgment of 21 May 1999, para. 88; ILC Commentary to Articles on State Responsibility, Article 40(4) and Article 26(5); Commentary to Draft Articles on the Law of Treaties, Ybk ILC 1966-II, Article 50(3); Waldock, Second Report, Ybk ILC 1963-II, 52–53.

[71] *Application of the Convention on the Prevention and Punishment of the Crime of Genocide, (Bosnia and Herzegovina v. Yugoslavia)* Provisional Measures, Order of 13 September 1993, 1993 ICJ Reports 325, Separate Opinion of Judge ad hoc Lauterpacht, para. 100.

have peremptory status, Judge Tanaka, for example, arguing that 'surely the law concerning the protection of human rights may be considered to belong to the *jus cogens*.'[72] International law has not yet moved to that position, so which fundamental human rights have the status of *jus cogens* norms? There is general agreement over the right to self-determination,[73] the prohibitions against slavery and the slave trade,[74] and against racial discrimination and apartheid.[75] Others with varying degrees of support are the prohibition of torture,[76] the right to life,[77] and the right to equality and non-discrimination.[78] Linked with fundamental human rights are the prohibition of crimes against humanity,[79] and the prohibition of piracy as peremptory norms.[80]

Fundamental rules of international humanitarian law may also lay claim to peremptory status. This has the support of the ILC and individual judges of the Court.[81] Again, however, we are left with the issue of precisely which rules have peremptory status. In concrete terms, this has been said to include the prohibition of hostilities directed at the civilian population and the execution of prisoners of war.[82] Rather more broadly, it has been contended to include the 'fundamental

---

[72] *South West Africa, Second Phase*, 1966 ICJ Reports 6, Dissenting Opinion of Judge Tanaka 298.

[73] *Barcelona Traction*, 1970 ICJ Reports 3, Separate Opinion of Judge Ammoun 72; Commentary to Articles on State Responsibility, Article 40(5) and Article 26(5).

[74] Waldock, Second Report, Ybk ILC 1963-II, 53 ('slave trade'); Commentary to Draft Articles on the Law of Treaties, Ybk ILC 1966-II, Article 50(3) ('trade in slaves'); Commentary to Articles on State Responsibility, Article 26(5) ('slavery') and Article 40(4) ('Slavery and the Slave Trade'); *Rights of the Undocumented Migrants*, IACtHR, Advisory Opinion OC-18 of 17 September 2003, Series A No. 18, Separate Opinion of Judge Cançado Trindade, para. 72.

[75] Commentary to Articles on State Responsibility, Article 40(4) and Article 26(5).

[76] *Al-Adsani v. United Kingdom* (App. No. 35763/97), ECtHR, Judgment of 21 November 2001, (2002) 34 EHRR 11, ECHR 2001-XI, para. 61; *Prosecutor v. Furundžija*, ICTY-95-17/1-T, Judgment of 10 December 1998, paras 153–154; Commentary to Articles on State Responsibility, Article 40(5) and Article 26(5); HRCt, General Comment No. 29, UN Doc. CCPR/C/21/Rev.1/Add.11, para. 11.

[77] *Victims of the Tugboat '13 de Marzo' v. Cuba*, IACmHR, Report No. 47/96, Case 11.436, OEA/Ser. L/V/II.95 Doc. 7 rev. at 127 (1997), para. 79; HRCt, General Comment No. 24, UN Doc. CCPR/C/21/Rev.1/Add.6, para. 10 (the prohibition of the 'arbitrary deprivation of life') and General Comment No. 29, UN Doc. CCPR/C/21/Rev.1/Add.11, para. 11.

[78] *Rights of the Undocumented Migrants*, IACtHR, Advisory Opinion OC-18 of 17 September 2003, Series A No. 18, paras 100–101.

[79] Commentary to Articles on State Responsibility, Article 26(5); Commentary to Draft Articles on the Law of Treaties, Ybk ILC 1966-II, 248, para. 3 ('acts criminal under international law'). See also *Prosecutor v. Kupreškić et al*, IT-95–16-T, para. 520 (14 January 2000).

[80] Commentary to Draft Articles on the Law of Treaties, Ybk ILC 1966-II, Article 50(3); Waldock, Second Report, Ybk ILC 1963-II, 52–53; *Application of the Convention of 1902 Governing the Guardianship of Infants (Netherlands v. Sweden)*, Judgment of 28 November 1958, 1958 ICJ Reports 55, Separate Opinion of Judge Moreno Quintana 106–107.

[81] Commentary to Articles on State Responsibility, Article 40(5); *Legality of the Threat or Use of Nuclear Weapons*, Advisory Opinion of 8 July 1996, 1996 ICJ Reports 226, Declaration of Judge Bedjaoui 273, Dissenting Opinion of Judge Koroma 574, Dissenting Opinion of Judge Weeramantry 496.

[82] Study Group of the ILC, Fragmentation of International Law, UN Doc. A/CN.4/L.682, para. 374 and Fitzmaurice, Third Report, Ybk ILC 1958-II, 39, respectively.

principles' of the 1949 Geneva Conventions,[83] 'most norms of international humanitarian law'[84] or 'most of the principles and rules of humanitarian law'.[85] A counterpart to this is the suggestion that the prohibition of war crimes has peremptory status.[86]

5. The Impact of Peremptory Norms

Peremptory norms are thus by and large human rights norms. This shows the concern of the international community for the protection of the human person. Certain human rights norms are non-negotiable; they cannot be bartered away or trumped. These norms represent the values of the international community and serve as its foundation. But how far does international law go in respect of these norms? It is one thing to pay lip service to their existence and another altogether to use them in practice.

The principal effect of *jus cogens* norms remains in the law of treaties. Article 53 of the Vienna Convention on the Law of Treaties, entitled '[t]reaties conflicting with a peremptory norm of general international law (*jus cogens*)' provides that:

A treaty is void if, at the time of its conclusion, it conflicts with a peremptory norm of general international law. For the purposes of the present Convention, a peremptory norm of general international law is a norm accepted and recognized by the international community of States as a whole as a norm from which no derogation is permitted and which can be modified only by a subsequent norm of general international law having the same character.

Similarly, Article 64 provides that '[i]f a new peremptory norm of general international law emerges, any existing treaty which is in conflict with that norm becomes void and terminates.'

The conclusion of these Articles was not without a certain amount of hostility. Although members of the ILC were almost entirely in agreement with the existence of peremptory norms, the same could not be said of states.[87] While many states did support the inclusion of provisions on *jus cogens* norms, others were less enthusiastic.[88] The same was true of the 1986 Vienna Convention on the Law of Treaties between States and International Organizations which contains

---

[83] Waldock, Second Report, Ybk ILC 1963-II, 59.

[84] *Prosecutor v. Kupreškić et al*, ICTY-95–16-T, Judgment of 14 January 2000, para. 520.

[85] *Nuclear Weapons* Advisory Opinion, 1996 ICJ Reports 226, Declaration of Judge Bedjaoui 273.

[86] *Prosecutor v. Kupreškić et al*, ICTY-95-16-T, Judgment of 14 January 2000, para. 520.

[87] For a helpful overview of the various positions, see L. Hannikainen, *Peremptory Norms (Jus Cogens) in International Law* (Lakimiesliiton Kustannus, Helsinki 1988) 166.

[88] For an exposition of the French position, see O. Deleau, 'Les positions françaises à la conférence de Vienne sur le droit des traités' (1969) 15 AFDI 7, 16. See also the references cited in Ragazzi, *The Concept of International Obligations Erga Omnes* (1997) 70, n. 104.

provisions on *jus cogens* norms similar to those of the 1969 Vienna Convention. The ILC took the view that the application of peremptory norms to international organizations was unsurprising,[89] and states were generally receptive subject to a few exceptions.[90]

The rules set out in the 1969 Vienna Convention have been reiterated many times in judicial decisions. Instances of application of the rule, however, remain few and far between, the oft-cited exceptions being the 1978 Treaty of Friendship, Goodneighborliness and Cooperation between the USSR and Afghanistan and a treaty between Germany and the Vichy regime relating to the use of French prisoners of war in the armament industry.[91]

Another aspect of the impact of peremptory norms on the law of treaties is the extent to which a reservation may be entered to a treaty, the subject of which is a peremptory norm. In the *North Sea Continental Shelf* cases, Judge Padilla Nervo took the view that '[c]ustomary rules belonging to the category of *jus cogens* cannot be subjected to unilateral reservations.'[92] A similar view has been expressed by the UN Human Rights Committee, to the effect that reservations that 'offend peremptory norms would not be compatible with the object and purpose of the Covenant' on Civil and Political Rights and would accordingly be prohibited.[93] There has also been some discussion as to whether a reservation to a compromissory clause may be incompatible with the object and purpose of a treaty.[94] These issues are not uncontroversial,[95] and the entire subject is currently under consideration by the International Law Commission.[96]

Today, it is generally agreed that peremptory norms also have a life outside the law of treaties, penetrating almost all areas of international law.[97] The Inter-American Court of Human Rights, for example, has taken the view that

[89] Commentary to Draft Articles on the Law of Treaties between States and International Organizations or between International Organizations, Ybk ILC 1982-II, 56.

[90] United Nations Conference on the Law of Treaties between States and International Organizations or Between International Organizations, UN Doc. A/CONF.129/16, 18 and 185–191.

[91] See the memorandum from the Legal Advisor of the United States State Department to the Acting Secretary of State on the Soviet-Afghan Treaty, (1980) 74 AJIL 418, 419; *United States of America v. Alfred Krupp et al.* (1948) 15 AD 620, 626–627.

[92] *North Sea Continental Shelf (Federal Republic of Germany v. Netherlands; Federal Republic of Germany v. Denmark)*, Judgment of 20 February 1969, 1969 ICJ Reports 3, Separate Opinion of Judge Padilla Nervo 97. See also the Dissenting Opinion of Judge Tanaka at 182.

[93] HRCt, General Comment No. 24, UN Doc. CCPR/C/21/Rev.1/Add.6, paras 6, 8.

[94] *Armed Activities on the Territory of the Congo (Congo v. Rwanda)*, Judgment of 3 February 2006, 2006 ICJ Reports 6, para. 67 and Joint Separate Opinion of Judges Higgins, Kooijmans, Elaraby, Owada, and Simma.

[95] See e.g. the response of France to the General Comment of the HRCt, Report of the Human Rights Committee, Vol. I, UN Doc. A/51/40, 104, para. 3.

[96] See Report of the International Law Commission: Fifty-ninth session, UN Doc. A/62/10 (2007) 99–104.

[97] See generally G. Gaja, 'Jus Cogens Beyond the Vienna Convention' (1981-III) 172 RdC 271; A. Orakhelashvili, *Peremptory Norms in International Law* (Oxford University Press, Oxford 2006).

jus cogens norms have influenced 'the basic principles of the international legal order.'[98] So what is the effect of a norm of *jus cogens* outside the law of treaties?

In the context of state responsibility, the ILC's articles provide for 'additional consequences, not only for the responsible State but for all other States' as a result of a serious breach of an obligation arising under a peremptory norm.[99] As the Special Rapporteur noted, violations of peremptory norms shock the conscience of mankind and this should be reflected in the consequences of their breach.[100] These additional consequences are that 'States shall cooperate to bring to an end through lawful means any serious breach' of an obligation arising under a peremptory norm, that '[n]o State shall recognize as lawful a situation created' by such a breach and that no state should 'render aid or assistance in maintaining that situation.'[101] In *the Wall* opinion, the Court stated that '[g]iven the character and the importance of the rights and obligations involved', namely the right to self-determination and certain obligations of international humanitarian law, 'all States are under an obligation not to recognize the illegal situation resulting from the construction of the wall... They are also under an obligation not to render aid or assistance in maintaining the situation created by such construction.'[102] Although no reference to *jus cogens* norms was made, the matter being treated as stemming from obligations *erga omnes*, the parallel with the ILC's articles on state responsibility is clear.[103]

There is a growing view that respect for peremptory norms also constitutes a limit on the powers of the Security Council. The most widely known statement is that of Judge ad hoc Lauterpacht in the *Bosnia Genocide* case who reasoned that Article 103 of the UN Charter, which provides that member states' obligations under the Charter prevail over their other obligations, could not apply to a conflict between a resolution of the Security Council and a *jus cogens* norm.[104] According to the Judge, a resolution that violated a *jus cogens* norm becomes 'void and legally ineffective.'[105] For a while an isolated dictum, the Court of First Instance of the European Communities has recently held that a resolution that fails to observe peremptory norms 'would bind neither the Member States of the United Nations nor, in consequence, the Community.'[106] The latter Court has gone as far as to

---

[98] *Rights of the Undocumented Migrants*, IACtHR, Advisory Opinion OC-18 of 17 September 2003, Series A No. 18, para. 99. See Separate Opinion of Judge Cançado Trindade, para. 68.

[99] Commentary to Articles on State Responsibility, Part two of Chapter III, para. 7.

[100] J. Crawford, Fourth Report on State Responsibility, UN Doc. A/CN.4/517 (2001), para. 47.

[101] Articles on State Responsibility, Article 41.

[102] *Legal Consequences of the Construction of a Wall in the Occupied Palestinian Territory*, 2004 ICJ Reports 136, para. 159.

[103] This was noted in the Separate Opinion of Judge Kooijmans, para. 40.

[104] *Application of the Convention on the Prevention and Punishment of the Crime of Genocide*, Provisional Measures Order of 13 September 1993, 1993 ICJ Reports 325, Separate Opinion of Judge ad hoc Lauterpacht, para. 100.

[105] Ibid., para. 104.

[106] Case T-315/01 *Kadi v. Council of the European Union and Commission of the European Communities* (CFI 21 September 2005), para. 230; Case T-306/01, *Yusuf and Al Barakaat v. Council*

note that it 'is empowered to check, indirectly, the lawfulness of the resolutions of the Security Council in question with regard to *jus cogens*'.[107]

Other areas in which international tribunals have recognized a role for *jus cogens* norms are—with various degrees of cogency—the recognition of states,[108] jurisdiction,[109] and the prosecution of crimes.[110]

It is equally important to note certain areas of international law in which *jus cogens* norms have not, or not yet, had an impact. Three such areas may be cited. First, as with obligations *erga omnes*, the International Court does not automatically have jurisdiction simply because the dispute relates to a peremptory norm; the usual rules of jurisdiction apply.[111] Secondly, the Special Rapporteur of the ILC on Diplomatic Protection sought to introduce a duty on states to exercise diplomatic protection on behalf of nationals suffering from a grave breach of a *jus cogens* norm in certain limited circumstances.[112] However, this caused some concern among members of the ILC who wished for more state practice and *opinio juris* on point and so the provision was dropped from the final text.[113] Thirdly, an area undergoing some movement is that of the law on immunity. At present, the rules on immunity have not been overridden by allegations of a violation of a peremptory norm but there exists a body of opinion expressing the contrary view.[114]

6. Conclusion

Obligations *erga omnes* have had a decisive impact on jurisdictional *locus standi* and the way in which a claim may be espoused. There has been a move away from the injured state as restrictively conceived and a widening of the traditional

---

of the European Union and Commission of the European Communities (CFI 21 September 2005), para. 281.

[107] *Kadi,* paras 226, 282; *Yusuf,* paras 277, 337.

[108] Commentary to Articles on State Responsibility, Article 41(2). Opinion No. 10 of the Arbitration Commission advising the Conference for Peace in Yugoslavia, 92 ILR 206, 208 refers to 'compliance with the imperatives of general international law'.

[109] *Prosecutor v. Furundžija*, ICTY-95–17/1-T, Judgment of 10 December 1998, para. 156.

[110] Ibid., para. 155.

[111] *Armed Activities on the Territory of the Congo (Democratic Republic of the Congo v. Rwanda),* Judgment of 3 February 2006, 2006 ICJ Reports 6, paras 64 and 125.

[112] J. Dugard, First Report on Diplomatic Protection, UN Doc. A/CN.4/506 (7 March 2000) 27–34.

[113] Report of the International Law Commission on the work of its fifty-second session, UN Doc. A/55/10 (2000) 77–79. For comment, see J. Dugard, 'The Future of International Law: A Human Rights Perspective—With Some Comments on the Leiden School of International Law' (2007) 20 LJIL 729, 732.

[114] *Arrest Warrant of 11 April 2000 (Democratic Republic of the Congo v. Belgium),* Judgment of 14 February 2002, 2002 ICJ Reports 3, Dissenting Opinion of Judge Al-Khasawneh, para. 7, Dissenting Opinion of Judge Van den Wyngaert, para. 28; *Al-Adsani v. United Kingdom* (App. No. 35763/97), ECtHR, Judgment of 21 November 2001, (2002) 34 EHRR 11, ECHR 2001-XI, Joint Dissenting Opinion of Judges Rozakis and Caflisch, Joined by Judges Wildhaber, Costa, Cabral Barreto, and Vajić.

response of diplomatic protection. A state may now intervene in a judicial forum on behalf of a foreign national, a considerable shift by any measure. At the same time, this movement evidences a shift from the bilateral legal obligation towards certain community interests and community values, interests and values that are primarily concerned with respect for the human person. As with obligations *erga omnes*, human rights norms form the bulk of *jus cogens* norms. These human rights norms, through the lens of *jus cogens*, may void inconsistent treaty provisions, render invalid Security Council resolutions and give rise to special consequences in the area of state responsibility. These are no small effects.

The concepts of obligations *erga omnes* and *jus cogens* norms accordingly have restructured international obligations. There has been a shift away from narrow self-interest towards community interests and from consensualism to the compulsory. The significance of the new structure, though, should not be overstated. The restructuring has not been followed by the institution of judicial proceedings taking advantage of the new structure; the concepts of *jus cogens* and *erga omnes* are still met with scepticism.[115] Even if used infrequently by states in their arguments before the Court, the work of the Court, the ILC and the *Institut de droit international* does show that certain human rights norms, as community interests, form part of the international legal architecture. The concepts themselves represent evidence of a maturing of the international legal system.

Two wider observations may be made in conclusion. First, unlike many other areas of international law, the impact of human rights on the structure of international obligations did not start out in a human rights treaty body or a regional human rights court before moving to the International Court or the ILC. The idea of obligations *erga omnes* was shaped by the Court and the concept of *jus cogens* norms by the ILC. Both have been embraced subsequently by the human rights regime. The influence of human rights on international law thus cannot be seen solely as a movement from the human rights regime to the public international regime, for international law comprises human rights and the Court and the ILC are bodies that consider human rights in their work. Secondly, the developments have not been about human rights alone. One of the key peremptory norms is that of the prohibition of aggression; a purported obligation *erga omnes* is one prohibiting atmospheric nuclear testing. Ideas of *jus cogens* and *erga omnes* are more about the broader values of the international community of which the protection of the human person forms but part, albeit an important part.

---

[115] Dugard, 'The Future of International Law' (2007) 20 LJIL 729, 732.

8

Impact on the Immunity of States and their Officials

*Thilo Rensmann**

1. The Resilience of the Traditional Rules

The *Pinochet* decision of the House of Lords, which held that the former Chilean head of state *Augusto Pinochet* did not enjoy immunity from criminal prosecution in Britain,[1] was hailed by many as a landmark case paving the way for the acceptance of a general 'human rights exception' to the traditional immunities granted to foreign states and their officials. Ten years later, the promise of a 'humanized'[2] immunity regime, which would enable national courts to prosecute and punish foreign state officials for severe human rights violations and to grant compensation to their victims, does not, however, seem to have been realized.

The venerable principle of *par in parem non habet imperium*[3] proved to be surprisingly resilient to claims that the traditional rules on the immunity of states and their officials should yield to the dictates of a new 'humanized' international legal order. The European Court of Human Rights in the *Al-Adsani* case, albeit by a very narrow majority, refused to extend the 'human rights exception' to tort proceedings against foreign states.[4] The International Court of Justice in its *Arrest Warrant* decision maintained that the *Pinochet* holding was strictly limited to former heads of state and that, accordingly, incumbent heads of state, heads of government and foreign ministers remained immune from criminal proceedings

---

* Dr. iur. habil. (University of Bonn); LL.M. (University of Virginia); Associate Professor of Law (Privatdozent) at the University of Bonn; Visiting Professor at the Ludwig-Maximilians-University, Munich.
  [1] *R v. Bow Street Metropolitan Stipendiary Magistrate, Ex parte Pinochet Ugarte (No. 1)* [1998] 3 WLR 1456; *R v. Bow Street Metropolitan Stipendiary Magistrate, Ex parte Pinochet Ugarte (No. 3)* [1999] 2 WLR 827.
  [2] On the notion of 'humanization' see T. Meron, *The Humanization of International Law* (Martinus Nijhoff, Leiden/Boston 2006).
  [3] Bartolus, *Tractatus Repressalium*, Question I/3, para. 10 (1354).
  [4] *Al-Adsani v. United Kingdom* (App. No. 35763/97), ECtHR, Judgment of 21 November 2001, (2002) 34 EHRR 11, ECHR 2001-XI; see also *Kalegoropoulou v. Greece and Germany* (App. No. 50021/00), ECtHR, Judgment of 12 December 2002, ECHR 2002-X.

abroad even if they were accused of having perpetrated war crimes and crimes against humanity.[5] National courts in Canada,[6] France,[7] Germany,[8] and Greece[9] showed a similar reluctance towards any extension of the *Pinochet* holding beyond the specific circumstances of that case. Recent decisions in the United States similarly upheld the immunity of states and their officials despite the *jus cogens* nature of the human rights alleged to have been violated.[10] It was finally the House of Lords itself which in *Jones v. Saudi Arabia* delivered the latest blow to the high hopes and expectations raised by the *Pinochet* precedent when it unequivocally endorsed the *Al-Adsani* decision and insisted that state immunity barred British courts from hearing tort claims against foreign states and their officials.[11]

It cannot, however, be considered as finally settled whether the 'humanization' of the traditional rules on the immunity of states and their officials will in the long run remain limited to the specific constellation of the *Pinochet* case or whether the ambit of the 'human rights exception' will gradually be extended to other immunity claims. In this context it has to be borne in mind that the *Al-Adsani* case was decided by the narrowest possible majority of nine to eight, that the categorical holding of the *Arrest Warrant* judgment was significantly qualified by a host of separate and dissenting opinions,[12] and that national courts have to date also not

---

[5] *Arrest Warrant of 11 April 2000 (Democratic Republic of the Congo v. Belgium)*, Judgment of 14 February 2002, 2002 ICJ Reports 3.

[6] Canada, Court of Appeal of Ontario, *Bouzari v. Islamic Republic of Iran* [2004] 243 OR (4th) 406; see also Canada, Superior Court of Ontario, *Arar v. Syrian Arab Republic* [2005] OJ No. 752.

[7] French Court of Cassation (*Cour de Cassation*), Judgment of 13 March 2001, Clunet 2001, 804 (*Gaddafi* case). A complaint lodged against the decision before the European Court of Human Rights was struck off the list, see *Association SOS Attentats and de Boery v. France* (App. No. 76642/01), ECtHR, Decision of 4 October 2006.

[8] German Supreme Court (*Bundesgerichtshof*), *Greek Citizens v. Federal Republic of Germany* (2003) 42 ILM 1030; German Federal Constitutional Court (*Bundesverfassungsgericht*), 2 BvR 1476/03, Decision of 15 February 2006, para. 18, available at <http://www.bverfg.de>.

[9] Greek Special Supreme Court (Ανώτατο Ειδικό Δικαστήριο), *Margellos v. Federal Republic of Germany* (2007) 129 ILR 525. A complaint filed against the decision of the Greek Court of Cassation before the ECtHR was declared inadmissible, *Kalegoropoulou v. Greece and Germany* (App. No. 50021/00), ECtHR, Judgment of 12 December 2002 . See also ECJ, Case C-292/05 *Lechouritou, V. Karkoulias, G. Pavlopoulos, P. Bratsikas, D. Sotiropoulos, G. Dimopoulos v. Dimosio tis Omospondiakis Dimokratias tis Germanias* [2007] ECR I-1519 holding that the Brussels Convention on Jurisdiction and the Enforcement of Judgments in Civil and Commercial Matters (1968), [1978] OJ L 304/36 was not applicable to the proceedings before Greek courts.

[10] See with regard to civil proceedings against foreign states *Princz v. Federal Republic of Germany* 26 F 3d (DC Cir 1994); *Sampson v. Federal Republic of Germany* 250 F 3d 1145 (7th Cir 2001); with regard to civil proceedings against foreign state officials *Matar v. Dichter* 2007 WL 1276960 (SDNY 2 May 2007) (former director of Israel's General Security Service)*; Yousuf v. Samantar* 2007 US Dist LEXIS 56227 (ED Va 1 August 2007) (former Somali Prime Minister and Minister of Defence); *Belhas v. Ya'alon*, No. 07–7009 (DC Cir, 15 February 2008) (former Israeli Head of Army Intelligence); with regard to tort actions against incumbent heads of state *Tachiona v. United States*, 386 F 3d 205 (2d Cir 2004); *Wei Ye v. Jiang Zemin*, 383 F.3d 620 (7th Cir 2004).

[11] *Jones v. Ministry of the Interior of Saudi Arabia* [2007] 1 AC 270.

[12] See also *Armed Activities on the Territory of the Congo* (*New Application: 2002*) (*Democratic Republic of the Congo v. Rwanda*) (Jurisdiction and Admissibility) Judgment of 3 February 2006, 2006 ICJ Reports 6, Separate Opinion Dugard, paras. 11–12 arguing that the Court should reconsider the *Arrest Warrant* decision in the light of the fact that it had now for the first time given express

spoken in a single voice on this issue. Most notably the Italian *Corte di Cassazione* in a tort case brought by victims of war crimes committed by German troops during World War II refused to pay allegiance to the prevailing restrictive approach and considered any claims to immunity by the Federal Republic of Germany to be overridden by the *jus cogens* nature of the crimes at issue.[13] In a similar vein, the UN Committee Against Torture[14] in its concluding observations on Canada's periodic report—with obvious reference to the *Bouzari* case in which Canadian courts had denied compensation claims of torture victims against Iran on account of state immunity[15]—urged Canada to reconsider its position in the light of its obligations under Article 14 of the UN Torture Convention.[16]

The 2004 UN Convention on Jurisdictional Immunities of States and their Property,[17] which has not yet entered into force but may nevertheless *cum grano salis* be considered the most authoritative restatement of current customary law on state immunity, has left the issue undecided.[18] Upon ratification, Norway explicitly added the understanding that 'the Convention is without prejudice to any future international development in the protection of human rights'.[19] In fact, the International Law Commission has recently embarked upon a project of codifying the 'immunity of State state officials from foreign criminal jurisdiction'[20] with the intention of making 'a contribution to ensuring a proper balance'

recognition to the concept of *jus cogens*. Such an opportunity might present itself to the Court in the case concerning *Certain Criminal Proceedings in France (Republic of the Congo v. France)*, see order of 17 June 2003 (Provisional Measures), 2003 ICJ Reports 102. On 18 April 2007 Rwanda filed an application with the Court in a dispute with France concerning arrest warrants issued by French authorities against three Rwandan officials; see ICJ Press Release 2007/11.

[13] Italian Court of Cassation (*Corte di Cassazione*), *Ferrini v. Federal Republic of Germany*, Judgment of 11 March 2004, (2005) 99 AJIL 242, (2006) 128 ILR 658. A similar line of reasoning was followed by the Greek Court of Cassation in *Prefecture of Voiotia v. Federal Republic of Germany* (Case No. 11/2000) (2007) 129 ILR 513 which was, however, later overruled by a special chamber of the Greek Supreme Court, see *Margellos v. Germany* (2007) 129 ILR 525.

[14] CAT, Conclusions and Recommendations of the Committee against Torture: Canada, 7 July 2005, CAT/C/CR/34/CAN, para. 5 (f). See also the Committee's decision in *Guengueng v. Senegal*, 19 May 2006, CAT/C/36/D/181/2001, which held that Senegal had violated its obligations under Art. 5 para. 2 and Art. 7 of the UN Torture Convention by failing to prosecute the former President of Chad Hissène Habré for alleged acts of torture. Note, however, that the Senegal Court of Cassation in its decision of 20 March 2001, (2004) 125 ILR 569, had based the dismissal of the charges against Habré on the lack of universal jurisdiction under the law of Senegal rather than on considerations of immunity.

[15] *Bouzari* [2004] 243 OR (4th) 406.

[16] Convention Against Torture and Other Cruel, Inhuman or Degrading Treatment or Punishment, 10 December 1984, 1465 UNTS 85.

[17] United Nations Convention on Jurisdictional Immunities of States and Their Property (adopted by the UN General Assembly on 2 December 2004) UNGA Res. 59/38 annex.

[18] See Report of the Working Group on Jurisdictional Immunities of States and Their Property, in ILC, Report of the ILC on the Work of its 51st Session, UN Doc. A/54/10 (1999), Annex, 171–172.

[19] Declaration made by Norway upon ratification (27 March 2006), in UN Office of Legal Affairs, Status of Multilateral Treaties Deposited with the Secretary General, Part 1, Chapter III, No. 13, available at <http://untreaty.un.org>.

[20] See GA Res. 62/66 of 6 December 2007, para. 7 and ILC, Report of the ILC on the Work of its 59th Session, UN Doc. A/62/10 (2007), para. 376.

between the fight against impunity and the need for stable and predictable inter-state relations.[21]

While international human rights law has not yet effectuated a general immunity exception with regard to serious human rights violations it should not be forgotten that human rights played a significant catalytic role in the gradual transformation from an absolute to today's restrictive understanding of immunity.[22] International human rights law continues to exert pressure on the international legal system to constantly review the extent to which the interest of preserving the stability of international relations may justify perpetrators of human rights violations going unpunished and their victims remaining without redress. This is not only witnessed by the incessant flow of court cases in which judges are faced with the argument that the traditional immunity rules have to give way to the imperatives of human rights, but also by recent initiatives to introduce a 'human rights exception' into international and domestic instruments on state immunity. The Secretary-General of the Council of Europe recently called for a 'Council of Europe instrument on State immunity and serious human rights violations' with a view to ensuring that '[t]orturers and perpetrators of other serious human rights violations... [will no longer] be able to hide behind the veil of immunity.'[23] In the aftermath of the *Jones* decision a bill was introduced in the House of Lords in February 2008 (Torture (Damages) Bill) which would add a specific caveat to the British State Immunity Act[24] in order to allow torture victims access to British courts.[25] Similar proposals are under consideration in Canada.[26]

2. A 'Human Rights Exception' to the Traditional Rules?

If one were to limit the present enquiry to assessing the *lex lata* in the light of the traditional sources of international law the analysis would not need to be taken a lot further. As yet there is insufficient state practice to support a general 'human

---

[21] See the preliminary study by the rapporteur Roman A. Kolodkin in ILC, Report of the ILC on the Work of its 58th Session, UN Doc. A/61/10 (2006), Annex A, paras. 1, 17, 18.

[22] See R. van Alebeek, *The Immunities of States and Their Officials in International Criminal Law and International Human Rights Law* (Oxford University Press, Oxford 2008), 47, 308; H. Lauterpacht, 'The Problem of Jurisdictional Immunities of Foreign States' (1951) 28 BYIL 220, 235.

[23] Council of Europe, Follow-up to the Secretary General's report under Article 52 ECHR on the question of secret detention and transport of detainees suspected of terrorist acts, notably by or at the instigation of foreign agencies, Proposals made by the Secretary General, 30 June 2006, SG (2006) 01, paras. 17, 19. For a similar proposal with regard to the UN Convention on State Immunity (n. 617) see C. Hall, 'UN Convention on State Immunity: The Need for a Human Rights Protocol' (2006) 55 ICLQ 411.

[24] State Immunity Act 1978 (c 33).

[25] Torture (Damages) HL Bill (2007–08) 30.

[26] See D. Black, 'A Canadian Law That Helps Outlaws', *Toronto Star* (Toronto 10 February 2008), available at <http://www.thestar.com>; N.B. Novogrodsky, 'Immunity for Torture: Lessons From *Bouzari v. Iran*' (2007) 18 EJIL 939, 948–952.

rights exception'. The majority of the Law Lords in the final and decisive *Pinochet* judgment rested their argument on the narrow ground that with regard to criminal prosecution for acts of torture the immunity of former heads of state must be considered to have been waived by virtue of the UN Torture Convention.[27] Beyond the *Pinochet* precedent human rights violations can only serve as a justification for disregarding immunity if one of the traditional immunity exceptions applies.[28] Specific exceptions for human rights violations amounting to crimes against humanity or war crimes only exist with regard to criminal proceedings before certain international and internationalized criminal tribunals.[29]

While the *Pinochet* precedent has hence not brought about a general 'human rights exception', it has still had a considerable impact on the discourse about the immunity of states and their officials. National and international judges have since constantly been faced with the challenge that the traditional ambit of immunities should be restricted in view of the progressive development of international human rights law.[30] This judicial discourse thus provides a valuable case study on the interaction between international human rights law and general international law. In particular it sheds light on the conditioning factors that determine the receptiveness of general international law to the charms of international human rights. Understanding why the immunities granted to states and their officials have, to date, proved so resilient to the impact of human rights will help both to provide a basis for predicting the future development of the law of immunity and offer a conceptual framework for devising realistic strategies for overcoming the obstacles that traditional immunities pose to the effective realization of human rights.

---

[27] *Pinochet (No. 3)* [1999] 2 WLR 827, 859 (per Lord Goff), 881 (per Lord Hope), 902 (per Lord Saville), 906–7 (per Lord Millet), 924 (per Lord Phillips).

[28] See below notes 46–49.

[29] See Art. 7, para. 2 of the Statute of the International Criminal Tribunal for the Former Yugoslavia, UN Doc. S/25704, annex (1993) reprinted in (1993) 32 ILM 1192; Art. 6, para. 2 of the Statute of the International Criminal Tribunal for Rwanda, SC Res. 955, annex (1994), reprinted in (1994) 333 ILM 1602; Art. 27, para. 2 of the Rome Statute of the International Criminal Court, 17 uly 1998, (1998) 37 ILM 1002; Art. 6, para. 2 of the Statute of the Special Court for Sierra Leone, 16 January 2002 available at <http://www.sc-sl.org/Documents/scsl-statute.html>. Note, however, that the Agreement between the United Nations and the Lebanese Republic on the establishment of a Special Tribunal for Lebanon, SC Res. 1757 (2007), Annex, reprinted in (2007) 46 ILM 989, does not contain any comparable immunity exception. On the issue of immunity before international and internationalized Tribunals see also Special Court for Sierra Leone (Appeals Chamber), *Prosecutor v. Charles Taylor*, Case No. SCSL-2003, Decision on Immunity from Jurisdiction, 31 May 2004, (2007) 128 ILR 239; *Arrest Warrant* Case 2002 ICJ Reports 3, para. 61. As to the disputed foundation and extent of immunities before international courts see Van Alebeek, *The Immunity of States and Their Officials* (2008) 275–295; D. Akande, 'International Law Immunities and the International Criminal Court' (2004) 98 AJIL 407; K. Schmalenbach, 'Immunität von Staatsoberhäuptern und anderen Staatsorganen' (2006) 61 *Zeitschrift für öffentliches Recht* 397, 427–429; T. Stein, 'Limits of International Law Immunities for Senior State Officials in Criminal Procedure' in C. Tomuschat and J-M. Thouvenin (eds.), *The Fundamental Rules of the International Legal Order* (Martinus Nijhoff, Leiden/Boston 2006) 249, 251–254.

[30] See above notes 4–13.

In reviewing the case law since the *Pinochet* decision of the British House of Lords, there appear to be two main conditioning factors defining the impact of human rights on the immunity of states and their officials: firstly the forum and the perspective from which the problem is addressed and secondly the methodology employed.

3. The Perspective of the Forum

3.1 International courts

The International Court of Justice in the *Arrest Warrant* case approaches the issue from the perspective of general international law. After having established that an incumbent foreign minister when abroad enjoys 'full immunity from criminal jurisdiction',[31] the Court holds that current state practice does not support any exemption from immunity on account of the seriousness of the alleged human rights violations.[32] Human rights are thus not considered as principles and rules in their own right which, in a given case, have to be reconciled with the traditional immunities of states and their officials. Rather they become only relevant if referred to in an immunity exception recognized under customary international law.[33]

In contrast, the specific mandate of the European Court of Human Rights requires the Strasbourg judges to take human rights as their point of departure.[34] Rather than asking whether there is a 'human rights exception' to state immunity the Strasbourg Court sets out to establish whether there is a 'general international law exception' to the right of access to a court (Article 6(1) of the Convention).[35] Any restriction imposed on this right would in principle only be justified if it pursued a legitimate aim and were proportionate to that aim.[36] The Court has to date, however, refrained from subjecting the rules on state immunity to such a balancing test.[37] Instead it assumes the right of access to a court (Article 6(1) of the Convention) to be inherently limited by general international law[38] and considers compliance with general international law *per se* a legitimate and proportionate limitation of the Convention guarantees.[39] Consequently, the Strasbourg court restricts its role to establishing the *status quo* of immunity law and in this sense switches back to the International Court of Justice's general international law perspective.

Whether the European Court of Human Rights would be prepared to assert a residual power to intervene if compliance with general international law were

---

[31] *Arrest Warrant*, 2002 ICJ Reports 3, para. 54.
[32] Ibid., para. 58.
[33] As to the underlying methodological assumptions see below.
[34] *Al-Adsani* (App. No. 35763/97) ECHR 2001-XI, paras. 35–67.
[35] Ibid., paras. 52–56.   [36] See ibid., paras. 53–54.
[37] A strict balancing approach is favoured by Judge Loucaidis, see ibid. (diss. op. Loucaidis).
[38] Ibid., para. 56.   [39] Ibid., paras. 54, 56.

severely to compromise the very essence of the Convention guarantees[40] remains to be seen. The extreme self-restraint the Court recently exercised in the *Behrami* decision, which in effect appears to give the Security Council *carte blanche* to brush away all human rights restraints laid down in the European Convention on Human Rights,[41] seems rather to raise the spectre of a non-reviewable 'general international law exception'.[42]

3.2 National courts

Due to their very nature questions of immunity are most frequently argued before national courts. National court decisions therefore constitute an extremely important source for ascertaining the extent to which customary international law shields states and their officials from subjection to foreign jurisdiction.[43]

The willingness of national courts to allow the traditional immunities of states and their officials to be set aside in cases of severe human rights violations depends both on the legal basis on which immunity is granted and on the status accorded to human rights under the domestic legal order in question. In jurisdictions such as the United Kingdom, the United States and Canada, in which the law of state immunity has been codified by an act of Parliament,[44] the approach to this question is largely determined by the domestic immunity statute.

Since such statutes typically do not provide for a specific 'human rights exception' immunity may only be disregarded if the violation of human rights fits one of the exceptions enumerated in the statute.[45] Typically, however, none of these exceptions apply. Efforts to argue that human rights violations can be qualified as commercial acts,[46] go beyond the official capacity of state

---

[40] See ibid., para. 53 ('the Court…must be satisfied that the limitations applied do not restrict or reduce the access left to the individual in such a way or to such an extent that the very essence of the right is impaired') and para. 56 ('It follows that measures taken by a High Contracting Party which reflect generally recognised rules of public international law on state immunity cannot *in principle* be regarded as imposing a disproportionate restriction on the right of access to a court as embodied in Article 6 § 1.' [Emphasis provided]).

[41] *Behrami and Behrami v. France* and *Saramati v. France, Germany and Norway* (App. No. 71412/01 and 78166/01), ECtHR, Decision of 2 May 2007. See in this context also the opinion delivered by A.G. Maduro in C-402/05, *Kadi v. Council and Commission* (16 January 2008).

[42] See also Judge Ress's criticism of the Court's self-restraint in European Court of Human Rights (Grand Chamber), *Bosphorus Hava Yolları Turizm ve Ticaret Anonim Şirketi (Bosphorus Airways) v. Ireland* (App. No. 45036/98), ECtHR, Judgment of 30 June 2005, ECHR 2005-VI, Concurring opinion of Judge Ress, para. 5.

[43] See R. Higgins *Problems & Process: International Law and How We Use It* (Clarendon Press, Oxford 1994) 81.

[44] See (British) State Immunity Act (1978); (US) Foreign Sovereign Immunities Act, 28 USC §§ 1602–1611; (Canadian) State Immunity Act, RSC 1985, c S-18.

[45] *Bouzari* [2004] 243 OR (4th) 406, paras. 57–58; *Jones* [2007] 1 AC 270, para. 13 (per Lord Bingham), paras. 39, 64 (per Lord Hoffmann); *Saudi Arabia v. Nelson*, 507 U.S. 349, 355 (1993).

[46] Rejected in *Bouzari* [2004] 243 OR (4th) 406 , paras. 48–55; *Saudi Arabia v. Nelson* 507 U.S. 349, 355 (1993) 356–363.

officials,[47] constitute an implied waiver,[48] or fall under the tort exception[49] have for the most part failed. To date only the United States of America[50] has enacted a specific immunity exception allowing tort actions against foreign states responsible for (or complicit in) certain serious human rights violations (torture, extrajudicial killing, aircraft sabotage, or hostage taking).[51] This exception is, however, only applicable if the plaintiff is a US citizen and the respondent state has been designated by the State Department as a 'sponsor of terrorism'.[52]

Both in Italy and in Greece, where the highest courts have assumed that state immunity cannot be invoked in tort proceedings involving alleged war crimes and crimes against humanity,[53] the judges are not confined by the straitjacket of a domestic immunity statute but are rather free to determine the reach of immunities with direct reference to customary international law. The absence of domestic codification allows a more activist approach which opens up the possibility of taking note of the progressive development of international human rights law and of the international legal order at large, in particular with regard to the legal consequences attached to breaches of *jus cogens*.[54] In contrast, those common law courts which must adjudicate on the basis of a domestic immunity statute are often effectively insulated from such new developments at the international level.[55] Since the limits of statutory interpretation hinder such courts from responding to the progressive 'humanization' of international law their jurisprudence cannot contribute to the state practice necessary to support an emerging 'human rights exception'. Domestic immunity statutes thus exercise a considerable 'ossifying' effect on customary international law.

---

[47] Rejected in *Jones* [2007] 1 AC 270, paras. 72–97 (per Lord Hoffmann); *Matar v. Dichter* 2007 WL 1276960 (SDNY 2 May 2007); *Samantar* 2007 US Dist LEXIS 56227 (ED Va 1 August 2007); *Belhas* (n. 10).

[48] Rejected in *Princz* 26 F 3d (DC Cir 1994) 1173; *Sampson* 250 F 3d 1145 (7th Cir 2001) 1156.

[49] Rejected in *Bouzari* [2004] 243 OR (4th) 406, paras. 45–47; *Al-Adsani v. Government of Kuwait* (1996) 107 ILR 536 CA.

[50] Note, however, that Iran and Cuba, which have both been branded 'State sponsors of terrorism' by the United States Government appear to have enacted similar legislation with a view to permitting civil actions against the United States as a reaction to the 1996 amendment of the Foreign Sovereign Immunities Act, see Congressional Research Service (J. Elsea), Suits Against Terrorist States By Victims of Terrorism, RL 31258 (17 December 2007), 53–54.

[51] 28 USC § 1605 (a)(7).

[52] See 28 USC § 1605 (a)(7)(B). For references to the case law based on this exception and subsequent legislation aimed at enabling the plaintiffs to enforce the awarded compensation see Congressional Research Service (Elsea) RL 31258 (17 December 2007). Currently the list of 'State sponsors of terrorism' includes Cuba, Iran, North Korea, Sudan, and Syria. Iraq and Libya have been struck off the list, see 22 CFR §126.1(a) (2002).

[53] *Ferrini* (2006) 128 ILR 658; *Prefecture of Voiotia* (Case No. 11/2000) (2007) 129 ILR 513, later overruled by *Margellos* (2007) 129 ILR 525.

[54] See e.g. the reference in *Ferrini* (2006) 128 ILR 658, para. 9, to Arts. 40 and 41 of the International Law Commission's Draft Articles on Responsibility of States for Internationally Wrongful Acts, UN GA Res. 56/83 Annex (12 December 2001).

[55] *Bouzari* [2004] 243 OR (4th) 406, para. 67: 'Even if Canada's international law obligations required that Canada permit a civil remedy for torture abroad by a foreign state, Canada has legislated in a way that does not do so.... Canada has clearly legislated so as not to create this exception to state immunity whether it has an international law obligation to do so or not.'

The status of human rights within the domestic legal order provides another important conditioning factor. Courts, such as the Italian courts in the *Ferrini* case, which are familiar with arguments based on human rights values[56] and corresponding protective duties will be particularly receptive to the argument that immunity claims must be balanced against the countervailing interests of the international community to avoid impunity and provide redress to the victims of serious human rights violations.[57]

It is interesting to observe that since the Human Rights Act[58] entered into force in 2000, British courts have also displayed a more dynamic approach to ascertaining the proper balance between state immunity and human rights. A case in point is *Jones v. Saudi Arabia*.[59] The Human Rights Act, by virtue of which the United Kingdom incorporated the European Convention on Human Rights into domestic law, requires British courts to interpret statutes as far as possible in the light of the Convention rights.[60] In consequence, the State Immunity Act must now be construed in the light of international human rights as they have been incorporated by the Human Rights Act. In this sense, human rights—regardless of whether they are *jus cogens* or not—are accorded *de facto* a hierarchically superior position in relation to state immunity. By virtue of this elevated status British courts must take into account human rights standards when determining the ambit of the (national) rules on state immunity.

This was precisely the conceptual starting point adopted by the Court of Appeal in the *Jones* case.[61] Whereas the Court felt compelled by the Human Rights Act[62] to follow the *Al-Adsani* precedent in granting Saudi Arabia immunity from jurisdiction, it held that the State Immunity Act did not extend immunity to the acting state officials, a constellation which, to date, has not been explicitly covered by the jurisprudence of the Strasbourg court. The fact that the House of Lords later overruled the Court of Appeal on this point[63] does not detract from the more general observation that the domestic incorporation of human rights has enticed British judges to break the mould of traditional statutory interpretation

---

[56] On the role of human rights values and protective duties in Italian law see T. Rensmann, *Wertordnung und Verfassung* (Mohr Siebeck 2007) 171–173, 295–298.

[57] The activist approach followed by the Italian *Corte di Cassazione* in *Ferrini* (2006) 128 ILR 658 is in stark contrast to the judicial self-restraint exercised by British and Canadian courts, see *Bouzari* [2004] 243 OR (4th) 406, para. 95 ('In future perhaps as the international human rights movement gathers greater force, this balance [between the condemnation of torture and the principle that states must treat each other as equals] may change, either through domestic legislation of states or by international treaty. . . . this is not a change to be effected by a domestic court.'); *Jones* [2007] 1 AC 270, para. 63 (per Lord Hoffmann) ('It is not for a national court to "develop" international law by unilaterally adopting a version of that law which, however desirable, forward-looking and reflective of values it may be, is simply not accepted by other states.').

[58] Human Rights Act 1998 (c 42).

[59] Infra, n. 61.

[60] Section 3 Human Rights Act (1998).

[61] *Jones v. Ministry of Interior of Saudi Arabia* [2005] QB 699.

[62] See Section 2(1)(a) Human Rights Act (1998).

[63] *Jones* [2007] 1 AC 270, paras. 29–34 (per Lord Bingham), paras. 65–101 (per Lord Hoffmann).

and to explore the impact of human rights on the immunity of states and their officials beyond the confines of a narrow reading of the State Immunity Act. Had it not been for the *Al-Adsani* precedent of the European Court of Human Rights, which must be taken into account by virtue of the Human Rights Act,[64] British courts might have even been more daring in adjusting the immunities of states and their officials to the demands of today's 'humanized' international legal order.

4. Methodology

The quest for a 'human rights exception' to the immunity of states and their officials pits the time-honoured principle of *par in parem non habet imperium*, one of the most immediate expressions of the sovereign equality of states, against the fledgling normative aspiration of the international community to fight the impunity of perpetrators of serious human rights violations[65] and to ensure that their victims are adequately compensated.[66] In this sense we are apparently faced with a head-on collision between classical state-oriented international law based on the axiom of state sovereignty and the modern 'humanized' international law which seeks to protect the 'dignity and worth of the human person'.[67] Due to the fundamental nature of this conflict which forces the decision-maker to reveal his basic assumptions about the dogmatic foundations of modern international law, the substantive conflict between immunity and human rights goes hand in hand with a methodological dispute as to the sources and the proper rules of interpretation in international law. The inevitability of having to reveal and defend one's methodological creed accounts for the intensity and passion with which the judicial and academic discourse about the propriety of a 'human rights exception' is conducted.

While the traditionalists set out to ascertain the will of the sovereign states with the dowsing rod of Article 38(1) of the ICJ Statue[68] and resolve any *non liquet* in favour of immunity, the (self-appointed) methodological avant-garde instead conjures up the new anthropocentric values of the international community and postulates their precedence over the 'old' state-centred immunity rules. Between these outer methodological poles various 'intermediate' approaches can be discerned which share the conviction that the traditional immunities must be

---

[64] Section 2(1)(a) Human Rights Act (1998).

[65] See Updated Principles for the Protection and Promotion of Human Rights Through Action to Combat Impunity, UN Doc. E/CN.4/2005/102/Add.1, Addendum.

[66] United Nations Basic Principles and Guidelines on the Right to a Remedy and Reparation for Victims of Gross Violations of International Human Rights Law and Serious Violations of International Humanitarian Law, GA Res. 60/147, 16 December 2005.

[67] Charter of the United Nations, Preamble, para. 2.

[68] Statute of the International Court of Justice, 24 October 1945, 961 UNTS 183, 280.

carefully adapted to the emergence of human rights as 'constitutional values' in modern international law.

The following analysis will attempt to review the current discourse on the impact of international human rights law on immunity of states and their officials through the lens of these three basic methodological approaches (the 'traditional', the value-driven 'hierarchical', and the 'intermediate' approach). The primary aim of this exercise is to gain some general insights into the mutual relationship between methodology and the integration of human rights values into general international law. At the same time an attempt will be made to identify the dangers and opportunities which each of the three methodological 'ideal-types' entails for the further development of international law.

At the outset it is important to note that the case law under review is concerned with a number of different constellations to which the body of traditional international law has responded with different sets of rules in order to accommodate the interests involved in each of these specific situations.[69] Hence civil proceedings[70] need to be distinguished from criminal proceedings;[71] court actions against states from those against state officials. If state officials are involved the extent of the immunities enjoyed depends on their respective functions since special immunity regimes have evolved for diplomats,[72] heads of state, heads of government, and certain cabinet members.[73] Acting state officials[74] may be entitled to more extensive immunities than former state officials.[75] Finally, different considerations apply depending on whether the case is heard before a national or an international court.[76]

In each of the cases under review it was argued by at least one of the parties that in the event of the violation of certain human rights, the human rights values at issue should trump the traditional immunity rules regardless of the nature of the proceedings. If this argument were followed, the new anthropocentric values would brush aside in one fell swoop all the sophisticated distinctions traditional international law has developed with regard to the immunity of states and their officials.[77] Whereas the emergence of the international

[69] As to the importance of these distinctions in assessing the influence of international human rights law on the immunities enjoyed by states and their officials see the in-depth study of Van Alebeek, *The Immunity of States and Their Officials* (2008).

[70] See e.g., *Al-Adsani* (n. 4); *Bouzari* [2004] 243 OR (4th) 406; *Ferrini* (2006) 128 ILR 658; *Jones* [2007] 1 AC 270.

[71] See e.g., *Arrest Warrant*, 2002 ICJ Reports 3; *Pinochet* [1999] 2 WLR 827.

[72] Vienna Convention on Diplomatic Relations, 18 April 1961, 500 UNTS 95.

[73] *Arrest Warrant*, 2002 ICJ Reports 3; Institut de Droit International, Immunities from Jurisdiction and Execution of Heads of State and of Governments in International Law, 26 August 2001, available at <http://www.idi-iil.org/idiE/resolutionsE/2001_van_02_en.PDF>.

[74] See *Arrest Warrant*, 2002 ICJ Reports 3; *Tachiona v. United States* (n. 10); *Wei Ye v. Jiang Zemin* (n 627).

[75] *Pinochet* [1999] 2 WLR 827.

[76] See above n. 29.

[77] See e.g., *Al-Adsani* (App. No. 35763/97), ECHR 2001-XI, Dissenting opinion Rozakis and Caflisch joined by Wildhaber, Costa, Cabral Barreto, and Vajić: '[T]he distinction made by the

community's interest in protecting 'the worth and value of the human person'[78] may indeed require the adjustment of these rules, careful consideration must be given to whether the 'humanization' of international law should indeed go as far as to reverse Oliver Wendell Holmes's famous observation that '[t]he life of the law has not been logic' but rather 'experience'.[79] Should the experience encapsulated in traditional international law really have to yield unremittingly to the 'logic of values'?[80]

4.1 The traditional approach

Before looking more closely at the radical value-driven approach, it is, however, necessary to assess the mainstream methodology on this issue. The traditional approach is based on the assumption that the detection of the relevant rules of immunity is essentially an empirical exercise of identifying the collective will of the international community of states as it has crystallized in the traditional sources of international law spelled out in Article 38(1) of the ICJ Statute.[81] In this sense the traditional methodology is indeed 'formalistic'.[82] The case law on the interaction between immunity and human rights which proclaims to adhere to this approach reveals, however, that the mainstream, despite its formalistic creed, is in the last analysis also value-driven.

With the exception of diplomatic immunities, the immunity of states and their officials rests largely on customary international law. The UN Convention on Jurisdictional Immunities of States and Their Property[83] is not yet in force and the European Convention on State Immunity[84] has only been ratified by eight states. Typically, the assessment of whether international law provides for a 'human rights exception' to state immunity hinges, therefore, on establishing

---

majority between civil and criminal proceedings, concerning the effect of the rule of the prohibition of torture, is not consonant with the very essence of the operation of the *jus cogens* rules. It is not the nature of the proceedings which determines the effects that a *jus cogens* rule has upon another rule of international law, but the character of the rule as a peremptory norm and its interaction with a hierarchically lower rule. The prohibition of torture, being a rule of *jus cogens*, acts in the international sphere and deprives the rule of sovereign immunity of all its legal effects in that sphere. The criminal or civil nature of the domestic proceedings is immaterial.'

[78] See above n. 67.

[79] Oliver Wendell Holmes, *The Common Law* (1881) 1.

[80] On the 'logic of values' see C. Schmitt, 'Die Tyrannei der Werte' in S. Buve (ed.), *Säkularisation und Utopie, Erbracher Studien, Ernst Forsthoff zum 65 Geburtstag* (Kohlhammer, Stuttgart 1967) 37, 60.

[81] This traditional approach is followed by the courts in *Arrest Warrant*, 2002 ICJ Reports 3; *Al-Adsani* (App. No. 35763/97) ECHR 2001-XI; *Bouzari* [2004] 243 OR (4th) 406; *Jones* [2007] 1 AC 270.

[82] *Al-Adsani* (App. No. 35763/97) ECHR 2001-XI (diss. op. Ferrari Bravo); *Arrest Warrant*, 2002 ICJ Reports 3, Dissenting opinion Van den Wyngaert, para. 28.

[83] See above n. 17.

[84] European Convention on State Immunity, 16 May 1972, ETS No. 74.

sufficient state practice to this effect which, in turn, needs to be supported by a corresponding *opinio juris*.[85]

Whereas in tort cases the rule of immunity finds a solid basis in state practice, the *Arrest Warrant* case demonstrates that in other instances it may be difficult, if not impossible, to corroborate the postulated immunity rule by sufficient state practice. The contention of the International Court of Justice that an incumbent foreign minister enjoys absolute immunity in criminal proceedings could not be bolstered by any significant state practice.[86] The Court instead relied on a functional analogy to recognize diplomatic immunities.[87] The lack of state practice was thus compensated for by relying on the value judgment of the international community in favour of the stability and smooth functioning of international relations. The realization of this value was in the further course of the Court's reasoning 'optimized'[88] by following a functional approach in determining the extent of the foreign minister's immunities: the foreign minister was considered to enjoy such immunities as are necessary for the effective fulfilment of his functions. Due to the special role international law accords to him by virtue of his portfolio, the Court considered a foreign minister to enjoy absolute immunity during his term of office.[89]

Significantly, however, the International Court of Justice did not follow this functional, value-oriented approach to customary international law when assessing the question as to whether an incumbent foreign minister would also enjoy immunity in the event of serious human rights violations amounting to crimes against humanity. The acceptance of a 'human rights exception' faltered due to the lack of supporting state practice.[90] At this stage in the analysis the Court suddenly lost its receptiveness to functional, value-oriented reasoning as a means to filling gaps in state practice. The majority declined to attach any normative significance to the firm commitment of the international community to a core of fundamental human rights. In the last analysis this selective reliance on values in the process of ascertaining the applicable rules of general international law amounts to the same syllogistic hierarchical reasoning as that advocated by some proponents of an all-encompassing 'human rights exception'.

4.2 The 'hierarchical' approach

Both from the bench and in academia, reliance is increasingly placed on the argument that states and their officials may not claim immunity in civil or criminal

---

[85] Art. 38(1)(b) ICJ Statute (1945).

[86] *Arrest Warrant*, 2002 ICJ Reports 3, paras. 51–53.

[87] Ibid., paras. 53–54.

[88] On the 'optimizing function' of principles see R. Alexy, *A Theory of Constitutional Rights* (Oxford University Press, Oxford 2002).

[89] *Arrest Warrant*, 2002 ICJ Reports 3, para. 54.

[90] Ibid., para. 58.

proceedings in which the violation of *jus cogens* is at issue.[91] This line of reasoning found its classical expression in the dissenting opinion by Judges Rozakis and Caflisch in the *Al-Adsani* case. In the eyes of the dissenters, the *jus cogens* nature of the prohibition of torture, for the violation of which Suleiman Al-Adsani had sought damages before British courts, provided the key to dismissing the validity of Kuwait's claim to immunity:

> The acceptance... of the *jus cogens* nature of the prohibition of torture entails that a State allegedly violating it cannot invoke hierarchically lower rules (in this case, those on State immunity) to avoid the consequences of the illegality of its actions. In the circumstances of this case, Kuwait cannot validly hide behind the rules on State immunity to avoid proceedings for a serious claim of torture made before a foreign jurisdiction; and the courts of that jurisdiction (the United Kingdom) cannot accept a plea of immunity, or invoke it *ex officio*, to refuse an applicant adjudication of a torture case. Due to the interplay of the *jus cogens* rule on prohibition of torture and the rules on State immunity, the procedural bar of State immunity is automatically lifted, because those rules, as they conflict with a hierarchically higher rule, do not produce any legal effect. In the same vein, national law which is designed to give domestic effect to the international rules on State immunity cannot be invoked as creating a jurisdictional bar, but must be interpreted in accordance with and in the light of the imperative precepts of *jus cogens*.[92]

Despite its seemingly logical rigour, the argument is seriously flawed because neither the alleged normative conflict nor the presumed hierarchy between human rights and state immunity can be demonstrated to exist.

4.2.1 The lack of normative conflict

The rules on state immunity forbid the *forum* state from exercising its jurisdiction over foreign states and their officials. A normative collision could accordingly only be assumed if the prohibition of torture (or any other *jus cogens* rule) implied the *duty* to establish jurisdiction over foreign states and their officials in order to provide compensation to the victims (or to initiate criminal proceedings against the responsible state officials).[93]

As international law stands today such a general duty to establish criminal or civil jurisdiction with a view to providing judicial remedies for the violation of fundamental human rights endowed with the status of *jus cogens* (*mandatory* universal jurisdiction) only exists in exceptional circumstances.

---

[91] See e.g., *Ferrini* (2006) 128 ILR 658; *Al-Adsani* (App. No. 35763/97) ECHR 2001-XI, Dissenting opinion Rozakis *et al. Arrest Warrant*, 2002 ICJ Reports 3, Dissenting opinion Van den Wyngaert), paras. 24–28; A. Orakhelashvili, 'State Immunity and Hierarchy of Norms: Why the House of Lords Got it Wrong' (2007) 18 EJIL 955.

[92] *Al-Adsani* (App. No. 35763/97) ECHR 2001-XI, dissenting opinion Rozakis *et al.*, para. 3.

[93] See *Jones* [2007] 1 AC 270, paras. 43–45. As to the opposite view which criticizes the 'formalistic' distinction between *jus cogens* as 'substantive' and 'procedural' rules see L. McGregor, 'Torture and State Immunity: Deflecting Impunity, Distorting Sovereignty' (2007) 18 EJIL 903, 906–907; Orakhelashvili, (2007) 18 EJIL 955, 964.

The positive obligations laid down in regional and international human rights treaties in principle only require the states parties to provide judicial remedies for human rights violations which have been committed within their jurisdiction.[94]

Under customary international law there is no rule of *mandatory* universal jurisdiction with regard to criminal or tort proceedings. Even in relation to crimes against humanity, customary international law merely allows criminal prosecution (*permissive* universal jurisdiction) but does not make it obligatory.[95]

Such mandatory universal jurisdiction cannot be read into the positive obligation which the ILC Draft Articles on State Responsibility[96] provide for in Article 41(1) in the event of a serious violation of peremptory rules of international law. Even if it were assumed that such a protective duty could already be considered *lex lata* it merely requires states to 'cooperate'. This cannot reasonably be understood to encompass a duty unilaterally to establish jurisdiction.[97] Equally the negative duty not to recognize as lawful the consequences of a *jus cogens* violation set forth in Article 41(2) of the ILC Draft cannot be construed as establishing a positive duty to exercise jurisdiction.[98]

Treaties which lay down obligatory universal jurisdiction to prosecute or extradite (*aut dedere aut iudicare/prosequi*)[99] do not necessarily displace the traditional immunity rules. The intention of the contracting parties to this effect cannot simply be assumed but would have to be established by ordinary means of treaty interpretation. The UN Torture Convention provides such an exceptional case because, according to the Convention, torture can only be committed by state officials or individuals acting in an official capacity.[100] The *aut dedere aut iudicare* obligation would accordingly be rendered meaningless if such officials or agents were granted immunity from criminal jurisdiction. The House of Lords in the *Pinochet* case therefore considered the UN Torture Convention as an implied waiver of immunity in criminal proceedings relating to torture.[101]

The House of Lords in the *Jones* case convincingly argued that having regard to the wording and the *travaux préparatoires,* Article 14 of the UN Torture Convention does not provide for mandatory universal tort jurisdiction.[102]

---

[94] *Al-Adsani* (App. No. 35763/97) ECHR 2001-XI, para. 37 *et seq.*

[95] See C. Tomuschat, 'The Duty to Prosecute International Crimes Committed by Individuals' in H. J. Cremer et al. (eds.), *Tradition und Weltoffenheit des Rechts: Festschrift für Helmut Steinberger* (Springer, Berlin 2002) 315, 327 *et seq.*

[96] See above n. 54.

[97] Schmalenbach (2006) 61 *Zeitschrift für öffentliches Recht* 397, 415–416. *Contra Ferrini* (2006) 128 ILR 658, para. 9; A. Orakhelashvili, 'State Immunity and International Public Order Revisited' (2007) 50 GYIL 327, 358–363; id. (2007) 18 EJIL 955, 968–971.

[98] T. Giegerich, 'Do Damages Claims Arising from *Jus Cogens* Violations Override State Immunity from the Jurisdiction of Foreign Courts?' in Tomuschat/Thouvenin (2006) 203, 235.

[99] See e.g., Art. 7(1) of the UN Torture Convention.

[100] Art. 1 of the UN Torture Convention.   [101] See above n. 27.

[102] *Jones* [2007] 1 AC 270, paras. 25 (per Lord Bingham), paras. 46, 56–57 (per Lord Hoffmann). See also *Bouzari* [2004] 243 OR (4th) 406, paras. 69–83. *Contra* Committee Against Torture,

Even if one were to assume that certain human rights treaties provided for the obligation to exercise universal civil or criminal jurisdiction such an obligation would not (necessarily) have *jus cogens* quality.[103] The conflict between the treaty norm demanding, and the immunity rule forbidding, the exercise of jurisdiction would therefore in principle have to be resolved in accordance with the established rules of international law for accommodating conflicting normative commands (*lex posterior derogat legi priori, lex specialis derogat legi generali,* etc.).[104]

4.2.2 The lack of hierarchical relationship between the rules

The *jus cogens* approach advocated by the dissenters in the *Al-Adsani* case presupposes that the immunity of states and their officials does not have the same intrinsic value for the international legal order as certain human rights. However, what Judges Higgins, Kooijmans, and Buergenthal in their separate opinion in the *Arrest Warrant case* state with regard to the immunities of high state officials applies *mutatis mutandis* to the general rules on state immunity:

Immunities are granted to high State officials to guarantee the proper functioning of the network of mutual inter-State relations, which is of paramount importance for a well-ordered and harmonious international system.[105]

The rules on the immunity of states and their officials hence have a 'constitutional' quality in the sense that they are considered indispensable for the proper functioning of the international legal order. Lightly sacrificing such a decisive pre-condition for the effectiveness of the network of international cooperation to allegedly superior values would attain merely a Pyrrhic victory for human rights.[106] Human rights violations, in particular, if they are committed on a large scale, cannot exclusively be remedied, let alone prevented, through judicial proceedings (be it at national or international level). Interstate cooperation through political and diplomatic dialogue plays an important role in the prevention, but also in the remedying of human rights violations (e.g. by means of a negotiated lump sum settlement). In this sense the conflict between state immunity and

---

CAT/C/CR/34/CAN; C.K. Hall, 'The Duty of States Parties to the Convention Against Torture to Provide Procedures Permitting Victims to Recover Reparations For Torture Committed Abroad' (2007) 18 EJIL 921.

[103] See *Jones* [2007] 1 AC 270, para. 45 (per Lord Hoffmann).

[104] See Conclusions of the Work of the Study Group on the Fragmentation of International Law—Difficulties Arising from the Diversification and Expansion of International Law, in: ILC, Report of the ILC on the Work of its 58th session, UN Doc. A/61/10 (2006), 407.

[105] *Arrest Warrant*, 2002 ICJ Reports 3, Separate opinion Higgins, Kooijmans, and Buergenthal, para. 75. See also International Court of Justice, *United States Diplomatic and Consular Staff in Tehran (Tehran Hostages Case) (United States v. Iran)*, Judgment of 24 May 1980, 1980 ICJ Reports 3, 43, with regard to diplomatic immunities: 'There is no more fundamental prerequisite for the conduct of relations between States than the inviolability of diplomatic envoys and embassies, so that throughout the history nations of all creeds and cultures have observed reciprocal obligations for that purpose.'

[106] *Al-Adsani* (App. No. 35763/97) ECHR 2001-XI, concurring opinion Pellonpää and Bratza.

human rights is really about finding the most effective *method* of human rights protection. This is indeed the most serious flaw of the *jus cogens* approach: it loses sight of the fact that we are not faced with a battle between human rights and immunity but that, in reality, human rights are on both sides of equation.

4.3 The intermediate approach

Having discarded both the traditional consent-based methodology and the self-proclaimed methodological avant-garde, which seeks reassurance in a static model of value hierarchies, the right way forward in adapting international law to the challenges of a 'humanized' international legal order must lie in an intermediate approach.

Such a balanced methodology was applied by Judges Higgins, Kooijmans, and Buergenthal in their separate opinion in the *Arrest Warrant* decision.[107] Their approach is based on the assumption that, in the conflict between immunity and human rights, none of the underlying principles or values deserves priority *per se*.[108] This contention is, on the one hand, directed against the traditional approach, which assumes that immunity is the rule and that the interest of avoiding impunity and providing redress to victims of serious human rights violations are an exception to that rule requiring a high threshold of proven state practice. That this assumption is not unassailable becomes evident if one does not view the immunity of states and state officials as a 'special regime' but rather in the wider context of the entire international legal system: immunity then suddenly becomes an exception to the rule of jurisdiction.[109] On the other hand, Higgins, Kooijmans, and Buergenthal also reject the humanitarian 'logic of values' which indiscriminately sacrifices the traditional immunities of states and their officials on the altar of *jus cogens*:

[I]mmunities serve…purposes which have their own intrinsic value…International law seeks the accommodation of this value with the fight against impunity, and not the triumph of one norm over the other.[110]

This insight does not, however, mean that judges and other decision-makers in a 'humanized' international legal order should have an unfettered mandate to balance competing values of the international community without paying regard to the traditional sources of law.[111] In this sense Lord Hoffman's observation in the *Jones* case is certainly true that in applying international law, national and international judges must be less 'activist' than when adjudicating domestic law:

As Professor Dworkin demonstrated in *Law's Empire*…the ordering of competing principles according to the importance of the values which they embody is a basic technique

---

[107] *Arrest Warrant*, 2002 ICJ Reports 3, separate opinion Higgins *et al.*, paras. 70–85.
[108] Ibid., para. 79.   [109] Ibid., para. 71.   [110] Ibid., para. 79.
[111] See also *Armed Activities on the Territory of the Congo*, 2006 ICJ Reports 1, Separate opinion of Judge ad hoc Dugard, para. 12.

of adjudication. But the same approach cannot be adopted in international law, which is based upon the common consent of nations. It is not for a national court to 'develop' international law by unilaterally adopting a version of that law which, however desirable, forward-looking and reflective of values it may be, is simply not accepted by other states.[112]

Lord Hoffman's comment needs to be qualified, however, since he establishes an artificial wall of separation between 'values' and the 'common consent of nations'. Ronald Dworkin's observation that every legal system is made up of both rules and principles (or values) and that principles play a decisive role in the creation and identification of specific rules[113] also applies to the international legal order. Therefore, as long as rules and principles find a firm basis in the 'common consent of nations', they will both have to be applied by the judge in adjudicating questions of international law.[114] This is also the main contention of the proponents of the 'constitutionalization' of international law: According to the constitutional approach international law is considered to be based on a number of foundational principles or values 'accepted and recognized by the international community of States as a whole'[115] which (in a substantive sense) form the constitution of the international community.[116]

As Higgins, Kooijmans, and Buergenthal demonstrate in their separate opinion, the task of the judge in ascertaining the will of the sovereign states relates to both rules and principles (values). It is first and foremost the prerogative of the states to accommodate conflicting values by formulating specific rules in treaties or through their state practice. The judicial function of interpreting those rules and filling possible gaps requires, however, the identification of the basic value judgments or principles which underpin those rules.[117] In those areas in which the international community has not yet formulated rules specific enough to resolve value conflicts the role of accommodating these values is, so to speak, passed on to the judge. In the *Arrest Warrant* case such points of entry for a genuine judicial mandate to balance competing values was, for example, provided for by the lack of state practice with regard to the immunities of an incumbent foreign minister.[118] Higgins, Kooijmans, and Buergenthal argued that the functional test, which was employed by the Court majority to compensate for the lack of state practice, would have to take into account both the value of the proper functioning of international relations and the value of avoiding impunity.[119] Whereas they agreed with the majority that a foreign minister needs to enjoy absolute immunity on

[112] *Jones* [2007] 1 AC 270, para. 63 (per Lord Hoffmann).
[113] See R. Dworkin, *Taking Rights Seriously* (Duckworth, London 1977) 14–45, 46–86.
[114] See also *Armed Activities on the Territory of the Congo*, 2006 ICJ Reports 1, Separate opinion of Judge ad hoc Dugard, paras. 9–10.
[115] Art. 53 Vienna Convention on the Law of Treaties, 23 May 1969, 1155 UNTS 331.
[116] See Rensmann, *Wertordnung und Verfassung* (2007) 360–405.
[117] See *Armed Activities on the Territory of the Congo*, 2006 ICJ Reports 1, Separate opinion of Judge ad hoc Dugard, paras. 9–10, 12.
[118] See above n. 86.
[119] *Arrest Warrant*, 2002 ICJ Reports 3, Separate opinion of Judge Higgins *et al.*, para. 79.

official missions, they appeared to suggest that, in view of the important conflicting values at stake, such immunities could be restricted while undertaking private journeys during his term of office.[120] The decisive lever, however, in order to give effect to the human rights consideration of avoiding impunity, is the limitation of a foreign minister's immunities once he has left office. Higgins, Kooijmans, and Buergenthal adopted the view held by certain national courts[121] that the 'official functions' to which the immunities of former high state officials are restricted do not encompass the commission of crimes against humanity.[122] The indeterminate notion 'official' is hence filled with substantive content which takes account of the values of the international community.[123] This approach is in keeping with the increasing tendency in international law to define normative standards of legitimacy for the exercise of governmental power.[124]

5. Conclusion

It seems that only now, a decade after the seminal judgments of the House of Lords in the *Pinochet* case, we are beginning to fully understand the wisdom of the Law Lords' reasoning. In their wisdom the Law Lords were, however, assisted by the 'cunning of reason' which forced them to set aside and reconsider their first judgment in order to base *Pinochet*'s exemption from immunity on a far more narrowly tailored argument than the blanket immunity exception for serious human rights violations which they initially favoured.

In the case law that has sprung from the House of Lord's precedent, the initial misunderstanding that *Pinochet* marked the victory of human rights over traditional immunities is gradually giving way to a more sophisticated approach that attempts to balance, in each individual case, the need for stable inter-state relations on the one hand and the interest of fighting impunity and of providing redress for the victims of serious human rights violations on the other. This complex task of finding the right balance between these fundamental interests of the international community will also in future primarily lie with the judiciary, since it is not to be expected that recent initiatives to codify a 'human rights exception' in national statutes or international treaties[125] will be successful.

---

[120] Ibid., paras. 83–84.

[121] See e.g., Israel Supreme Court, *Eichmann* case, (1962) 36 ILR 312; *Pinochet No. 1* [1998] 3 WLR 1456 (per Lord Hutton and Lord Phillips); *Pinochet No. 3* [1999] 2 WLR 827 (per Lord Steyn and Lord Nicholls); Court of Appeal of Amsterdam, *Bouterse* case, (2001) 51 Nederlandse Jurisprudentie 302.

[122] *Arrest Warrant*, 2002 ICJ Reports 3, Separate opinion of Judge Higgins *et al.*, para. 85.

[123] For a similar approach see Van Alebeek, *The Immunities of States and Their Officials* (2008) 222–265.

[124] See e.g., G. Fox and B. Roth (eds.), *Democratic Governance and International Law* (Cambridge University Press, London 2000).

[125] See above notes 23, 25, 26.

In his separate opinion in the *Congo v. Rwanda* case, John Dugard pointed to the fact that judges are, however, ill-equipped for this task:

In national law there is a wealth of literature on judicial lawmaking and the nature of the judicial process. International law, on the other hand, is characterised by a dearth of literature on this subject.... This explains why little attention has been paid to the place of *jus cogens* in the judicial process despite the pivotal role that it could—and should—play.[126]

In the intense judicial discourse in the aftermath of the House of Lords' *Pinochet* decision, the first contours of such a theory of judicial law-making in the age of *jus cogens* have emerged. *Pinochet's* legacy for the next ten years should be to provide national and international judges with more solid methodological guideposts which will enable them, when applying general international law, to give due effect to international human rights law and its underlying values.

---

[126] *Armed Activities on the Territory of the Congo*, 2006 ICJ Reports 1, Separate opinion of Judge ad hoc Dugard, para. 9.

9

Impact on the Right to Consular Notification

*Christina M. Cerna**

1. Introduction

The issue of the right to consular notification, set forth in Article 36 of the Vienna Convention on Consular Relations (Vienna Convention)[1] and the differing considerations of this right by the International Court of Justice (ICJ) and the Inter-American Court of Human Rights (Inter-American Court), provide material for a case study of the impact of international human rights law on general international law, to gauge what some have termed the 'humanization' of general international law.[2] The ICJ judgments, when contrasted with the advisory opinion of the Inter-American Court, also provide an interesting case study on the results of a multiplicity of international jurisdictions dealing with the same facts.

Legal interpretations as to whether there is a right to notification of the right to consular assistance, and if so what 'kind' of a right, are diverse enough to create doubt as to the status of the norm in international law. The status of a 'human' right is clearly greater than the status of an individual right derived from a particular treaty.[3] For the right to notification of the right to consular assistance to

* Principal Specialist at the General Secretariat of the Organization of American States' Secretariat for the Inter-American Commission on Human Rights. The opinions expressed in this paper are in the author's personal capacity and are not to be attributed to the Inter-American Commission on Human Rights, the General Secretariat of the Organization of American States, or to the Organization of American States.

[1] Vienna Convention on Consular Relations, Apr. 24, 1963, 21 UST 77, 596 UNTS 261 (hereinafter Vienna Convention).

[2] For example, Judges Theodor Meron and Antonio Cancado Trindade.

[3] Cf. e.g., A. Cançado Trindade, 'The Humanization of Consular Law: The Impact of Advisory Opinion No. 16 (1999) of the Inter-American Court of Human Rights on International Case Law and Practice', (2007) 6 Chinese J Intl L 1–2: 'In my recent General Course on Public International Law, which I delivered in 2005 at The Hague Academy of International Law, I developed my *leitmotiv* [sic] of identification of a *corpus juris* increasingly oriented to the fulfillment of the needs and aspiration of human beings, of peoples and of humankind as a whole.'; T. Meron, *Human Rights And Humanitarian Norms As Customary Law* (Clarendon Press, Oxford 1989) 94: 'Empiric studies of state practice are therefore of the highest importance in establishing whether a particular right

acquire the status of a 'human' right, as a component of the fundamental right to due process for a fair trial, for example, failure to provide this right would have to call into question the legitimacy of the final judgment in the alien's trial. What would be the appropriate reparation for such a violation? And further, for the right to have crystallized into a 'human' right and not merely a 'treaty' right, one would expect that the alien's state of nationality would be obliged to actually provide the alien with assistance. When considered as a mere 'individual' or 'treaty' right, any obligation would have to be set forth in the treaty, and no such obligation on the part of the national state is provided for in the Vienna Convention.

The oral arguments presented by the United States in the *LaGrand* case[4] addressed the issue as to whether Article 36 of the Vienna Convention endowed the detained foreign national with human rights. Specifically, Professor Stefan Trechsel, a Swiss national and former President of the European Commission of Human Rights, a specialist in criminal law and international human rights, argued for the US, quite remarkably, that 'the present case does not concern the problem of capital punishment', despite the fact that the two *LaGrand* brothers had been executed.[5] Dr. Trechsel argued that no human rights instrument or document mentioned the right to consular 'contact' as a human right and that the right to consular assistance does not have the characteristics of a 'fundamental' right 'which all human beings should enjoy by virtue of their human existence.'[6] Human rights, Dr. Trechsel added, 'are not conferred on their beneficiaries, they are innate, and are merely "recognised" by international treaties.'[7] Dr. Trechsel's most persuasive argument was that no state in the world considered this Vienna Convention 'right' to be a human right and the proof thereof was that the US was unable 'to find a single decision quashing a judgment for contravening the Vienna Convention.'[8]

None of these arguments may be considered conclusive, however, when one examines the evolution of 'fundamental' human rights.[9] In the United States,

has matured into customary law. It is of course to be expected that those rights which are most crucial to the protection of human dignity and of universally accepted values of humanity, and whose violation triggers broad condemnation by the international community, will require a lesser amount of confirmatory evidence.'

[4] *LaGrand (Germany v. United States of America)*, Judgment of 27 June 2001, 2001 ICJ Reports 466; see also 40 ILM 1069 (2001).

[5] ICJ, *LaGrand*, Argument of Dr. Stefan Trechsel, CR 2000/29 (translation), Tuesday 14 November 2000 at 3 p.m., para 6.3.

[6] Ibid., para. 6.11.   [7] Ibid., para. 6.13.

[8] Ibid., para. 6.33. Cf. Argument of Ms. Catherine Brown of the US State Department in *LaGrand*, Verbatim Record, 14 November 2000 at 10 a.m. at para. 4.27 to the effect that 'the prevailing practice of the over 165 States party to the Vienna Consular Convention overwhelming supports our position.' Ms. Brown added later that the 'LaGrands were treated in every manner as if they had been United States citizens' (at para 1.21) and given that Germany does not have the death penalty, the possibility of becoming subject to the death penalty in the United States, places the alien at a risk that his state of nationality has an interest in preventing.

[9] Cf. Meron, *Human Rights* (Clarendon Press, Oxford 1989) 99: 'Given the rapid, continued development of international human rights, the list as now constituted should be regarded as

for example, an indigent's right to a lawyer in state court criminal proceedings or the right of an arrestee to be informed of his so-called 'Miranda' rights, both of which date from the 1960s, are today considered an essential part of the components of the fundamental right to due process, whereas prior to the 1960s they were not considered rights at all. The US argued that in its criminal justice process, an alien receives due process on an equal footing with that of any US citizen rendering any further protection by his consulate unnecessary. Regrettably, the inadequate defence provided by public defenders in the US, even in capital cases, and the inability, on appeal, to correct the errors committed in the courts of first instance due to the procedural default rule, are at the heart of the problem.

Judge Cançado Trindade, a Brazilian Judge, at the time President of the Inter-American Court of Human Rights, was of the view, in his Concurring Opinion in Advisory Opinion No. 16, that the right to consular assistance had crystallized into a human right:

At this end of century, we have the privilege to witness the process of *humanisation* of international law, which today encompasses also this aspect of consular relations. In the confluence of these latter with human rights, the subjective individual right to information on consular assistance of which are *titulaires* all human beings who are in the need to exercise it, has crystallised such individual right, inserted into the conceptual universe of human rights, is nowadays supported by conventional international law as well as by customary international law.[10]

The International Court of Justice, on the other hand, in the *LaGrand* case held that the right of the individual to be informed without delay of his right to communicate with his consulate upon detention was an 'individual' right.[11] Germany, in oral argument, had contended before the ICJ that it had assumed the character of a 'human' right and submitted that the UN Declaration on the Human Rights of Individuals Who are not Nationals of the Country in which They Live, adopted by General Assembly resolution 40/144 on 13 December 1985, confirmed the view that the right of access to the consulate of the home state, as well as the information on this right, constitute individual rights of foreign nationals and are to be regarded as human rights of aliens, equating the concept of 'individual' and 'human' rights.[12] Given the views of other judges and

essentially open-ended. Human rights are undergoing a stage of continuing evolution....Many other rights will be added in the course of time.' See also at 95–96: 'I accept the Restatement's list [of norms with customary international law status] as far as it goes, but I believe that it is, perhaps, somewhat too cautious, especially concerning due process guarantees.'

[10] *The Right to Information on Consular Assistance in the Framework of the Guarantees of the Due Process of Law*, IACtHR, Advisory Opinion OC-16/99 of 1 October 1999, (1999) Series. A No.16, Dissenting opinion of Judge Cançado Trindade, para. 35. Available on the IACtHR website: <http://www.corteidh.or.cr>.

[11] ICJ, *LaGrand*, 2001 ICJ Reports 466, para. 78.

[12] Ibid., para. 75. The Declaration on the Human Rights of Individuals Who are not Nationals of the Country in which They Live, Adopted by General Assembly resolution 40/144 of 13 December 1985 provides in Article 10: 'Any alien shall be free at any time to communicate with the consulate

jurists, however, it appears that 'individual' and 'human' rights are not equivalent concepts.

The ICJ's decision in the *LaGrand* case established that Article 36(1)(b) of the Vienna Convention created obligations of the receiving state towards the sending state *and the detained person*.[13] The existence of this latter obligation was a matter of some dispute.

Germany, in its Application dated 16 September 1999, had not taken the position that the rights of any individuals had been violated. Germany presented a classic interstate case and argued that the US had 'violated its international legal obligations to Germany in its own right and in its right of diplomatic protection of its nationals'.[14] Germany claimed to have suffered a direct injury in that the US allegedly violated its treaty obligations towards Germany under Article 36 of the Vienna Convention, and also an indirect injury in the form of violations of the rights of its nationals.[15] Article 36 of the Vienna Convention provides:

1. With a view to facilitating the exercise of consular functions relating to nationals of the sending State:

    a. Consular officers shall be free to communicate with nationals of the sending State and to have access to them. Nationals of the sending State shall have the same freedom with respect to communication with and access to consular officers of the sending State;

    b. If he so requests, the competent authorities of the receiving State shall, without delay, inform the consular post of the sending State if, within its consular district, a national of that State is arrested or committed to prison or to custody pending trial or is detained in any other manner. Any communication addressed to the consular post by the person arrested, in prison, custody or detention shall be forwarded by the said authorities without delay. The said authorities shall inform the person concerned without delay of his rights under this subparagraph;

---

or diplomatic mission of the State of which he or she is a national or, in the absence thereof, with the consulate or diplomatic mission of any other State entrusted with the protection of the interests of the State of which he or she is a national in the State where he or she resides.' Also cf. the Charter of Fundamental Rights of the European Union signed by the Presidents of the European Parliament, the Council and the Commission at the European Council meeting in Nice on 7 December 2000, in Article 46: 'Every citizen of the Union shall, in the territory of a third country in which the Member State of which he or she is a national is not represented, be entitled to protection by the diplomatic or consular authorities of any Member State, on the same conditions as the nationals of that Member State.' It is noteworthy that both of these instruments provide for the diplomatic/consular protection and not merely 'notification' of the right to consular assistance.

[13] Ibid., paras. 77 and 128.

[14] Ibid., para. 12. Had the German consulate been duly informed, Germany's Application notes that 'its officials would have immediately provided protection, support and assistance to their nationals, helping in the preparation of their defence, in obtaining competent counsel and in collecting mitigating evidence.... In fact, however, Karl and Walter LaGrand were poorly represented, none of this evidence was produced, and the brothers were sentenced to death.' See *LaGrand*, Memorial of the Federal Republic of Germany, Vol. I, Text of the Memorial, 16 September 1999 at para. 1.01.

[15] Ibid., paras. 11, 12 and 75.

    c. Consular officers shall have the right to visit a national of the sending State who is in prison, custody or detention, to converse and correspond with him and to arrange for his legal representation. They shall also have the right to visit any national of the sending State who is in prison, custody or detention in their district in pursuance of a judgment. Nevertheless, consular officers shall refrain from taking action on behalf of a national who is in prison, custody or detention if he expressly opposes such action.

2. The rights referred to in paragraph 1 of this Article shall be exercised in conformity with the laws and regulations of the receiving State, subject to the proviso, however, that the said laws and regulations must enable full effect to be given to the purposes for which the rights accorded under this Article are intended.

Judge Oda, the Japanese Judge on the ICJ panel, dissented from the Court's judgment and suggested that Germany had erred in bringing the case before the ICJ, as there was no 'dispute' within the meaning of the Optional Protocol and that the US had erred by not bringing preliminary objections to the suit. Judge Oda was of the view that the holding of the ICJ in the *LaGrand* case, which affirmed that the Vienna Convention created individual rights that may be invoked before the ICJ by the national state of the detained person, was a mistake:

[T]he Court has confused the right, if any, of the arrested foreign national accorded under the Vienna Convention with the rights of foreign nationals to protection under general international law or other treaties or conventions, and, possibly, even with human rights.[16]

2. Setting the Stage

The International Court of Justice, in *LaGrand* and then again in *Avena*,[17] stated that Article 36 of the Vienna Convention on Consular Relations created individual rights for the detained alien in addition to the rights accorded to the state of the individual's nationality. It is the contention of this paper that these ICJ decisions were strongly influenced by the Inter-American Court's Advisory Opinion No. 16. The Inter-American Court considered the right to consular notification to be part of the evolving package of minimum guarantees of due process required for a fair trial and, consequently, if consular notification had not been provided by the host state, the state's violation of the human right to due process constituted a violation of the alien's human rights and incurred the state's obligation to make reparations.[18]

---

[16] ICJ, *LaGrand*, 2001 ICJ Reports 466, Dissenting Opinion of Judge Oda, para. 19.
[17] *Avena and Other Mexican Nationals (Mexico v. United States of America)*, Judgment of 31 March 2004, 2004 ICJ Reports 12. See also 43 ILM 581 (2004).
[18] Ibid., at Opinion, para. 141(7).

How did the Vienna Convention on Consular Relations, an interstate treaty, designed to facilitate consular relations, become the source of a new international human right?

The US had argued before the Inter-American Court that neither the Vienna Convention, nor any international human rights instrument, created a human right to consular assistance and, in its view, non-observance could not invalidate criminal proceedings that otherwise satisfied relevant human rights norms, as reflected in national law.

In addition, the United States urged the Inter-American Court to decline to exercise jurisdiction over Mexico's request for an advisory opinion on the right to consular notification, arguing that Paraguay had brought a contentious case against the US before the ICJ, and that the subject matter and issues were similar to at least some of those involved in the request. Further, the US was concerned that 'an advisory opinion would create confusion, be detrimental to the legal positions of the parties and could create the risk of inconsistency between the findings of the Inter-American Court and those of the principal judicial organ of the United Nations.'[19]

The US concern was warranted. The ICJ and the Inter-American Court reached different conclusions, but the Inter-American Court reaffirmed that it was 'autonomous' and brushed aside concerns that inconsistency between its findings and those of the ICJ amounted to a problem. It reiterated its jurisprudence on this point, stating:

[T]he possibility of conflicting interpretations is a phenomenon common to all those legal systems that have certain courts which are not hierarchically integrated. Such courts have jurisdiction to apply and, consequently, interpret the same body of law. Here it is, therefore, not unusual to find that on certain occasions courts reach conflicting or at the very least different conclusions in interpreting the same rule of law. On the international law plane, for example, because the advisory jurisdiction of the International Court of Justice extends to any legal question, the UN Security Council or the General Assembly might ask the International Court to render an advisory opinion concerning a treaty which, without any doubt, could also be interpreted by this Court under Article 64 of the Convention. Even a restrictive interpretation of Article 64 would not avoid the possibility that this type of conflict might arise.[20]

The judicial proceedings on the issue of consular notification began in 1996 with the filing of a case by Paraguay before the ICJ against the United States. A chronological review of the decisions will assist in assessing the impact of the Inter-American Court's Advisory Opinion on the litigation conducted before the ICJ.

---

[19] IACtHR, *The Right to Information on Consular Assistance*, Advisory Opinion OC-16/99, para. 26.

[20] Ibid., at para. 61; also see the US Memorial dated 1 June 1998.

3. Chronology of the Jurisprudence

ICJ: The *Breard* case (Paraguay v. United States)
3 April 1998–4 November 1998

In 1996, Paraguay learned that one of its nationals, Angel Francisco Breard, had been tried and convicted for murder and attempted rape on 24 June 1993, and sentenced to death by a Virginia Court on 24 August 1993.[21] During the proceedings, Mr Breard was never informed of his right to request consular assistance pursuant to the Vienna Convention. On 20 August 1996, Paraguay assisted Mr Breard in filing a petition for *habeas* relief in the US Federal District Court. In that motion, Mr Breard argued for the first time that his conviction and sentence should be overturned because of an alleged violation of his Vienna Convention right. The District Court rejected his claim, concluding that he had 'procedurally defaulted' the claim since he had failed to raise it before the state court. Mr Breard appealed, and the Fourth Circuit Court of Appeals rejected it for the same reason. He then filed a petition for *certiorari* to the US Supreme Court.

Some sixteen months later, on 9 December 1997, Mexico sought an Advisory Opinion before the Inter-American Court on several treaties concerning the protection of human rights in the American states. The application concerned the 'issue of minimum judicial guarantees and the requirement of due process when a court sentences to death foreign nationals whom the host State has not informed of their right to communicate with and seek assistance from the consular authorities of the State of which they are nationals.'[22] On 9 March 1998, the President of the Court convened a public hearing on the request to be held on 12 June 1998. The Court invited OAS member states to present their points of view on the issue;[23] Paraguay, in its presentation to the Court, noted that:

States must respect the minimum guarantees to which foreign nationals accused of capital offences are entitled. Non-observance generates international responsibility. The Vienna Convention on Consular Relations contains obligations incumbent upon the host State and not the individual charged; failure to fulfil those obligations effectively denies the individual his rights;

 A host State's failure to comply with Article 36(1) (b) of the Vienna Convention on Consular Relations renders a detained foreign national's right to the due process illusory; when the defendant is charged with a crime punishable with the death penalty, the host

---

[21] See *Vienna Convention on Consular Relations (Paraguay v. United States)*, Provisional Measures, Order of 9 April 1998, 1998 ICJ Reports 248. See also 27 ILM 810 (1998).

[22] IACtHR, *The Right to Information on Consular Assistance*, Advisory Opinion OC-16/99, para. 1.

[23] Eight states responded to the Inter-American Court's request for their views: Mexico, Costa Rica, El Salvador, Guatemala, Honduras, Paraguay, the Dominican Republic, and the United States.

State's failure to comply with its obligations under Article 36(1) (b) is all the more serious, and constitutes a violation of the 'human right *par excellence*', the right to life, and

The involvement of consular officers from the time a foreign national is arrested is essential, especially when one considers how the legal systems differ from State to State and the potential language problems the arrested foreign national might have. Consular assistance can significantly influence the outcome of the process in the accused's favour. (Emphasis added).[24]

Paraguay, in its request to the ICJ for provisional measures, dated 3 April 1998, maintained that by violating its obligations under Article 36, the United States prevented Paraguay from exercising the consular functions provided for in Articles 5 and 36 of the Vienna Convention. Paraguay claimed, as no state before it ever had, that because of a failure to inform the detainee of his right to consular access under the Vienna Convention, resulting in a breach thereof, the results of the criminal trial, conviction and appeal should be voided.

On 9 April 1998, the International Court of Justice issued provisional measures in the *Breard* case, which stated that: 'The US should take all measures at its disposal to ensure that Angel Francisco Breard is not executed pending the final decision in these proceedings and should inform the Court of all measures which it has taken in the implementation of this Order.'[25]

For 11 days, from 3 to 14 April 1998, the *Breard* case was pending both before the US Supreme Court and the International Court of Justice. Breard's lawyers had filed a petition and applied for a stay of execution before the US Supreme Court to 'enforce' the ICJ's order of provisional measures.

In a six to three decision on 14 April 1998, the US Supreme Court rejected the Vienna Convention claim on 'procedural default' grounds and implicitly rejected any rights argument noting that: 'Even were Breard's Vienna Convention claim properly raised and proven, it is extremely doubtful that the violation should result in the overturning of a final judgment of conviction without some showing that the violation had an effect on the trial.'[26]

Although the US, in its brief dated 1 June 1998, recommended that the Inter-American Court defer its consideration of the request for an advisory opinion until the ICJ rendered its decision on the *Breard* case, interpreting the obligations of states parties to the Vienna Convention, its request was not persuasive since one and a half months earlier, on 14 April 1998, the US had executed Angel Breard.

Although Paraguay asserted that the ICJ's order was legally binding, at the time of the *Breard* case, the ICJ provisional measures were *not* considered legally binding by the states parties, yet states were considered obliged to take them into

---

[24] IACtHR, *The Right to Information on Consular Assistance*, Advisory Opinion OC-16/99, para. 27.

[25] Provisional Measures, Order of 9 April 1998, 1998 ICJ Reports 258.

[26] *Breard v. Greene*, 523 US 371, 118 S. Ct. 1352, 140 L.Ed.2d 529 (1998).

account.[27] On 3 November 1998, following Mr Breard's execution, the United States issued a formal apology to Paraguay over the failure of US authorities to notify him of his treaty based right to seek consular assistance following arrest on capital murder charges. The United States acknowledged having violated the Vienna Convention but denied that the violation warranted the provision of any reparations or guarantees of non-repetition. One day after receiving the apology, Paraguay withdrew its case against the United States at the ICJ and, consequently, no merits judgment was ever issued.

ICJ: The issuance of provisional measures (*LaGrand* Case, Germany v. United States) 3 March 1999

Four months later, on 2 March 1999, the German Government requested the ICJ to issue provisional measures of protection for Mr Walter LaGrand. The LaGrand brothers had been tried and convicted for murder in 1982 in Arizona and, as in the *Breard* case, they had not been informed by the US authorities of their right to seek consular assistance. Mr Karl LaGrand was executed on 24 February 1999, and on the evening of 2 March 1999, the German Government instituted proceedings before the ICJ requesting the Court to order a stay of execution for Walter, Karl's brother, whose execution date was set for the next day, 3 March 1999.

The morning of 3 March 1999, the Vice President of the ICJ was informed by the German Government's representative that the Governor of Arizona had rejected the Mercy Committee's recommendation to stay Walter's execution, and that he would be executed at 3 p.m. Phoenix time. Given his imminent execution, the German Government's representative asked the Court 'to indicate' forthwith, and *without holding a hearing*, provisional measures, *proprio motu*, pursuant to Article 75.1 of the Court's Rules. The United States objected, pointing out that the case had been the subject of lengthy proceedings in the US and the late request for provisional measures would result in the Court issuing an order without having first heard the parties. Despite the US's request for caution, the urgency of the impending execution led the ICJ to indicate provisional measures. On 3 March 1999, the ICJ unanimously issued provisional measures in exactly the same terms as in the *Breard* case one year earlier:[28]

1. The United States of America should take all measures at its disposal to ensure that Walter LaGrand is not executed pending the final decision in these

---

[27] It is noteworthy that Paraguay, in its Application claimed that the US breached Article 36(1) of the Vienna Convention 'by denying to both Paraguay *and its nationals* their rights of consular notification and access during the course of a criminal proceeding by which Mr Breard was sentenced to death.' (Emphasis added). *Vienna Convention on Consular Relations (Paraguay v. United States of America)* 1998 ICJ Reports 248, Memorial of the Republic of Paraguay, 9 October 1998.

[28] ICJ, *LaGrand (Germany v. United States of America)*, Provisional Measures, Order of 3 March 1999, 1999 ICJ Reports 9, para. 29.

proceedings, and should inform the Court of all the measures which it has taken in implementation of this order.
2. The Government of the United States of America should transmit this Order to the Governor of the State of Arizona.

The second part of the measures was new and added a requirement that the United States authorities transmit a copy of the Order to the Governor of Arizona. Despite the issuance of the ICJ's provisional measures, however, Walter LaGrand was executed on 3 March 1999.

Germany argued in its Memorial dated 16 September 1999, as Paraguay had before it, that the provisional measures, issued by the ICJ on 3 March 1999, were legally binding on the United States. The ICJ's judgment on the merits in *LaGrand* did not appear for another two years, until 27 June 2001, at which time the ICJ declared, for the first time, that its provisional measures, issued two years earlier, were indeed legally binding on the United States. One can only speculate whether the ICJ's decision was influenced by the Inter-American Court's conventional authority to issue legally binding provisional measures.[29]

Germany, following the execution of Walter LaGrand in disregard of the ICJ's provisional measures order, amended its complaint and requested the ICJ to hold that the US violation of the Court's provisional measures entailed state responsibility.

Inter-American Court of Human Rights: *Advisory Opinion No. 16,* 9 December 1997–1 October 1999

The Inter-American Court's Advisory Opinion No. 16 is surprisingly bold given the extent of its reach and the fact that cases involving similar issues were pending before the ICJ. The Inter-American Court held that the rights conferred in Article 36 of the Vienna Convention apply 'to all cases in which a national of a sending state is deprived of his freedom, regardless of the reason,' and not just for cases involving persons subject to the imposition of the death penalty.[30]

The Inter-American Court looked to the jurisprudence of the UN Human Rights Committee and concluded that if the requirements of procedural and substantive due process are not met, then the state violates not only Article 14 (due process) but also Article 6(2) (right to life) by imposing the death penalty.[31]

---

[29] The Inter-American Court is the only judicial body specifically authorized by treaty (Article 63(2) of the American Convention) to issue legally binding provisional measures. For an evaluation of the impact of Advisory Opinion No. 16 on the ICJ, from the viewpoint of one of the Inter-American Court's judges, see A.A. Cançado Trindade, 'The Humanization of Consular Law: The Impact of Advisory Opinion No. 16 (1999) of the Inter-American Court of Human Rights on International Case Law and Practice' (2007) 6 Chinese J Intl L. 1, 5, at paras. 19 and 20.

[30] IACtHR, *The Right to Information on Consular Assistance*, Advisory Opinion OC-16/99, para. 101.

[31] Cf. *Mbenge v. Zaire* (16/1977), HRCt, 25 March 1983, *Restrictions to the Death Penalty (Arts. 4(2) and 4(4) of the American Convention on Human Rights)*, Advisory Opinion OC-3/83 of 8

Because the imposition of the death penalty is irreversible, the strictest enforcement of judicial guarantees is required to prevent the arbitrary taking of a life in violation of Article 4 of the American Convention or Article 6 of the UN International Covenant on Civil and Political Rights.[32] The Court concluded that the failure to observe a foreign national's right to information, recognized in Article 36(1)(b) of the Vienna Convention, is prejudicial to the due process of law and, in such circumstances, imposition of the death penalty is a violation of the right not to be deprived of life 'arbitrarily', as stipulated in the relevant provisions of the international human rights treaties.[33]

In so doing, the Inter-American Court aggressively *created* a 'human right' in finding that whenever a foreign national is detained, he has the fundamental human right, recognized in the Vienna Convention, to be informed by the authorities that he may contact the consular agents of his own country, and that failure to do so, *even without a showing of prejudice* (since the prejudice is presumed)[34] constitutes a violation of the human right to due process sufficient to incur international responsibility and the duty to make reparation.

The Inter-American Court established that it had jurisdiction to consider the case since it concerned the protection of human rights in the American states and determined that the Vienna Convention on Consular Relations 'recognises assistance to a national of the sending State for the defence of his rights before the authorities of the host State to be one of the paramount functions of a consular officer. Hence, the provision recognising consular communication serves a dual purpose: that of recognising a State's right to assist its nationals through the consular officer's actions and, correspondingly, that of recognizing the correlative right of the national of the sending State to contact the consular officer to obtain that assistance.'[35]

The possessor of the rights, the Inter-American Court stated, is the individual, and the individual may decide that he expressly opposes any action on his behalf from the state of his nationality. The Court concluded that it may 'be inferred... that exercise of this right is limited only by the individual's choice, who may expressly oppose any intervention by the consular officer on his behalf. This confirms the fact that the rights accorded under Article 36 of the Vienna Convention on Consular Relations are rights of individuals.'[36]

Although the Vienna Convention does not require the national's state to provide assistance to its national once it is informed of his or her detention in the

September 1983, (1983), IACtHR, Series A No. 3. The Inter-American Court took jurisdiction over this request for an advisory opinion because the case concerned the right to life of Mexican nationals, but the United States, the country accused, had not ratified the American Convention, so although it might be considered a 'disguised contentious case' it could not come before the Court for that reason. Unable to apply the American Convention to the US, the Court looked to the ICCPR, which the US had ratified and the jurisprudence of the UN Human Rights Committee for the applicable human rights norms and precedents.

[32] IACtHR, *The Right to Information on Consular Assistance*, Advisory Opinion OC-16/99, para. 134.
[33] Ibid., para. 137.   [34] Ibid., para. 129.   [35] Ibid., para. 80.
[36] Ibid., para. 83.

host state, (and the US repeatedly invoked the discretionary nature of the nation-al's state's obligations in its arguments before the ICJ), the Inter-American Court, having received this request for an advisory opinion from Mexico, a state that was enthusiastic in its eagerness to assist its nationals, found that as regards 'the real situation of the foreign nationals facing criminal proceedings . . . it is obvious that notification of one's right to contact the consular agent of one's country will considerably enhance one's chances of defending oneself and the proceedings conducted in the respective cases, including the police investigations, are more likely to be carried out in accord with the law and with respect for the dignity of the human person.'[37] The Court, in creating (or recognizing) this human right to consular notification did not offer any opinions as to whether the national's state (as well as the host state) owed any obligations to its national, in light of the reconfiguration of the right as a 'human' right and not simply a treaty right.

Judge Oliver Jackman of Barbados agreed with the majority of the Court's opinion that consular notification was a human right. He disagreed, however, in his 'partially' dissenting opinion, in that in 'every' case in which the host state failed to notify the alien of his right to contact his consulate that the criminal conviction must, *per se,* be considered arbitrary and therefore nullified. He stated that 'it is difficult to see how a provision such as Article 36(1)(b) of the Vienna Convention, which is essentially a right on the part of an alien accused in a crimi-nal matter to be informed of a right to take advantage of the possible availability of consular assistance, can be elevated to the status of a fundamental guaran-tee, universally exigible as a *conditio sine qua non* for meeting the internation-ally accepted standards of due process.'[38] Judge Jackman, despite considering the right to consular notification a 'human' right, did not endow the right with any additional attributes. The majority of the Court had presumed 'prejudice' in the failure to afford the right to an alien detainee, whereas Jackman focused on the question of actual prejudice, thereby diminishing his earlier characterization of the right as a 'human' right.

Judge Antonio Cançado Trindade, in his Concurring Opinion, leaves no doubt about the aggressive posture of the Court in the creation of this 'human right' in Article 36(1)(b) of the Vienna Convention. Judge Cançado proclaims that the 'Advisory Opinion . . . represents an important contribution of the International Law of Human Rights to the evolution of a specific aspect of contemporary inter-national law, namely, that pertaining to the right of foreigners under detention to information on consular assistance in the framework of the guarantees of [the] due process of law.'[39] Citing the jurisprudence of the European Court of Human Rights, Judge Cançado suggests that the impact of international human rights law, evolving over the past fifty years, has influenced national laws, for example those that discriminated against 'natural' as opposed to 'legitimate' children, and

---

[37] Ibid., para. 121.
[38] Ibid., see Partially Dissenting Opinion of Judge Oliver Jackman.
[39] Ibid., see Concurring Opinion of Judge A.A. Cançado Trindade.

that criminalized homosexual conduct between consenting adults. The Court, he suggested, was pursuing an 'evolutive interpretation' in its Advisory Opinion, taking into consideration the crystallization of the right to information on consular assistance in time, and its link with human rights.

According to Judge Cançado, the profound transformations undergone by international law in the last five decades under the impact of the recognition of universal human rights are widely known and acknowledged. It is in the context of the evolution of the law over time, as a function of the new needs of protection of the human being that Judge Cançado considers the insertion of the right to information on consular notification into the conceptual universe of human rights.

In the ambit of the international law of human rights, the action of protection, Judge Cançado affirms, does not seek to govern the relations between equals, but rather to protect those ostensibly weaker and more vulnerable. Foreigners in detention in a social and juridical milieu and in an idiom different from their own are particularly vulnerable, which the right to information on consular assistance, inserted into the conceptual universe of human rights, seeks to remedy.

The international juridical personality of the human being, emancipated from the domination of the state, Judge Cançado suggests, is today a reality. The Westphalian model of the international order appears exhausted and overcome, he submits, and the access of the individual to justice at the international level represents a true juridical revolution, perhaps the most important legacy which mankind will be taking into the next century.

The direct access of the individual to international human rights courts is perceived by Judge Cançado to be the key to what he terms the process of 'humanization' of international law. The intermingling of public international law and human rights law testifies, he asserts, to the recognition of the centrality of universal human rights in this new *corpus juris*, which is a new ethos of our times. In the *civitas maxima gentium* of our days, he concludes, it has become indispensable to protect foreigners in detention from discriminatory treatment, thus linking the right to information on consular assistance with the guarantees of due process of law set forth in the instruments of international protection of human rights.

Judge Sergio Garcia Ramirez of Mexico, in his Concurring Opinion, suggested that the Inter-American Court had not created a new human right, but simply identified one that had been there all along: 'The relatively new right of an accused alien to be informed of his right to seek consular protection was not invented by this Court in Advisory Opinion OC-16. The Court merely took a right already established in the Vienna Convention and made it part of that dynamic body of law that constitutes due process in our time.'[40]

Judge Garcia Ramirez also grounds his argument on the 'evolutive and expansive character of human rights.'[41] He suggests that the lofty declarations of the late 18th century established fundamental rights, but as time passed, new

---

[40] Ibid., see Concurring Opinion of Judge Sergio Garcia Ramirez at para. 11.
[41] Ibid., para. 4.

rights would emerge and be proclaimed, that have not been incorporated into an extensive body of national constitutions and international instruments. Article 36 of the Vienna Convention is simply one more addition to that list.[42]

Judge Garcia Ramirez suggests certain examples of this 'evolutive' development of the corpus of international human rights law. For example, the right to have a defence lawyer at one's trial has been expanded and enriched with the addition of the right to have an attorney present from the time of one's arrest; the right to know the charges against you, has expanded to include the right to have an interpreter if you do not speak the language; the right to testify on one's behalf is matched, he suggests, by the right not to incriminate oneself.

Judge Garcia Ramirez noted that '[D]ue process is undone when the accused does not have those rights and guarantees or is unaware of them. Their absence is not remedied by attempts to prove that even though the guarantees of a fair trial were lacking, the sentence that the court handed out at the end of the bogus criminal proceedings was fair.'[43]

The 'no need to prove actual prejudice' view, echoed by Judge Garcia Ramirez, prevailed among the judges of the Inter-American Court. In summary, any failure to notify an alien detainee of his right to consular assistance is a violation of Article 36(1)(b) of the Vienna Convention and amounts to a due process violation sufficient to invalidate a conviction. The concepts of relevance, proportionality, adequacy and above all, necessity, suggested by Judge Jackman, were dismissed as superfluous; the right, having been identified as a 'human' right rendered a finding of prejudice redundant. The prejudice was inherent in the failure to notify. The Inter-American Court sought the creation of a kind of international 'Miranda' rule to place alien detainees on an equal footing with nationals as regards their access to justice anywhere.[44]

Questions Provoked by Advisory Opinion No. 16

This Advisory Opinion raises a number of questions. First, was the right to consular notification in the American states created on 1 October 1999, with the issuance of the Court's Advisory Opinion, or was it created with the entry into force of the Vienna Convention on Consular Relations? Judge Garcia Ramirez

---

[42] Ibid., para. 5.

[43] Ibid.

[44] Later, claims would come that aliens received greater advantages than nationals, in violation of the right to equal protection before the law, since nationals did not receive the same assistance provided by foreign governments when subjected to criminal proceedings. This claim has particular force in cases involving assimilated aliens. See Concurring Opinion of Judge Hervey of the Texas Court of Criminal Appeals, in which he notes that defendant José Ernesto Medellín has lived in the United States since the age of three and does not claim that he did not rape and murder two teenage girls with fellow gang members. Nevertheless, Judge Hervey points out, the applicant maintains that 'he is entitled to an immunity heretofore not afforded to any citizen or non-resident under Texas or Federal law—immunity from procedural default. He argues that he has this immunity simply because he happened to be born on foreign soil approximately 28 years ago and, for whatever reason, has elected not to apply for United States citizenship.' See 2006 SL 3302639.

seems to be saying that the right to consular assistance always existed. This is important as regards the questioning of convictions prior to 1 October 1999, in cases where there was no consular notification.

The Inter-American Court acknowledges that it is creating a 'human right' in Article 36(1)(b) of the Vienna Convention, but the only obligation it recognizes is on the part of the host state to advise the alien of his right to consular assistance. The Court does not posit an obligation on the part of the alien's state of nationality to provide any assistance to the alien once it is contacted. The assistance to be provided, *at the state's discretion*, may involve various measures to assist in the detainee's defence, such as providing legal representation, obtaining evidence in favour of mitigation of the sentence in the country of origin, etc., but there is no treaty requirement for the state of nationality to assist its national.

When the 'right' is termed a 'human right', however, one is authorized to inquire into a corresponding state obligation to give substance to the right. If the right in question is a right to receive information regarding access to consular assistance, isn't the failure to receive that assistance as significant a breach as the failure to receive the notification? For what is the value of the notification, in 'human rights' terms, if there is no guarantee of assistance? Also, in the alternative, doesn't the nature of 'diplomatic and/or consular protection' require that the state afford the requisite protection to its national?

The logic is that the alien experiences real disadvantages in the foreign country which necessitate countervailing measures by the state of his nationality to place him on an equal footing with nationals in their access to courts. The Inter-American Court held that a defendant must be able to exercise his rights and defend his interests effectively and in full procedural equality with other defendants. To protect the individual and see justice done, the Court stated, the historical development of the judicial process has introduced new procedural rights such as the right not to incriminate oneself and to have an attorney present when one speaks. These rights have evolved gradually and are recognized today. Other guarantees should be added to ensure equality and non-discrimination, to protect and ensure the exercise of the right to a fair trial. The judicial process must recognize and correct any real disadvantages foreign detainees may suffer. The presence of real disadvantages necessitates countervailing measures to eliminate the obstacles that limit the defence of their interests.[45] But what about aliens, such as the LaGrand brothers, who were so totally assimilated into the host state's culture that they did not inform anyone of their foreign nationality and appeared not to even know that they were aliens when detained? Should they also be entitled to consular assistance from the country of their nationality and doesn't such assistance skew the playing field as regards similarly situated nationals who do not receive such assistance?

---

[45] IACtHR, *The Right to Information on Consular Assistance*, Advisory Opinion OC-16/99, paras. 117–119.

Furthermore, the Inter-American Court considered possible violations of due process and the right to life under the UN International Covenant on Civil and Political Rights, since 'articles 2, 6, 14 and 50 of the ICCPR concern the protection of human rights in the American States.'[46] The Court states that 'failure to observe a detained foreign national's right to information, recognised in Article 36(1)(b) of the Vienna Convention on Consular Relations, is prejudicial to the due process of law and, in such circumstances, imposition of the death penalty is a violation of the right not to be deprived of life "arbitrarily" as stipulated in the relevant provisions of the human rights treaties (e.g. American Convention, Article 4; ICCPR, Article 6) with the juridical consequences that a violation of this nature carries, in other words, those pertaining to the State's international responsibility and the duty to make reparations.'[47] Does this opinion open the door to the possibility of the Court considering cases involving OAS member states coming from the UN Human Rights Committee or challenging decisions of that Committee? Is a failure of consular notification sufficient to vitiate any criminal conviction, even one not involving a death sentence?

In my view, this remarkable Opinion can only be understood in the context of the frontal attack launched by Europe and Latin America against the continued imposition of the death penalty by the United States. Germany noted in its Memorial to the International Court of Justice in the *LaGrand* case that the US is the only Western industrialized nation to still impose the death penalty.

In addition, Judge Buergenthal, a US national, is currently a judge at the International Court of Justice. Judge Buergenthal was formerly a judge of the Inter-American Court (and a member of the UN Human Rights Committee), and requested a set of the documents of OC-16 from the, then, President of the Inter-American Court.[48] Unfortunately OC-16 is not cited in the ICJ's *LaGrand* judgment, but then how could the pre-eminent interpreter of international law cite an inferior regional human rights court? Since 1991, the Inter-American Court has been issuing provisional measures, pursuant to Article 63(2) of the American Convention, and one can only assume that the ICJ looked closely at the practice of the Inter-American Court in issuing provisional measures and decided that it was time to declare that the measures issued by the ICJ are also legally binding on states, on the grounds that they were necessary to preserve the subject matter of the case until such time as the Court could eventually issue a decision on the merits.[49]

---

[46] Ibid.., at para. 141, Opinion at para. 5.

[47] Ibid., Opinion at para. 7.

[48] Information provided by Judge A.A. Cançado Trindade to the author.

[49] The UN Human Rights Committee on 29 October 2000, in *Piandiong et al. v. Philippines* (869/1999), for the first time declared that failure to respect its 'interim measures' constituted a grave breach of a state's obligations under the Optional Protocol. This 'domino effect' is most apparent in the European system: the European Court of Human Rights on 6 February 2003, in the First Section's judgment in *Mamatkulov and Askarov v. Turkey* (App. Nos. 46827/99 and 46951/99), Judgment of 6 February 2003 (later confirmed in 2005 by the Grand Chamber), after

ICJ: The *LaGrand Case*—merits—27 June 2001

The International Court of Justice issued its judgment in the *LaGrand* case on 27 June 2001 and in that judgment noted, for the first time, that its provisional measures order, issued on 3 March 1999, was legally binding.[50] The ICJ held that the US had breached a binding obligation in executing Walter LaGrand, in defiance of the provisional measures Order, and that it had breached its obligations to Germany and to the LaGrand brothers under Article 36 of the Vienna Convention on Consular Relations.

It is worth noting that the provisional measures in *LaGrand* are in language that is virtually identical to the language of the provisional measures issued in the *Breard* case, approximately one year earlier. There was no explanation proffered by the ICJ as to why the provisional measures are now considered 'binding'.

The ICJ criticized the US for merely transmitting its provisional measures order to the Governor of Arizona without urging the Governor to issue a temporary stay.[51] Although the ICJ engaged in an interpretation of Article 41 of its Statute to substantiate its holding on the binding nature of the provisional measures, there is no explanation in the judgment as to why the order was considered binding in *LaGrand* but not in *Breard*. One can only surmise that the Court was frustrated by the attitude of the United States. The ICJ criticized the United States for informing its Supreme Court that 'an order of the International Court of Justice indicating provisional measures is not binding and does not furnish a basis for judicial relief.'[52] Earlier, in the *Breard* Case, the United States had evidenced some slight ambiguity as to the binding nature of a provisional measures order, for which the ICJ noted that 'the same Solicitor General had declared less than a year earlier that "there is substantial disagreement among jurists as to whether an ICJ order indicating provisional measures is binding. (...) The better reasoned position is that such an order is not binding." '[53] By the time of the *LaGrand* case however, any such ambiguity had vanished and one can only speculate that the ICJ considered it necessary to reaffirm its competence to issue legally binding decisions. Consequently, the ICJ found that 'various competent United States authorities failed to take all the steps they could have taken to give effect to the Court's order and found a violation because the US did not take all measures at its disposal to ensure that Walter LaGrand was not executed while the Court's judgment was pending.[54]

The provisional measures were issued unanimously, but President Stephen Schwebel, a US national, noted that although the Court may indicate provisional

a thorough review of the practice of the inter-American system, the International Court of Justice, the UN Human Rights Committee and the UN Torture Committee, changed its jurisprudence and held that a state's failure to observe an 'interim measure' constituted a violation of Article 34 of the European Convention.

[50] ICJ, *LaGrand*, 2001 ICJ Reports 466, para. 128.   [51] Ibid., para. 112.
[52] Ibid.   [53] Ibid.   [54] Ibid., para. 115.

measures *proprio motu*, pursuant to Article 75.1 of its Rules, since Germany had known of the situation since 1992, it could have brought its application months, weeks or days earlier, rather than on the eve of the execution. By necessity, the ICJ granted Germany's request without affording the US a hearing or the opportunity to present written observations. Also Judge Oda appended a 'declaration', noting that the Court was departing from its functions as a tribunal set up to settle interstate disputes and was intervening directly in the fate of an individual. He agreed 'on humanitarian grounds' to the provisional measures, but stated that the ICJ could not act as a court of criminal appeal and could not be petitioned for writs of *habeas corpus*. 'Whether capital punishment would be contrary to Article 6 of the 1996 ICCPR is not a matter to be determined by the ICJ—at least not in the present situation,' he warned.[55]

On 2 March 1999, when Germany instituted proceedings against the US for violations of the Vienna Convention, the Inter-American Court had not yet declared the right to consular assistance to be a 'human right'. Germany argued that the US violated its international legal obligation to Germany, by direct injury, in breaching its treaty obligations under Article 36, and by indirect injury, in violating the rights of its nationals, which it protected by means of diplomatic protection.[56] As regards the indirect injury, Germany alleged that 'the breach of Article 36 by the United States did not only infringe upon the rights of Germany as a State party to the [Vienna] Convention but also entailed a violation of the individual rights of the LaGrand brothers.'[57] It argued that the US, by applying rules of its domestic law, in particular the doctrine of procedural default, which barred the LaGrand brothers from raising their claims under the Vienna Convention, and by ultimately executing them, violated its legal obligations to Germany under Article 36(2) of that Convention, which obligates the US to give full effect to Article 36 rights. Furthermore, Germany amended its complaint following the execution of Walter LaGrand, and argued that the US, by failing to prevent the execution of Walter LaGrand, violated its international legal obligation to comply with the order on provisional measures issued by the Court on 3 March 1999, and it requested the Court to ensure that in any future cases the US would ensure, in law and practice, the effective exercise of the rights under Article 36 of the Vienna Convention, by requiring the US to provide effective review of and remedies for criminal convictions impaired by a violation of these rights.

The facts of the *LaGrand* case, given the brothers' complete assimilation into US culture, were hardly ideal for an emblematic case demonstrating the necessity

---

[55] Ibid., see Dissenting Opinion of Judge Oda.

[56] Ibid., para. 12.

[57] Ibid., para. 75. Germany argued that the UN Declaration on the Human Rights of Individuals who are Not Nationals of the Country in which They Live, adopted by General Assembly resolution 40/144 on 13 December 1985, confirms the view that the right of access to the consulate of the home state, as well as the information on this right, constitute individual rights of foreign nationals and are to be regarded as human rights of aliens.

of consular assistance to level the playing field in achieving fair access to justice for aliens.

The LaGrand brothers were born in Germany and were German nationals, but hardly knew it. They were brought to the US by their mother when they were approximately 4 and 5 years of age, having returned once for 6 months when they were approximately 11 and 12 years of age. In all respects, their demeanour and speech appeared to be that of Americans rather than Germans. Neither was known to speak German. In 1982, at the time of their arrest for an attempted armed bank robbery in Arizona, which resulted in the killing of the bank manager and another employee, neither of the LaGrands identified himself to the US authorities as a German national and the US contends that Walter LaGrand affirmatively identified himself as a US citizen.[58] The US maintained that it did not become aware of their German nationality until mid-1983 or by late 1984, but was not aware of their nationality at the time of their arrest as maintained by the German Government.[59]

On 17 February 1984, the LaGrand brothers were convicted of murder in the first degree, attempted murder in the first degree, attempted armed robbery and two counts of kidnapping. The brothers were represented by Court-appointed counsel because they could not afford legal counsel of their own choice. The LaGrand brothers' attorneys failed to raise the issue of violations of the Vienna Convention, nor did they raise or investigate mitigating circumstances linked to the upbringing of the brothers under extremely difficult social circumstances. On 14 December 1984 both brothers were sentenced to death for first degree murder and to concurrent jail sentences for the other charges. On 30 January 1987, the Arizona Supreme Court rejected their appeals.

The German consular post only became aware of the case in June 1992; it was informed by the LaGrands, who learned of their rights from sources other than the Arizona authorities. In December 1992 a German official visited the LaGrand brothers in prison for the first time. On 24 January and 16 February 1995, the Federal US District Court for the District of Arizona rejected the *habeas corpus* claims of the brothers in four separate orders. In these proceedings the attorneys raised for the first time the lack of consular notification and the violations of Article 36 of the Vienna Convention. The Court rejected the assertion of this and other claims on the basis of the doctrine of procedural default, deciding that, because the LaGrand brothers had not asserted their rights under the Vienna Convention in the previous legal proceedings at the state level, they could not assert them in the federal *habeas corpus* proceedings. As the German Government pointed out in its Memorial, the doctrine of procedural default barred relief even

---

[58] Ibid., para. 16.

[59] The German Government maintained that the Arizona state attorney disclosed on 23 February 1989, the fact that the state authorities had known since 1982 that the LaGrand brothers were German. See *LaGrand (Germany v. United States of America)* Memorial of the Federal Republic of Germany, Volume I, 16 September 1990 at 1.03.

though it was obvious that the LaGrand brothers were unaware of their rights under the Vienna Convention during the state court proceedings. Further, the brothers were unaware of their rights because the authorities failed to inform them thereof, without delay, as they were obligated to pursuant to the Vienna Convention.[60]

The US did not deny that it had violated Article 36(1)(b) of the Vienna Convention, but it contended that the rights of consular notification and access under the Vienna Convention are rights of states and not of individuals, even though these rights may benefit individuals by permitting states to offer them consular assistance. It maintained that the treatment due to individuals under the Convention is inextricably linked to and derived from the right of the state, acting through its consular officer, to communicate with its nationals and does not constitute a fundamental right or a human right.[61] Germany contended that Article 36(1)(b) was not only an individual right but has assumed the character of a human right. It is noteworthy, however, that Germany, in its application, claimed only that the US had violated its international legal obligations to Germany—in its own right and in its right of diplomatic protection of its nationals, although that position evolved and Germany argued that the breach 'entailed a violation of the individual rights of the LaGrand brothers.'[62] At the oral hearings, Germany further contended that the right of the individual to be informed without delay has assumed the character of a human right, adding that 'the character of the right under Article 36 as a human right renders the effectiveness of this provision even more imperative.'[63]

The ICJ did not accept the US's argument that Article 36(2) of the Vienna Convention applies only to the rights of the sending state and not also to those of the detained individual. The Court determined that Article 36(1) creates individual rights for the detained person, in addition to the rights accorded to the sending state and that consequently the reference to the 'rights' in paragraph 2 must be read as applying not only to the rights of the sending state, *but also to the rights of the detained individual*.[64] This is the ICJ's closest approximation to finding

---

[60] On 24 February 1999 the Ninth Circuit Court of Appeals rejected a second *habeas corpus* claim of Karl LaGrand based on the omission of consular notification. The Court held that the claim was procedurally defaulted. On 23 February 1999, the Arizona Superior Court in Pima County rejected Walter LaGrand's second petition for post-conviction relief based on the lack of consular advice.

[61] Ibid., para. 76.

[62] Ibid., paras. 11, 12 and 75.

[63] Ibid., para. 78. The hearings on this case were held from 13–17 November 2000, a year after the issuance of the Inter-American Court's Advisory Opinion, which may explain Germany's 'human rights' argument. Support for this interpretation can be found in the statement by Bruno Simma on behalf of Germany. See *LaGrand* Hearing, 13 November 2000 at 10 am and 3 pm; CR2000/26, para. 7, in which Simma (Germany) states that Article 36 has acquired the character of a human right for aliens and, para. 9, in which reference is made to the Inter-American Court's Advisory Opinion No. 16.

[64] Ibid., paras. 77 and 89.

that a human right of the LaGrand brothers had been violated and it is submitted that the ICJ's willingness to consider the rights of the individuals was motivated by the Advisory Opinion of the Inter-American Court. The ICJ found that the US violated the rights accorded by Article 36(1)(b) to the LaGrand brothers and determined that it was not necessary 'to consider the additional argument developed by Germany in this regard.'[65]

The ICJ held that by failing to inform the LaGrand brothers without delay following their arrest of their rights under the Vienna Convention and thereby depriving Germany of the possibility of rendering consular assistance, the US breached its obligations to Germany *and to the LaGrand brothers* under Article 36(1).[66] The ICJ dismissed the requirement of a finding of actual prejudice to the purported victim in the failure to provide consular notification and held that the failure to provide notification was sufficient to constitute a violation of the Vienna Convention:

It is immaterial for the purposes of the present case whether the LaGrands would have sought consular assistance from Germany, whether Germany would have rendered such assistance, or whether a different verdict would have been rendered. It is sufficient that the Convention conferred these rights, and that Germany and the LaGrands were in effect prevented by the breach of the United States from exercising them, had they so chosen.[67]

Generally, when a violation of human rights is determined, state responsibility to provide reparations is appropriate. In Germany's application to the ICJ it requested reparation in the form of compensation and satisfaction for the execution of Karl LaGrand on 24 February 1999.[68] The Court, however, notes that the US apologized to Germany for the breach of Article 36(1), and that Germany (in the amended application) had *not requested* material reparation for this injury to itself and to the LaGrand brothers.[69] Later, in the *Avena* case, the ICJ stepped back from the position of presuming prejudice in the failure of notification to a requirement of a showing of actual prejudice.

Judge Shi, the Chinese Vice President of the ICJ, was of the view that the US had violated its obligation to Germany under Article 36(1) but had doubts as to the Court's finding that the US also violated its obligations to the LaGrand brothers.[70] Judge Oda was of the view that ICJ jurisdiction was wrongly assumed in that there was no dispute in this case. Most judges, he alleged, accepted this case because the US raised no preliminary objections to the application. In addition, Judge Oda was against the 3 March 1999 order on provisional measures,

---

[65] Ibid., para. 78. In *Avena*, the ICJ repeats this hesitation to comment on whether or not consular notification is a human right, but offers a hint of its opinion that it is not a human right, quite different from the earlier implications in *LaGrand*.

[66] Ibid., para. 128.   [67] Ibid., para. 74.

[68] Ibid., para. 10.   [69] Ibid., para. 125.

[70] Ibid., para. 2 of the Separate Opinion of Vice-President Shi.

having voted for them for 'humanitarian' reasons.[71] Both Judges Shi and Oda questioned the majority's finding that an obligation *to individuals* had been breached, rather than solely an obligation to the state.

The ICJ did not issue its judgment on the merits in *LaGrand* until 27 June 2001, whereas on 1 October 1999, the Inter-American Court had issued its Advisory Opinion on the right to information on consular assistance. It is one of the unverifiable presumptions of this paper that the ICJ would not have considered the prejudice to the victim to be presumed in the failure of the host state to provide notification of consular assistance but for the Inter-American Court's Advisory Opinion terming the right a 'human' right. Despite the ICJ's unwillingness to unambiguously discuss the issue, the presumption of prejudice leads to the conclusion that the ICJ considered the right to be more than a treaty right.[72]

Despite ICJ President Guillaume's declaration in the *LaGrand* case of what has been termed 'the doctrine of the impermissibility of an *a contrario* contention', after pointing out that the judgment only rules on the obligations of the United States in relation to German nationals, he states that the ruling:

Does not address the position of nationals of other countries or that of individuals sentenced to penalties that are not of a severe nature. However, in order to avoid any ambiguity, it should be made clear that there can be no question of applying an *a contrario* interpretation to this paragraph.[73]

It has been suggested that the effect of this doctrine is that an interpretation of a multilateral convention in a judgment on a bilateral dispute will apply generally, although the application of that interpretation will remain a bilateral matter between the parties to the litigation.[74] Instead of controlling the litigation in the subsequent case, *Avena,* the reasoning of the judgment was somewhat modified although the doctrine was reiterated in that judgment.[75]

ICJ: The issuance of provisional measures (*Avena* case, Mexico v. United States) 5 February 2003

On 9 January 2003, Mexico brought a case to the ICJ against the United States, alleging violations of Articles 5 and 36 of the Vienna Convention on Consular

---

[71] Ibid., paras. 15 and 9 of the Dissenting Opinion of Judge Oda.

[72] There is now a continuous stream of these cases. On 10 October 2002, the Inter-American Commission decided the *Ramón Martinez Villareal* case (IACmHR, Report No 52/02, Case 11.753, 10 October 2002), in which it held that the US failure to inform a Mexican national of his right to seek consular assistance violated his right to due process, as protected by the American Declaration of the Rights and Duties of Man (American Declaration) and should the US execute him it will also incur a violation of the right to life provisions of the American Declaration. Mr Martinez-Villareal's death sentence was subsequently vacated due to his mental retardation.

[73] Ibid., Declaration of President Guillaume.

[74] Shabtai Rosenne, *The Law And Practice Of The International Court 1920–2005 Volume III, Procedure* (Martinus Nijhoff Publishers, Leiden/Boston 2006) 1378.

[75] *Avena*, 2004 ICJ Reports 121, para. 150.

Relations with respect to 54 Mexican nationals who had been sentenced to death in California, Texas, Illinois, Arizona, Arkansas, Florida, Nevada, Ohio Oklahoma, and Oregon.[76] In its application, Mexico alleged that the US was systematically violating its obligation under Article 36 of the Vienna Convention to inform Mexican nationals of their 'human' right to seek consular assistance and violating Mexico's own right to provide consular protection to its nationals by failing to provide adequate relief to redress these violations.

Mexico, with the Inter-American Court's recently issued Advisory Opinion No. 16 validating its position, in its January 2003 application to the ICJ alleged that the US and Mexico held 'irreconcilable views regarding the interpretation and the application of Article 36'. Mexico and the US disagreed, according to the Mexican application, both 'on the scope and the nature of the rights conferred by Article 36'.[77]

Mexico contended that even if a Mexican national raised a Vienna Convention claim in a state court, the state courts in the US declined 'to provide a remedy for Convention violations on the ground that the Convention does not create 'fundamental' rights on a par with constitutional rights (e.g. the right to counsel) that would justify judicial relief'.[78]

Further, Mexico argued, the US Federal Courts of Appeal have consistently held that the Vienna Convention does not confer individual rights on foreign nationals in the first place.[79] Citing US law Professor Joan Fitzpatrick, Mexico argued that the Federal Courts of Appeals have continued to rely on pre-*LaGrand* interpretations by the Department of State that the 'Vienna Convention does not create individual rights'.[80]

Following the 27 June 2001 *LaGrand* judgment, Texas executed Mexican national, Javier Suarez Medina on 14 August 2002.[81] Mexico supported Mr Suarez's petition to the Inter-American Commission and the Commission issued precautionary measures to the US to stay his execution, which were ignored by the US. As a result of Mr Suarez's execution, the President of Mexico cancelled his announced official visit to Texas to formally protest the violation of international law.[82]

[76] Mexico's Application and its request for the indication of provisional measures are also available on the International Court of Justice's website: (<http://www.icj-cij.org>).

[77] Mexico's Application dated 9 January 2003 at para. 5.

[78] Ibid., para. 33.

[79] Ibid., para. 41.

[80] Ibid., para. 65.

[81] Earlier, on 9 November 2000, Texas had executed Mexican national Miguel Angel Flores. Texas officials conceded that they had violated Mr Flores' Vienna Convention rights under Article 36(1)(b), and the Department of State on 9 November 2000, after his execution, apologized to Mexico for the 'failure' of Texas authorities to comply with the Vienna Convention. Mexico noted that it had supported Mr Flores' petition to the Inter-American Commission on Human Rights, which had issued precautionary measures to stay his execution that were ignored by the US.

[82] Unlike in the Flores case, the US did not formally apologize to Mexico for the violation of Mr Suarez's rights in this case (see Application of Mexico, para. 60).

Faced with this 'continuing pattern and practice of Vienna Convention violations by the US authorities', Mexico noted in its application that it had sought a declaration of its rights in the Inter-American Court of Human Rights.[83] Mexico noted that the Inter-American Court's Advisory Opinion No. 16 had 'had no apparent effect on United States policy and practice'.[84]

On the basis of the ICJ's judgment in *LaGrand*, Mexico could now assert that the state's failure to comply with Article 36 of the Vienna Convention ('the rights conferred by Article 36 ... are not rights without remedies') required the state to 'allow the review and reconsideration of the conviction and sentence by taking account of the violations set forth in the Convention'. Mexico alleged that US law, specifically, the procedural default rule, the need to show prejudice and the interpretation of the Eleventh Amendment by US Courts, rendered ineffective all actions brought before US Courts seeking relief for violations of the Vienna Convention when brought by Mexican nationals or by Mexico.

In at least 49 of these cases Mexico alleged that there was no evidence that the US authorities attempted to comply with Article 36 of the Vienna Convention before its nationals were tried, convicted and sentenced to death. Mexico also filed an urgent request for the indication of provisional measures, asking that, pending final judgment in the case, 'the Court indicate that the United States take all measures necessary to ensure that no Mexican national be executed and that no execution dates be set for any Mexican national; that the United States report to the Court the actions it has taken in that respect; and that it ensure that no action is taken that might prejudice the rights of the United Mexican States or its nationals with respect to any decision this Court may render on the merits of the case'.[85]

On 5 February 2003, the International Court of Justice indicated an order for provisional measures in the *Case concerning Avena and Other Mexican Nationals* for three of the Mexican nationals to preserve 'any rights that may subsequently be adjudged by the Court to belong to Mexico', clearly leaving aside the adjudication of any 'human rights' of the Mexican nationals.[86] The request alleges, however, that three of the Mexicans, Messrs. Fierro Reyna, Moreno Ramos, and Torres Aguilera, 'risk execution in the next few months and that many others could also be at risk of execution before the Court rules on the merits'.[87]

---

[83] Application of Mexico at para. 65.
[84] Ibid.   [85] Ibid.
[86] The request had originally been filed on behalf of 54 Mexican nationals, however, on 20 January 2003, Mexico informed the Court that following the decision of the Governor of the State of Illinois to commute the death sentences of all convicted individuals awaiting execution in that state, it was withdrawing its request for provisional measures on behalf of three of the 54, but that its request for provisional measures for the other 51 Mexican nationals would stand.
[87] *Avena and Other Mexican Nationals (Mexico v. United States of America)*, Provisional Measures, Order of 5 February 2003, 2003 ICJ Reports 77, at para. 28. On 11 May 2004, William H. Taft IV, the Legal Advisor of the US Department of State, sent Governor Brad Henry of Oklahoma a copy of the *Avena* judgment of the ICJ and requested that he give careful consideration regarding Osbaldo Torres' pending clemency request to the failure to provide consular information and notification. See discussion infra.

Although the United States argued that execution dates had not been set in any of these cases, the Court found that the condition of 'urgency', a requisite to grant the provisional measures, had been met. The Court noted that 'the fact that no such [execution] dates have been fixed in any of the cases before the Court is not *per se* a circumstance that should preclude the Court from indicating provisional measures.'[88] The Court only granted provisional measures for Messrs. Fierro Reyna, Moreno Ramos, and Torres Aguilera on the grounds that it seemed apparent from the information before the Court that only these three individuals were at risk of execution in the coming months, or possibly even weeks. It is difficult to discern why these three individuals out of the group of 51 were at greater risk than their fellow compatriots, since execution dates had not been set in any of these cases.

Judge Oda in his Declaration re the 3 February 2003 Order Indicating the Provisional Measures for the three Mexicans, noted that the 'present case...is in essence an attempt by Mexico to save the lives of its nationals who have been sentenced to death by domestic courts in the United States. This case concerns human rights, specifically those of the Mexican nationals on death row...'[89] In Judge Oda's view 'what this case is about is abhorrence—by Mexico and others—of capital punishment.'[90] He warned, as he had earlier in *LaGrand*, that 'the Court cannot act as a court of criminal appeal and cannot be petitioned for writs of *habeas corpus*. The Court does not have jurisdiction to decide matters relating to capital punishment and its execution, and should not intervene in such matters.'[91]

The Inter-American Commission, on 29 December 2003, issued its decision on the merits in the case of *Cesar Fierro*, one of the two cases pending before the Inter-American Commission of the three Mexican nationals who received provisional measures from the ICJ.[92] Since the Commission indicated in the pilot *Martinez Villareal* case that it could consider compliance with the Vienna Convention as a condition for determining whether there was a due process violation of the American Convention, it adopted that approach in this case.[93] As in the earlier case, the Commission looked for possible prejudice caused by the failure of notification and carried out its own evaluation of the alleged fairness of the proceedings.[94] Most interesting in this decision, however, is the discussion as to whether the Commission should take jurisdiction over this case, given the fact that it was simultaneously pending before the ICJ.

The Commission in interpreting its Rules of Procedure, prohibiting the consideration of cases that could be considered a 'duplication' of the consideration by other international bodies, concluded that the same parties were not involved in the

[88] Ibid., para. 54.   [89] Ibid., See Declaration of Judge Oda.
[90] Ibid.   [91] Ibid.
[92] *Cesar Fierro (United States)* (Merits), IACmHR, Report No. 99/03, Case 11.331, 29 December 2003. IACHR Annual Report 2003, 769, 769.
[93] Ibid., para. 37.   [94] Ibid., paras. 39–40.

proceedings before the Commission and the ICJ since Mr Fierro could not be considered a party to the ICJ proceedings,[95] nor could it be said that the same legal claims had been raised before both tribunals.[96] The issue before the ICJ was whether the US violated its international obligations to Mexico under Articles 5 and 36 of the Vienna Convention based upon its procedures in detaining, convicting, etc. Mr Fierro and the other Mexican nationals, whereas the issue before the Commission was whether the US violated Mr Fierro's rights, *inter alia*, to due process of law under the American Declaration on the Rights and Duties of Man (American Declaration). In the *Cesar Fierro* case, the Commission again found a violation of the guarantees of due process set forth in the American Declaration and warned the respondent state that it would violate Mr Fierro's right to life, if it proceeded to execute him.

ICJ: The *Avena* case—merits—31 March 2004

The ICJ's merits decision in *Avena* was issued on 31 March 2004. Mexico's application to the ICJ had requested the World Court to declare, *inter alia*, that the right to consular notification under the Vienna Convention is a human right. Mexico argued that the rights of the detained Mexican nationals had been violated by the authorities of the US, and that they had been 'subjected to criminal proceedings without the fairness and dignity to which each person is entitled'.[97] Mexico further requested the Court to declare that, pursuant to the US's international legal obligations, it should vacate the convictions and sentences of the Mexican nationals sentenced to death.

Mexico contended that 'consular notification has been widely recognised as a fundamental due process right, and indeed, a human right, relying on the authority of the Inter-American Court's Advisory Opinion'.[98] Mexico argued that the US had violated the Vienna Convention and that Mexico in its own right and in the exercise of diplomatic protection of its nationals is entitled to full reparation for those injuries in the form of *restitutio in integrum*.[99] Mexico argued that it was entitled to *restitutio in integrum*, and that the US was bound to vacate the convictions and sentences of the Mexican nationals concerned, to exclude from any subsequent proceedings any statements and confessions obtained from them, to prevent the application of any procedural penalty for failure to raise a timely defence on the basis of the Convention.[100]

Mexico asked the Court to declare that the United States in failing to comply with the Vienna Convention had 'violated its international legal obligations to Mexico, in its own right and in the exercise of the right of diplomatic protection

---

[95] Ibid., para. 56.

[96] This line of argument would never find the procedure of another international body to be duplicative of the Commission's procedure since no other body interprets the American Declaration or the American Convention except the Inter-American Court.

[97] *Avena*, 2004 ICJ Reports 12, para. 35.

[98] Ibid., para. 30.   [99] Ibid., para. 14.   [100] Ibid., para. 31.

of its nationals.'[101] The Court recalled that, in the *LaGrand* case, it recognized that the Vienna Convention creates *individual rights* for the nationals concerned, which may be invoked before the ICJ by the national state of the detained alien.

The United States argued that millions of aliens reside, legally or illegally in the US and that the language or appearance of a person does not precisely indicate that one is a foreign national. The US noted that some of its law enforcement authorities routinely ask persons taken in detention if they are US citizens. The ICJ considered that were each individual to be told at that time that should he be a foreign national, he is entitled to ask for his consular post to be contacted, compliance with this requirement under Article 36(1) would be greatly enhanced. The provision of such information, the ICJ suggested, could be added to the rights read to any person taken into custody in the United States, the so-called 'Miranda' rights.[102]

Mexico contended that the right to consular notification and consular communication under the Vienna Convention is a fundamental human right that constitutes part of due process in criminal proceedings and should be guaranteed in the territory of each of the contracting parties to the Vienna Convention. According to Mexico, this right is so fundamental that its infringement will *ipso facto* produce the effect of vitiating the entire criminal proceedings. The ICJ, although expressly prodded by Mexico to determine whether the right to consular notification is or is not a 'human right,' as the Inter-American Court had characterized it, demurred again, as it had in the *LaGrand* case, although this time, contrary to the attitude that it assumed in the *LaGrand* case, it suggested in *Avena* that it might not consider it a human right: 'Whether or not the Vienna Convention rights are human rights is not a matter that this Court need decide. The Court would, however, observe that neither the text nor the object and purpose of the Convention, nor any indication in the *travaux préparatoires*, support the conclusion that Mexico draws from its contention in that regard.'[103]

But, by not deciding, didn't the ICJ, in fact, decide? If the ICJ had agreed with the reasoning of the Inter-American Court's Advisory Opinion that the right to consular notification under the Vienna Convention is a fundamental human right that constitutes part of the minimum guarantees of due process in criminal proceedings, then it could easily have found that the criminal conviction should be vacated as a result of the breach of the treaty obligations. In fact, the ICJ suggests that it is not the convictions and death sentences of the Mexican nationals which are to be regarded as a violation of international law, 'but solely certain breaches of treaty obligations which preceded them'.[104]

The ICJ compares the *Arrest Warrant* case and states that the question of the legality under international law of the act of issuing the arrest warrant against the

---

[101] Ibid., para. 40.

[102] Ibid., para. 64. The 'Miranda' rights include the right to remain silent, the right to have an attorney present during questioning and the right to have an attorney appointed at government expense if the person cannot afford one.

[103] Ibid., para. 124.   [104] Ibid., para. 123.

Congolese Minister for Foreign Affairs by the Belgian judicial authorities was itself the subject matter of the dispute. Since the Court found the act to be in violation of the international law relating to immunity, the proper legal consequence was for the Court to order the cancellation of the arrest warrant in question. But the Court could have found the act (the failure to notify the detainee) in the *Avena* case to be in violation of the international law relating to human rights where the proper legal consequence for the Court, according to the law on state responsibility set forth in the *Factory at Chorzów* decision,[105] would have been *restitutio in integrum,* recreating the *status quo ante*, precisely by ordering the nullification of the conviction.

The ICJ in the *Avena* case found the US responsible for multiple violations of the Vienna Convention: 1) for not informing the 51 Mexicans of their rights, without delay, upon their detention; 2) for not notifying the appropriate Mexican consular post, without delay, of their detention and thereby depriving Mexico of the right to render the assistance provided for by the Vienna Convention to the individuals concerned; 3) for depriving Mexico of the right, in a timely fashion, to communicate with and have access to its nationals and to visit them in detention; and 4) for depriving Mexico of the right, in a timely fashion, to arrange for the legal representation of some of those nationals. The ICJ found that the 'appropriate reparation' in this case consists in the obligation of the US to provide, 'by means of its own choosing, review and reconsideration of the convictions and sentences of the Mexican nationals referred to'.[106]

This odd choice of what the ICJ termed 'appropriate reparation', however, did not provide the *restitutio in integrum* claimed by Mexico. Mexico sought to have the Court declare that depriving a foreign national facing criminal proceedings of the right to consular notification and assistance renders the proceedings fundamentally unfair, although Judge Gonzalo Parra-Aranguren, in his Separate Opinion, pointed out that Germany had accepted the fairness of the proceedings and the legitimacy of the convictions in the *LaGrand* case on the same facts.

Mexico lost the battle, which had been waged before it by Paraguay and Germany, to have the ICJ recognize the right to consular notification as a 'human' right, with the consequence that the failure to provide consular notification warranted the nullification of the death penalty conviction. Bernardo Sepulveda, the ad hoc Judge named by Mexico, described in his Separate Opinion in considerable detail the prejudice caused by the failure to provide the right to consular notification to the Mexican nationals.

Bernardo Sepulveda continued the argument of human rights set forth in Mexico's application. He argued that what was required was the incorporation of the right to consular notification into a Miranda style warning to be

---

[105] *Factory at Chorzów, Jurisdiction (Germany v. Poland)*, Judgment No. 8, 1927, PCIJ Series A, No. 9, 21.
[106] *Avena*, 2004 ICJ Reports 121, para. 153.

communicated to the detainee, without delay, upon arrest. The Miranda warning, a particularly American judicial invention, is linked in important part to the right to legal representation at the crucial moments following arrest. The argument that the right to consular notification forms part of the minimum guarantee of due process is thereby converted into a US constitutional law argument as well as an international human rights argument.

4. Impact on Litigation within the United States

The Vienna Convention was adopted in 1963 as a means of codifying customary international law. The US ratified the Vienna Convention in 1969 and according to the US Department of State the Convention was entirely self-executing and did 'not require any implementing or complementing legislation to come into force'.[107]

Under Article 94 of the UN Charter, a member state is obligated to comply with any decision to which it is a party. The US, until March 2005, was also a party to the Vienna Convention on Consular Relation's Optional Protocol Concerning the Compulsory Settlement of Disputes. The ICJ judgments in *LaGrand* case and *Avena* were both issued prior to the US withdrawal from the Protocol and held that Article 36 of the Vienna Convention confers an individually enforceable right to consular notification. In addition, the ICJ held that the procedural default rule should not bar the raising of Article 26 claims by aliens who were not provided with requisite consular information and were subsequently convicted in criminal proceedings. The Vienna Convention does not provide any specific remedy to a detained foreign national if he is not informed of his right to consular notification and the Department of State has historically taken the position that 'The [only] remedies for failures of consular notification under the [Vienna Convention] are diplomatic, political, or exist between states under international law.'[108]

Breard v. Greene (523 US 371) (1998) *(per curiam)*

In *Breard*, the US Supreme Court refused to stay the imminent execution of Angel Breard, a citizen of Paraguay, in compliance with the provisional measures ordered by the ICJ because the Court held that Breard procedurally defaulted his

---

[107] S.EXEC. REP. No. 91–9, App. At 5 (1969). See also Dissenting Opinion of Justice O'Connor in *Medellin v. Dretke,* 544 US 660 (2005) in which she points out that Article 36 of the Vienna Convention is self-executing. O'Connor also notes that a self-executing treaty does not necessarily confer standing on an individual to bring a judicially enforceable complaint before US courts; see also Dissenting Opinion of Justice Breyer in *Sanchez-Llamas v. Oregon,* 548 US 331 (2006) in which he states that it 'is common ground that the convention is "self execut[ing]".'; see also *Jogi v. Voges,* 425 F.3d 267, 376–378 (7th Cir. 2005) in which the Seventh Circuit finds that the Vienna Convention is a self-executing treaty.

[108] *See United States v. Li,* 206 F. 3d 56, 61 (First Circuit, 2000).

claim by failing to raise it in the Virginia state courts. Breard raised his claim in a post-conviction federal *habeas corpus* application that alleged that the Virginia authorities had failed to advise him of his rights under Article 36 of the Vienna Convention to have the Paraguayan Consulate notified of his arrest and trial. The Court found that neither the text nor the history of the Vienna Convention provided Breard with a private right of action in the US courts, to set aside a criminal conviction and sentence, based on the failure of the state officials to provide him with consular notification.

Torres v. Mullin (540 US 1035) (2003)

Osbaldo Torres was tried and convicted of first degree murder in an Oklahoma state court in 1993 and was sentenced to death. The Oklahoma Court of Criminal Appeals affirmed his conviction and the US Supreme Court denied his petition for *certiorari*.[109] He was one of the 54 defendants included in the *Avena* case decided by the ICJ (*supra*), and was one of the three Mexican nationals for whom the ICJ ordered provisional measures to stay his execution (*supra*). Justices Breyer and Stevens dissented from the decision not to grant *certiorari*, and would have granted his request for a review of his murder conviction. Justice Breyer noted that the ICJ in *LaGrand* held that the Vienna Convention creates individual rights, and that the ICJ interpretation of the Convention is authoritative. Further, since the Convention is self-executing, the ICJ's interpretation is part of the law of the United States. Justice Stevens noted that Torres may have failed to assert the Vienna Convention claim because he knew nothing about the treaty until after the state proceedings were concluded and opined that it is reasonable to presume that most foreign nationals were unaware of the provisions of the Vienna Convention and that is why the Convention places the notice obligation on the governmental authorities. In addition, Justice Stevens considered application of the procedural default rule to Article 36 claims to be not only in direct violation of the Vienna Convention but also to be manifestly unfair. Both Justices Breyer and Stevens noted that the Supremacy Clause of the Constitution (Article VI) specifies that all treaties shall be the supreme Law of the Land.

Osbaldo Torres, a 29-year-old, was scheduled to be executed on Tuesday, 18 May 2004, having lost all his applications for post-conviction relief. Five days before the scheduled execution date, on 13 May 2004, the Oklahoma Court of Criminal Appeals, in a three to two decision, stayed the execution and remanded the case for an evidentiary hearing to determine: 1) whether Torres was prejudiced by the state's violation of the Vienna Convention in failing to inform Torres, after he was detained, that he had the right to contact the Mexican consulate; and 2) ineffective assistance of counsel. The ICJ judgment in *Avena* had been issued less than two months earlier, on 31 March 2004. Judge Chapel of the Oklahoma Court considered that Torres was entitled to a review and reconsideration of

---

[109] This denial of *certiorari*, however, is prior to the ICJ's merits decision in *Avena*.

his conviction in light of the consequences of the treaty violation. Since Judge Chapel's consideration is exemplary in affording the review and reconsideration set forth in the ICJ's judgments, it is reproduced *verbatim:*

Torres argues that the violation of his Vienna Convention rights deprived him of the substantial investigative, legal and financial assistance which would have been, and eventually was, afforded him by the Mexican government. He claims that the information developed with this assistance would, if presented to a jury, have resulted in a different outcome. He also claims that trial counsel was ineffective for failing to inform him of his right to consular assistance under the Vienna Convention and was rendered ineffective by counsel's lack of experience and funds, which could have been remedied had the Mexican government been notified of his detention and the charges against him.

In determining the merits of these claims, I first look to see whether Torres has shown prejudice. In dicta, the United States Supreme Court has noted that any claim of error under the Vienna Convention is subject to a requirement of prejudice. Other courts, considering Vienna Convention claims brought initially in state and federal courts, have used a three-prong test to determine prejudice: (1) the defendant did not know he had a right to contact his consulate for assistance; (2) he would have availed himself of the right had he known of it; and (3) it was likely that the consulate would have assisted the defendant. I would adopt this test. The first of these prongs is uncontested. Regarding the second prong, Torres has provided this Court with an affidavit stating that he would have asked the Mexican consulate for help. This assertion is bolstered by the fact that Torres did request help from the Mexican government when he became aware of his right to do so, after his direct appeal had been filed.

Torres offers this Court a great deal of material regarding the third prong. The Mexican government has actively assisted Mexican nationals since well before Torres's 1993 arrest. This tradition of active assistance extends back to the 1920s. In 1993, the Mexican government monitored and participated in capital cases throughout the United States involving Mexican nationals through consulates, Mexican government departments, and retained counsel in the United States. Mexico has a systematic procedure to offer very specific consular assistance in defending these cases. Consular officials monitor defence counsel's efforts, speak regularly with defence counsel, the defendant and his family and attend court proceedings; officials often assist in gathering evidence in preparation for both stages of capital trials. Mexico provides funds for experts and investigators, particularly regarding discovery and presentation of mitigating evidence, but [sic] for DNA testing, jury consultants, and other specialized testimony where appropriate. Mexico obtains and provides official documents from institutions in Mexico such as schools and hospitals, searches for criminal records, and assists attorneys travelling in Mexico with logistical support, translators, and witness identification and preparation. In addition to aiding retained or appointed counsel, the consulate also helps capital defendants obtain qualified capital counsel. Taken as a whole, this material overwhelmingly indicates the ability of the Mexican government to assist Torres at the time of his arrest and trials, and the intention of the Mexican government to assist Mexican nationals charged with capital crimes in the United States at the time of Torres' arrest and trials.

Judge Chapel reviewed and reconsidered Torres' conviction and sentence in light of the consequences of the violation of the Vienna Convention and concluded that there was a possibility of a significant miscarriage of justice, as shown by

Torres' claims. The case was remanded to the state court for an evidentiary hearing on the Vienna Convention and ineffective assistance of counsel issues, a decision that would not have been possible but for the decision of the ICJ in *Avena*. On 14 May 2004, Oklahoma Governor Brad Henry commuted Mr Torres' death sentence to life without parole.

Sanchez-Llamas v. Oregon and *Bustillo v. Johnson*
548 US 331 (2006)

On 2 November 2005, the US Supreme Court granted *certiorari* in *Sanchez-Llamas v. Oregon* and *Bustillo v. Johnson*, two cases involving the review of state convictions for failure to provide consular notification under the Vienna Convention.

Sanchez-Llamas, a Mexican national, but not one of the defendants in the *Avena* case, was arrested for attempted murder and other offences after a shoot-out with Oregon police. He was informed of his Miranda rights, but not of his right of consular notification. During interrogation he incriminated himself and prior to his trial moved to have these statements suppressed because the authorities failed to inform him of his right to contact his consulate under the Vienna Convention. The trial court denied the motion and he was convicted. The Oregon State Court of Appeals and the State Supreme Court held that Article 36 of the Vienna Convention does not create judicially enforceable right to consular access. He appealed for *certiorari* to the Supreme Court.

Petitioner Bustillo, a Honduran national, was arrested and charged with murder in Virginia and not informed of his right to consular assistance. He was convicted and sentenced to imprisonment and his conviction and sentence were affirmed on appeal. He filed a post-conviction *habeas* petition in state court arguing that his right to consular notification had been breached. The court dismissed the claim as procedurally defaulted because he failed to raise it at trial or on appeal.

In an opinion by Chief Justice Roberts, joined by Justices Alito, Kennedy, Scalia, and Thomas, the Supreme Court denied the petitioners' claims for relief. The Court held that even assuming, without deciding, that the Vienna Convention creates judicially enforceable rights, suppression is not the appropriate remedy for a violation of the Convention and, following the *Breard* precedent, a state may apply its regular procedural default rules to Convention claims. According to the majority, it was unnecessary in this case to decide whether Article 36 grants the petitioners an individually enforceable right to request that their consular officers be notified of their detention and so it assumed that such a right existed, but held that suppression or application of the exclusionary rule would be a vastly disproportionate remedy for an Article 36 violation.[110] Judge Breyer dissented, joined by Justices Stevens, Souter, and Ginsburg, and on the

---

[110] Echoes of Judge Oliver Jackman's partial dissent in Advisory Opinion OC-16 (*supra*).

basis of the ICJ decisions in *LaGrand* and *Avena* read the Vienna Convention as authorizing an individual foreign national to raise an Article 36 violation at trial or in a post-conviction proceeding. The minority agreed with the majority insofar as it rejected the argument that the Convention creates a Miranda-style automatic exclusionary rule, yet considered that 'sometimes' suppression could prove to be the only effective remedy.

The *Medellín* case, oral argument—10 October 2007

José Ernesto Medellín was another of the 54 Mexican nationals on whose behalf Mexico filed the *Case concerning Avena and other Mexican Nationals*. He was convicted of having violently raped and murdered a fourteen-year-old and a sixteen-year-old girl with fellow members of his gang in Texas. Following his conviction he filed a writ of *habeas corpus* in a federal district court claiming that he should receive a new trial because he had not been advised of his right to consular notification under the Vienna Convention. The federal district court rejected the claim, holding that his failure to raise it at trial constituted an adequate and independent state ground barring federal *habeas* review. The court rejected Medellín's argument that Vienna Convention claims are exempt from the procedural default doctrine. Medellín alleged that his confession should not have been considered by the jury because it was obtained in violation of the Vienna Convention. The district court also found, in the alternative, that Medellín, as a private individual, did not have standing to bring a claim under the Vienna Convention because it is a treaty among nations and therefore does not confer enforceable rights on individuals. As an additional alternative, the district court determined that Medellín failed to show harm because he received effective legal representation and his constitutional rights had been safeguarded.

Medellín subsequently appealed to the Fifth Circuit. The ICJ had rejected Mexico's request to vacate the convictions, concluding that the remedy for the violations of the Vienna Convention was that the US must provide 'review and reconsideration' of the convictions and sentences of the Mexican nationals.[111] The ICJ had decided that the 'review and reconsideration' must take place within the judicial system of the United States and that the doctrine of procedural default could not bar such review. The Fifth Circuit acknowledged the ICJ's decisions in *Avena* and *LaGrand*, but concluded that it was bound instead by the Supreme Court's decision in *Breard* that Vienna Convention claims are subject to the procedural default rule.[112]

The Supreme Court granted *certiorari* in the *Medellín* case to resolve two questions: 1) whether a Federal Court is bound by the ICJ's *Avena* judgment that

---

[111] *Avena*, 2004 ICJ Reports 121, para. 152.
[112] The Fifth Circuit in *United States v. Jimenez-Nava* previously held that the Vienna Convention does not create individually enforceable rights.

US courts must consider Medellín's Vienna Convention claim without regard to procedural default doctrines; and 2) whether a Federal Court must give effect to the ICJ's *Avena* decision as a matter of judicial comity and uniform treaty interpretation.

While the case was pending before the Supreme Court, on 28 February 2005, President Bush issued a document styled as a 'Memorandum for the Attorney General,' which stated in pertinent part:

I have determined, pursuant to the authority vested in me as President by the Constitution and the laws of the United States of America, that the United States will discharge its international obligations under the decision of the International Court of Justice [*Avena*], by having State courts give effect to the decision in accordance with general principles of comity in cases filed by the 51 Mexican nationals addressed in that decision.[113]

The good will of the President to discharge the US's international obligations under the ICJ judgment in *Avena* was undermined by the US's withdrawal from the Optional Protocol to the Vienna Convention, thereby guaranteeing that the US would not be subject to future suits before the ICJ on this issue.

Although *Sanchez-Llama*s was decided after the issuance of the Presidential Memorandum, the Supreme Court in that case noted that the United States has agreed to discharge its international obligations in having state courts give effect to the decision in *Avena,* but it has not taken the view that the ICJ's interpretation of Article 36 is binding on US courts.

Medellín filed a *habeas* application following the issuance of the Presidential Memorandum, alleging the memorandum and the *Avena* decision as separate bases for relief that had not been available when he filed his first state *habeas* application. The Supreme Court dismissed the writ as improvidently granted stating that there is a possibility that Texas courts will provide Medellín with the review he seeks pursuant to the *Avena* judgment and the President's Memorandum.

In his subsequent *habeas* application Medellín argued that the *Avena* decision and the Presidential Memorandum constituted binding federal law that pre-empted the procedural default provision of the Texas Code of Criminal Procedure under the Supremacy Clause of the US Constitution. The Texas Court of Criminal Appeals, in an opinion issued on 15 November 2006, disagreed, and rejected the claim. Recognizing the competing arguments as to whether Article 36 of the Vienna Convention confers privately enforceable rights, the Court held that resolution of that issue was not required for its decision as to whether *Avena* is enforceable in the Texas courts. The Texas state court held that the Supreme Court's decision in *Sanchez-Llamas* was controlling authority to hold that the ICJ's judgment in *Avena* was not binding federal law and, therefore, does not pre-empt Texas's procedural bar. The court also found that the President's Memorandum violated the separation of powers doctrine by intruding into the

---

[113] President Bush, Memorandum for the Attorney General, Compliance with the Decision of the International Court of Justice in *Avena*, 28 February 2005, see 44 ILM 961 (2005).

domain of the judiciary and suggested that Texas's procedural bar might have been pre-empted by an executive agreement between Mexico and the United States permitting reconsideration of the sentences of the Mexican nationals by US courts.[114] Since the President acted unilaterally rather than with the acquiescence of Congress to an executive agreement, the Texas state court concluded that 'the President has exceeded his inherent constitutional foreign affairs authority by directing state courts to comply with *Avena*'.[115]

Sanchez-Llamas, of course, does nothing more than reaffirm the Supreme Court's holding in *Breard* that a *habeas* petitioner alleging a Vienna Convention violation has no remedy on a procedurally defaulted claim.

Two circuits (the Fifth and Sixth) have concluded that Article 36 of the Vienna Convention, in the context of a criminal proceeding, does not confer individual rights, whereas the Seventh Circuit was the first to be confronted directly with the question whether the Convention creates a private right for damages.[116] On 17 March 2007 the Seventh Circuit issued its decision in *Jogi v. Voges*, and taking the earlier decisions of the Fifth and Sixth Circuits into consideration, concluded that, given the 'unambiguous language' of the Vienna Convention, Article 36 confers individual rights on detained aliens from countries that are parties to the Convention who are in the United States.[117]

Jogi, an Indian national, appealed from the US District Court decision over whether he had any individual remedy if he was not informed of his right to consular notification under Article 36 of the Vienna Convention. This was not a capital case. Jogi had been charged with aggravated battery with a firearm, but had not been afforded information regarding his right to consular assistance. The Court's original opinion concluded that the district court had subject matter jurisdiction under both the general federal jurisdiction statute (28 USC § 1331) and under the Alien Tort Statute (28 USC § 1359). Following this decision the Supreme Court decided *Sanchez-Llamas* and the Seventh Circuit decided to have a second look at the Jogi case in the light of that decision.

In *Jogi II*, the three-judge panel of the Seventh Circuit Court asked whether § 1983[118] furnishes a remedy to Jogi and other such aliens. In an opinion by Circuit Judge Wood, it held that Jogi had a cause of action under § 1983, which

---

[114] Professor Frederic L. Kirgis astutely notes that they did not discuss Articles 59 and 60 of the ICJ Statute which provides that ICJ decisions have binding force as a matter of international law as between the parties to the specific case it has decided, although they may have no binding force beyond those parties. Kirgis notes that the ICJ Statute is an international agreement—in fact, a treaty approved by two-thirds of the Senate—among the United States, Mexico and many other nation states. See F. Kirgis, 'The Texas Court of Criminal Appeals Decides Medellin's Consular Convention Case', (2006) Vol. 10, Issue 32 ASIL Newsletter.

[115] 2006 WL 3302639 (Tex.Crim.App.)

[116] *See United States v. Jimenez-Nava*, 243 F.3d 192 (5th Cir. 2001) and *United States v. Emuegbunam*, 268 F.3d 377 (6th Cir. 2001).

[117] 480 F.3d 822 (7th Cir. 2007).

[118] Section 1983 refers to Title 42 of the US Code Section 1983 (42 USC 1983) and provides civil remedies for violations of federal civil rights (set forth in the US Constitution and federal statutes).

creates a private right of action for the violation by state officials of 'rights privileges, and immunities secured by the Constitution and Laws' of the United States. The United States, in an *amicus curiae* brief, had urged an interpretation of § 1983 that would limit its reach to statutes passed by Congress and not to treaties, but the Court rejected this restrictive interpretation. The Court cited as authority the Supreme Court's decision in *Baldwin v. Franks*,[119] where the Court considered whether the criminal counterpart to what has become § 1983 supported a claim by a class of Chinese aliens deprived of their rights under certain treaties by a conspiracy of local officials. The Supreme Court in that case decided that the statute did not reach that far, but for federalism reasons, not because 'treaties' fell outside the scope. Indeed, it indicated that a proper claim under the treaty would be cognizable.[120] Having decided that § 1983 was applicable the Court decided that it did not need to answer the question as to whether the Vienna Convention itself may be the source of an enforceable remedy.

On 24 September 2007, the Ninth Circuit challenged the Seventh Circuit's holding in *Jogi II* and affirmed a district court dismissal of an action on behalf of a class of foreign nationals who were arrested and detained without being advised of their right to have a consular officer notified as required by Article 36 of the Vienna Convention.[121] The Ninth Circuit agreed that Ezequiel Nuñez Cornejo, a Mexican national, could not bring a § 1983 claim for violation of the Vienna Convention because it creates no private rights of action or corresponding remedies. It declared that the signatory states did not choose to delegate enforcement of Article 36 to foreign nationals and echoing the Seventh Circuit noted that it could not see the 'unambiguous clarity' in the language of Article 36 implying that the states parties to the Convention conferred a private, judicially enforceable right upon individuals.[122] It held that Article 36 did not unambiguously give Cornejo a privately enforceable right to be notified. He should have been notified, the Seventh Circuit adds, however the 'rights' in Article 36 were intended to facilitate the exercise of consular functions. The Court concludes that while Article 36 may also benefit an individual, benefit is not enough to state a claim under § 1983.[123]

---

[119] *Baldwin v. Franks*, 120 US 678 (1887).

[120] *Jogi II*, 2007 US App. LEXIS 5713 at *10–11.

[121] See *Ezequiel Nuñez Cornejo v. County of San Diego et al.*, Opinion No. 05–56202 of September 24, 2007.

[122] Article 36(1)(b) of the Vienna Convention unambiguously provides: 'The said authorities shall inform the person concerned without delay of his rights under this subparagraph.'

[123] The more coherent opinion is the Dissent of D.W. Nelson, the Senior Circuit Judge, which supports the reasoning of the Seventh Circuit opinion. Judge Nelson states that 'I believe that the confusion in the majority opinion ultimately arises from the erroneous interpretation of *Gonzaga*. Contrary to the majority's view that there must be an intent to confer a privately enforceable individual right, *Gonzaga* only requires a demonstration that the statute confers an individual right.... The Supreme Court held in Gonzaga, '[o]nce a plaintiff demonstrates that a statute confers an individual right, the right is presumptively enforceable by § 1983.'

The US Supreme Court decision in *Medellín* 552 US (2008)

On 25 March 2008, the United States Supreme Court decided the *Medellín* case affirming the Texas Court of Criminal Appeals' dismissal of Medellín's application for a writ of *habeas corpus,* declaring that neither *Avena* nor the President's Memorandum constitutes directly enforceable federal law that pre-empts Texas' procedural default rule. The ICJ had held the procedural default rule to be an impermissible bar to the required 'review and reconsideration' of the claims raised by the Mexican nationals, but the Supreme Court found that the ICJ decision 'constitutes an international law obligation on the part of the United States' but that such obligation is not enforceable in US Courts and has no automatic domestic legal effect (p. 8 of the Opinion). The Supreme Court defined the issue as 'whether the *Avena* judgment has binding legal effect in domestic courts under the Optional Protocol, ICJ Statute, and UN Charter' and noted that it is unnecessary to resolve whether the Vienna Convention is 'self-executing'.[124] It determined that the Optional Protocol, the UN Charter, and the ICJ Statute did not create binding federal law in the absence of implementing legislation, which does not exist, and concluded that the *Avena* judgment is not automatically binding domestic law (p. 10 of the Opinion).

Although the Supreme Court recognized that ICJ judgments are 'binding only between . . . parties' it could find no legal basis to conclude that an ICJ decision requires the parties to comply, which, it noted, could only be deduced from language in the UN Charter that specified that a party 'shall' or 'must' comply. With regard to ICJ decisions, the Supreme Court noted that Article 94 of the UN Charter provides only that '[e]ach Member of the United Nations *undertakes to comply* with the decision of the ICJ in any case to which it is a party,' which it interpreted to mean that states will take *future* action, through *political,* not legal, branches, to comply. Such compliance, the Court suggested, must be sought by the aggrieved party at the UN Security Council, where the US retains its veto power. The most compelling point of the majority opinion, however, was that 'neither Medellín nor his *amici* have identified a single nation that treats ICJ judgments as binding in domestic courts' (p. 20), but it was noteworthy that the Supreme Court even looked to the practice of other states regarding the enforceability of ICJ judgments at the national level.[125]

---

[124] As in *Sanchez-Llamas (supra)* the Supreme Court assumed, without deciding, that Article 36 grants foreign nationals 'an individually enforceable right to request that their consular officers be notified of their detention, and an accompanying right to be informed by authorities of the availability of consular notification.'

[125] In the first Circuit Court case post *Medellín*, the Second Circuit in *Mora v. People of the State of N.Y.* (24 April 2008) held that a state's failure to notify a detained alien of his rights to consular notification does not create the basis for a suit under the Alien Tort Statute. The Court, however, noted that it requested that the United States, as amicus, provide the court with information regarding the judicial enforcement of alleged individual rights in the domestic courts of other states parties to the Convention. The United States informed the Court that in January 2007 the

In a reprise of the *Sanchez-Llamas* decision, the decision for the majority was written by Chief Justice Roberts (in which Scalia, Kennedy, Thomas, and Alito joined) and the minority dissenting opinion by Justice Breyer (in which Souter and Ginsburg joined). The dissenting opinion considered the *Avena* judgment automatically enforceable in US courts. Justice Stevens, however, filed an opinion concurring with the majority, in which he reiterated that the *Avena* decision constitutes an international law obligation on the part of the United States, but noted that although the judgment is 'binding' as a matter of international law this says nothing about its domestic legal effect. In his effort to explain how this international legal obligation should be complied with, Stevens, recognizing the improbability of any action by Congress, looked to the states. Invoking the Supremacy Clause, Stevens stated that the US is obliged to take action necessary to comply with the ICJ's judgment, but suggested that this obligation falls on each of the states as well as the Federal Government, and that 'sometimes States must shoulder the primary responsibility for protecting the honour and integrity of the Nation' (at p. 4). Comparing the action of Oklahoma's Governor in commuting Osbaldo Torres' death sentence, Stevens noted that '[t]he cost to Texas of comply with *Avena* would be minimal' (at p. 5), whereas the failure to act would jeopardize US interests in seeking reciprocal observance of the Vienna Convention and demonstrating commitment to the role of international law. Unfortunately Texas did not heed Justice Stevens' suggestion and has set 4 August 2008 as Medellín's execution date.

5. Epilogue

International human rights law, in particular, Advisory Opinion No. 16 of the Inter-American Court of Human Rights, has had a profound effect on the interpretation of the Vienna Convention on Consular Relations as regards the evolving content of the fundamental right to due process. Once a right is 'recognized' by an international judicial body, victims will begin to invoke it in many countries and claimants will allege that they have been harmed by a state's failure to respect it and will seek reparations for the violation. It is only a question of time

US Department of State surveyed US embassies worldwide asking whether 'an individual [can] sue in court if he or she did not receive consular notification and/or access?' The State Department received 96 responses, representing 91 of the 170 countries party to the Convention. With one possible exception, the State Department was unable to identify any country in which an individual litigant could sue for money damages for violation of the consular notification and access provisions of Article 36. And with a handful of possible exceptions, no other country's courts have construed the consular notification requirements of the Convention to create privately enforceable rights. A study of whether other states consider ICJ judgments as legally enforceable in domestic courts would be an interesting and important project for the International Law Association to pursue in the future.

for the contours of this right to fully emerge around the world and for individuals to defend it as a human right and, consequently, as a legal entitlement.

The US domestic climate, however, at present is one of disregard for the obligations imposed by international law. As Madeline Albright noted in a recent *Washington Post* Op-ed, the US is currently experiencing the 'politics of fear'. She noted that: 'We have been told to be afraid so that we might be less protective of our Constitution, less mindful of international law, less respectful toward allies, less discerning in our search for truth and less rigorous in questioning what our leaders tell us. We have been exhorted by the White House to embrace a culture of fear that has driven and narrowed our foreign policy while poisoning our ability to communicate effectively with others. One manifestation of fear is an unwillingness to think seriously about alternative perspectives. America's standing in the world has been in free fall these past few years because our country is perceived as trying to impose its own reality—to fashion a world that is safe and comfortable for us with little regard for the views of anyone else.'[126]

---

[126] M. Albright, 'Confidence in America, The Best Change the Next President Can Make' *Washington Post*, 7 January 2008.

10

Impact on the Law of Diplomatic Protection

*Riccardo Pisillo Mazzeschi**

1. The Traditional Concept of Diplomatic Protection

The norms on diplomatic protection have always been considered as secondary norms with respect to the breach of the primary norms on treatment of aliens. This is still true nowadays. However, as we shall see, with the passing of time many concepts have changed.

The traditional concept of diplomatic protection is well expressed in a very famous passage of the *Mavrommatis* judgment of 1924 of the Permanent Court of International Justice:

> It is an elementary principle of international law that a State is entitled to protect its subjects, when injured by acts contrary to international law committed by another State, from whom they have been unable to obtain satisfaction through the ordinary channels. By taking up the case of one of its subjects and by resorting to diplomatic action or international judicial proceedings on his behalf, a State is in reality asserting its own right—its right to ensure, in the person of its subjects, respect for the rules of international law.[1]

It is clear that the so-called '*Mavrommatis* principle' on diplomatic protection well reflects the more general concepts on which international law was based in that historical period (in the first half of the 20th century). According to those ideas, the primary norms on treatment of aliens regulate only inter-state relations. The individual is conceived only as a subject of the state and an object in the international legal order. On the other hand, the idea itself of an international human rights law does not exist.

To this particular conception of the primary norms on treatment of aliens, a similar conception of the secondary norms corresponds: diplomatic protection concerns only states; it is founded only on reciprocity; states have full discretion in exercising diplomatic protection and even in deciding whether or not to give the individual victim the possible reparation; the individual victim has no rights at all.

---

* Professor of International Law, University of Siena.
[1] *Mavrommatis Palestine Concessions Case (Jurisdiction) (Greece v. United Kingdom)* 1924 PCIJ Series A, No.2, 12. See also *Panevezys Saldutiskis Railway Case (Estonia v. Lithuania)* 1939 PCIJ Series A/B, No.76, 16.

It should be noted that these traditional ideas on the law on treatment of aliens and on diplomatic protection have not changed until very recently. For instance, in the *Nottebohm* judgment of 1955,[2] in the *Interhandel* judgment of 1959[3] and in the *Barcelona Traction* judgment of 1970,[4] the ICJ has substantially restated the *Mavrommatis* principle on diplomatic protection. This fact could seem surprising at a first glance, considering that almost 50 years passed from *Mavrommatis* to the *Barcelona Traction* judgment and considering also that, in the 1970s, the theory of international human rights had already quite developed. However, I believe that in the 1970s the time was not ripe for a change due to two fundamental reasons: 1) the individual was not yet considered as a holder of rights which directly derive from international norms; 2) the theory of human rights was not yet so strong as to exercise an impact on the field of treatment of aliens (primary norms) and on the field of diplomatic protection (secondary norms). Therefore, there was still a clear (conceptual and also practical) separation between the binomial treatment of aliens/diplomatic protection, on one side, and the binomial primary/secondary norms on human rights, on the other.

In other words, my argument is that, at the basis of the traditional conception of the norms on treatment of aliens and of the norms on diplomatic protection, there are, in substance, two very clear ideas: a) the individual is not a holder of individual rights in international law; and b) the legal regime of human rights is separate and does not affect the two interconnected legal regimes of treatment of aliens and diplomatic protection. However, as we shall see, in contemporary international law these two ideas have changed or, at least, are rapidly changing. I will try to examine (separately, for reasons of clarity) these two processes of change (although they are of course in many ways interconnected), and the way they have affected or are possibly going to affect the legal regime of diplomatic protection. I will examine, first, the new role of the individual and of individual rights in international law, and then the impact of human rights law.

2. The New Role of the Individual in International Law

The first process of change is well known: the ever growing role of the individual in contemporary international law is linked to three other phenomena of general and gradual change of international law which may be so summarized: a) a

---

    [2] *Nottebohm (Liechtenstein v. Guatemala)*, Judgment of 6 April 1955, 1955 ICJ Reports 24.
    [3] *Interhandel (Switzerland v. USA)*, Judgment of 21 March 1959, 1959 ICJ Reports 27.
    [4] *Barcelona Traction, Light and Power Company, Limited (New Application: 1962) (Belgium v. Spain)* Second Phase, Judgment of 5 February 1970, 1970 ICJ Reports 44, para. 79: 'The State must be viewed as the sole judge to decide whether its protection will be granted, to what extent it is granted, and when it will cease. It retains in this respect a discretionary power the exercise of which may be determined by considerations of a political or other nature, unrelated to the particular case. Since the claim of the State is not identical with that of the individual or corporate person whose cause is espoused, the State enjoys complete freedom of action.'

widening of the scope and of the material content of international law; b) a process of progressive narrowing of the 'private' normative nature of international law and of widening of its 'public' nature; c) a process of widening of the formal addressees of international law (or holders of international rights and bearers of international obligations).[5]

The international literature agrees on the great widening of the scope and the material content of international law. It is clear to everyone that traditional international law, which mostly regulated coexistence among states and matters concerning only inter-state relations, nowadays has been largely substituted by a new international law, which also governs cooperation among states and which *materially* regulates many relationships that take place inside national communities and which concern individuals.

Most of the doctrine also agrees on the process of progressive overcoming of the 'private' character of international law and widening of its 'public' nature. Traditional international law, basically founded on an individualistic and private law-oriented conception of inter-state relations, on the principle of reciprocity, on bilateralism, and on a 'egoistic' management of state interests, has slowly made room for a new international law, which is open to the protection of collective and even community interests of states.[6] One only has to think of the concepts of the 'international community on the whole', 'fundamental values of the international community', 'common heritage of mankind', '*jus cogens*', '*erga omnes* obligations', 'international crimes of states and of individuals' to demonstrate this. Of course, the protection of collective and community interests is linked, in many respects, to the protection of human rights and of the dignity of the person as a human being.

On the contrary, the doctrine does not agree on the existence of the third above-mentioned phenomenon of change: the broadening of formal addressees of international law. The disagreement comes, in my opinion, from the fact that the doctrine always links such a phenomenon to one of the most debated and controversial theoretical problems: *the international personality of the individual.* In my opinion, this problem constitutes a real obstacle, of purely theoretical character, that prevents the doctrine from finding an agreement on the above-mentioned phenomenon. In reality, the solution of the problem of the international personality of the individual essentially depends on the different theoretical starting premises (which are still under discussion and un-demonstrable) of different scholars.[7] Therefore, it is clear that the answer to the problem of the international

---

[5] On these three phenomena of general change of international law see, recently, R. Pisillo Mazzeschi, *Esaurimento dei ricorsi interni e diritti umani* (Giappichelli, Torino, 2004) 16–36; Id.; 'Responsabilité de l'Etat pour violation d'obligations positives relatives aux droits de l'homme' in (2006) RdC, Ch. I, (printing).

[6] Of course it is clear that this phenomenon of change has only integrated, without substituting, that part, still predominant, of international law which has an individualistic and private law-based nature.

[7] One wonders, for instance, whether international law has its own *ad hoc* rules to establish the conditions for personality, or whether one should conduct empirical research, based on the

personality of the individual changes depending on the answer that one gives, as a starting point, to the above-mentioned questions, which involve the very essence of the concept of personality. Everything depends, after all, on a problem of terminology and definition. In fact, the doctrine is still divided. Many authors, starting from a unitary concept of international personality and from the necessity of taking into account also secondary norms and international remedies, continue to deny that individuals may be international subjects. Other, more progressive, writers, starting from a non-unitary concept of international personality, define individuals as 'partial' or 'limited 'subjects of the international legal order. A third doctrinal view, in an attempt to solve the problem through a terminological choice, prefers to speak of the individual as an 'actor' in the international arena. Lastly, some authors, although still denying the international personality of individuals, have recently tried to theoretically construct, in an original way, the undeniable phenomenon of the new role of the individual in international law.[8]

In my opinion, it is better to recognize that the concept of international personality has by now become a *useless concept*, which we can leave aside in contemporary international reality.[9] Even more, I believe that its elimination from the conceptual background of international doctrine would serve to clear up many problems. The traditional concept of international personality should now

principle of effectiveness, to determine which are the protagonists of international social life. Moreover, one wonders whether, in order to be international subjects, it is sufficient to be holders of rights and obligations, or whether it is also necessary to dispose of remedies for enforcing rights at the international level and, inversely, to be concretely subjected to international responsibility for breach of obligations. One also wonders whether, in order to be international subjects, it is necessary to participate in the formation of international norms. Lastly, one wonders whether the concept of personality is a unitary and absolute one or whether a limited or partial (or even an *inter partes*) personality is conceivable.

   [8] One writer, by distinguishing between international subjects and addressees of international norms, maintains that only states and other sovereign entities are subjects, but that individuals may be addressees of norms (C. Dominicé, L'émergence de l'individu en droit international public (1987–1988) *Annales d'études internationales* 1.; Id., La personnalité juridique dans le système du droit des gens, in J. Makarczyk (ed.), *Theory of International Law at the Threshold of the 21st Century, Essays in Honour of Krzysztof Skubiszewski* (Martinus Nijhoff, The Hague/London/Boston 1996) 147, 154 and 164). Another scholar speaks of a dichotomy between the traditional international law and a new international inter-individual law—G. Arangio Ruiz, 'Dualism Revisited: International Law and Interindividual Law' (2003) Riv dir int 909, 992–993. Lastly another author suggests that there are two different concepts of international personality, both relating to the state, but the former concerning state activities in the fields of international law from which private individuals are excluded, and the latter concerning state activities in the fields in which the state acts in favour of individuals—M. Iovane, 'Soggetti privati, società civile e tutela internazionale dell'ambiente' in A. Del Vecchio and A. Dal Ri Junior (eds.), *Il diritto internazionale dell'ambiente dopo il vertice di Johannesburg* (Editoriale Scientifica, Naples 2005) 133, para. 21.

   [9] See R. Pisillo Mazzeschi, 'La dottrina pura di Kelsen e la realtà del diritto internazionale contemporaneo' (1994) *Diritto e cultura* 63; Id., *Esaurimento* (2004), *supra* note 5, 31. For a similar view see I. Brownlie, *Principles of Public International Law*, 4th ed. (Oxford University Press, Oxford 1990), 67 and 601; R. Higgins, *Problems and Process: International Law and How We Use It* (Oxford University Press, Oxford 1995) 48, 49–50 and 53.

be substituted by the concept, more limited but more useful and concrete, of *addressee* of single international norms or *holder* of single international rights or obligations.[10] On the basis of the latter concept, one should admit that international (primary, secondary, and tertiary) norms are now able to formally address (and indifferently create rights and obligations for) states, international organizations and individuals (or other non-state entities), although, of course, in a rather different quantity for each category of these entities.[11] In other words, while traditional international law was formally addressed only to states and other sovereign entities,[12] contemporary international law can be *formally* addressed also to individuals and can *directly* regulate relationships between states and individuals, without the need to be always implemented or incorporated through the domestic law of a state. The international norms on human rights are the best, but not the only, example of this process of change.

In conclusion, once the ground has been cleared from the obstacle made by the problem of the international personality of the individual, it is not difficult to recognize the phenomenon of the broadening of the formal addressees of international law. However, I do not want to insist further on this general and theoretical discussion. I will now try to show how the new role of the individual in international law has been recently confirmed by the ICJ and the Inter-American Court of Human Rights.

3. Individual Rights in the Law on Treatment of Aliens: the Judgments *LaGrand* and *Avena* and the Opinion *OC-16/99*

As it is well known, the International Court of Justice has recently recognized that the individual may be *a holder of rights which directly derive from international norms*. This has occurred just in that field of treatment of aliens in which we are particularly interested.[13]

In fact, the International Court of Justice, in the *LaGrand* case,[14] was requested to interpret Article 36(1)(b) of the Vienna Convention on Consular Relations of 24 April 1963, which obliges the authorities of the receiving state: a) to inform

---

[10] See Pisillo Mazzeschi, *Esaurimento* (2004), *supra* note 5, 18, 24–32; Id., 'The Marginal Role of the Individual in the ILC's Articles on State Responsibility', (2004) XIV Italian Ybk Intl L 42.

[11] In other terms, it is no more important, in my view, to establish who enters within the unitary category of international subjects. In fact, the differences between the legal positions (rights and obligations) of states, of international organizations and of individuals have by now become quantitative and not qualitative; and that makes useless the concept of international personality, which does not lend itself to be split up or relativized. Therefore, if necessary, it would be more correct to speak, instead of legal personality, of different legal *capacities* of those various entities.

[12] Therefore it created only rights and obligations for states, which the latter undertook to transform into rights and obligations for individuals within their domestic legal orders.

[13] The ICJ's case law in this area is discussed in more detail in Chapter 9 of this volume.

[14] *LaGrand (Germany v. USA), Merits*, Judgment of 27 June 2001, 2001 ICJ Reports 466.

without delay the consular post of the sending state if a national of that state is arrested, or committed to prison or custody, or detained in any other manner; b) to forward without delay to the consular post any communication addressed to it by the detained person; c) to inform the person concerned without delay of his above-mentioned rights.

Germany argued that the right of access to the consulate of the home state and the right to be informed on such access are individual rights that belong to every national of a state party to the Vienna Convention who enters the territory of another state party; and that they are to be regarded also as human rights of aliens.[15] On the contrary, the USA maintained the more traditional view, according to which the rights of consular notification and access under the Vienna Convention are only rights of states, and not of individuals, who are merely *de facto* beneficiaries of these rights.[16] The Court expressly stated that Article 36(1) (b) creates obligations of the receiving state both towards the sending state *and the detained person*.[17] Therefore this person's right of access to the consulate and his right to be informed without delay are *individual rights*, directly created by the Vienna Convention. However, the Court deemed that it was not necessary to take a position on the question whether the right to be informed, besides being an individual right, has also assumed today the character of a human right.[18] This is an important point, to which we shall return later on. It should be noted that the Court established that an international treaty norm can be *formally* addressed to an individual and can directly create individual rights, without any need to take a position on the problem of the international personality of the individual.

In the subsequent *Avena* case,[19] the ICJ took the same approach. The Court reaffirmed that Article 36(1) of the Vienna Convention on Consular Relations creates rights both for contracting states and for individuals.[20] It added that there is interdependence between the rights of states and those of individuals, so that a contracting state can, in submitting a claim in its own name, request the Court to rule on the violation of rights which it claims to have suffered both directly and through the violation of individual rights conferred on its nationals.[21] However, the Court, once again, deemed it unnecessary to decide on the question, raised by

---

[15] Ibid., para. 75.   [16] Ibid., para. 76.

[17] Ibid., para. 77: 'The Court notes that Article 36, paragraph 1(b) spells out the obligations the receiving State has towards the detained person and the sending State... The Court concludes that Article 36, paragraph 1, creates individual rights, which... may be invoked in this Court by the national State of the detained person.' See also para. 89.

[18] Ibid., para. 78.

[19] *Avena and Other Mexican Nationals (Mexico v. USA)*, Judgment of 31 March 2004, 2004 ICJ Reports 121.

[20] Ibid., para. 40: 'The Court... would further observe that violations of the rights of the individual under Article 36 may entail a violation of the rights of the sending State, and that violations of the rights of the latter may entail a violation of the rights of the individual.'

[21] Ibid., para. 40: 'Mexico may... request the Court to rule on the violation of rights which it claims to have suffered both directly and through the violation of individual rights conferred on Mexican nationals under Article 36, para. 1(b).'

Mexico, as to whether the right to consular notification and consular communication under the Vienna Convention is also a fundamental human right.[22]

The Inter-American Court of Human Rights had given a partially different answer in Advisory Opinion *OC-16/99* of 1 October 1999,[23] following a request by Mexico. In this case the Court also had to interpret Article 36 of the Vienna Convention on Consular Relations, in order to determine whether it creates individual rights.[24] The Court stated that Article 36 serves a dual purpose: that of recognizing a state's right to assist its nationals abroad through the consular officer's action and that of recognizing the correlative right of the national of the sending state to contact the consular officer to obtain that assistance.[25] Lastly, the Court established that Article 36 'is part of the body of international human rights law',[26] and, in particular, that the right of the individual to information on consular assistance contained in Article 36(1)(b) 'must be recognised and counted among the minimum guarantees essential to providing foreign nationals the opportunity to adequately prepare their defence and receive a fair trial'.[27] It therefore 'allows the right to the due process of law recognised in Article 14 of the International Covenant on Civil and Political Rights to have practical effects in concrete cases.'[28]

In conclusion, after the two judgments of the ICJ and the opinion of the IACtHR, it is not completely clear whether one may conclude that the individual is an addressee of *all* the norms in the field of treatment of aliens that concern individuals or only of *some* norms having a specific character, such as those considered by the ICJ and the IACtHR, dealing with the right to consular assistance and the right to information on such assistance. However, one fundamental point is clear: at least in certain cases, the international norms on treatment of aliens may directly attribute rights both to individuals and to their national states; and their breach may imply an internationally wrongful act that simultaneously breaches both individual and states' rights. In other words, these norms now regulate trilateral legal relationships, instead of bilateral ones. It is, certainly, a great change in the way of conceiving these norms.

---

[22] Ibid., para. 124.

[23] *The Right to Information on Consular Assistance in the Framework of the Guarantees of the Due Process of Law*, IACtHR, Advisory Opinion OC-16/99 of 1 October 1999, (1999) Series. A No.16, requested by the United Mexican States, (1999) Series A, No. 16 (reproduced also in *Inter-American Yearbook on Human Rights* (1999), Vol. 4, p. 4364).

[24] The Court first of all clarified that it was not requested by Mexico to decide whether the principal object of the Vienna Convention is the protection of human rights, but only whether one particular provision of that Convention concerns the protection of human rights (para. 76).

[25] Ibid., para. 80. More specifically, according to the Court, the bearer of the rights established by subparagraph (b) of Article 36(1), which concerns consular assistance to detained persons, is the individual; in this respect, Article 36 is an exception to the remaining part of the Vienna Convention, that essentially sets states' rights and obligations (paras. 81–82 and 84).

[26] Ibid., para. 141.

[27] Ibid., para. 122.

[28] Ibid., para. 141.

4. The Impact of Individual Rights on the Law of Diplomatic Protection

At this point, the problem is the following: is the above-described new conception of the primary norms on treatment of aliens destined to have an impact on the secondary norms of diplomatic protection?

In my opinion, the answer is yes. Let us reflect upon the relationship between primary norms and secondary norms on international responsibility. If a state breaches a primary norm which is directed not only towards another state but also towards an individual, it is only logical to maintain that such state commits an internationally wrongful act not only towards the other state but also towards the individual.[29] That means that individuals (and other non-state entities) may be holders of true rights deriving from secondary norms of international law. The principle of the international responsibility of the state towards the individual has not been expressly formulated by the ILC, in its Draft Articles on State Responsibility.[30] These do, however, provide for a saving clause, Art 33(2), in which that principle is implicitly recognized.[31] The principle is commonly applied in human rights practice: one may think, for instance, of the wide judicial and quasi-judicial practice of all international supervisory bodies, which clearly demonstrates that the state responsible for a violation has an *obligation to grant reparation to the individual victim.*[32]

---

[29] See Pisillo Mazzeschi, 'The Marginal Role of the Individual' (2004), *supra* note 10, 39, 44–50.

[30] UN Doc. A/CN.4/L.602/Rev.1, 26 July 2004. For a criticism to the limited approach of the ILC Draft Articles, see also E. Brown Weiss, 'Invoking State Responsibility in the Twenty-First Century', (2002) 96 AJIL 809.

[31] According to Article 33(2), the section of the Draft Articles on the content of responsibility 'is without prejudice to any *right*, arising from the international responsibility of a State, which may accrue *directly* to any person or entity other than a State' (italics mine). The ILC by this clause seems to recognize, even though indirectly, that individuals (and other non-state entities) can be holders of true rights deriving from state responsibility. See also Commentary on Article 33 (in UN Doc. A/56/10, p. 234), where it is stated: 'In cases where the *primary obligation is owed to a non-State entity*, it may be that some procedure is available whereby *that entity can invoke the responsibility* on its own account and without the intermediation of any State. This is true, for example, under human rights treaties which provide a right of petition to a court or some other body for individuals affected. It is also true in the case of rights under bilateral or regional investment protection agreements' (italics mine).

[32] On the right of the individual to obtain reparation from the state responsible for human rights violations, see R. Pisillo Mazzeschi, 'International Obligations to Provide for Reparations Claims?' in A. Randelzhofer and C. Tomuschat (eds.), *State Responsibility and the Individual: Reparation in Instances of Grave Violations of Human Rights* (Martinus Nijhoff, The Hague/London/Boston 1999) 149; Id., 'Reparation Claims by Individuals for State Breaches of Humanitarian Law and Human Rights: An Overview' (2003) JIJC 339; C. Dominicé, 'La prétention de la personne privée dans le système de la responsabilité internationale des Etats' in *Studi di diritto internazionale in onore di G. Arangio-Ruiz*, Vol. II (Editoriale Scientifica, Naples 2004) 729. Recently, the International Commission of Inquiry on Darfur, in its report to the UN Secretary General, pronounced in favour of a right to obtain reparation for individual victims of serious violations

In my view, it is clear that the principle of international responsibility of the state towards the individual for the breach of international obligations directed towards the individual is applicable today also in the field of treatment of aliens. The above-mentioned recent decisions of the ICJ and of the IACtHR clearly confirm this principle. Therefore, one may conclude that, in the case of an individual who has suffered an injury by a foreign state for a breach of an international rule on treatment of aliens, a relationship of international responsibility arises not only between the author state and the national state of the individual, but *also between the author state and the individual* (i.e., a trilateral relationship is set up also at the level of responsibility). An important consequence is that the individual has, at least in theory, his own right to receive reparation by the author state.[33]

As one can see, it is difficult to think that this new legal setting, in the field of international responsibility, is not destined to have an impact, in some way, also on the traditional situation of diplomatic protection; that is also on secondary norms other than those on responsibility. In other words, it is clear that the *Mavrommatis* principle is by now obsolete. If the norms on treatment of aliens, or some of those, are formally addressed also to the individual and if, moreover, the individual has suffered the injury of a personal right directly recognized by international law, that means that it is by now impossible to maintain the old fiction (so-called 'Vattelian fiction') that, at the level of international law, there exists only the right of the national state of the injured individual against the obligation of the offending state.[34] On the contrary, we must admit that there now exists, at the international level, *also the injury of an individual right* by the offending state.

In short, the great change (which we have described above) in conceiving the primary norms on treatment of aliens has inevitably produced a change in the legal positions of the three actors involved in the mechanism of diplomatic protection (the claiming state, the offending state, and the individual victim). How may such new situations have an impact on the traditional legal regime of

---

of fundamental human rights (International Commission of Inquiry on Darfur, Report to the Secretary General, 25 January 2005, paras. 597–598). See also UN General Assembly, Resolution 60/147 on Basic Principles and Guidelines on the Right to a Remedy and Reparation for Victims of Gross Violations of International Human Rights Law and Serious Violations of International Humanitarian Law (UN Doc. A/RES/60/147 of 21 March 2006).

[33] In my view, the principle of international responsibility of the state towards the individual may have applications that exceed the fields of human rights and treatment of aliens. In fact this principle implies that, following the breach of *all* international norms that are formally addressed both to states and individuals, the obligation of reparation by the responsible state creates a double series of holders of the corresponding right to receive reparation: the other states (injured or otherwise entitled to react) and the individual victims. Of course this is only a theoretical possibility; in practice it will be necessary to demonstrate, each time, that the international norm in question intends to directly confer on the individual a right to reparation at the international level.

[34] For a criticism of the 'Vattelian fiction' see also F. Orrego Vicuña, Interim Report on The Changing Law of Nationality of Claims, in *Report of the Sixty-ninth Conference of the ILA* (London, 2000) 631, 633–634.

diplomatic protection? In my view, one may envisage three possible and different perspectives.

4.1 Minimal changes in the law of diplomatic protection

According to a first, more conservative, perspective, one may think that the individual, even though he has become a direct addressee of the norms on treatment of aliens and a holder of a direct relationship of international responsibility vis-à-vis the state author of the wrongful act, can continue to use *only the traditional instruments* against that state, i.e. a) resort to local remedies before the authorities of that state; b) resort, if possible, to international monitoring organs only in the limited cases in which the injury is also a violation of a human right protected by international judicial or quasi-judicial organs admitting individual claims; and finally c) ask for diplomatic protection (but without any right) from his national state. In other terms, according to this perspective, the individual is addressee only of the primary international norms on treatment of aliens, and that does not produce innovative influence on the secondary norms on diplomatic protection. Moreover, according to the same perspective, the field of diplomatic protection (continuing to work only within the strictly inter-state conception) remains separate and autonomous with respect to the field of human rights protection, and the latter exercises no influence on the former.

This prospect leads to only very small ('cosmetic') changes to the legal regime of diplomatic protection, in order to better fit it to the more important role of the individual in contemporary reality. This minimalist approach, which has been approved by a part of the doctrine,[35] is well reflected by the 2004 ILC Draft Articles on Diplomatic Protection,[36] which had limited themselves to making only moderate updates to the traditional legal regime. In particular, they established an increase of states entitled to exercise diplomatic protection and more flexibility in the conditions for exercising diplomatic protection.[37]

However, this approach remains, in my opinion, too conservative and is not destined to last in time. In particular, it is difficult to think that the above-mentioned changes in the primary norms on treatment of aliens are not going to produce, sooner or later, an impact also on the secondary norms on diplomatic protection.

---

[35] See e.g. G. Gaja, 'Droits des Etats et droits des individus dans le cadre de la protection diplomatique', in J.F. Flauss (ed.), *La protection diplomatique—Mutations contemporaines et pratiques nationales* (Bruylant, Brussels 2003) 63. But see also the criticism by L. Condorelli, 'L'évolution du champ d'application de la protection diplomatique', ivi, 19–24; Id., 'La protection diplomatique et l'évolution de son domaine d'application actuelle', (2003) Riv dir int 20.

[36] UN Doc. A/CN.4/L.647 of 24 May 2004.

[37] See e.g. Article 8 of the Draft, that allows diplomatic protection of stateless persons and refugees by their state of residence, and Articles 6 and 7 of the Draft, that widen the number of states that may exercise diplomatic protection in respect of persons having multiple nationality. For other small modernizations attempted by the Draft Articles see P. Pustorino, 'Recenti sviluppi in tema di protezione diplomatica' (2006) Riv dir int 68.

4.2 More meaningful changes in the law of diplomatic protection

On the contrary, according to a second, more progressive, perspective, the concept of the individual as a direct addressee of the primary norms on treatment of aliens is destined to have an impact also on the secondary norms on diplomatic protection. One may think, in that case, of some meaningful, progressive developments of those latter norms. Of course, it is clear that the idea that the individual has directly suffered an internationally wrongful act by the author state, and that such wrongful act produces a true right to reparation in favour of the individual, cannot by itself cause a change to the typical interstate structure of diplomatic protection. However that idea can produce some meaningful changes in the conception of diplomatic protection, because it may give rise to the new concept that the state, by resorting to diplomatic protection, asserts not only its own right but *also the right of its national* (the right being directly conferred by international law).[38]

Therefore, starting from that new concept, one could hypothesize that the traditional discretionary power of the state in deciding whether to exercise diplomatic protection *can be limited*, through a judicial control on the *reasonableness* (or at least the *non-arbitrariness*) of the decision itself. The domestic case law and legislation of some states is moving in that direction.[39] One could also consider attributing to the individual victim at least *a procedural right to be informed* of the reasons for which his own state does not resort to diplomatic protection or, if the state decides to resort to it, a right to be informed on the various stages of the inter-state procedure. Lastly, one could even predict that, if the national state obtains monetary compensation through diplomatic protection, it has the duty *to transfer it to the individual victim*.[40]

---

[38] On this point see also C. Dominicé, 'Regard Actuel sur la Protection Diplomatique' in J.D. Bredin *et al.*, *Liber Amicorum Claude Reymond, Autour de l'Arbitrage* (Éditions du Juris-Classeur, Paris 2004) 73, 77.

[39] See the following domestic judgments: German Federal Constitutional Court (*Bundesverfassungsgericht*), *Rudolf Hess Case* (1980) 90 ILR 386; Spanish Supreme Court (*Tribunal Supremo de España*), Third Chamber, *Comercial F S A v. Council of Ministers* (1987) 88 ILR 691; Swiss Federal Tribunal (*Tribunal fédéral suisse*) *N. et consorts c. Confédération suisse*, 1996 *Schweizerische Zeitschrift für Internationales und Europäisches Recht* 614; Swiss Federal Council (*Conseil fédéral suisse*), *X c. Département fédéral des affaires étrangères*, decision JAAC 61/75 of 30 October 1996, available at: <http://www.jaac.admin.ch/franz/doc/61/61.75.html>; *Abbasi & another v. Secretary of State for Foreign and Commonwealth Affairs and Others* [2002] All ER (D) 70 (Nov); Civil Court The Hague (*Rechtbank 's-Gravenhage*), *M. Kuijt v. Netherlands* (2003) LJN. No. AF5930, Rolno. KG 03/137, para. 3.8; Swiss Federal Council (*Conseil fédéral suisse*), *Groupement X c. Département fédéral des affaires étrangères*, decision JAAC 68.78 of 14 January 2004, available at: <http://www.jaac.admin.ch/franz/doc/68/68.78.html>; Swiss Federal Tribunal (*Tribunal fédéral suisse*), *Groupement X c. Conseil fédéral*, 2005 RGDIP 407; Constitutional Court of South Africa, *S. Kaunda and Others v. President of the Republic of South Africa and Others*, 4 August 2004 (2005) 44 ILM, 173, especially paras. 23–35 and 58–81. See also the other cases cited by A.M.H. Vermeer-Künzli, *The Protection of Individuals by means of Diplomatic Protection—Diplomatic Protection as a Human Rights Instrument* (PrintPartners Ipskamp, Leiden 2007) 181–202.

[40] See Gaja, 'Droits des Etats' (2003) *supra* note 35, 69.

It should be noted that some of these innovations have been proposed by the ILC, as a progressive development of international law, in the ILC Draft Articles on Diplomatic Protection, which were definitively approved in May 2006.[41]

4.3 Radical changes in the law of diplomatic protection?

The two above-described perspectives are, in my opinion, those possible, if one starts from the new role of the individual in international law and from the new legal and theoretical conception of the norms on treatment of aliens. In fact both perspectives have been, albeit only partially, realized in the ILC Draft Articles on Diplomatic Protection.

Can one go further and maintain that the new role of the individual can even justify a *radical change* in the relationship between the national state and the individual, to such a point that the individual victim would have *a true right to obtain diplomatic protection* from his national state? In this case, would the national state (or any other state entitled to exercise diplomatic protection) have a corresponding *obligation* to exercise diplomatic protection? In other words, is it possible to reach the stage of modifying the vertical relationship between the individual victim and his national state?

I think the answer is negative. In fact, in theory, one can maintain that, although the individual is a direct addressee of the international norms on treatment of aliens and is a direct victim of an international breach of those norms, diplomatic protection still remains an instrument for redressing those breaches which is under the full and exclusive control of states. In other words, one can, in theoretical terms, argue that those changes in the conception of the primary norms and of the secondary norms on responsibility do not affect the relationship between the individual and his national state (i.e. the 'hard core' of the norms on diplomatic protection). This argument seems rather persuasive.

Therefore something more is needed in order to change the vertical relationship between the individual and his national state: that is, the theory of human rights. For this reason, it is now necessary to examine the second above-mentioned development: the impact of human rights law on the law of treatment of aliens and on the regime of diplomatic protection.

5. The Relationship between Human Rights Law and the Law on Treatment of Aliens

It is useless to spend many words on the great impact that the theory of human rights and the international law of human rights had exercised both on some

---

[41] UN Doc. A/CN.4/L.684 of 19 May 2006. See especially Article 19(b) and (c) of the Draft and the corresponding Commentary.

general and structural characters of the international legal order[42] and on some specific areas of international law, such as the sources of law, the law of treaties, the law of state responsibility, the law of immunity from jurisdiction, the law on the use of force, and other fields.

Here we are mostly interested in the relationship between human rights law and the law on treatment of aliens and the impact exercised by the former field on the latter. The topic is complicated and it would take too long to discuss it in depth. In short, I think that the theory of human rights has made a decisive contribution to letting the field of treatment of aliens overcome the strictly inter-state logic on which it was founded. Moreover, the idea (typical of the human rights theory) that the individual is protected by international law mostly as a human being, rather than as a subject of another state or as an alien, has inevitably produced a tendency of the human rights norms to gradually replace the norms on treatment of aliens, which tend to remain residuary and to regulate the property and the economic interests rather than the personal security of aliens.

In this process, the traditional and clear separation between the two legal regimes increasingly disappears, with the consequence, among others, that frequent cases of overlapping between the two regimes may occur; that is, an injury suffered by an individual in a foreign state may simultaneously give rise to a breach of the traditional norms on treatment of aliens and of the more recent norms on human rights. This simultaneous breach of different primary norms also entails, as we shall see,[43] the application of different secondary norms (i.e. norms on *diplomatic protection in a strict sense* and norms on state responsibility for human rights violations). The topicality of the problem of overlapping between the two legal regimes is symbolically demonstrated by the already cited opinion *OC-16/99* of the IACtHR and the recent case *Congo v. Uganda* decided by the ICJ in 2005,[44] of which I will speak later. The opinion *OC-16/99* and the *Congo v. Uganda* judgment show that, at least in certain cases, it has by now become artificial to maintain a rigid separation and a sort of incommunicability between the norms on treatment of aliens and diplomatic protection, on one side, and the primary and secondary norms on human rights, on the other side.

Furthermore, insofar as certain norms on treatment of aliens coincide with certain norms on fundamental human rights, the concepts of *erga omnes* obligations and *jus cogens* also apply indirectly. The consequence may be that certain breaches by a state of norms on treatment of aliens, if they are also grave violations of fundamental human rights, legitimate other states, including the national state

---

[42] It is worth mentioning that the theory of human rights has had a great influence also in developing the three general phenomena of change of international law that we briefly described speaking of the new role of the individual. See *supra* para.2.

[43] See *infra*, para.6.

[44] *Armed Activities on the Territory of the Congo (Democratic Republic of the Congo v. Uganda)*, Judgment of 19 December 2005, 2005 ICJ Reports 168.

of the individual victim, to intervene in the interest of the victim.[45] In my opinion, one cannot exclude that, in certain exceptional circumstances, this *right* of the national state of the victim, to intervene in the interest of the victim, may be transformed into a true *obligation*, which could affect, as we shall see, the discretionary power of that state in the exercise of diplomatic protection.

6. The Impact of Human Rights Law on the Law of Diplomatic Protection

Now the question is the following: has the impact of human rights law on the law of treatment of aliens (primary norms) already affected (or in any case is destined to affect very soon) the law of diplomatic protection (secondary norms)? I think the answer is positive. In my opinion, that impact manifests itself in two different ways:

A) In certain exceptional circumstances, it may lead to a change in the vertical relationship between the national state and the individual citizen. In fact the individual, as we shall see, may claim a 'procedural' human right to obtain diplomatic protection, when such protection is the only available instrument for the protection of his basic human rights.

B) In a more general way, the aforesaid impact may lead to a tendency to conceive diplomatic protection as a means for the protection of human rights; that is, as one of the international instruments at the disposal of the national state of the individual injured by another state to invoke and implement the responsibility of the latter state for human rights violations. However, as we shall see, this 'new form' or 'new function' of diplomatic protection (hereinafter *diplomatic protection in a wide sense*) may produce remarkable complications in its coordination with 'traditional' diplomatic protection (hereinafter also *diplomatic protection in a strict sense*).

Let us examine these two aspects, starting with the former.

6.1 A human right of the individual to diplomatic protection?

We have seen that, notwithstanding the impact of individual rights in international law, resort to diplomatic protection remains, as a rule, a right belonging only to the state, to which neither a right of the individual victim to obtain diplomatic protection from his national state nor an obligation of the same state correspond.

---

[45] See especially Arts. 41, 48 and 54 of the ILC Draft Articles on State Responsibility, *supra* note 30.

However Special Rapporteur Dugard, in his First Report on Diplomatic Protection, suggested introducing in the Draft Articles, as a progressive development of international law, an exception to that rule for violations of *jus cogens*.[46] The Rapporteur especially had in mind gross violations of basic human rights, but his proposal was not accepted by the ILC.

In spite of that, in 2006, the Italian Government, sending its observations on the Draft Articles approved by the ILC at the first reading in 2004, made a proposal which adopted and made clearer the original idea of Dugard.[47] According to the Italian proposal,[48] a state has *a legal duty* to exercise diplomatic protection on behalf of the injured person, if two requirements are fulfilled: a) the injury results from a grave violation, attributable to another state, of fundamental human rights (right to life, prohibitions of torture, slavery, and racial discrimination); b) in addition, the injured person cannot bring a claim for such injury before a competent international judicial or quasi-judicial organ. The underlying idea of the proposal was that an exception to the rule of the discretionary power of the state is appropriate, in these limited circumstances, because here fundamental values, concerning the dignity of the human being and recognized by the international community as a whole, are at issue. Moreover, primary norms on human rights certainly having the nature of *jus cogens* have been violated. Finally, in these exceptional circumstances, one should also consider the fact that diplomatic protection is the only remedy available for the individual, so that its denial by the state would prejudice those fundamental principles on human dignity that the international community firmly intends to protect. In other terms, the protection of a substantive fundamental human right, to be effective, needs also a procedural remedy in case of its breach: when diplomatic protection is the only available remedy, the individual victim must have a 'procedural' human right to obtain diplomatic protection by his own state.

The proposal of the Italian Government was welcomed by some governments and criticized by others; but was not adopted, as such, by the ILC in the 2006 Draft Articles on Diplomatic Protection.[49] However, I think it has produced some results in the final Draft. In fact, Article 19 of the Draft, which has the interesting title 'Recommended Practice', reads:

A State entitled to exercise diplomatic protection according to the present draft articles, should:

(a) give due consideration to the possibility of exercising diplomatic protection, especially when a significant injury has occurred.

---

[46] See J. R. Dugard, First report on diplomatic protection, (A/CN.4/506 of 7 March 2000), Article 4 and comment, 27–34.

[47] Perhaps the main difficulty of the proposal made by Dugard was represented by the generality and broadness of the concept of *jus cogens*.

[48] UN Doc. A/CN.4/561/Add.2 of 12 April 2006, pp. 2–8.

[49] See note 41.

If we read the Commentary to Article 19,[50] we may note that the ILC looks at that rule especially from the point of view of the protection of human rights. In fact the Commentary states:

There are certain practices on the part of States in the field of diplomatic protection which have not yet acquired the status of customary rules... Nevertheless they are desirable practices... that add strength to diplomatic protection as a means for the protection of human rights... These practices are recommended to States for their consideration in the exercise of diplomatic protection in draft article 19... Subparagraph (a) recommends to States that they should give consideration to the possibility of exercising diplomatic protection on behalf of a national who suffers significant injury. The protection of human beings by means of international law is today one of the principal goals of the international legal order... There is growing support for the view that there is some obligation, however imperfect, on States, either under international law or national law, to protect their nationals abroad when they are subjected to significant human rights violations... In these circumstances it is possible to seriously suggest that international law already recognises the existence of some obligation on the part of a State to consider the possibility of exercising diplomatic protection on behalf of a national who has suffered a significant injury abroad. If customary international law has not yet reached this stage of development then draft article 19, subparagraph (a) must be seen as an exercise in progressive development.[51]

Article 19(a) is something less than what was asked by the original Dugard proposal and by the subsequent Italian proposal, but it is, in any case, a very interesting rule, which opens the way to a progressive development of international law.

It should be noted that recently the Court of First Instance of the European Communities seems to have moved in that direction, since, in the *Hassan* and *Ayadi* cases,[52] it has maintained that, within the European Union's legal system, when an individual does not have a judicial remedy against an order restricting his fundamental rights, the EU member states have an obligation to exercise diplomatic protection in favour of the individual; and that such an obligation derives from Article 6 of the EU Treaty, which imposes on member states the protection of human rights.[53]

---

[50] ILC Report on the work of its fifty-eighth session (2006) (UN Doc. A/61/10), Chapter IV: Diplomatic Protection, 94.

[51] Ibid., pp. 94–96, paras. 1–3.

[52] Court of First Instance, Judgment of 12 July 2006 in case T-49/04, *Hassan v. Council of the EU and Commission of the EC*, paras. 114–119; and Judgment of 12 July 2006 in case T-253/02, *Ayadi v. Council of the EU*, paras. 144–149, available at: <http://curia.europa.eu>.

[53] See also Human Rights Chamber for Bosnia and Herzegovina, Decision of 11 October 2002, Case CH/02/8679, *Boudellaa, Lakhdar, Nechle and Lahmar v. Bosnia and Herzegovina and The Federation of Bosnia and Herzegovina*, para. 330, available at: <http://www.hrc.ba/database/decisions/CH02–8679%20BOUDELLAA%20et%20al.%20Admissibility%20and%20Merits%20E.pdf>; and the judgment of the South African Constitutional Court in the *Kaunda case*, (2005) 44 ILM 173. In this case the Court held that there is 'a duty on the government, consistent with its obligations under international law, to take action to protect one of its citizens against a gross abuse of international human rights norms' (para.69).

6.2 Diplomatic protection and actions invoking responsibility for human rights violations

Let us come to the second aspect of the impact of human rights law on the legal regime of diplomatic protection: the tendency to use diplomatic protection to address human rights violations. This is, in other words, the conception of diplomatic protection (that is, resort by a state to international actions or procedures against another state to secure redress for injury suffered by its nationals) as one of the means available to the state in order to protect the human rights of its nationals who have been injured by a foreign state.[54] This tendency to broaden the concept of diplomatic protection (that we have called *diplomatic protection in a wide sense*) has been underlined also by the ILC. However, the ILC does not clarify the exact legal content of this 'new form' of diplomatic protection and, consequently, leaves unresolved a series of difficult problems. In particular, it is not clear from the ILC Draft whether this 'new mechanism' is similar in substance to the old, traditional and well-known mechanism of *diplomatic protection in a strict sense*, or whether, as is more likely, the national state can also resort to the rules on invocation and implementation of state responsibility for internationally wrongful acts, which have been established by the ILC Draft Articles of 2001,[55] and which are applicable to human rights violations.

It should be noted that the choice, by the national state, between actions of 'traditional' diplomatic protection and actions invoking responsibility for human rights violations entails, in my opinion, different legal consequences. For instance, according to existing international law, the individual victim will, only in the latter scenario, have a right to obtain the monetary compensation possibly awarded to his national state from the offending state.

Moreover, within the framework of the actions invoking responsibility for human rights violations, it is still not clear which is the legal status of the claiming state. One could consider the national state of the individual victim of a human rights violation as an 'injured' and 'specially affected' state, under Article 42(b) (i) of the ILC Draft Articles on State Responsibility[56] (because the state espouses

---

[54] On this topic see Dugard, *First report, supra* note 46, paras.22–32; Id., Seventh report on diplomatic protection (A/CN.4/567 of 7 March 2006), 3; J.-F. Flauss, 'Protection diplomatique et protection internationale des droits de l'homme' (2003) *Rev. suisse de dr. int. et europ.* 1; Condorelli, 'L'évolution du champ d'application de la protection diplomatique' (2003); G. Cohen-Jonathan, 'La responsabilité internationale pou atteinte aux droits de l'homme: sur quelques tendances récentes' in *Studi di diritto internazionale in onore di G. Arangio-Ruiz* (Editoriale Scientifica Naples, 2004) 699; S. Forlati, 'Protection diplomatique, droits de l'homme et reclamations 'directes' devant la Cour internationale de justice—Quelques réflexions en marge de l'arrêt Congo/Ouganda' (2007) RGDIP. 89; Vermeer-Künzli, *The Protection of Individuals by means of Diplomatic Protection* (2007).

[55] See *supra* note 30.

[56] Article 42: 'A State is entitled as an injured State to invoke the responsibility of another State if the obligation breached is owed to:

(a) That State individually; or

the injury suffered by his national), or else as a 'State other than an injured State', under Article 48 (1) of the same ILC Draft[57] (because the state asserts the violation of an *erga omnes* obligation). This alternative, as we shall see, entails very different consequences as to the standing of the claiming state, as to the admissibility requirements for the claim, and as to the possibility of countermeasures or 'lawful measures' against the state responsible for the wrongful act.

One would think that the national state, in case of violation of norms pertaining only to the human rights field, would prefer to act by invoking responsibility for human rights violation, instead of resorting to 'traditional' diplomatic protection. However the ICJ seems to hold a different opinion, since in the recent *Ahmadou Sadio Diallo* judgment of 2007,[58] it has maintained that the scope of application of 'traditional' diplomatic protection, originally limited to breaches of minimum standard of treatment of aliens, has now become larger in order to include 'internationally guaranteed human rights'.[59]

The problem of choice and/or coordination between *diplomatic protection in a strict sense* and invocation of responsibility for human rights violations arises not only when the primary norms violated pertain exclusively to the field of human rights. The same problem arises also in cases of overlap between primary norms on treatment of aliens and primary norms on human rights. In fact, as I already said,[60] today it may frequently occur that an individual suffers an injury in a foreign state which gives rise *simultaneously* to a breach of a norm on treatment of aliens and a norm on human rights. This situation too creates the possibility of two different kinds of state action, at the level of secondary norms: a) resort to *diplomatic protection in a strict sense*; b) invocation and implementation of responsibility for human rights violations.

This problem of overlapping is well illustrated by two recent and already-mentioned cases. In its opinion *OC-16/99*, as we saw,[61] the IACtHR established that the right to information on consular assistance is an individual right directly conferred by international law (in the field of treatment of aliens) *and also a human right*, and that its breach implies a wrongful act concerning *both fields*.

A similar, and even more interesting, problem had arisen in the well-known *Congo v. Uganda* case, decided by the ICJ on 19 December 2005.[62] Uganda, as a

(b) A group of States including that State, or the international community as a whole, and the breach of the obligation:

    (i) specially affects that State...'

[57] Article 48: '1. Any State other than an injured State is entitled to invoke the responsibility of another State in accordance with paragraph 2 if:

(a) The obligation breached is owed to a group of States including that State, and is established for the protection of a collective interest of the group; or
(b) The obligation breached is owed to the international community as a whole'.

[58] *Ahmadou Sadio Diallo (Republic of Guinea v. Democratic Republic of Congo)*, Judgment of 24 May 2007, 2007 ICJ Reports. Available at <http://www.icj-cij.org/>.

[59] Ibid., para. 39.　　　[60] See *supra*, Section 5.　　　[61] See *supra* para. 3.

[62] *Armed Activities on the Territory of the Congo (Democratic Republic of the Congo v. Uganda)*, 2005 ICJ Reports 168.

second counter-claim, contended that the Congolese armed forces, by attacking the premises of the Ugandan Embassy, maltreated not only Ugandan diplomats, but also other Ugandan nationals present on the premises of the mission and at Ndjili Airport.[63] The Democratic Republic of the Congo (DRC) argued that the claim based on the inhumane treatment of Ugandan nationals could not be admitted, because the requirements for admissibility of a diplomatic protection claim (evidence of Ugandan nationality of the persons and prior exhaustion of local remedies) were not satisfied.[64] The ICJ decided that, with respect to maltreatments of diplomats and other persons present at the Embassy, the counter-claim was admissible under Article 22 of the Vienna Convention on Diplomatic Relations (because it was a direct injury between states). Instead, with regard to maltreatment of persons not enjoying diplomatic status at Ndjili Airport, the Ugandan counter-claim was based on diplomatic protection (i.e., it was not a direct injury between states); therefore that part of the counter-claim was inadmissible, since Uganda had not satisfied the requirements for diplomatic protection, and in particular had not given evidence on the Ugandan nationality of the victims.[65]

However, in an interesting separate opinion,[66] Judge Simma argued that, if one had applied international human rights law to the individuals maltreated at Ndjili Airport, one should have concluded, on the basis of Article 48 of the ILC Draft Articles on State Responsibility (which allows states other than the injured state to invoke responsibility for breach of *erga omnes* obligations), that Uganda would have had standing to raise before the ICJ violations of the relevant human rights of individuals, without any need to give evidence that they were its own nationals.

This separate opinion raises an important point concerning the standing and requisites to bring judicial claims. In my view, Uganda could have based its claim for the individuals maltreated at Ndjili Airport on a violation of international human rights law, either by applying Article 42(b)(i) or Article 48(1) of the ILC Draft Articles on State Responsibility. It would have been more logical to apply Article 42(b)(i), which identifies the legal category of the 'specially affected' state when, *inter alia*, 'the obligation breached is owed to . . . a group of States including that State, or the international community on the whole, and the breach of the obligation . . . specially affects that State.' The state that invokes responsibility of another state for human rights violations committed against its nationals seems a good example of a 'specially affected' state, because of a breach of an obligation having an *erga omnes* or *erga omnes partes* character.[67] But, in that case, in my view, the claiming state has to prove the nationality link with the victim, in order to justify his status of 'specially affected' state. That may create a disadvantage from a procedural point of view. For instance, returning to the *Congo v. Uganda*

---

[63] Ibid., paras. 306–313 and 316–317.
[64] Ibid., para. 315.
[65] Ibid., paras. 328–333.
[66] Ibid., Separate Opinion of Judge Simma, paras. 32–41.
[67] For a similar view see Forlati, (2007) RGDIP 89, *supra* note 54, 97, 114.

case, Uganda, by invoking Article 42(b)(i), would not have obtained a procedural advantage with respect to the action based on 'traditional' diplomatic protection. Instead, the application of Article 48 (as suggested by Judge Simma), by giving the standing to invoke responsibility to states *other than the injured one* for breaches of *erga omnes* obligations, would have conveyed a procedural advantage exempting Uganda from proving the nationality link of the victims.[68]

6.3 Which coordination between the two categories of actions?

It is clear that international practice, in the areas of treatment of aliens and of human rights, will create more and more of a problem of coordination between actions of *diplomatic protection in a strict sense* and actions invoking state responsibility for human rights violations. As I said, the ILC has perhaps seen the problem, but has not been able to resolve it. In fact, Article 16 of the ILC Draft on Diplomatic Protection reads:

The rights of States, natural persons, legal persons or other entities to resort under international law to actions or procedures other than diplomatic protection to secure redress for injury suffered as a result of an internationally wrongful act, are not affected by the present draft articles.

However, Article 16 is only a saving clause, as made clear by the Commentary.[69] Therefore the problem has remained unsettled and one may try to propose some solutions. In my opinion, one may envisage three general hypotheses.

The first general hypothesis is that there has been only the breach of a norm belonging to the field of treatment of aliens. In this case I think that the national state of the individual victim can only resort to *diplomatic protection in a strict sense*. It must prove the nationality link (or any other link now admitted by the ILC Draft Articles on Diplomatic Protection); and it must prove prior exhaustion

---

[68] See also Vermeer-Künzli, *The Protection of Individuals by means of Diplomatic Protection* (2007) 117, 125, who criticizes the separate opinion of Judge Simma because it does not distinguish between application of Article 48(1)(a), dealing with obligations *erga omnes partes*, and application of Article 48(1)(b), dealing with obligations *erga omnes*. According to Vermeer-Künzli, when the claimant state acts under Article 48(1)(b), it claims its own right as a member of the international community, it thus exercises a 'direct claim' and therefore the rule of exhaustion of local remedies is not applicable.

[69] The Commentary on Article 16 reads: 'The customary international law rules on diplomatic protection and the rules governing the protection of human rights are complementary. The present draft articles are therefore not intended to exclude or to trump the right of States, including both the State of nationality and States other than the State of nationality of the injured individual, to protect the individual under either customary international law or a multilateral or bilateral human rights treaty or other treaty... Draft article 16 makes it clear that the present draft articles are without prejudice to the rights that States... may have to secure redress for injury suffered as a result of an internationally wrongful act by procedures other than diplomatic protection. Where, however, a State resorts to such procedures, it does not necessarily abandon its rights to exercise diplomatic protection in respect of a person if that person should be a national or person referred to in draft article 8.' (ILC Report on the work of its fifty-eighth session, *supra* note 50, 86–89).

of local remedies by the individual. The national state does not have, at the actual stage of international law, the duty to transfer the possible compensation to the individual victim.[70] In other words, *diplomatic protection in a strict sense* should still apply to violations of traditional norms on treatment of aliens.[71]

The second general hypothesis is that there has been only the violation of a norm belonging to the field of human rights law. In this case, I think that the national state of the individual victim can, first of all, raise the violation of human rights law by invoking, as a 'specially affected State', under Article 42(b)(i) of the ILC Draft on State Responsibility, the responsibility of the offending state.[72] It should, even in this case, prove the nationality link in order to justify its particular status of 'specially affected' state. It should also prove the prior exhaustion of local remedies by the individual (but the rule on exhaustion is more flexible in the human rights field with respect to the field of treatment of aliens).[73] It must be underlined that the national state, being an 'injured' state, is entitled to take countermeasures[74] against the state responsible for the wrongful act. Finally, in my opinion, the national state probably has a duty to transfer the monetary compensation to the individual victim (since the individual has, according to contemporary international law, a true right to reparation for human rights violations).[75]

In the second place, the national state of the individual may also, in my view, choose to raise the violation of human rights law by invoking, as a 'State other than an injured State', under Article 48 of the ILC Draft Articles on State Responsibility, the responsibility of the offending state.[76] In this case, the national state has the procedural advantage (as I already said) that it does not have to prove the nationality link with the individual victim.[77] But, on the other hand, the state, having renounced his quality of 'injured State', cannot take countermeasures against the state responsible for the wrongful act, but only 'lawful measures . . . to ensure cessation of the breach and reparation in the interests of the . . . beneficiaries of the obligation breached'.[78]

Instead, still speaking of the second general hypothesis, I think it is useless to envisage that the national state may resort to *diplomatic protection in a strict sense*. It would not give the state, in any case, any further advantage with respect to the

---

[70] See Article 19 (c) of the ILC Draft, which only recommends the trasfer of compensation to the injured person.

[71] See also Forlati, (2007) RGDIP 89, 114.

[72] Of course this applies in the case of *erga omnes* obligations, but international norms on human rights usually impose on states *erga omnes* (conventional or customary) obligations.

[73] See Pisillo Mazzeschi, *Esaurimento* (2004), *supra* note 5, *passim*.

[74] See Article 49 of the ILC Draft Articles on State Responsibility.

[75] See *supra* para. 4.

[76] Still in case of *erga omnes* human rights obligations.

[77] According to some authors, the claimant state, when acting under Article 48(1)(b), has also the procedural advantage that it does not have to prove exhaustion of local remedies by the individual victim. See *supra* note 68.

[78] Article 54 of the ILC Draft Articles on State Responsibility.

action under Article 42(b)(i) of the ILC Draft Articles on State Responsibility and it would, instead, give some disadvantages to the individual (non-right to reparation, a more rigid application of the rule of exhaustion of local remedies).

Lastly, one should also consider that any action by the national state of the individual victim does not exclude the possibility of other actions against the offending state undertaken by the victim itself (in certain treaty regimes) or by other states. But we shall come back to this point.

The third general hypothesis is that there has been a *simultaneous* breach of a norm on treatment of aliens and a norm on human rights. This is the most problematic hypothesis. A first solution could be to give the national state of the individual victim the possibility to choose whether to have resort to *diplomatic protection in a strict sense* or to invoke responsibility for human rights violation under Article 42(b)(i) or even under Article 48 of the ILC Draft Articles on State Responsibility; with different consequences concerning standing to act, prerequisites and possible measures against the offending state. A second (in my view, much worse) solution could be to apply the *lex specialis* criterion, which is somehow suggested by the combination of Articles 16 and 17 of the ILC Draft Articles on Diplomatic Protection.[79] However, it is not clear which is more special between an action of 'traditional' diplomatic protection for breach of a norm on treatment of aliens and an action of responsibility for violation of a norm on human rights. Perhaps one should look at the more or less special character of the substantive rule, which of course could vary in each concrete case. It should be noted that the ILC rejected a proposal of one of its members aimed at considering the remedies on human rights violations as being *lex specialis* with respect to the rules on 'traditional' diplomatic protection.[80]

Finally, there may be a further complication: what happens if, in addition to the action by the national state in protection of the individual victim, other states and also the individual himself decide to act against the offending state? How should the actions by the latter be coordinated with the action by the former? It seems logical that the action by the national state should prevail over the actions by other states, at least insofar as the former acts by means of 'traditional' diplomatic protection or by invoking responsibility as a 'specially affected State'. Perhaps an action by the national state should also prevail over an action by the individual victim. However, this rule should have an exception when the 'third' state or the individual victim have resorted to an action before an international judicial organ; i.e., when they have started a procedure which entails a binding legal decision adopted by an independent and impartial judge, like, for instance,

---

[79] Article 17: 'The present draft articles do not apply to the extent that they are inconsistent with special rules of international law, such as treaty provisions for the protection of investments'. Some members of the ILC have expressed the view that Articles 16 and 17 should be merged.

[80] See ILC Report on the work of its fifty-sixth session (2004) (UN Doc. A/59/10), Chapter IV: Diplomatic Protection, 88, para. 7. Article 17 of the 2004 Draft corresponds in substance to Article 16 of the 2006 Draft.

the European Court of Human Rights. In fact, in that case, the right of the national state to exercise diplomatic protection, in a strict or in a wide sense, should give way to the fact that the action before a judge provides a better guarantee of eliminating the consequences of any wrongful act that might have been committed.[81]

7. Conclusion

In my opinion, the theory of human rights, once applied at the international level, has introduced into the international legal system some 'revolutionary' elements which have produced and are progressively producing profound changes to the system itself.

First of all, from the point of view of its material content, international law, which dealt traditionally only with matters of interest for diplomats, now deals also with matters of interest for each individual. Secondly, classic international law, from the point of view of its legal nature, was basically founded on a reciprocal, private law-based idea of interstate relations. Now the theory of human rights has opened the floor to the idea of protecting solidarity interests of the international community which are superior to single interests of states, and therefore to a public law-based or 'constitutional' conception of international law, which supplements the private law-based one. Thirdly, from the perspective of the formal addressees of the norms, contemporary international law has considerably re-evaluated the role of the individual. Under this respect, the above-mentioned decisions of the ICJ and the IACtHR give a remarkable contribution, because they confirm the existence of a phenomenon of progressive development of international law, concerning the broadening of the holders of international rights and obligations.

These three interconnected structural developments of the whole international legal system, and the third one most of all, have necessarily had an impact on the old law on treatment of aliens. In its turn, the recent adjournment of that law, in order to recognize the new role of individual rights, has already had some impact (although for the moment not very impressive) on the law of diplomatic protection. However now other steps forward are needed; the ever increasing integration of human rights law into the law on treatment of aliens is destined, sooner or later, to bring the 'new' philosophy of human rights also into the 'old' field of diplomatic protection. But these developments seem, for the moment, rather difficult to materialize. On the other hand, that should not be surprising; diplomatic protection is a typical inter-state mechanism which is governed by international secondary norms; and therefore it tends, by its own nature, to strongly resist the incentives to change that are exercised by human rights norms.

---

[81] See the proposal of the Italian Government, *supra* note 48.

11

Impact on State Responsibility

*Robert McCorquodale**

1. Introduction

The law of state responsibility distinguishes 'public' actions for which the state is accountable from those 'private' ones for which it does not have to answer internationally. Thus the conduct of persons not acting on the state's behalf, or which is not attributable to the state, generally is not considered an act of state.[1]

One of the core elements of an international legal system concerns the extent to which states have international legal responsibility for their actions. A significant body of law has developed to clarify the extent of a state's responsibility under international law. As just demonstrated, this law has tended to be limited to certain actions by a state and to certain conduct by some persons.

This chapter will explore the extent to which general international law principles of state responsibility have been influenced by international human rights law, rather than the impact of state responsibility on international human rights law.[2] It will focus on the two core aspects of state responsibility: attribution to a state, and the extent of the obligations on a state for which it has international legal responsibility.[3] It will also consider the general impact that international

* Director, British Institute of International and Comparative Law, and Professor of International Law and Human Rights, University of Nottingham. I am very grateful for the research assistance of Mehnaz Yoosuf and for the insights of Associate Professor Penelope Simons of the Faculty of Law, University of Ottawa.

[1] H. Charlesworth and C. Chinkin, *The Boundaries of International Law: A Feminist Analysis* (Manchester University Press, Manchester 2000) 148.

[2] There is still a need to address fully the impact of state responsibility on international human rights law, though it has been dealt with to some extent. See, e.g., N. Jägers, *Corporate Human Rights Obligations: In Search of Accountability* (Intersentia, Antwerp 2002) 175, who indicates that '[t]he law of state responsibility offers an interesting, yet under utilised tool for addressing human rights violations resulting from corporate activities'; M. Sornarajah, 'Linking State Responsibility for Certain Harms Caused by Corporate Nationals Abroad to Civil Recourse in the Legal Systems of Home States' in C. Scott (ed.), *Torture as Tort* (Hart, Oxford 2001) 491–512; and O. De Schutter, 'The Accountability of Multinationals for Human Rights Violations in European Law', in P. Alston (ed.), *Non-State Actors and Human Rights* (Oxford University Press, Oxford 2005).

[3] This chapter will not deal with the (albeit important) procedural and remedial issues arising from state responsibility, such as the exhaustion of local remedies, remedies, or defences (sometimes

human rights law may have had upon the broader understanding of state responsibility. In so doing, the issue of whether it is appropriate in any event to engage in an evaluation of the impact of international human rights law on the general international law of state responsibility, especially considering the apparently 'private' nature of many human rights abuses, will be considered.

2. State Responsibility v. Human Rights

The general international law of state responsibility is a law created by states in which states themselves determine their own obligations for certain public acts in relation to other states and how a state can then enforce these obligations against other states. Thus it is a law *by states for states* about when states are legally responsible to other states. The principles developed by this law would therefore seem unable to engage with international human rights law, where the focus of protection is the human person.

Further, at a time when international human rights law is being strongly criticized for its lack of direct responsibility on non-state actors for violations of human rights,[4] any direct connections with general international law in regard to state responsibility principles could be problematic:

> The narrow focus of human rights law on state responsibility is not only out of step with current power relations, but also tends to obscure them. The exclusive concern with national governments not only distorts the reality of the growing weakness of national-level authority, but also shields other actors from greater responsibility. The focus on state responsibility also creates a false sense of rigidity or inevitability about social and political hierarchies and existing inequities.[5]

This concern may be alleviated to some extent if it is shown that international human rights law approaches have had a positive impact on some of these aspects of the general international law of state responsibility. In addition, the International Law Commission (ILC) was clear that the international law of state responsibility—as set out in its Articles on State Responsibility—expresses secondary rules that 'indicate the consequences of a breach of an applicable primary obligation.'[6] Thus it is an issue as to whether the secondary rules of state

---

called, rather coyly, 'circumstances precluding wrongfulness'): International Law Commission's Articles on Responsibility of States for Internationally Wrongful Acts, Report of the International Law Commission Report, 53rd sess., UN Doc. A/56/10, August 2001, s. 4.

[4] See e.g., R. McCorquodale, 'An Inclusive International Legal System' (2004) 17 LJIL 477.

[5] C. Jochnick, 'Confronting the Impunity of Non-State Actors: New Fields for the Promotion of Human Rights' (1999) 21 HRQ 56, 59.

[6] ILC, Commentaries on the Report of the International Law Commission, 53rd sess., UN GAOR, 56th sess., Supp. No. 10, UN Doc. A/56/10 (SUPP) (2001) (ILC Commentary), reproduced in J. Crawford, *The International Law Commission's Articles on State Responsibility: Introduction, Text and Commentaries* (Cambridge University Press, Cambridge 2002) 16, 74.

responsibility are relevant at all in regard to the primary obligations established in international human rights law through treaties and customary international law. Indeed, it is Clapham's view that 'human rights law has developed a set of state obligations that cannot be understood by the application of the primary rules of diplomatic protection of foreigners and the secondary rules of state responsibility.'[7] Whilst there may be strength in this view at one level, it does not deal with the issue of whether the secondary rules of state responsibility may be understood by reference to the primary rules of international human rights law, and the practice of the international human rights bodies must also be considered.

Despite these concerns, it is clear that the ILC itself considered that international human rights law was relevant to the development of the general provisions about state responsibility when it (finally) completed its Articles on State Responsibility. The ILC's Commentary to these Articles notes that these provisions are relevant to all areas within the international legal system, though there may be different compliance mechanisms for its enforcement in parts of that system—such as with human rights treaty monitoring bodies.[8] Whilst there is an exclusion of the application of the Articles where the existence, content or implementation of state responsibility is governed by special rules (*lex specialis*) of international law[9]—and international human rights law clearly has special rules and procedures—the ILC has considered that areas of international law such as human rights are 'special regimes' and are not outside the framework of general international law.[10] The ILC has commented that these Articles are generally applicable to 'the whole field of the international responsibility of States, whether the obligation is owed to one or several States, to an individual or a group, or to the international community as a whole.'[11] Indeed, the potential impact of international human rights law on the general international law of state responsibility is seen in the number of references in the ILC Commentary to human rights examples and cases.[12]

A clear demonstration of the connection between international human rights law and the general principles of state responsibility is seen in the fact that human rights treaty monitoring bodies have applied the general law of state responsibility to key aspects of human rights matters before them. Sometimes they have done this explicitly, for example, the Inter-American Court of Human Rights

---

[7] A. Clapham, *Human Rights Obligations of Non-State Actors* (2006) 318. See also the critiques of R. Pisillo Mazzechi, 'The Marginal Role of the Individual in the ILC's Articles on State Responsibility' (2004) 14 Italian Ybk Intl L 39, 47; D. Bodansky, J.R. Crook and E. Brown Weiss, 'Invoking State Responsibility in the Twenty-First Century' (2002) 96 AJIL 798, 809; and Charlesworth and Chinkin, above n. 1, 148.

[8] See ILC Commentary, above n. 6, in relation to Part II and III of the ILC Articles on State Responsibility.

[9] See ILC Articles on State Responsibility, above n. 3, Art. 55.

[10] See International Law Commission Study Group on Fragmentation of International Law, First Report: Study on the Function and Scope of Lex Specialis Rule and the Question of 'Self-Contained Regimes', UN Doc. ILC(LVI)/SG/FIL/CRD.1/Add.1 (2004) [134].

[11] ILC Commentary, above n. 6, 76.

[12] See e.g., ibid., 129.

stating that: 'According to the rules of law pertaining to the international responsibility of the State and applicable under international human rights law, actions
or omissions by any public authority, whatever its hierarchic position, are charge-
able to the State which is responsible under the terms set forth in the American
Convention [on Human Rights].'[13] The Grand Chamber of the European Court
of Human Rights has added: '[The Court] must also take into account relevant
rules of international law when examining questions concerning jurisdiction
and, consequently, determine State responsibility in conformity and harmony
with the governing principles of international law of which [the European
Convention on Human Rights] forms a part, although it must remain mindful of
the Convention's special character as a human rights treaty.'[14]

More often, however, human rights treaty monitoring bodies have applied
the general law of state responsibility implicitly.[15] In fact, in the development
of jurisprudence in this area, international legal dispute settlement bodies of all
kinds have rarely set out clearly the influence of one law on the other, or even
distinguished clearly between the concepts of attribution or the scope of a state's
obligations.[16] Nevertheless, there is no reason why international human rights
law and general international law principles of state responsibility cannot be considered as being of relevance to each other, such that it is possible to evaluate the
impact of the former on the latter.

3. Attribution to a State

The first two articles of the ILC Articles on State Responsibility provide:

Article 1: Every internationally wrongful act of a State entails the international
responsibility of that State.

Article 2: There is an internationally wrongful act of a State when conduct
consisting of an action or omission:

(a) is attributable to the State under international law; and
(b) constitutes a breach of an international obligation of the State.[17]

---

[13] *The Mayagna (Sumo) Awas Tingni Community v. Nicaragua*, IACtHR, Judgment of 31 August
2001, Series C No. 79, (2003) 10 *International Human Rights Reports* 758, para. 154.

[14] *Behrami and Behrami v. France* and *Saramati v. France, Germany and Norway* (App. Nos.
71412/01 and 78166/01), ECtHR, Decision of 2 May 2007, para. 122.

[15] R. Lawson, 'Out of Control. State Responsibility and Human Rights: Will the ILC's
Definition of the "Act of State" Meet the Challenges of the 21st Century?' in M. Castermans, F. van
Hoof and J. Smith (eds.), *The Role of the Nation-State in the 21st Century* (1998), 115, who notes that
'the [ECHR] has consistently applied the principles articulated in the ILC Draft Articles on State
Responsibility, without, however, referring expressly to the Draft Articles.'

[16] See J. Cerone, 'Out of Bounds? Considering the Reach of International Human Rights Law,
Center for Human Rights and Global Justice' New York School of Law, Working Paper Number 5
(2006) 26 at <http://www.chrgj.org/publications/docs/wp/WPS_NYU_CHRGJ_Cerone_Final.
pdf>.

[17] ILC Articles on State Responsibility, above n. 3, Arts. 1, 2.

These two Articles, which establish that there is state responsibility for an internationally wrongful act where that act is attributable to the state and it is a breach of an international obligation of the state, are generally considered to represent customary international law.[18]

3.1 General attribution

The relevant actions and omissions that are attributable to a state are the acts and omissions of its officials and organs:

The conduct of any state organ shall be considered an act of that state under international law, whether the organ exercises legislative, executive, judicial or any other functions, whatever position it holds in the organization of the state, and whatever its character as an organ of the central government or of a territorial unit of the state.[19]

A state is responsible for the actions of its executive, legislative, judicial and other state organs and officials, including police, military, immigration, and similar officials. This is the position even where those actions are committed outside the scope of the state official's or organ's apparent authority if they 'acted, at least apparently, as authorised officials or organs, or that, in so acting, they...used powers or measures appropriate to their official character.'[20]

This customary international law position is confirmed by international human rights law, in which treaty monitoring bodies have consistently found a state responsible for actions and omissions of its organs or officials, even when acting outside their official authority, such as in cases of violation of human rights in detention and for torture.[21] In addition, states have been found responsible for a violation even where, under the state's constitutional system, that state does not have direct control over the organ or official who violated the human right concerned.[22] It is also clear that when such individuals act for the state, there is no restriction on the types of obligation for which the state itself may be

[18] See e.g., *Factory at Chorzów (Claim for Indemnity) Case (Germany v. Poland)* (Merits) (1928) PCIJ Series A, No. 17. Not all the ILC Articles can be considered to be customary international law, though most of them—including those relevant to this paper—have been adopted by international tribunals as reflective of customary international law: See H. Duffy, 'Towards Global Responsibility for Human Rights Protection: A Sketch of International Developments', (2006) 15 *Interights Bulletin.* 104.

[19] ILC Articles on State Responsibility, above n. 3, Art. 4.

[20] *Caire Claim (France v. Mexico)* (1929) 5 RIAA 516. However, 'much depends on the type of activity and the related consequences in the particular case': I. Brownlie, *Principles of Public International Law*, 5th ed. (Oxford University Press, Oxford, 1998) 454.

[21] See e.g., the series of cases discussed in S. Joseph, J. Schultz and M. Castan, *The International Covenant on Civil and Political Rights: Cases, Commentary and Materials*, 2nd ed. (Oxford University Press, Oxford, 2004), esp. 198–207, 275–7.

[22] For example, the (federal) Australian government was internationally responsible for the actions of the (sub-national) Tasmanian government in *Toonen v. Australia*, (488/1992), HRCt, 4 April 1998, UN Doc. CCPR/C/50/D/488/1992. This is because the responsibility of a state cannot be avoided by use of its national law or practice: Article 27, *Vienna Convention on the Law*

responsible should the official occasion a breach. Hence, in the *Case concerning the Application of the Convention on the Prevention and Punishment of the Crime of Genocide* ('*Genocide Case*'), the International Court of Justice (ICJ) accepted that a state could be held directly responsible for genocide even though the actual events were ordered or carried out by individuals (and the individuals were also directly responsible under international law).[23]

In contrast, the acts of private persons and other non-state actors are not generally attributable to the state under the principles of state responsibility,[24] even where the private entity is wholly-owned by the state or the state has a controlling interest in it.[25] Yet it has long been the case that there has been attribution to a state of the acts of private entities that are exercising public or governmental functions.[26] One specific exception where a state may be responsible for the acts of non-state actors is where the state could be considered to adopt the actions of non-state actors.[27] An example is the *Case concerning United States Diplomatic and Consular Staff in Tehran (United States of America v. Iran)*, where the ICJ found the acts of militants, who seized control of the US Embassy in Tehran, were attributable to the Iranian Government since the authorities took no steps to try to prevent the seizure and subsequently endorsed the actions of the militants.[28] This approach has been reflected in the decisions of international human rights treaty bodies, which have attributed to the state the acts of private entities, especially with the growth in privatization of those state entities that retain some public functions.[29] Thus it would appear that the practices and principles found in international human rights law reinforce the general principles of state responsibility, so that there is development and confirmation of the customary international law principles relating to attribution.

3.2 State control

A key issue concerns whether a non-state actor is under the control of a state or not, because there is attribution to a state under Article 8 of the ILC Articles on State Responsibility where: '[T]he person or group of persons is in fact acting on

---

of Treaties 1969, which represents customary international law: *Free Zones of Upper Savoy and the District of Gex Case (France v. Switzerland)* (1932) PCIJ Series. A/B, No. 46, 167.

[23] *Application of the Convention on the Prevention and Punishment of the Crime of Genocide (Bosnia and Herzegovina v. Serbia and Montenegro)*, Judgment of 26 February 2007, 2007 ICJ Reports, para. 565.

[24] ILC Commentary, above n. 6, 91, 121.

[25] Ibid., 110, 112.

[26] See the discussions at the League of Nations Conference for the Codification of International Law 1929, referred to in ibid. 100–101.

[27] Ibid. 92.

[28] *United States Diplomatic and Consular Staff in Tehran (United States of America v. Iran)*, 1980 ICJ Reports 3, paras. 57, 69–71.

[29] See A. McBeth, 'Privatising Human Rights: What Happens to the State's Human Rights Duties when Services are Privatised?' (2004) 5 Melbourne J Int L 133.

the instructions or under the direction or control of that State in carrying out the conduct.'[30]

In relation to the attribution to the state of the actions of non-state actors acting extraterritorially, the ICJ established in the *Military and Paramilitary Activities in and against Nicaragua (Nicaragua v. United States of America) (Merits) (Nicaragua Case)*[31] a test for the degree of control over non-state actors that was needed by the state for attribution to be found. In that case, the United States of America (US) had, *inter alia*, financed, trained, supplied, and equipped the *contras*, who were an armed opposition group opposed to the Nicaraguan Government. The ICJ decided that, while the US could be held responsible for the particular acts of financing, training, etc., of the group, and that therefore some of the acts of the *contras* were attributable to that state, there was insufficient evidence to find that the US exercised 'effective control', being 'such a degree of control in all fields as to justify treating the *contras* as acting on its behalf [and thus] that the United States directed or enforced the perpetration of the acts contrary to human rights and humanitarian law' as Nicaragua had alleged.[32] The Court held that, even if the US' participation in such acts was 'preponderant or decisive', it was still insufficient for the general attribution of the acts of the *contras* to the US.[33]

This approach was criticized by the Appeals Chamber of the International Criminal Tribunal for the Former Yugoslavia (ICTY) in *Prosecutor v. Tadić* ('*Tadić*').[34] In that case, the ICTY found that the adoption of the 'effective control' test by the ICJ 'as an exclusive and all embracing test', was out of line with state practice, the decisions of international tribunals, and with the rules on attribution of conduct in relation to the acts of non-state actors which 'are not based on rigid and uniform criteria.'[35] Instead, it considered that a lower threshold of 'overall control' was applicable, which would be found to exist where a state had 'a role in organising, coordinating or planning the military actions of [a] military group, in addition to financing, training and equipping or providing operational support to that group',[36] on the grounds that the state could not be

---

[30] ILC Articles on State Responsibility, above n. 3, Art. 8; See also ILC Commentary, above n. 6, 91, 121.

[31] *Military and Paramilitary Activities in and against Nicaragua (Nicaragua v. United States of America) (Merits)*, Judgment of 27 June 1986, 1986 ICJ Reports 14.

[32] Ibid., paras. 109, 115.

[33] Ibid., More recently, in *Armed Activities on the Territory of the Congo (Democratic Republic of the Congo v. Uganda)*, Judgment of 19 December 2005, 2005 ICJ Reports 168, at 116, the ICJ found that Uganda was responsible for its assistance and control of forces in the DRC.

[34] *Prosecutor v. Tadić*, ICTY-94-1-A, Judgment of 15 July 1999.

[35] Ibid., paras. 117, 124. The ILC maintains the test set out in *Nicaragua* as the only test of 'effective control' and distinguishes the decision in *Tadić* on the basis that the mandate of the tribunal was to deal with individual rather than state responsibility. However, the Appeals Chamber in *Tadić* expressly states that '[w]hat is at issue is not the distinction between two classes of responsibility', i.e. a distinction between individual and state responsibility: Ibid., para. 104. See D. Chirwa, 'The Doctrine of State Responsibility as a Potential Means of Holding Private Actors Accountable for Human Rights' (2004) 5 Melbourne J Intl L 1.

[36] *Tadić*, para. 137.

expected to control every aspect of the group's actions within the territory of another state. The ICTY indicated that the '*degree of control* may . . . vary according to the factual circumstances of the case',[37] and so the 'effective control' test in the *Nicaragua Case* might be appropriate in relation to private individuals or a group that was not militarily organized,[38] and that where the conduct in question is extraterritorial, it will require 'more extensive and compelling evidence' in support of the claim of control.[39]

Another test of state control for attribution purposes was applied by the European Court of Human Rights in *Ilaşcu v. Moldova and Russia (Ilaşcu)*[40] in relation to the attribution to Russia of conduct of a Moldovian separatist regime. In that case, the alleged violations occurred in Transdniestria, a region of Moldova under the control of a group calling itself the 'Moldavian Republic of Transdniestria' (MRT), which was a separatist regime not recognized by any state. One of the claims was that Russia had been assisting and supporting the MRT through military and political means, including by Russian soldiers participating in the arrests of the applicants in the MRT. When considering the responsibility of Russia, the Court took into account the history of the situation in which Russia had given military and political support to the MRT, which included its participation in the fighting to help the separatists set up their regime. The Court also considered specific acts by Russia, in particular, the fact that Russian soldiers participated in the arrest and detention of the applicants, and the fact that Russian agents had transferred the applicants to the Transdniestrian authorities with the full knowledge 'that they were handing them over to an illegal and unconstitutional regime . . . and knew, or at least should have known, the fate which awaited them.'[41] As a result, the Court held that:

All of the above proves that the 'MRT', set up in 1991–1992 with the support of the Russian Federation, vested with organs of power and its own administration, remains under the *effective authority, or at the very least under the decisive influence*, of the Russian Federation, and in any event that it survives by virtue of the military, economic, financial and political support given to it by the Russian Federation . . . That being so, [there was] a continuous and uninterrupted link of responsibility on the part of the Russian Federation for the applicants' fate.[42]

---

[37] *Tadić*, para. 117 (emphasis in original).

[38] *Tadić*, para. 137. M. Milanović, 'State Responsibility for Genocide' (2007) 17 EJIL 553, 585–586, argues that the Appeals Chamber in *Tadić* 'unnecessarily attempted to deal with questions which were immaterial to its basic purpose of assigning individual criminal responsibility,' and that the cases it cites 'do not support its test of overall control.'

[39] *Tadić*, para. 138.

[40] *Ilaşcu v. Moldova and Russia* (App. No. 48787/99), ECtHR, Judgment of 8 July 2004.

[41] *Ilaşcu*, paras. 392–393.

[42] *Ilaşcu*, para. 394 (emphasis added). It should be noted that the Court is not always clear in its decision in this case as to whether it means 'responsibility' in the sense of the general international law of state responsibility or in sense of an obligation under a human rights treaty—see also Cerone, above n.16.

Thus, the acts of the MRT were attributable to Russia, bringing the applicants within the jurisdiction of Russia under Article 1 of the European Convention on Human Rights (ECHR) and engaging Russian international legal responsibility.[43]

So the Court considered that the necessary degree of control for the purposes of attribution was shown in this case where Russia had provided political and military support to the MRT and the latter remained 'under the effective authority, or *at the very least the decisive influence*, of the Russian Federation.'[44] This seems to indicate that the Court is not requiring a high degree of control—and certainly not territorial or 'effective control'—or even 'overall control'—for it to find that the actions of non-state actors in another territory can be attributed to a state in such a way that a state is considered to have jurisdiction over such actors and, hence, has extraterritorial obligations under the ECHR.

These threshold tests of control for attribution purposes were not accepted by the ICJ when it came to consider the question in the *Genocide* case.[45] The relevant issue in that case concerned the extent of the responsibility of the state of Serbia (as it now is) for alleged acts of genocide by Bosnian-Serb paramilitary forces against the Bosnian Muslim population in Bosnia-Herzegovina during the armed conflict in 1992–1995. The Court expressly affirmed the decision in the *Nicaragua* case that the appropriate test for the purposes of attribution under Article 8 of the ILC Articles on State Responsibility was that of 'effective control.' This test required that the 'state's instructions be given, in respect of *each* operation in which the alleged violations occurred, *not generally* in respect of the overall operations taken by the persons or group having committed the violations.'[46] On this basis, the ICJ found that Serbia did not have 'effective control' over the Bosnian-Serb paramilitary forces accused of the purported acts of genocide, despite the Court acknowledging that Serbia provided up to 90 per cent of the material needs of the Republic of Srpska (the Bosnian-Serb region), that a substantial portion of the Bosnian-Serb paramilitary forces were being paid salaries by Serbia, and that the economies of the two entities were effectively completely integrated.[47]

The Court explicitly rejected the 'overall control' test as propounded in *Tadić* on two main grounds. First, it held that in dealing with a question of state responsibility, the ICTY—as an international criminal tribunal with jurisdiction over individual persons—'addressed an issue [of general international law] which was not indispensable for the exercise of its jurisdiction.'[48] Thus, the Court held that it was free not to take into account ICTY decisions when they concerned issues of general international law 'which do not lie within the specific purview of its

---

[43] *Ilaşcu*, paras. 392–394.
[44] *Ilaşcu*, para. 392 (emphasis added).
[45] *Genocide Case*, paras. 398–407.
[46] *Genocide Case*, para. 404 (emphasis added).
[47] M. Gibney, 'Genocide and State Responsibility' (2007) 7(4) Human Rights L Rev 760, 763.
[48] *Genocide Case*, para. 403.

jurisdiction and, moreover, the resolution of which is not always necessary for deciding the criminal cases before it.'[49]

Second, the ICJ considered that the 'overall control' test was not applicable to the issues concerned in the *Genocide* case in any event. The first reason given was that, unlike the ICTY in *Tadić*, the ICJ was not deciding whether a conflict should be characterized as 'international' for the purposes of an armed conflict but a specific issue of state responsibility.[50] Thus the Court questioned whether logic 'required the same test to be adopted in resolving the two issues, which [were] very different in nature.'[51] The second reason offered was that the 'overall control' test 'has the major drawback of broadening state responsibility well beyond the fundamental principles governing the law of international responsibility.'[52] Its reasoning was simply that a state could only be held responsible for the acts of third parties where the third party was either a *de jure* or *de facto* organ of the state or if the party was being directed and controlled by the state pursuant to customary international law as embodied in Article 8 of the ILC Articles on State Responsibility and as clarified by the ICJ in the *Nicaragua* case.[53]

The decision by the ICJ in the *Genocide* case has been widely and strongly criticized, not least because it established an exceedingly high threshold for a finding of control of non-state actors by a state for the purposes of attribution to the state of the acts of those non-state actors, such that 'if extraterritorial state responsibility could not be established in this particular case, it is difficult to imagine under what circumstances it could ever be established.'[54] Further, Cassese has argued that the Court failed to justify sufficiently the imposition of two different tests for the two areas of law[55] and, in order to prove that a different test should have existed, the Court ought to have shown that judicial and state practice evinced the existence of the 'effective control' test; something which it did not do.[56] It simply predicated its arguments on the fact that such a test would go beyond established jurisprudence—that is, its own earlier decision—as a justification: clearly circular reasoning. Indeed, the Court did not prove—as it only asserted— that the 'overall control' test would stretch 'too far, almost to breaking point, the connection which must exist between the conduct of a State's organs and its international responsibility.'[57] Indeed, such a statement appears to have the interests of states alone in mind and not those of individuals (such as the Bosnian Muslims here) whose human rights are violated. In such a way, it also seems inconsistent

---

[49] *Genocide Case*, para. 403.
[50] *Genocide Case*, para. 404.
[51] *Genocide Case*, para. 405.
[52] *Genocide Case*, para. 406.
[53] *Genocide Case*, paras. 406–407.
[54] Gibney, above n. 47, 771. See also, Milanović, above n. 38, 585–586.
[55] A. Cassese, 'The *Nicaragua* and *Tadić* Tests revisited in light of the ICJ Judgment on Genocide in Bosnia' (2007) 18 EJIL 649.
[56] Ibid.
[57] *Genocide Case*, para. 406.

with the development of international law as a body of rules that is cognizant and reflective of a community of different interests and broad spectrum of actors.[58] While the case before it raised difficult political issues that the Court tried hard to negotiate, its decision on this issue remains problematic for the future development of the general law on state responsibility.

The *Genocide* case firmly and pointedly rejected any test of control in terms of attribution to a state under the international law of state responsibility beyond the 'effective control' test. It rejected directly and indirectly the approaches adopted by an international criminal tribunal deciding a human rights and humanitarian issue and a respected regional human rights court. In fact, the ILC had taken a similar position even prior to the *Genocide* case.[59] Thus there has been no impact by international human rights law on the general international law of state responsibility in regard to the issue of state control for the purposes of attribution.

Nevertheless this does not mean that human rights treaty monitoring bodies cannot themselves require a lower level of control by a state over a non-state actor than that found in general international law. Indeed, the ICJ in *DRC v. Uganda* indicated that international human rights law applies to a state's conduct extraterritorially even when the level of control is less than that of an occupying power.'[60] In reaching this conclusion, the ICJ is appearing to allow the possibility of there being a lower test of control under international human rights law, while not adopting it under general international law. This approach could become even more important since the beginning of the (illegal) action by the 'occupying' forces in Iraq, where it is clear that many private corporations were contracted by the states involved to provide a wide variety of services—from providing intelligence to recreating state infrastructure to support such military action—and that some of those corporations abused human rights.[61] So international human rights law could be accepted as taking a different approach—due to its subject matter and aim—from the general application of the international law of state responsibility in relation to aspects of attribution.

Overall international human rights law has had a minimal impact on the general international law of state responsibility in regard to attribution to the state. While its interpretations and practices have largely supported the development of the general international law of attribution, in the area of attribution

---

[58] See A. Cassese, 'The Impact of Human Rights on Traditional International Law', in *International Law*, 2nd ed. (Oxford University Press, Oxford 2005) 396; T. Meron, *The Humanization of International Law* (Nijhoff, Leiden/Boston 2006). For a fuller discussion, see R. McCorquodale, 'An Inclusive International Legal System' (2007) 17 LJIL 477.

[59] ILC Commentary, above n. 6,

[60] *DRC v. Uganda*, above n. 33, para. 179–180, 219–220.

[61] See e.g., S. Gibson, 'Lack of Extraterritorial Jurisdiction over Civilians: A New Look at an Old Problem' (1995) 148 *Military Law Review* 114; M. Bina, 'Private Military Contractor Liability and Accountability after Abu Ghraib' (2005) 39 *John Marshall Law Review* 1237; and M. Schmitt, 'Humanitarian Law and Direct Participation in Hostilities by Private Contractors or Civilian Employees' (2005) *Chicago Journal of International Law* 511.

through control by the state of the acts of non-state actors extraterritorially, its approach has been rejected by the ICJ as not applicable to the general rules on state responsibility.

4. International Obligations of a State

Attribution is one of the two key aspects of the general principles of state responsibility; the other concerns an international obligation. Under general international law, a state is responsible only if there is a breach of its international obligations. Article 12 of the ILC Articles on State Responsibility provides that: 'There is a breach of an international obligation by a State when an act of that State is not in conformity with what is required of it by that obligation, regardless of its origin or character.'[62] The human rights treaty monitoring bodies' role is to examine the obligations of states under the relevant human rights treaty. In so doing they have clarified the extent of these obligations.

4.1 Positive obligations in international human rights law

International human rights law has consistently recognized that there are different types of obligations that states enter into for the protection of human rights. All the major global and regional human rights treaties place an obligation on states party to the treaty to adopt legislation or other measures to 'ensure' or 'realize' the rights in the human rights treaty, whether immediately or progressively.[63] As all states are party to at least one of the major treaties then this obligation could be considered to apply to all states.[64] This obligation has been expressed as a threefold responsibility on states to respect, protect, and fulfil human rights.[65]

---

[62] It should be noted that there is no consensus in international law as to whether there should be a subjective element to the finding of international wrongfulness by a state for which it incurs responsibility, with the final ILC Articles on State Responsibility offering no definite position: ILC Commentary, above n. 6, 67–70. For a discussion of this position as reflecting 'the current transitional state of international law', see A. Gattini, 'A Return Ticket to "Communitarisme", Please' (2002) 13 EJIL 1181.

[63] See e.g., Art 2 of both the International Covenant on Economic, Social and Cultural Rights (ICESCR) and the International Covenant on Civil and Political Rights (ICCPR).

[64] This is also implied by the approaches to the United Nations Human Rights Council Universal Periodic Review (see <http://www.ohchr.org/EN/HRBodies/UPR/Pages/UPRMain.aspx> (last accessed 03 September 2008). The issue of reservations is not considered here because no state has argued that it has no obligation to adopt any measures to comply with its international human rights treaty obligations.

[65] See e.g., the analysis by the United Nations Committee on Economic, Social and Cultural Rights, General Comment No. 13 on the Right to Education, 7 *International Human Rights Reports* (2000) 303, where the Committee states at para. 46: 'The right to education, like all human rights, imposes three types or levels of obligations on states parties: the obligations to respect, protect and fulfill. In turn, the obligation to fulfill incorporates both an obligation to facilitate and an obligation to provide.'

These types of obligations require states not only to refrain from acting to prevent violations of human rights but also to take active steps to ensure compliance with their responsibilities towards all those within their jurisdiction (and not just within their territory).[66] These latter obligations on states are often called 'positive' obligations, where a state has a constant and ongoing obligation to exercise 'due diligence' to prevent human rights violations by all persons within that jurisdiction. This means that unlawful acts *and* omissions by a state (and those whose acts are attributed to the state) may breach provisions of international law,[67] and that the state may breach a human rights obligation even when the acts of the non-state actor cannot be attributed directly to the state.[68] Thus international human rights law obliges a state to take measures—such as by legislation and administrative practices—to control, regulate, investigate, and prosecute actions by non-state actors that violate the human rights of those within the territory of that state. For example, in *Velásquez Rodriguez v. Honduras*,[69] the Inter-American Court of Human Rights held that the international responsibility of a state may be occasioned:

[N]ot because of the act itself, but because of a lack of due diligence to prevent the violation or to respond to it as required by [the human rights treaty] ... The state is obligated to investigate every situation involving a violation of rights under the Convention. If the state apparatus acts in such a way that the violation goes unpunished and the victim's full enjoyment of such rights is not restored as soon as possible, the state has failed to comply with its duty to ensure the free and full exercise of those rights to persons within its jurisdiction. The same is true when the state allows private persons or groups to act freely and with impunity to the detriment of the rights recognised in the Convention.[70]

As a consequence, states have been found to be in breach of their international human rights obligations in relation to activities of non-state actors (such as corporations) within their territory, because the acts or omissions by the state

---

[66] 'Jurisdiction' is the key term used in human rights treaties and is more extensive than territory: See, e.g., American Convention on Human Rights, Art 1(1) European Convention on Human Rights, Art 1, and HRCt, General Comment No. 31(80), Nature of the General Legal Obligation Imposed on States Parties to the *Covenant*, UN Doc. CCPR/C/21/Rev.1/Add.13 (26 May 2004) [3]. In *Drozd and Janousek v. France and Spain* (App. No. 12747/8), ECtHR, Judgment of 26 June 1992, (1992)14 EHRR 745, para, 91, the ECHR held that 'The term "jurisdiction" is not limited to the national territory of the High Contracting Parties, their responsibility can be invoked because of their authorities producing effects outside their own territory.'

[67] The ILC considers that cases in which the responsibility of states has been invoked on the basis of an omission have been 'as least as numerous' as those based on positive conduct: ILC Commentary, above n. 6, para. 82. Note that the obligation of due diligence seems to have been developed initially within the general law of state responsibility in relation to issues of, for example, transboundary pollution, but has been developed much more substantially within international human rights law.

[68] See generally A. Clapham, *Human Rights in the Private Sphere* (Oxford University Press, Oxford 1993) and A. Clapham, 'Revisiting *Human Rights in the Private Sphere*: Using the European Convention to Protect the Right of Access to the Civil Court' in C. Scott (ed.), above n. 2, 513.

[69] *Velásquez Rodriguez v. Honduras*, IACtHR, Judgment of 29 July 1989, Series C No. 4, 28 ILM 291 (henceforth *Velásquez Rodriguez*).

[70] *Velásquez Rodriguez*, paras. 172, 176.

enabled the corporation to act as it did. These have included situations where corporations dismissed or victimized employees for joining a trade union,[71] chemical and oil corporations have been found to have polluted the air and land,[72] and corporations have used indigenous peoples' land.[73] In all these cases, the state was in breach of its obligations under the relevant human rights treaty because its acts or omissions enabled the non-state actor to act as it did. In a similar way, states have been found in breach of their human rights obligations where the actions of paramilitaries, armed groups and individuals have violated human rights within the state's jurisdiction.[74] In such cases, international human rights law expects states to undertake fact-finding, criminal investigations and, perhaps, prosecution, in a transparent, 'accessible and effective manner',[75] and to provide redress[76]—all of which require considerable state resources and positive action.

These obligations extend extraterritorially, as the state's obligation is not limited to its territory, as noted above.[77] So states have been held to violate their obligations where a state's security forces support illegal action and administration in another territory,[78] where the state confiscates its own citizen's passport at one of its consulates in another state,[79] and in relation to detention in Guantánamo Bay.[80] The United Nations Human Rights Committee (HRC) has also taken

---

[71] See e.g., *Young, James and Webster v. United Kingdom* (App. No. 7601/76), Judgment of 13 August 1981, Series A No. 44. (1982) 4 EHRR 38.

[72] See e.g., *López Ostra v. Spain* (Application No. 16798/90), ECtHR, Judgment of 9 December 1994, Series A No. 303-C and *Social and Economic Rights Action Centre for Economic and Social Rights v. Nigeria*, African Commission, Communication No. 155/96 (2001).

[73] See e.g., *The Mayagna (Sumo) Awas Tingni Community v. Nicaragua*, above, n. 13.

[74] See e.g., *Herrera Rubio v. Colombia* (161/1983) , HRCt, 2 November 1987, UN GAOR, 43rd Sess, Supp. 40, 190 [11] (1988) and decisions of the ECtHR in *Ergi v. Turkey* (App. no. 23818/94) ECtHR, Judgment of 28 July 1998 and *Timurtas v. Turkey* (App. No. 23531/94), ECtHR, Judgment of 13 June 2000, and the further extension of this obligation in *A v. United Kingdom*, (1999) 27 EHRR 611. See also, CEDAW, General Recommendation 19, Violence against Women (1992), para. 9; 1 IHRR 25 (1994).

[75] *Jordan v. United Kingdom* (App. No. 24746/94) ECtHR, Judgment of 4 May 2001, para. 143, where the ECHR considered that the conduct of the investigation, the coroner's inquest, delay, the lack of both legal aid for the victim's family and the lack of public scrutiny of the reasons of the Director of Public Prosecutions not to prosecute, was a violation of Art. 2 of the European Convention. See also *Halimi-Nedzibi v. Austria* (8/1991), CAT, 1(2) IHRR 190 (1994), para. 13.5.

[76] See *Z v. United Kingdom* (App. No. 29392/95) ECtHR, Judgment of 10 May 2001, para. 109, and *Keenan v. United Kingdom* (App. No. 27229/95), ECtHR, Judgment of 3 April 2001. See also N. Rhot-Arriaza, 'State Responsibility to Investigate and Prosecute Grave Human Rights Violations in International Law' (1990) 78 *California Law Review* 449; O. Mendez, 'Accountability for Past Abuses' (1997) 19 HRQ 261; and *United Nations Declaration on the Elimination of Violence against Women*, UNGAOR 48/104 (20 December 1993) 33 ILM 1049 (1994).

[77] For an excellent range of analyses of the position see F. Coomans and M. Kamminga (eds), *Extraterritorial Application of Human Rights Treaties* (Intersentia, Antwerp 2004).

[78] *Loizidou v. Turkey (Preliminary Objections)* (App. No. 15318/89), Judgment of 23 March 1995, (1995) Series A No. 310, 20 EHRR 99, para. 62. This decision was confirmed in *Cyprus v. Turkey* (App. No. 25781/94), ECtHR, Judgment of 10 May 2001, (2002) 35 EHRR 30.

[79] HRCt, *Montero v. Uruguay* (106/81) 31 July 1983.

[80] *Detainees at Guantánamo Bay, Cuba* (Precautionary Measures), IACmHR, 41 ILM 532 (2002), 533 where the Commission considered that, although the detainees were outside the territory of the US they were subject to its jurisdiction because they were 'wholly within the authority and control of the United States government.'

the position that Israel has obligations under the ICCPR in relation to individuals within its Occupied Territories,[81] and that Belgium has such obligations in relation to its forces operating as UN peacekeepers in Somalia,[82] on the basis that: 'A State party must respect and ensure the rights laid down in the [ICCPR] to anyone within the power and effective control of that State Party, even if not situated within the territory of the State Party... regardless of the circumstances in which such power or effective control was obtained.'[83] Thus a state may be responsible for a violation of an international human rights treaty obligation where 'acts of their authorities, whether performed within or outside national boundaries... produce effects outside their own territory'[84] and for 'the extraterritorial consequences of its intraterritorial decisions.'[85]

International human rights law has interpreted the nature of a state's obligations and extended the scope and depth of those obligations. As a consequence, there could be some impact by international human rights law on the general international law of state responsibility.[86]

4.2 Positive obligations in state responsibility

The ICJ has had to consider the nature of positive obligations under international human rights law. In its *Advisory Opinion on the Legal Consequences on the Construction of a Wall in the Occupied Palestinian Territory*,[87] the ICJ stated that Israel had obligations under the ICCPR, ICESCR and the CRC in relation to the occupied Palestinian territories, and that the ICCPR was 'applicable in respect of acts done by a State in the exercise of its jurisdiction outside its own territory.'[88] This position was confirmed by the ICJ in its decision in *DRC v. Uganda*, in finding that the ICCPR, the CRC and the African Charter on Human and Peoples' Rights (ACHPR) all applied in relation to Uganda's actions within the territory of the Democratic Republic of Congo.[89] Indeed, in this latter case, the Court went further in stating that: '[I]nternational human rights instruments are applicable in respect of acts done by a state in the exercise of its jurisdiction outside its own territory, particularly in occupied territories.'[90]

In reaching this conclusion, the ICJ is determining that the obligations of all states (and not only occupying powers) under *all* international human rights

---

[81] Concluding Observations of HRCt on Israel (1999), UN Doc. CCPR/C/79/Add.93, 10.
[82] Concluding Observations of HRCt on Belgium (1999), UN Doc. CCPR/C/79/Add.93, 12.
[83] HRC, *General Comment No. 31(80)*, above n. 66, para. 10.
[84] *Loizidou v. Turkey (Preliminary Objections)* (App. No. 15318/89), Judgment of 23 March 1995, (1995) Series A No. 310, 20 EHRR 99, 62.
[85] S. Joseph, J. Schultz and M. Castan, above n. 21, 96.
[86] See M. Sornarajah, above n. 2, and P. Alston (ed.), *Non-State Actors and Human Rights* (Oxford University Press, Oxford 2005).
[87] *Legal Consequences of the Construction of a Wall in the Occupied Palestinian Territory*, Advisory Opinion of 9 July 2004, 2004 ICJ Reports 136.
[88] *Advisory Opinion on the Wall*, paras. 107–113.
[89] *DRC v. Uganda*, para. 217.   [90] *DRC v. Uganda*, para. 216.

instruments to which a state is a party—and necessarily, all human rights that are part of customary international law—are applicable in relation to the acts of a state outside its territory. This obligation is only limited by the phrase 'in the exercise of its jurisdiction', which, as seen above, concerns all actions in relation to anyone within the power, 'effective control', or authority of a state, and does not depend on the acquiescence of the territorial state. This obligation is also seen to apply beyond international human rights law, such as to actions where there are transboundary environmental impacts and the state should have had control over the activities that led to these impacts.[91]

This acceptance by the ICJ that a state has positive obligations—both territorially and extraterritorially—was expanded upon by the ICJ in the *Genocide* case. Whilst, as noted above, the Court did not find that Serbia had 'effective control' of the Bosnian-Serb paramilitary forces, it did decide that Serbia breached its positive obligation to prevent genocide. Article 1 of the Convention on the Prevention and the Punishment of the Crime of Genocide provides: 'The Contracting Parties confirm that genocide, whether committed in time of peace or in time of war, is a crime under international law which they undertake to prevent and to punish.'

In defining the scope of this duty, the ICJ held that the Serbian Government was under a duty to 'employ all means reasonably available to them, so as to prevent genocide so far as possible.'[92] This obligation required a level of 'due diligence', which would vary from state to state depending on its 'capacity to influence effectively the action of persons likely to commit or already committing genocide.'[93] This would in turn depend on factors such as the geographical distance of the state concerned from the scene of the events; the strength of the links between authorities of the state and the main actors in the events; and the particular legal position of the state towards the situations and people facing the threat or the reality of the genocide.[94]

The scope of this duty is significant in that it means that each state can be held accountable for breaching the duty to prevent genocide, including by omission. Therefore, whilst a state may avoid legal responsibility for the actual commission of genocide due to the strict 'effective control' test in relation to attribution, it may still be held responsible for acts *and* omissions that violate an international legal obligation.[95] This may mitigate to some degree and in some circumstances, the restrictive consequences of the 'effective control' test for attribution in regards to individuals under threat.

---

[91] See e.g., *Trail Smelter Arbitration (US v. Canada)* 3 RIAA (1941) 1905. See also, *The Rainbow Warrior (New Zealand v. France)*, Arbitral Tribunal (1990) 82 ILR 449 and N. Jägers, above n. 2.

[92] *Genocide Case*, para. 430. The Court also asserted that Serbia had an obligation to cooperate with the ICTY by transferring Ratko Mladić for trial and it was in breach of its duty to punish offenders under Article 6 of the Genocide Convention.

[93] *Genocide Case*, para. 430.   [94] *Genocide Case*, para. 430.

[95] A. Gattini, 'Breach of the Obligation to Prevent and Reparation thereof in the ICJ's Genocide Judgment' (2007) EJIL 712.

In this way, the ICJ has adopted the approach of international human rights law as to the scope of a state's obligations under the general international law of state responsibility to include positive obligations. Whilst the ICJ has not explicitly acknowledged that it was following an approach taken under international human rights law, it is evident that there have been important effects of the development of international human rights law on the law of state responsibility in regard to the extent and nature of a state's obligations. This expansion in the understanding of a state's obligations for which it incurs international responsibility could occur in other areas of international law, especially trade, investment, and the environment, as there is growing support for the view that '[w]here a state knows that its national's activities will cause, or are causing, harm to other states or peoples, it is consistent with this [general] duty that it should prevent such harm.'[96]

At the same time, the concept of positive obligations appears to have had an impact on the secondary rules of general international law.[97] The concept was incorporated, for example, into Article 41 of the ILC Articles on State Responsibility, as '[s]tates shall cooperate to bring to an end through lawful means any serious breach within the meaning of Article 40 [being a serious breach of a peremptory norm of international law].' If this reflects customary international law,[98] then it is a clear effect of international human rights law on the general understanding and application of the general law of state responsibility. In addition, the 'responsibility to protect' was recognized by the United Nations General Assembly in the World Summit Outcome,[99] and more recently, by the Security Council, which has reaffirmed states' 'responsibility to protect populations from genocide, war crimes, ethnic cleansing, and crimes against humanity.'[100]

Therefore, it has become accepted within the general international law of state responsibility that states have positive obligations. This position arises primarily from the practices and principles developed within international human rights law. In this way, international human rights law has had a significant, and potentially long-lasting, impact on the general international law of state responsibility.

---

[96] Sornarajah, above n. 2, 507: Sornarajah makes this assertion in relation to acts that violate *jus cogens* norms. See also, N. Jägers, above n. 2, 170–172, and C. Scott, 'Multinational Enterprises and Emergent Jurisprudence on violations of Economic, Social and Cultural Rights' in A. Eide, C. Krause and A. Rosas (eds), *Economic, Social and Cultural Rights: A Textbook* 2nd ed. (Nijhoff, Dordrecht 2001) 563, 587. See also I. Seidl-Hohenfeldern, *International Economic Law* (Nijhoff, Dordrecht 1989) 159–160: Seidl-Hohenfeldern maintains that despite the lack of a general rule there may be situations in which a state could be held responsible for the acts of its national corporations, 'for example, the export tolerated by the authorities of the home country, of goods, whose sale in the home country is banned on account of health risks.'

[97] I acknowledge the work of my colleagues in the ILA Committee for their insights in this paragraph.

[98] ILC Commentary, above n. 6, 249, expresses hesitation whether the positive obligation of cooperation in Art. 41 is already part of general international law or whether it reflects progressive development of the law.

[99] UN Doc. A/Res/60/1, (2005) paras. 138–139.

[100] UN SC Res. 1674 (2006), Protection of civilians in armed conflict, para. 4.

5. State Responsibility and the Individual

Some of the earliest litigation concerning the extent of the obligations under state responsibility dealt with the issue of the 'treatment of aliens', which was the terminology used within state responsibility in relation to non-nationals of that state.[101] These cases arose when one state brought a case against another state before an international dispute settlement body in regard to the action taken by the second state against one of the first state's own nationals. The case law consistently held that states were responsible for failing to exercise due diligence within their territorial jurisdiction either in preventing injury to non-nationals or in ensuring due process of law.[102]

This method of action, where the claim is brought by one state against another state, is known as 'diplomatic protection' because: '[B]y resorting to diplomatic action or international judicial proceedings on his behalf, a State is in reality assert-ing its own right, the right to ensure in the person of its nationals respect for the rules of international law.'[103] As noted by the Permanent Court of International Justice in that case, it was not the individual who was asserting their rights under international law but the state asserting its rights on the basis of nationality pow-ers. As a consequence, the law of state responsibility has developed intricate rules regarding the nationality of people in terms of their relationship to states, as deter-mined by the degree of connection they have to the territory of a state.[104] Even then, this nationality connection may be insufficient if there are other interna-tional rules that override it or if the state chooses not to take action.[105]

This position has been dealt with differently in international human rights law. Both conceptually and substantially, international human rights law is not limited to the nationality of an individual or group. Human rights protection is not based on nationality.[106] The necessary link with a state is now jurisdic-tion. If a state has jurisdiction over an individual then that individual can bring a claim against that state—if that state has ratified the relevant human rights

---

[101] See e.g., G. Hackworth, *Digest of International Law* (1943) vol. 5.

[102] I. Brownlie, *System of the Law of Nations: State Responsibility, Part I* (Clarendon Press, Oxford 1983) 161. It should be noted that these cases were usually brought by the economically powerful states against less economically powerful states in relation to physical or economic actions by the latter states.

[103] *Panevezys-Saldutiskis Railway Case (Estonia v. Lithuania)* (Preliminary Objections), 1939 PCIJ Series. A/B (1939) No. 76. For a more detailed analysis of diplomatic protection, see Chapter 10 of this volume.

[104] See e.g., *Nottebohm (Liechtenstein v. Guatemala)* 1955 ICJ Reports 4 and *Iran-United States Case No. A/18*, 5 Iran-United States Claims Tribunal Reports (1984) 251.

[105] Indeed, the ICJ has stated that '[t]he State must be viewed as the sole judge to decide whether its protection will be granted, to what extent it is granted, and when it will cease....Should the natural or legal persons on whose behalf it is acting consider that their rights are not adequately protected, they have no remedy in international law': *Barcelona Traction, Light and Power Company Limited Case (Belgium v. Spain)*, 1970 ICJ Reports 3, paras. 78–79.

[106] For a summary of a wealth of this material, see P. Alston (ed.), *Human Rights Law* (1996) and R. McCorquodale (ed.), *Human Rights* (2002).

treaty—irrespective of whether that individual is a national of that state. This also applies if the individual is only temporarily in that state,[107] and even where that state's jurisdiction over the individual is unlawful.[108] The state of which that individual is a national does not have to be a party to the treaty and the individual could be a stateless person. Therefore a state has obligations to protect all non-nationals within their jurisdiction and is subject to claims by individuals rather then deciding for itself whether to make a claim (though the latter is still possible, if rare).[109] This change in understanding of the obligations to individuals for which state responsibility extends within international human rights law, represents 'a momentous advance in the world community.'[110]

This change by international human rights law of the international legal relationship between a state and those within its jurisdiction has had an impact on the general understanding and application of the obligations of state responsibility. For example, in the *LaGrand Case (Germany v. USA) (Merits)*,[111] the ICJ expressly acknowledged that the obligations under the Vienna Convention on Consular Relations gave rise not only to rights by the state to protect its own interests (through traditional diplomatic protection) but also 'creates individual rights, which... may be invoked in this Court by the national State of the detained person.'[112] This is confirmed by the decision of the UK Court of Appeal in *Abassi v. Secretary of State for Foreign and Commonwealth Affairs*,[113] where the Court held that there was a legitimate expectation by nationals that their government would make representations to another government to assist them (though, in that instance, the Court found that the UK Government's actions were sufficient). This indicates a step towards making a state directly responsible for its decisions as to the diplomatic protection of its nationals.[114]

6. Conclusions

To establish state responsibility under general public international law, it is necessary to confirm the attribution to the state of the act or omission under

---

[107] See e.g., *Miha v. Equatorial Guinea* (414/90), HRCt, 8 July 1994 and *Soering v. United Kingdom* (Judgment of 7 July 1989) and *Soering v. United Kingdom* (1989) 11 EHRR 439. Indeed the persons do not have to be in the territory of the state at the time that any complaint is made: *Massiotti and Baristussio v. Uruguay* (25/78), HRCt, 26 July 1982.

[108] *Loizidou v. Turkey* (Preliminary Objections) (App. No. 15318/89), Judgment of 23 March 1995, (1995) Series A No. 310, 20 EHRR 99.

[109] See e.g., *Ireland v. United Kingdom* (Application no. 5310/71), Judgment of 18 January 1978, 2 EHRR 25.

[110] A. Cassese, *International Law in a Divided World* (Clarendon Press, Oxford 1986) 102.

[111] *LaGrand (Germany v. United States of America)*, Judgment of 27 June 2001, 2001 ICJ Reports 466.

[112] *Ireland v. United Kingdom* (Application no. 5310/71), Judgment of 18 January 1978, (1978) 2 EHRR 25 [77].

[113] *R (Abassi) v. Secretary of State for Foreign and Commonwealth Affairs*, 42 ILM 358 (2003).

[114] See further the discussion on *jus cogens* in Chapter 7 of this volume.

consideration, and confirm that the act or omission was in breach of an international legal obligation. International human rights law has developed a range of interpretations, practices and principles that have elaborated on these two core aspects of state responsibility. Whilst some of this law has not been adopted within general international law (and some even rejected), other aspects have influenced, sometimes significantly, the general international law of state responsibility. This is seen most clearly in the acceptance that states have positive obligations.

However, whilst state responsibility may be changing, it is still a flawed law. It is flawed because, as noted above, it is a law created for states by states within a state-based legal framework. Allott strongly criticizes it:

Two especially vicious consequences result from using responsibility as a general and independent category in international law. First, it consecrates the idea that wrongdoing is the behaviour of a general category known as 'states' and is not the behavior of morally responsible human beings. It therefore obscures the fact that breaches of international law are attributable formally to the legal persons known as states but morally to the human beings who determine the behaviour of states.

Second, if responsibility exists as a legal category, it must be given legal substance. In particular, general conditions of responsibility have to be created which are then applicable to all rights and duties. The net result is that the deterrent effect of the imposition of responsibility is seriously compromised, not only by notionalizing it (the first vicious consequence) but also by leaving room for argument in every conceivable case of potential responsibility (the second vicious consequence). When lawyers leave room for argument there is much room for injustice.[115]

The hope is that the influence of international human rights law may reduce some of these problematic aspects of the general law of state responsibility. After all, as Cassese views it:

[Human rights] operate as a potent leaven, contributing to shift the world community from a reciprocity-based bundle of legal relations, geared to the private pursuit of self-interest, and ultimately blind to collective needs, to a community hinging on a core of fundamental values, strengthened by the emergence of community obligations and community rights and the gradual shaping of public interests.[116]

The impact of international human rights law on the general international law of state responsibility may be both direct and indirect. It may directly influence the core principles of the law of state responsibility, such as the extent and nature of a state's obligations, and so influence other areas of international law. It may also indirectly influence the general law of state responsibility through its impact on the nature of the international legal system itself.

---

[115] P. Allott, 'State Responsibility and the Unmaking of International Law' (1988) 29 Harv Intl LJ 1.

[116] A. Cassese, above n. 58, 396.

Index